MODERN HUMANITIES RESEARCH ASSOCIATION

DISSERTATION SERIES

VOLUME 8

Editors:

F. J. STOPP   R. A. WISBEY

(*Germanic*)

ARRIGO SUBIOTTO

Bertolt Brecht's Adaptations for the Berliner Ensemble

BERTOLT BRECHT'S ADAPTATIONS FOR THE BERLINER ENSEMBLE

by

ARRIGO SUBIOTTO

Professor of German, University of Birmingham

Published by

THE MODERN HUMANITIES RESEARCH ASSOCIATION

LONDON

1975

ISBN 0 900547 37 5

Printed by
W. S. MANEY AND SON LTD   LEEDS   ENGLAND

FOR FRANKIE

CONTENTS

Contents (continued)

PREFACE

This study is the extensively revised and rewritten version of a dissertation for which the Degree of Ph.D. was awarded by the University of Aberdeen in 1969. I am deeply grateful to Professor W. Witte for his generous help and advice, given at every stage. My thanks are also due to the Bertolt Brecht Archiv and the late Helene Weigel for permission to use the facilities of the archives and to quote some passages from unpublished material. The first chapter appeared in an extended form in *Forum for Modern Languages Studies*, April 1966. For the convenience of readers the titles of several recent works related to this study have been inserted in the bibliography; none of them have necessitated a revision of my argument. In preparing this book for publication, the printers have shown remarkable patience and painstaking accuracy, for which I thank them.

I owe the greatest debt to my wife for her sensitive criticism, wide-ranging discussions and unceasing encouragement during the writing of this book.

Birmingham, September 1975   A.S.

ABBREVIATIONS

Brecht's works are referred to by the abbreviated title, with volume and page number, as follows:

> *GW* = *Gesammelte Werke* (Werkausgabe), 20 vols, Suhrkamp (Frankfurt, 1967)
>
> *Th* = *Theaterarbeit*, Henschelverlag (Berlin, 1961)
>
> **BBA** = Bertolt-Brecht-Archiv MS, with number of folder and sheet, Berlin
>
> *Programmheft* — Detailed programme notes provided for every production of the Berliner Ensemble.

CHAPTER I

BERTOLT BRECHT AND THE DIALECTIC
OF TRADITION

Brecht's lifelong efforts to evolve a consistently new approach to the theatre
seem to have created the erroneous impression that he was therefore a contemptuous arch-enemy of the classics, especially of German classical plays.
But it is wrong to see Brecht as the gratuitous literary firebrand and revolutionary iconoclast of the popular image; a feature of his work, from the first
to the last plays and theoretical writings, is his concern with a literary tradition; many of his own dramas are stimulated by existing models or are
counterpoints to them. Brecht's quarrel is seldom with his literary ancestors
(Shakespeare, *Urfaust*, *Die Räuber* are frequently cited as admirable past
models of playwriting technique and involvement outside literature), but he
does not spare his scorn for the traditional ways of performing the classics
and makes virulent attacks on the misappropriation of past drama by society.
An early move in his career to counter the hallowed lifeless approach to the
classics was Brecht and Feuchtwanger's adaptation of Marlowe's *Edward II*,
on which Brecht later commented that it was an attempt to break away from
the ossified Shakespeare of the German stage, 'jenem gipsig monumentalen
Stil, der den Spießbürgern so teuer ist'. Brecht had of course to contend with
the particularly German notion of the theatre as a place of serious moral
edification. Formal attire for the audience and generous subsidy by public
authority are only two aspects of this quasi-religious character of the theatre in
Germany; and religion requires ritual, which is paralleled on the stage by
norms of production that are stultifying in their rigidity. As late as 1954
Brecht's essay *Einschüchterung durch die Klassizität* carried a biting attack
on this deadening tradition:

Es fällt sozusagen durch Vernachlässigung mehr und mehr Staub auf die großen
alten Bilder, und die Kopisten kopieren mehr oder minder fleißig diese Staubflecken
mit. Hauptsächlich verloren geht dabei die ursprüngliche Frische der klassischen
Werke, ihr damalig Überraschendes, Neues, Produktives, das ein Hauptmerkmal
dieser Werke ist.[1]

The exasperated critic was well aware that there were plenty of producers
(such as Max Reinhardt) capable of giving the theatre an illusory new slant
by making what were, in the last analysis, merely peripheral innovations in
staging to tease a semblance of life out of worn-out conventions. Such purely
formalistic titillation was condemned by Brecht as even more damaging than

traditional productions in that the feverish search for novel and sensational effects blunted and indeed distorted the import of a play.

Never content with solely negative criticism, Brecht sought to define the true greatness of the dramatic heritage that was so frequently obscured by unimaginative convention: he saw it as a 'human greatness', not something detached and superficial, and he complained that the tradition handed down from the court theatres had diverged more and more from this human greatness, while formalistic experiments had only made matters worse. In 1952 Brecht described how *Urfaust* is 'killed' by the conventional view that a classic must be solemn and therefore stiff, and concluded:

Die lustigen Partien sind, der 'Würde des Ortes' (nämlich des meist staatlichen Theaters) entsprechend und Rechnung tragend der 'Bedeutung eines Klassikers', matt, trocken und vor allem ideenlos geworden. Der wahre Respekt vor den klassischen Werken muß aber der Größe ihrer Ideen und der Schönheit ihrer Formen gelten, und er wird auf dem Theater dadurch gezollt, daß die Werke produktiv, phantasievoll und lebendig aufgeführt werden.[2]

Brecht was not only inimical to the reverential type of production but altogether sceptical of the whole approach to literary ranking and the allocation of the title 'genius'. Empirically and realistically he was prepared to rummage in neglected corners if there was the likelihood of unearthing bits of tradition meaningful to the present. In his view a heaven studded with stars of the first rank only was not a heaven, and though Goethe offered things that Lenz did not have, the converse was also true. Already in 1929 Brecht was implicitly aware of the contradictions inherent in reverence for the classics, and how, as objects of worship, they became blackened by incense and covered with dust:

Es wäre ihnen besser bekommen, wenn man ihnen gegenüber eine freiere Haltung eingenommen hätte, wie die Wissenschaft sie zu den Entdeckungen, auch zu großen, eingenommen hat, die sie doch immerfort korrigierte oder sogar wieder verwarf, nicht aus Oppositionslust, sondern der Notwendigkeit entsprechend.[3]

The analogy with science is significant for this is the critical point at which the dialectic of scientific (i.e. experientially ascertainable) progress begins to be applied to literary tradition. Brecht's later yardstick for gauging the significance for us of a drama from another epoch is almost exclusively based on the dialectical feed-back between the portrayal given of that epoch, the seminal ideals contained in the play, and the historical time-dimension between then and now. The social applications of this dialectic are the content and its working out is the form.

Before elaborating on Brecht's endeavours to impose a fundamentally dialectical function on the literary heritage, it is as well to consider first his reiterated demands between 1926 and 1929 concerning the material offered by classics. The simplest call seemed to be for a fearless pillaging of accepted classics in order to appropriate basic material (such as the rough outline of *Herodes und Mariamne*, despite Brecht's rabid disparagement of Hebbel

3

elsewhere) wherever it might serve the needs of a repertoire in the 1920s. The criterion of choice was to be positive value in a contemporary theatrical context. He was not, as he put it, prepared to take over the classics blind. Noticeably, Brecht advocates no out-of-hand rejection of the classics but a guarded respect for the social and artistic ethos from which they sprang. In *Vorrede zu 'Macbeth'*, 1927, Brecht saw Shakespeare's drama as absolute material, and though it called for a different theatre from what was now customary, it was still the best classical quarry for the theatrical renaissance of a generation that in 1914 had had of necessity to make a clean break with the past. Brecht's concern with the fate of the classical repertoire was fully voiced in 1926 in the more or less programmatic *Wie soll man heute Klassiker spielen?* in which he announced where the potential lay and in what terms it could be realized:

Wirklich brauchen davon konnte man nur mehr den Stoff . . . Durch Anwendung eines politischen Gesichtspunktes konnte man irgendein klassisches Stück zu mehr machen als einem Schwelgen in Erinnerungen.[4]

The young and exuberant playwright of those years, sparking off plans and new ideas in many directions, boldly claimed that there was actually a plethora of modern material available in all sorts of places which would enable him to write all the plays needed for a repertoire to last a generation — all this without even tapping the rich mines of dramatic material we had inherited, though the latter lay always ready to hand and afforded a wealth of possibilities. Indeed, Brecht characterizes as 'bourgeois escapism' the demands of certain aesthetes to cease producing old plays. It is debatable whether at this stage Brecht himself was at all clear about the fresh points of view he advocated: on the one hand he talked of applying a political viewpoint to classics, on the other he stated they should not be used to put over any message. Presumably, if the tendency were inherent in the work, it was permissible to bring this out with the aid of a political point of view, whereas it would be wrong to impose it from outside. This procedure would, of course, lay the onus of determining the original tendency on the adaptor — a responsibility that Brecht sometimes only too readily assumed!

Of central importance in Brecht's consideration of dramatic material is the concept of ownership and plagiarism: he regarded any work, once in existence, as lawful plunder for a subsequent writer who could make use of it, and spoke with irritation of the 'mania for possession' that hindered a fresh approach to the classics by treating them as sacrosanct. Brecht had earlier described how the bourgeois theatre was nevertheless unwittingly (and, of course, fundamentally for the wrong reasons) promoting the habit of collective ownership of plays by its own practice of arbitrary cutting. While welcoming 'diese unbedenkliche praktische Anwendung eines neuen kollektivistischen Besitzbegriffs', Brecht emphasizes that hacking out organic parts of literary works is, 'bürgerlich betrachtet, ein Raub, ganz gleich, ob die herausgehackten oder die übriggebliebenen Teile verwendet werden'. The cause of this ironical pat on the back for the bourgeois theatre is seriously and radically analysed in *Das Theater als öffentliche Angelegenheit: Funktionswechsel des Theaters*, 1929, where Brecht develops the idea that 'nationalisation' of the heritage of dramatic material would, by embedding this material in the national consciousness, make it easier than in the case of drama aimed at the individual to work out its gestic content (i.e. the social implications of scenes, situations, actions) as a collective phenomenon and to define the function of the latter in promoting new attitudes. This whole process would obviate the role of the spectator as the autonomous emotional 'consumer'. In conversation with the critic Ihering at this time, Brecht indicated how he strove in productions of classics to extract the gestic content and explained that he found the task too arduous in most cases because the classics showed not the world but themselves, with a narrow bourgeois horizon. The sociologist Fritz Sternberg, with whom Brecht frequently argued to thrash out problems he was struggling with, describes the attempts at bringing out the specific social import of *Julius Caesar* and outlines the way of thinking that could lead to a free hand in the use of the material. Brecht had rejected as inadequate both the omission of extensive stretches of Shakespeare's text and the emphasizing of sociological aspects, and Sternberg had then suggested:

Wenn Sie bereit sind, Shakespeare durch Überbetonung gewisser Stellen und Weglassen von anderen zu ändern; wenn Sie somit schon etwas anderes bringen als jener Dichter, der unter Elisabeth seine Stücke schrieb und inszenierte — warum können Sie dann nicht auch, wenn Sie offen darauf hinweisen, neuen Text hinzufügen? Warum können Sie nicht ein Drama auf die Bühne bringen: *Julius Cäsar*, nach Motiven von Shakespeare, zum Teil neu geschrieben von Bertolt Brecht? Wenn Shakespeare selber für seine Dramen auf Stoffe der Weltliteratur, wie sie zu seiner Zeit bekannt war, zurückgriff und sie umformte — warum sollen wir unsererseits seine Dramen heute nicht ebenfalls umformen? Und zwar gerade den Cäsar, da ja die Tragödie des Brutus — daß man mit der Ermordung des Diktators die Diktatur nicht tötet — eine ganz gewaltige, uns noch heute aufs stärkste aufwühlende Angelegenheit ist.[5]

Whether or not this memoir was coloured by hindsight it is difficult to say; certainly it prefigures exactly much of what Brecht later did with his adaptations. At any rate, Brecht grew very thoughtful at that point, according to Sternberg.

It is relevant to compare Brecht's attitude to classics with that of Erwin Piscator who shared Brecht's left-wing ideology and in addition was actively engaged, as a producer, in trying to establish a *political* theatre in Berlin in the 1920s. Brecht had great sympathy with Piscator's efforts and collaborated with him to some extent (e.g. in the adaptation of Hašek's *Schwejk* for Piscator's Volksbühne). As he was building up a repertoire Piscator had necessarily to grapple with the question of the dramatic tradition. In his account of the rise and fall of the Volksbühne (*Das politische Theater*, 1929) he tackles it by first of all repudiating the hollow externals of modernization and replacing them by the point of view that to revitalize the classics one must give them the relevance to present life that they had to their own times by setting them in the same relationship to us as they had to their original age. But his real aim is the promotion of the proletarian revolution:

Der geistige Visierpunkt ist und bleibt für mich das Proletariat und die soziale Revolution. Sie ist der Gradmesser meiner Arbeit. Nicht im luftleeren Raum sind innere und geistige Probleme zur Diskussion zu stellen. Fruchtbar kann sie nur werden, wenn ein Zweck vorhanden ist, ein Zweck, der sich auf das Gesellschaftliche richtet.[6]

Under the rubric *Grundsätzliches* Piscator goes on to make certain programmatic points about the reshaping of classical works to fit the needs of present-day society. In the first place he sees a dramatic work (in contrast to a lyric) as rooted in the actuality of its time, yet not for that reason evanescent; rather, succeeding ages will shift its meaningfulness from one aspect to another according to changing circumstances and will throw into relief the elements they find apposite to their own conditions. It is not enough, however, for the play itself to have the quality that enables it to evolve and acquire changed significance; the producer is of overriding importance in adopting a viewpoint from which to lay bare the essentials of the drama — and in demanding that the producer be a servant of his age, not of the play, Piscator had already stated quite unambiguously that this viewpoint must be ideological. At this time Brecht might have gone along with Piscator in ransacking classics for those elements that would suit our era and in demanding a clear-cut ideological standpoint from which the producer would, after all, interpret the play. Two decades later, however, engaged now in evolving a 'responsible' repertoire for the Berliner Ensemble, Brecht was more circumspect and subtle. In 1952 he adapted and produced Molière's *Dom Juan*, wrestling with the temptation to interpret, posing and answering his own questions:

Wie soll man Molière spielen? Wie den *Don Juan*? Ich denke, die Antwort muß sein: So, wie er nach möglichst genauer Prüfung des Textes unter Berücksichtigung der Dokumente von Molières Zeit und seiner Stellung zu dieser Zeit gespielt werden muß. Das heißt, man darf ihn nicht verdrehen, verfälschen, schlau ausdeuten; man darf nicht spätere Gesichtspunkte über die seinen stellen und so weiter.[7]

Two years later the essay *Einschüchterung durch die Klassizität* emerged from the problems involved in staging *Urfaust* in 1954. Towards the end of his life Brecht showed great respect for classics and instead of imposing modern political ideas by constraint on the historical situation, sought now to release similar political attitudes latent in the original. The ideas embedded in the play, the contemporary documents and historical situation, the particular individuality and attitude of the author towards his time — all these elements take precedence over Piscator's primacy of the present ideological context. Not that Brecht abandoned the political dimension: the Marxist point of view provides for him the intellectual and emotional focus in which the content of the classics acquires perspective and relevance. Whereas Piscator was first and foremost interested in the *immediate* uses of the past to further the proletarian advance in the class war, Brecht brought to bear a genuinely felt and cogently argued philosophy of history in his conception of tradition and its function.

It is the Marxist philosophy of history that leads directly to the core of Brecht's aesthetic; the approach to the past based on the broad theory of historical materialism was made productive by the dialectical method developed through Hegel and Marx. In the first place Brecht categorically accepted (in the *Kleines Organon für das Theater*) the admissibility of differing structural and stylistic principles in the theatre according to the epoch involved: the tyrant-dominated Greek populace in its arena had to be entertained in a different way from the feudal court of Louis XIV. Fruitful in a modern context are the many modes of presenting society that can still give us pleasure, even those that are now superseded because of their inaccuracies and improbabilities. However, the productiveness of works handed down is not intrinsic to them in an absolute sense, it is only released by setting them in their historical situation, in contrast to the present; that is, by being looked at historically they become meaningful *because of* and *for* the present. In Brecht's dialogue on drama, *Der Messingkauf*, the Philosopher refers to the impossibility of producing Shakespeare for the spectator who is totally devoid of a historical sense, and indeed claims that the old plays cease to have any true substance if they are not seen in the context of our own time.

The historical attitude is the crucial requisite for the whole of Brecht's theory and practice; it is as central to the making of a new, contemporary play as to looking at or adapting past literature. In both cases, observation of present or past, it determines the relationship between observer and situation. The Marxist critic, Georg Lukács, lucidly described the shortcomings in this respect not only of earlier literary periods but also of the Naturalists who thought they had pre-empted the secret of truly objective historical description:

Die Unmittelbarkeit des Naturalismus stellt die Welt dar, so wie sie in den Erlebnissen der Figuren selbst direkt erscheint. Um eine vollendete Echtheit zu erlangen, geht der naturalistische Schriftsteller weder inhaltlich noch formell über den Horizont seiner Gestalten hinaus; ihr Horizont ist zugleich der des Werks . . . Selbst bei Hauptmann wird der Bauernkrieg für uns nur so weit sichtbar, als sein Florian Geyer imstande ist, ihn zu erleben.[8]

Like most Naturalist writers, who more often than not were only emotionally involved with socialism as 'sympathizers', Hauptmann, according to Lukács, failed to grasp and convey the historical dialectic of his material in *Florian Geyer* — the Peasant Wars and Germany's social failure at a point of transition from medieval to modern times. Lukács further maintains that peripheral refinements in language and atmosphere were of no weight at all in overcoming the limitations of Naturalism if there were not present the wider 'objective' dimension that encompassed and made comprehensible the 'subjective' individual vision. Brecht differed radically from both Naturalists

— in going aggressively beyond a straightforward reproducing of circumstances — and also earlier writers — in so far as the objective forces of life
(which Lukács held to be the basis of their writing) were quite inadmissible
in the light of the historical dialectic which could not allow only absolutes,
and as it was wholly irrelevant to the earlier writers whether their personages
had a 'horizon' at all. Brecht can be seen to have widened the historical
consciousness of the 'hero' beyond the situation in which he finds himself, to
make it coincide (wherever possible) with the hindsight of the modern playwright and audience. As late as 1954, on reconsidering his earliest plays,
Brecht had exactly the same criticism of his presentation of the proletarian
revolution in *Trommeln in der Nacht* as Lukács had of the depiction of
the Peasants' Revolt in *Florian Geyer*:

... es war mir nicht gelungen, den Zuschauer die Revolution anders sehen zu lassen,
als der 'Held' Kragler sie sah, und er sah sie als etwas Romantisches. Die Technik
der Verfremdung stand mir noch nicht zur Verfügung.[9]

There are, however, indications of a burgeoning if not yet subtle alienation in
this play, and before many years had passed Brecht was developing this
technique in great strides as the most appropriate method for achieving the
double perspective congruent with a dramatic action in its immediate reality
on the stage and, simultaneously, its determination in a historical context.
The clash between empathy and alienation which many regard as a rejection
of so-called Aristotelian principles by Brecht is, looked at in other terms, a
conflict of claims between the subjective individualizing approach that seeks
its justification solely within the compass of the play, and the historicizing
sense that casts its anchors in other waters than apparently purely aesthetic
ones. Brecht felt that empathy diverts our attention from significant aspects
and allows us only partly to grasp and enjoy the full import of past plays, and
that we are encouraged to concentrate on such accessories as beauty of
language and elegance of plot, devices often used to conceal discrepancies in
the story. He even accuses the theatre of having lost the desire or capacity to
make credible the concatenation of events. In a significant addendum to these
ideas in the *Organon* Brecht explicitly selected the historical sense as the prime
element in aesthetic appreciation suited to our times, implying its dominance
as a structural principle and demanding that it should be developed 'into true
sensuousness'. It may seem surprising to find sensuousness and the historical
sense linked so closely; the explanation lies in the enjoyment felt by Brecht in
analysing any situation, past or present. Pleasure is generated in this process of
applying the reasoning powers, and is akin to the mathematician's delight
in an elegant solution to a problem or the excitement of discovery. To this
function of the historical sense Brecht added the idea that it should in fact
contribute to retaining an awareness of change, thereby increasing our grasp
of the dialectic of reality.

One pioneering application of the historical sense to a classic had been
Piscator's production of *Die Räuber* in 1926 at the Berlin Staatstheater. The

2

critic Ihering quickly noted the significance of Piscator's manhandling of Schiller's text: by shifting the accent from Karl Moor, the centripetal hero, to Spiegelberg, the convinced revolutionary, he had widened the 'horizon' of the play beyond its time. In *Gespräch über Klassiker* Brecht commented that this production was a promising experiment, opening up possibilities and allowing Schiller's text to blossom with a fresh appeal. Earlier Brecht quoted Piscator as having told him that his aim had been to impress on the spectators' minds, when they left the theatre, that 150 years was no mean space of time. In the *Gespräch* Ihering went on to describe how, as early as his adaptation of *Edward II*, Brecht himself had broken the ground in replacing 'greatness' by 'distance', and by a process of 'cooling' had brought the old play closer in the very act of distancing it:

Sie verkleinerten die Menschen nicht. Sie atomisierten die Figuren nicht. Sie entfernten sie. Sie nahmen dem Schauspieler die Gemütlichkeit, die sich temperamentvoll anbiedert. Sie forderten Rechenschaft über die Vorgänge. Sie verlangten einfache Gesten. Sie zwangen zu klarem, kühlem Sprechen. Keine Gefühlsmogelei wurde geduldet. Das ergab den objektiven, den epischen Stil.[10]

Up to a point the historical sense is the objective, aloof viewpoint of the historian (*pace* Croce and Collingwood) who, ideally, attempts to analyse logically and elucidate any factual situation on the basis of available documentary evidence. But this historical attitude is indiscriminate, in that it does not inherently evaluate the past or see it in a changing perspective because of the present. In contrast, Brecht's historical sense is different in quality from that of the historian because it is the active factor in promoting the social function of the theatre, and as such central to his dramaturgy. Ultimately, and paradoxically, Brecht's historical sense can only be considered subjective for, being goal-directed, it attempts to establish on the stage reciprocal effects between 'then' and 'now'. Brecht historicizes from particular situations and is indeed highly selective in choosing suitable ones. He made this clear with reference to classic plays in answering a question put to him by a West German theatre director concerning the feasibility of an epic manner of production. He saw the greatest possibility of success with Shakespeare or the early plays of the classics, depending in each instance on how the social function had been tackled. There is indeed no significant distinction to be made between Brecht's use of historical material or of an existing play. If anything, the latter has perhaps a greater degree of unique reality (*Coriolan* is about a specific war situation, not the wrongness of war; *Der Hofmeister* contains the particular relationship of a tutor to his masters at a strictly defined historical time) whereas the plays that are entirely Brecht's have a paradigmatic, generalizing quality even when based on historical facts (war in general is thematic in *Mutter Courage*, the Catholic Church stands for *any* authority in *Leben des Galilei*). In both cases the selection of material is governed by the degree of its usefulness in promoting the social function of the stage.

In the productions and adaptations of classics this social function —
'Abbildung der Wirklichkeit zum Zweck der Einflußnahme auf die Wirklichkeit' — can be of a threefold nature: the original playwright may have
intended an effect at his time, the adaptor could be trying to condition
the present audience's appraisal of history, or attempting on the basis of a
shifted reaction to the past to alter our attitude to present reality. The triple
perspective is clearly evident, for example, in *Der Hofmeister*. The sub-title,
Vorteile der Privaterziehung, and the fact that the play is called a 'Komödie'
(that is, not a comedy but a non-tragedy) are sufficient indications in themselves, given the content, that Lenz was adopting a very definite critical
attitude to certain contemporary social facts. In his re-working of the play
Brecht achieves the remaining two perspectives by the device of adding a
prologue and epilogue spoken by the Hofmeister himself. In *Die Dramaturgie
des späten Brecht* Walter Hinck has pointed out the functional (and consequent formal) difference between the personage in the prologue and in the
play, the former having essentially the dual role of typifying all the private
tutors of his time and of commenting on this from a modern standpoint.
Further, the influencing of the reality of our present time is projected in the
exhortation of the epilogue which transmits an impulse or stimulus to the
audience that may be used productively; the drama itself is therefore only one
part of a process that is left to the audience to carry further in direct application to its own time. The question of topicality is especially pertinent
in productions of plays where the society depicted no longer exists or has
changed beyond recognition. Brecht asked himself this question about his own
play, *Herr Puntila und sein Knecht Matti*, 'nach der Vertreibung der Guts-
besitzer bei uns', and decided it was still relevant, 'weil man nicht nur aus dem
Kampf lernt, sondern auch aus der Geschichte der Kämpfe'. Being
conditioned by the notion of social progress, Brecht's idea of topicality was
distinctly ideological, and had been so for many years; he had already in 1928
talked of the need to alter our conception of existing plays in the light of social
developments:

Das Schicksal der Rose Bernd, der Weber und so weiter kann nicht mehr als tragisch
empfunden und also auch nicht als tragisch vorgegeben werden in einer Zeit, welche
diese Katastrophen schon auf einen bloßen Mangel der Zivilisation zurückführt,
den zu beheben sie schon höchst praktische Vorschläge ausgearbeitet hat.[11]

This statement carries the implicit corollary that a meaningful production
of such plays would have to be slanted in such a way as to disclose the motives
for which they *could* once be felt as 'tragic fates'. This leads us back to the
problem of selection of material: there is a gradation of latent topicality in
classics, usually stronger and more immediate in the first works of authors
or in those heralding a new tradition, as these tend to contain more substance
of a social nature.

Crucial in Brecht's attitude to literature is his belief that a work of art is
tantamount to a historical event and, once created, belongs to history. This

viewpoint prevented him from omitting *Trommeln in der Nacht* when his collected plays were published, despite the fact that he expressed great dissatisfaction with this drama, as it contained attitudes which he later condemned and repudiated. Since literature is part of history, which must not be falsified, and since his present ideas would be of less value without the knowledge of his earlier ones, Brecht decided to admit this play. To suppress it would not be enough — what is wrong must be corrected. The value of an existent work, as of history, does not then lie in our ability to learn from the past (though this may appear to be the case at first glance) but in creating a perspective for fresh work; it is didactic in opening the way to a correction of false ideas, and active in its intention to influence. If an original play is seen as an event (which is what it is in the history of literature) then the adaptation must be regarded as a historical analysis; any alterations made are an intervention in the facts or the evidence for facts in order to illustrate and elucidate the situation more trenchantly. The degree of 'correction' would reflect Brecht's divergence from the standpoint of the original author or the social system concerned, or it would be in inverse proportion to the significance of the productive impulses that Brecht finds latent in the subject-matter.

Though Brecht did not hold the naive view that the study of history enables men to learn from the past in order not to repeat mistakes, the idea of progress is constantly to the fore in all his cogitations. This is, however, not the ebullient material optimism of nineteenth-century historians beguiled by technological advances, but a philosophical idea of progress derived from Hegel's exposition of the historical dialectic based on the axiom 'daß die Vernunft die Welt beherrscht, daß es also auch in der Weltgeschichte vernünftig zugegangen ist'. In keeping with this meaning or 'purpose' of history Brecht does not apply a definite criterion in selecting classics for modern production. He believes that humanity retains the plays that give artistic form to its steps 'in der Richtung auf immer kräftigere, zartere und kühnere Humanität'; thus, such plays must possess progressive ideas in some measure which will provide the dynamic of any present-day 'rendering'.

Apart from his practical creative activity in adapting and producing plays from previous epochs for the theatre in Berlin, there are many notes that indicate how preoccupied Brecht must have been in his last years with this question of the function of the classical repertoire. A year before his death he took an observation by Marx as the starting-point for a statement on the essentially dialectical function of great art. Marx had pointed out the surprising capacity people have for being affected by even very ancient works of art. Though Brecht agreed with him in rejecting as a reason for this 'the hackneyed formula of the timelessness of art', he brushed aside Marx's supposition that humanity likes to recall its early stages. He suggested instead that great works of art are born in times of struggle and change, and progress is an overcoming of previous progress, so that humanity has a constant nostalgia for what has been sacrificed for the sake of new achievements. Brecht here deploys the same dialectical notion as in his 1929 analogy with the sciences, where the modification or rejection of previous discoveries is dictated by the necessities of scientific evolution. That this is not simply theory but an active force in a live theatre is corroborated in a letter, written in 1955 to the Central Committee of the SED, in which Brecht describes the efforts of the Berliner Ensemble 'die Errungenschaften der Klassik im dialektischen Sinn "aufzuheben" ' as one of their characteristics that cause misunderstanding. This concern to alter the function of *familiar* material, a highly developed and conscious procedure of the Ensemble, had its seeds back in 1929 in Brecht's call to bring out the gestic content of well-known subject-matter in order to determine the correct attitudes that conflicted with that subject-matter. It is evident that dialectic became increasingly the *mode* of Brecht's thought and activity, and it is well-known that he reduced a life-time's work to the succinct formula 'dialectic theatre'. Dialectic for Brecht is by no means purely philosophical but is rooted in the fairly rigorous training in historical materialism he acquired, especially from the Marxist theorist Karl Korsch. The critic Wolfdietrich Rasch has described the influence of Korsch on Brecht's dramaturgical thought and referred to the possibilities latent in applying Heisenberg's 'uncertainty principle' to the function of art in the field of sociology:

Vollzieht sich in der Dichtung eine Veränderung des Bewußtseins, so ist damit bereits die Wirklichkeit selbst verändert. Genau dies ist die Grundlage der dramaturgischen Theorie Brechts . . . In den *Flüchtlingsgesprächen* beruft sich Ziffel auf Heisenbergs Feststellung, daß die wissenschaftliche Beobachtung der physischen Objekte diese bereits verändert, und er findet das gleiche Phänomen in der sozialen Welt . . . Das gilt nach Brechts Überzeugung auch von der Umsetzung gesellschaftswissenschaftlicher Erkenntnisse im Drama.[12]

This 'uncertainty principle', however inconvenient it may be to the quantum physicist, was certainly assessed as a positive factor by Brecht, since it can reasonably be assumed that he was voicing his own ideas through Ziffel. The analogy with the scientific principle is undoubtedly imperfect, but it served Brecht's purpose in defining a phenomenon he was aware of, and so he inserted the uncertainty factor into the dialectical process, at least as regards its social application. It is fruitful to take Brecht's analogy further, into the playwright's own domain. It calls to mind, for instance, Brecht's definition of the social function of drama — 'Abbildung der Wirklichkeit zum Zweck der Einflußnahme auf die Wirklichkeit' — and explains in a certain degree the special nature of his adaptation of plays. In effect, he developed a quite individual technique of treating classics not as independent absolutes but as events in history, and therefore with a causation and dynamic linked to the society they sprang from and explicable in its terms. The second factor to come into play is the modern observer, with his point of view conditioned by the time-gap, who then enters into a dialectic with the potential of the original work and alters it. Thus far Brecht really shared Piscator's approach, though exploiting it more thoroughly. What Brecht was overridingly alive to was, however, the third factor, necessarily integral to the dialectical process, namely that the revealed dynamic of the play inevitably altered and enriched the viewpoint of the modern observer, this effect taking place concurrently and interdependently with that in the reverse direction, to become a unique synthesis in the play in its new form.

The dialectical principle that enabled Brecht to effect this triple perspective originates in Hegel's concept of 'Aufhebung', the importance of which is stressed by Hans Mayer in a discussion of Brecht's relationship with tradition in *Bertolt Brecht und die Tradition*. Mayer equates 'Emporheben' and 'Um-gestaltung' within the trinity of meaning contained in 'Aufhebung'; this corresponds to the Hegelian synthesis which can be seen as a 'raising up' on to a higher level, and is indeed the manner in which the dialectical process evolves in a time-value dimension. There is no doubt that the oscillatory feed-back between a classic and its adaptation by Brecht produces a dialectically dynamic third force that Mayer subsumes under the term 'Umfunktionierung klassischer Werke' as the solution to the disparate attitudes displayed in the two essays *Wie soll man heute Klassiker spielen?* and *Einschüchterung durch die Klassizität*:

Klassik als Stoff oder als Gehalt? Brecht entscheidet sich für den Gehalt. Eine neue Auffassung also von der klassischen Substanz. Neue Vorstellungen aber auch von ihrer Funktion . . . Man hat den Eindruck, als bemühe sich der Dialektiker Brecht bei seinen Bearbeitungen klassischer Werke, den realen Gehalt zu vernachlässigen, um einen virtuellen Gehalt 'in Freiheit zu setzen'.[13]

Another Marxist critic, Hans Kaufmann, claims that there are two conflicting intentions at work in the adaptations:

Das überlieferte Stück wird *bühnengerecht* und — bei ausländischen Werken — in neuem sprachlichen Gewand *vorgeführt, damit die dem Stück eigenen Züge deutlicher werden*, und zugleich benutzt es Brecht *als Material für seine poetischen Zwecke*.[14]

Kaufmann reasons that these conflicting tendencies must be mutually ex-clusive, and concludes (in contradiction to Mayer) that, since Brecht added textual matter that altered the meaning intended by the original author, he was after the matter not the content of the work as the starting-point of his interpretation. Unlike Mayer, Kaufmann overlooks the dialectic inherent in both theory and practice of the adaptations, for Brecht had stated that one of his intentions had been to bring out the original ideas and the social comment of a work, and this activity might very easily reveal a *latent* content that could only be apprehended with an alert historical sense functioning from a present standpoint. Kaufmann's analysis operates altogether in sharply delimited opposites which are nevertheless nebulous and marks off Brecht's later 'critical appropriation' of classics from an earlier 'dissociation from the culture of the past'. Yet even in his more belligerent and uncompromising youthful attitudes (as drama reviewer of the left-wing Augsburg newspaper *Volkswille*, for instance) Brecht directed his opposition not to the classics themselves in any absolute sense, but always to falsifying conceptions and misuses of them. For apparent discrepancies to be resolved we must define more closely what Brecht meant by classics. He had stated in 1929: 'Die Form unserer Klassiker ist nicht klassisch. Zu frühe Stabilisierung, Prinzip der Ruhe und Abgeklärtheit.' It has been pointed out that Brecht was inclined to look on first works as true classics in his sense of the word, that is, works setting the pace, surging forward, holding the seeds of an epoch capable of fruitful dialectical semination, not the formal crowning and ossification of a style or an era. These reveal the points in history where the dialectical leap from quantity to quality occurs — an example of the Hegelian 'Umschlag'. Here the accumulated energy is released on a higher level, and the social movement forward is reflected in the drama of the time. In this context it is fully understandable that the pioneers of Marxist thought should always be termed classics by Brecht.

The special nature of Brecht's view of what constitutes classics sheds an important light on his adaptations: no play is haphazardly chosen, the potential of its social and political orientation weighs more than any attributed literary merit, and it fits integrally into the pattern of the Hegelian historical dialectic that Brecht applied ever more stringently in his work up to the end of his life. The mainsprings of dialectic that were the motive force of historicizing in his own work provided the criterion by which Brecht chose plays for adaptation, with a consequent and sometimes radical change in their dramatic form and function. It can be no coincidence that Brecht selected plays that dealt with or appeared at nodal points in social and cultural history. They were suited to the encouragement of the productive attitude of change in the mind of the spectator, because an artistic inculcation of the historical sense could be achieved through them. This impulse to constant change is one of the many aspects of the dialectical theatre present in Brecht's adaptations. Another is that of criticism both *with* and *of* Lenz which Mayer sees in Brecht's version of *Der Hofmeister*. A further structural force of a dialectical nature, that of 'sowohl — als auch' or 'nicht — sondern', was fully exploited to indicate how a particular image of reality implied, in the very way it was shaped, what it did *not* depict and what might be considered desirable. The triadic movement of thesis, antithesis and synthesis was probably more clearly realizable by Brecht in the utilization of historical material rather than invented situations, as one side of the movement — the positive affirmation — was thus already set and determined through its historical reality.

In the last instance, whatever intellectual tools may have served Brecht to prepare himself for constructing his plays and may help the critic to analyse them, there remains the irrefutable but often overlooked fact that Brecht wrote *plays* — not political or sociological pamphlets. However much a man may be slotted into sociological pigeon-holes, smelted statistically, mechanically unravelled by psychology and biology, each man yet remains *one* man, an individual, irreducibly *there* as more than and different from all his separate aspects added together. As a playwright first and foremost Brecht does justice to the intimate coherence between the individuality of the human being and that of a play. The latter is a structure of words forming an image of human attitudes and relationships and serving as a vehicle and focal point for the gestures of actors and the attention of an audience (particularly for Brecht there was a powerful dialectical traffic between stage and public); as such the play is a unique, empirical, particular thing. Contrary to common belief, Brecht never derived his practice from theory; indeed, he would handle the printed text of a play as if it were theory, subjecting it in rehearsal to the most rigorous test of visual reality and probability, as Käthe Rülicke, a close collaborator in the Berliner Ensemble productions, has clearly stated. The dual misconception that Brecht's plays are either overweighted with ideological matter or good theatre despite their tendentiousness arises in part from Brecht's own ample, able and polemical inquiries into the meaning and function of his plays *after* they had come into existence.

Marx's 'correction' of the Hegelian dialectical principle in its application to man in a historical context (i.e. that man cannot be considered only conceptually as an absolute in metaphysical terms, but that a man is with equal importance a moment, an integral bit in the flow of humanity, and his reality is in the dialectical interrelation of these two aspects) can help determine the nature of an adaptation by Brecht. The latter is the re-siting of an original in a new historical context, with all the accumulated knowledge, events and experience of intervening years actually altering it, to produce something radically different. (The same relationship can be said to hold between a play and historical 'facts' on which it is based — as in *Leben des Galilei*, where the historical Galileo is not portrayed as an absolute fixed figure pre-determined by a skeleton cage of facts and events circumscribing his life, but as a changeable reality essentially made up of our shifting reactions to what he was and achieved: 'das "atomarische Zeitalter" machte sein Debüt in Hiroshima in der Mitte unserer Arbeit. Von heute auf morgen las sich die Biographie des Begründers der neuen Physik anders.')[15] However many lines survive unbruised and whatever else may be residual from the original, the Brechtian adaptation is unique in that the changes are qualitative rather than quantitative, and, once the specific adaptation has been created, a dialectic is set up between the two plays and the social realities that generated them and which in turn they affect.

NOTES

1 *GW*, 17/1275.
2 *GW*, 17/1280.
3 *GW*, 15/178.
4 *GW*, 15/113.
5 F. Sternberg, *Der Dichter und die Ratio* (Göttingen, 1963), pp. 35 f.
6 E. Piscator, *Das politische Theater*, revised edition (Hamburg, 1963), p. 90.
7 *GW*, 17/1257.
8 G. Lukács, 'Deutsche Literatur im Zeitalter des Imperialismus', in *Skizze einer Geschichte der neueren deutschen Literatur* (Berlin, 1964), pp. 160 ff.
9 *GW*, 17/946.
10 *GW*, 15/181.
11 *GW*, 15/173.
12 W. Rasch, 'Bertolt Brechts marxistischer Lehrer', *Merkur*, 17 (1963), 996 f.
13 H. Mayer, *Bertolt Brecht und die Tradition* (Pfullingen, 1961), p. 17.
14 H. Kaufmann, *Bertolt Brecht. Geschichtsdrama und Parabelstück* (Berlin, 1962), p. 198.
15 *GW*, 17/1106.

CHAPTER II

DER HOFMEISTER

It is not surprising that in 1950 Brecht should have chosen J. M. R. Lenz's *Der Hofmeister* (1774) as the first guinea-pig to be submitted to his experiments in creating a repertoire for the newly-instituted Berliner Ensemble amid the ruins of the German capital. With his appreciation of the dynamism in first works, his abhorrence of what he considered the dead balance that 'classical' implied and the desire to open the way again to Shakespeare (without whom he could not conceive a national theatre) Brecht naturally turned to the beginnings of German classicism, where it is still realistic and poetic at the same time. Shakespeare is the guiding star and in *Der Hofmeister*, said Brecht, we find in full measure the 'natural disorder' characteristic of the Shakespearian play, where ideas have not yet dominated the material. A leading representative of the Sturm und Drang, maligned, neglected and eccentric, Lenz could and did hold his own in a frenetic Shakespearian creativity that matched the restlessness and miserable curtailment of his life. As aware as any contemporary of the social inequalities and human degradation of his time, he succeeded in conveying criticism through a depiction of the rich variety of human affairs without which all theatrical shaping is lifeless. The social-critical attitude so dear to Brecht is inherent in *Der Hofmeister* in the conjunction of rebellious Sturm und Drang ideas and Lenz's theatre note calling for the individual human being to be the focus of attention, where the Greeks had eyes only for an immutable fate and its effects. In this account of the private tutor who succumbs to the physical attractions of his employer's daughter and castrates himself out of despair at being unable to control his sexual urges, the intervention of fate is almost non-existent and the dramatic pressure arises from the collision of an individual with class distinctions, within a well-defined social reality.

Another factor drawing Brecht's attention to the pre-classical Sturm und Drang is that this is the high point of that form of German society generally described by left-wing commentators as 'die deutsche Misere', a nodal period of social and intellectual repression in the painful transition from a feudal structure dominated by the aristocracy to the emergence of the modern bourgeois society. Brecht consistently held an unequivocally critical attitude to this epoch, seeing in it the bourgeois acquiescence in the ideology of feudal society, thus prolonging its existence beyond the 'natural' limit the Hegelian dialectic of history would have allowed it. Lenz himself is not absolved from blame for this acquiescence, and indeed the discrepancy between his attack on a contemporary state of affairs and Brecht's criticism of the idealistic lack of consistency in this attack provides the mainspring for Brecht's adaptation and a ready-made frame for 'epic' theatre:

So werden wir gezwungen (oder instand gesetzt), die Vorgänge zwischen seinen Personen zu spielen und die Äußerungen davon abzusetzen — wir brauchen sie nicht zu unseren eigenen zu machen. Auf diese Weise sind die Personen auch nicht entweder ernst oder komisch, sondern bald ernst, bald komisch. Der Hofmeister selbst erntet unser Mitgefühl, da er sehr unterdrückt wird, und unsere Verachtung, da er sich so sehr unterdrücken läßt.[1]

Der Hofmeister is significant as Brecht's first adaptation for the Berliner Ensemble in so far as it is a native play and not one by Shakespeare, despite the pride of place Brecht accords the latter in any repertoire. The adaptation of a German play was bound to be more revealing than that of a foreign one; both for adaptor and audience there were far closer links and a subtler coming to terms with a native tradition than could be conceivable with alien subject-matter, which would lack the deeper familiarity with psychological, socio-political and cultural factors at work in a significant era of native history.

To say why Brecht selected *Der Hofmeister* for adaptation is to say something about his purpose: he wanted explicitly to lay bare the workings of a certain social situation, to indicate that it was open to alteration and in what way this could be achieved. In effect Brecht's version was to be an interpretation of history (that is, of the theme and its handling by Lenz) from his own twentieth-century standpoint, and, containing as it does three portraits of schoolmasters and three of aspiring schoolmasters from the time when the German middle class was establishing the shape of its educational system, he believed it would give 'ein anregendes satirisches Bild dieses Teils der deutschen Misere'[2] and be a practical contribution to the great reform in education now under way in the German Democratic Republic. In a letter to Hans Mayer written during the rehearsals of his *Hofmeister*, Brecht enumerates the aspects of the play that he found specially relevant. First of all he censures the faint-heartedness of German classicism for failing to clinch the revolutionary realism set in motion by the Sturm und Drang and for creating a great dramatic style only for idealistic works. In defiance of the neglect literary history has shown for Lenz, Brecht claims that any realistic dramatic style must start with him. Secondly, he stresses the parabolic nature of Läuffer's act of self-castration:

Natürlich ist die Fabel keine symbolische schlechthin: es wird einfach ganz realistisch (es liegt ja ein grausiges wahres Ereignis in Ostpreußen dem Stück zugrunde) die Selbstentmannung der Intellektuellen, die zu dieser Zeit mehr oder weniger alle, also als Kaste in den Lehrerberuf gedrängt waren, an einem Exempel in Fleisch und Blut vorgeführt, d.h. die körperliche Selbstentmannung *bedeutet* nicht nur eine geistige Selbstentmannung, sondern ist selber als der groteske Ausweg aus der sozialen Situation Läuffers dargestellt.[3]

Most significantly, Brecht lays special weight on the fact that it is a real *comedy*, and it is this that determines a radical shift in the conceptual and aesthetic postulates of the play. It is true that the first edition of Lenz's play in 1774 carried the title and sub-title *Der Hofmeister oder Vorteile der Privater-ziehung. Eine Komödie*, the author supplying his own definition of comedy (in *Rezension des neuen Menoza*) as 'a picture of human society', in the same way as Dante or Balzac. But he had originally intended it as a *Lust- und Trauerspiel*, and indeed Brecht restricts the description even more in one of the 'socio-critical sonnets' he wrote in 1940 entitled 'Über das bürgerliche Trauerspiel *Der Hofmeister* von Lenz':

> Hier habt ihr Figaro diesseits des Rheins!
> Der Adel geht beim Pöbel in die Lehre
> Der drüben Macht gewinnt und hüben Ehre:
> So wirds ein Lustspiel drüben und hier keins.
>
> Der Arme will, statt in die Literatur
> Der reichen Schülrin in die Bluse schau'n.
> Doch statt den Gordischen Knoten zu durchhau'n
> Haut er, Lakai, nur über seine Schnur.
>
> Nun er gewahrt, daß sich mit seinem Glied
> Zugleich sein Brotkorb in die Höhe zieht.
> So heißt es denn zu wählen, und er wählt.
>
> Sein Magen knurrt, doch klärt auch sein Verstand sich.
> Er flennt und murrt und lästert und entmannt sich.
> Des Dichters Stimme bricht, wenn er's erzählt.

This sonnet indicates an ironic use of the term 'bürgerliches Trauerspiel'. The social requisite for the establishment of this type of tragedy in eighteenth-century Germany had been the emergence of the middle class as a possible challenge to political absolutism; it combined the imperious ignoring of class barriers by the sexual urge with the poaching from the middle class by a privileged and powerful aristocracy. But Lenz's hero reverses the situation: it is *he* who first thrusts into forbidden territory but then succumbs to econo-mic pressures brought to bear on him. Brecht calls particular attention to this factor and would see Lenz's play more as a 'tragedy of the middle class' were he not criticizing that class for the inability to fulfil what a Marxist would see as its historical function. Thus the sonnet prefigures the main lines along which Brecht's adaptation was to move: 'Lustspiel drüben' (the French absolutist state was undermined and toppled before the close of that century); 'Lakai' (the seemingly 'fixed stars' of masters and servants); 'Glied/Brotkorb' (conflict between the drives of the individual and the pressures of society); 'des Dichters Stimme bricht' (emotional involvement of the author through personal experience). But Brecht, with the advantage of a time perspective on his side, alters the fundamental premisses of Lenz and disengages himself from sympathetic identity with the hero in order to make a true comedy.

Mayer describes how, in doing so, Brecht becomes a critic both *with* and *of* Lenz:

Wo Lenz mit brechender Stimme berichtet, zeigt Brecht heitere Gelassenheit. Das jedoch ist nur möglich, wenn der Bearbeiter das Einverständnis mit den sozialen Postulaten des ersten Stückschreibers, des Stürmers und Drängers, aufgekündigt hat ... Brechts Bearbeitung des Schauspiels von Lenz wird zur Kritik an Lenz. Der Bearbeiter bleibt dort ein Gegner, wo bereits Lenz ein Gegner war. Er wird aber auch dort zum Gegner, wo Lenz noch Freunde gesucht hatte.[4]

However, in depicting dispassionately, 'epically', Brecht does not relinquish the positive emotional effect on an audience: by making the comedy satirical he seeks to engender passion in the spectator, but a passion stemming from discernment and judgement of the situation and not from the personal misfortunes of the hero — in short, the critical passion aroused by a historical view. There is no room in Brecht's adaptation for the sentimentality attendant on Gustchen's plight; by unequivocally presenting the unpitying haughtiness of her class in her dealings with Läuffer Brecht totally switches off our sympathy. The hollow insincerity of her traditional gesture in attempting suicide turns the scene into comic satire — the pathos is pricked by Gustchen's conscious, self-assured action on hearing her father approach:

MAJOR *von weitem*: Gustel! Gustel!
Gustchen stellt ihre Schuhe hin und watet mit zurückgewandtem Antlitz in den Teich.[5]

Similarly, by guying the subsequent family reunion of the aristocrats, Brecht makes their position suspect and lays them open to ridicule in the same way that he debunks Läuffer's pathological self-castration by utilizing its grotesque symbolism.

Since Brecht published *Der Hofmeister* as one of his own plays it is pertinent to look first at the purely numerical ratio between the original text and Brecht's insertions. Brecht's *Hofmeister* is only two-thirds the length of the original and well over half of this is new. This means that he kept only a third of the text more or less in its existing state, the discarded remainder being supplanted by fresh material vigorously remoulding the play to his own specifications. Yet, since the adaptor did not do such violence to the content, plot, action and individual scenes, it is easy to be misled into thinking that Brecht only tinkered with the original. Though Mayer, too, seems wrongly to think that Brecht retained a large amount of Lenz's text, he does realize the far more important effect of what he calls 'change of function'. Even where Lenz's lines do survive they are frequently shifted into another context in which they acquire a quite different, and sometimes opposite, meaning.

The adaptor has kept the division into five acts, but this is neutralized by the scenes (seventeen in all; one of them, Scene 14, being split into three sub-scenes and occupying the whole of Act IV) being numbered straight through in Brecht's usual manner, and by the displacement of nodal points in the action (the seduction of Gustchen moves from Act II to Act III; the castration scene is brought forward from Act v to Act iv). Furthermore, Brecht seizes on the structural element of the 'happy ending'[6] with which Lenz rounded off his comedy but injects into it a completely new content that swings the line of force of the play into a totally new direction. The function of the happy ending here is identical with that in *Pauken und Trompeten* where champagne corks pop and a pheasant shoot is announced against the aural background of an ominous, lugubrious song in the street below as pressed soldiers march off to the colonial war in America. In *Der Hofmeister*, too, the future is toasted with the participating presence of the servants, the absence of the tutor himself being pointedly underlined by the falling snow which evokes the earlier scene of his self-castration. As Brecht remarked: 'Das von Bergsche Haus ist tragödiensicher',[7] and he wrapped the 'wohlgelittene Innigkeit'[8] of the scene in the patronizing futility of the Major's wife:

MAJORIN: Berg, mich dünkt, Sie gewarten, daß ich was Volkstümliches zum Besten gebe. *Singt am Spinett, während alle trinken*:

> O stille Winterzeit!
> Wenns auf die Erde schneit!
> Der Mensch, er schauet bloß
> Seine Hände ruhn im Schoß
> Und still im Stall stehn Ochs und Kuh
> Und hörn der großen Stille zu.[9]

By these means Brecht ensures an aesthetic rounding off to the action in terms of the society depicted, but in so doing he throws into sharp relief the indefensible state of that society and keeps the way open to its explicit indictment in one of his favourite formal devices, the epilogue.

In order to reduce the total length of his adaptation to roughly two-thirds of the original Brecht obviously had to jettison much of the latter; he achieved this largely by sacrificing many intricacies of the plot, allowing the essential action to emerge the more powerfully. Among the personages, the meddling young gentleman Seiffenblase and his own private tutor disappear, as do the blind old woman Marthe, who had turned out to be Pätus's grandmother, and his conscience-stricken father. The lute-teacher Rehaar, who had caused complications with his grovelling demands for compensation from the students for his seduced daughter, is also done away with, while the tattling trio of Frau Hamster, her daughter and Jungfer Knicks are replaced by the Misses Watten, Müller and Rabenjung, the object of their social derision now no longer Pätus wearing a wolf-skin in the summer heat but Läuffer's gaucheness on ice-skates. Brecht added Karoline, the university rector's daughter whom Pätus ultimately marries, and she assumes much of the function that had devolved on Rehaar's daughter in the original; and he expanded the part of Bollwerk (into whom the swashbuckling fire of Pätus is drained) — indeed, his function is now exactly parallel to that of Läuffer: the private tutor without a penny but with sexual potency to spare. The omission of incidents and whole scenes (mainly connected with the dropped characters) enabled Brecht to tighten the overall structure of the play so as to establish a tauter link between motivation and effect, and to emphasize the clean lines of the action. It has been argued that the *commedia dell' arte*, with its surprise twists of plot and superfluous scenes, left its mark on the episodic structure of Lenz's play, and that another relic appears in stereotyped characters such as the blustering Major, his comical wife and the ridiculous Graf. These traits are not used in the adaptation. The Major's excessive histrionics throughout the Lenz text, his reiterated concern for his daughter's health, the ravings of a dishonoured father, all disappear, though a vestige is turned to account as exaggerated gesture in Scene 11 to dissociate the actor from his role and to indicate the Major's insincerity. This is the point at which he lays about him with a stick at the news of his daughter's seduction. The fuller use made of Bollwerk (who now vicariously seduces Rehaar's daughter) releases Pätus from his altercation with her father and from Fritz's high-minded challenge to a duel, while the latter's unrealistic idealism is whittled away even more by his not being allowed to go to prison for Pätus's debts; this in turn renders redundant the *deus ex machina* of Pätus's lottery win that had enabled both young men to travel to Insterburg and participate in the general reconciliation with Gustchen and Jungfer Rehaar. The removal of Pätus's outcast grandmother obviates the sentimental thread which is reminiscent of a similar dichotomy of sentimentality and realism in Dickens and ill fits the biting satire. Finally, Brecht suppressed much of the pedantic village schoolmaster Wenzeslaus's meandering speeches — an aesthetic gain — but in doing the same with the enlightened educational ideas of the Geheimer Rat he had only one aim — to force that personage into the strait-jacket of a new, tendentious presentation, and the result is caricature. Most critics interpret the figure of the Geheimer Rat as a positive expression by Lenz: 'Prototyp des Aufklärers, Adliger, hoher preußischer Beamter mit allen Titeln und Orden'.[10] Mattenklott argues that he is not a 'Vertreter der Ausbeuterklasse', his relatively independent economic position separating him from the petty middle class and even from his equals.[11] Brecht's adaptation reserves no such serene role for the Geheimer Rat who now, like every other character, is conditioned by and speaks for his class which is seen wholly in a negative light. Several other factors that contribute overt or submerged effects to Lenz's play are eroded or altogether suppressed in the adaptation. Such are the Rousseauesque excess of feeling connected with Pietism and Lenz's own situation as a clergyman's son; the motif of the Prodigal Son that has been seen as the basic pattern in the substructure of the play; the various consequences of atmosphere and symbolism of eighteenth-century 'melancholy'.[12]

The streamlining of the original play was a necessary preliminary and gave Brecht a clean stock on to which he could graft fresh shoots in the form of outright additions or changes in the function of existing material. A major structural alteration is met with immediately in the Prologue (supplanting the expository opening monologue by Läuffer in the original) and its formal corollary, the Epilogue. However, the change is not so much in the structure

as in the nature of the Hofmeister: he is no longer *entirely within* the play
(as an individual) but also presents himself beforehand in front of the curtain
('Geehrtes Publikum . . .') as a type ('des deutschen Schulmeisters Urahn').[13]
The Prologue is effectively Brecht's declaration of intent, seeking to divert
the attention of the audience from the purely private circumstances of the
Hofmeister to his behaviour as the typical representative of a group within a
certain social structure.[14] Even a visual correlate was found in rehearsal by
getting the Hofmeister to move and speak jerkily, a marionette-like figure
subservient to the will of others. This is echoed in the course of the play by
Läuffer's physical gaucheness whenever he finds himself amongst his masters.
The speaker in the Prologue explicitly mentions the 150 years that have
elapsed since Lenz's play appeared and defines the historical context: though
himself 'vom niederen Stand' he serves the nobility 'mit kargem Gewinst',
and this causes him seriously to consider entering the service of the middle
class which is growing powerful in the land; he can promise that the latter
would find in him 'allezeit einen dienenden Geist' as he has been so well
clipped and trained by the nobility:

> Daß ich nur lehre, was genehm
> Da wird sich ändern nichts in dem.

But in the following, final couplet Brecht suddenly switches the emphasis
and indicates, in the quite different application of the word 'lehre', that this is
going to be a didactic play viewed historically, that is, epically:

> Wills euch verraten, was ich lehre:
> Das ABC der Teutschen Misere![15]

The epic quality of Brecht's play impinges immediately, as the actor, having
assured himself in the Prologue of the complicity of the audience, is enabled,
the moment the curtain rises, to act Läuffer in a detached alienating manner
throughout.

Another formal aspect of the epic theatre is exploited in the insertion
between Acts III and IV (Scenes 13 and 14) of the *Zwischenspiel*, consisting of
four brief scenes in dumb show depicting the passage of a year in the lives of
the protagonists. This is neatly done by the use of a revolving stage so that the
quick succession of scenes adds a controlled realism to the play where Lenz
relied conventionally on the imagination of the spectator when confronting
him with the sudden appearance of Gustchen's new-born infant in Act IV, 2.
Brecht plainly depended on this 'interlude' to give the audience a breathing-
space (and time to disengage their feelings) before the dramatic knots were
untied, but avowedly seized on it, too, as an elegantly simple way of conveying
the parallel time-pattern of the plot.

Brecht sought to integrate *Der Hofmeister* into the historical complex
of thought of the revolutionary, and he is inevitably more extreme than Lenz
was with his somewhat aimless or impractical reforming tendencies. From his
radical point of departure Brecht saw fresh aspects of various characters and

situations: he gave bite to Wenzeslaus by turning Lenz's circumlocutory, well-meaning dominie into an exploiter of the Hofmeister who unexpectedly seeks asylum with him; the progressive ideas of the Geheimer Rat disappear in a specious vindication of the status quo (and the actor taking this role is specifically enjoined to emphasize the grandiose hollow phrases); Läuffer's reason for his self-castration is no longer remorse but fear for his job, so that his private misfortune (occasioned by a physical instinct) is seen to be socially determined as well. Brecht motivated the key action of seduction more convincingly than Lenz and also developed a complete reorientation of the character of Pätus in rehearsal, making him the focus of a wholly new theme — the attack on Kantian idealism and its consequences — as both a parallel and a symbolic accentuation of Läuffer's situation.

Brecht found in Lenz many germs of the critical attitudes he then elaborated unambiguously in his adaptation. Läuffer's humble position, for instance, already a motive force in the original, is kept by Brecht constantly to the fore in speech, situation and gesture. Not only is special attention devoted to the overall elegance of a stage production, but particular scenes and objects serve at every turn to ram home the comment that may or may not be explicit in the text. In the very first scene Läuffer bows obsequiously and repeatedly as he passes the Geheimer Rat and his brother, the Major, in conversation outside the former's ornamental garden; he gets no acknowledgement of his servility, and Brecht adds to the original text:

LÄUFFER: Der Teufel hol euch, Flegel.
GEHEIMER RAT: Wer ist der Speichellecker?
MAJOR: Ein gewisser Läuffer, ich hör, ein Pastorensohn. Meine Frau hat ihn wollen zu sich bestellen, sie braucht für Leopolden einen Hofmeister, er mag vielleicht dienen so gut wie ein anderer.[16]

The Hofmeister expresses his powerless anger in a muttered curse while his social superiors impatiently return to the subject of their conversation, the common fern, which interests the Major more than his son's future teacher. Läuffer's second appearance — to be interviewed and told his duties by the Majorin — differs little from Act I, 3 in Lenz, yet even here the Hofmeister's submission is given a visual impact as well. The original stage directions: *Frau Majorin auf einem Kanapee. Läuffer in sehr demütiger Stellung neben ihr sitzend. Leopold steht.* is altered to: *Frau Majorin (am Spinett). Läuffer (in sehr demütiger Haltung neben ihr stehend). Leopold (steht und fängt Fliegen).* While Läuffer stands Brecht adds to the speech of the Majorin Läuffer's daily time-table, as if he were just another menial:

Und nun Ihr Taglauf: Sie nehmen Ihre Schokolade um sieben Uhr mit dem jungen Herrn und sehen zu, daß er ordentlich ißt, er ist von zarter Gesundheit. Schule von acht bis zwölf. Nachmittag: Spaziergang im Stadtpark und ihn nicht von der Hand gelassen, er ist lebhaften Geistes. Von sechs bis zum Nachtmahl mögen Sie sich in den Erker setzen und sich weiterbilden. Abends rechne ich mit Ihnen für die Unterhaltung der Gäste.[17]

Leopold, whom Läuffer is to 'serve', stands in the background catching flies, while Läuffer receives the catalogue of his duties 'eagerly bowing and scraping', and goes on to perform the complicated and degrading minuet bow demanded by the Majorin:

In sehr gerader Haltung, die Fäuste in die Hüften gestützt, vollführt er einige vollendete Schritte an der Rampe entlang, die Beine sehr hoch hebend ... Sein Kopf erscheint etwas verdreht, auf die Schulter geschraubt. Er geht wie zwischen Eiern, jedoch hat seine Schulterhaltung etwas Herausforderndes, er schreitet sozusagen wie ein gebändigter Tiger, mit einer wilden Grazie. In Rampenmitte vollzieht er eine Wendung und arrangiert, der Majorin zugewendet, ein Kompliment von einem Umfang der Planung, als habe er dafür ein ganzes Ballett zur Verfügung ... Die Szene erhält ihre Bedeutung durch Gauglers [the actor in this role] Kunst, die aufsässige, brutale Vitalität des niedriggeborenen Läuffers in den Schnürstiefel der feudalen Etikette geschnürt aufzuzeigen. Der Keim der Tragikomödie ist nun angedeutet.[18]

Läuffer's self-abasement ensures him the post (which was his anyway, he was so cheap) but not less demeaning treatment: Lenz had already pin-pointed the Hofmeister's status in the household when he ventured a contradictory opinion:

MAJORIN: Merk Er sich, mein Freund! daß Domestiken in Gesellschaften von Standespersonen nicht mitreden.[19]

Brecht seizes on this oral reprimand and underpins it with every resource of gesture and facial expression.

In the entirely new Scene 4 of the adaptation the humbling of Läuffer is transferred from the social to the sexual sphere: he is trying to show off his virtuosity on ice-skates to three giggling, whispering young ladies who hint at his bad reputation in the town and ignore his overtures. Läuffer's uneasy exhibitionism ends in humiliation, indicated in the stage directions: *Läuffer ist ihnen* [the girls] *ohne Leopold gefolgt und zieht den Hut. Sie stehen steif und grüßen nicht zurück ... Läuffer ist zornig zu Leopold zurückgelaufen und wird von dem Ungeschickten niedergezogen. Die Fräuleins lachen.*[20] The rebuff to Läuffer's culture by the Majorin is now underscored by his discomfiture on the ice, which prompts further hypocritical submission in the next scene where he asks for the loan of a horse after the Major has just coerced him into accepting a lower salary than had been promised:

LÄUFFER: Herr Major, wärs recht kühn, eine untertänigste Bitte vorzubringen—...
MAJOR: Nun, das könnte beredet werden.
LÄUFFER *springt auf und vollführt Verbeugungen*: O gnädigster Herr Major —[21]

The Major's evasive answer foreshadows his subsequent prevarication in this matter, and so Läuffer, in desperation, makes one more bid to obtain the half-promised horse. This is in Scene 8 (Lenz: Act II, 1) where Brecht has Läuffer present at his pastor father's interview with the Geheimer Rat about the scandalous pay his son receives. While his father is only concerned for prestige and dignity of position (and gets sidetracked into an argument on the merits of private tutors) the son is desperate for a horse. The setting is now again the ornamental garden of Scene 1 and the Geheimer Rat, bucolically dressed, carries on clipping his box-trees: 'Sorglich knipst er hie und da einen übermäßigen Sprößling des Buchsbaums mit der großen Schere ab.'[22] This action not only indicates the imposition of discipline on the world around, but provides as well a visual correlate to point the contrast between the freedom mouthed by the Geheimer Rat and its curtailment in reality. The trimmed box-tree becomes the object of the will of the Geheimer Rat, anticipates the castration of Läuffer and finally fits an epoch in which a dominant motif is the constraint of nature such as is found in formal gardens and architectural landscaping. The dehumanizing of Läuffer by his submission to the upper class is already suggested by Brecht in the jerky, marionette-like movements of the private tutor in the Prologue ('Der Adel hat mich gut trainiert/Zurechtgestutzt und exerziert') and is taken up by his bowing and scraping, the minuet performance, the ice-skating figures, the catechism lesson with Gustchen, the pen-and-ruler work for Wenzeslaus — all images of artificial drilling and training that constrict natural expression. Läuffer's 'unnatural' situation is further underlined by the increased frequency with which Brecht has him present in a scene where he is ignored although he is the subject of the conversation: the Geheimer Rat talks to his brother about Läuffer outside the ornamental garden, in which he later talks to Läuffer's father about his salary; the young women take no notice of him on the ice; the Majorin and the mincing Graf talk over his head in the drawing-room; Wenzeslaus and the Geheimer Rat make dispositions about the wounded tutor lying before them; finally Läuffer is represented *in absentia* by his petitioning letter, on the contents of which the aristocrats crudely and cruelly comment.

The degrading of Läuffer to the status of a puppet is carried through more consistently and mercilessly by Brecht than Lenz and it might therefore seem that he is trying to secure the sympathy of the modern audience for this hero trapped in a situation that he is powerless to change. But Brecht is in fact critical of Läuffer's motives and sees his position as resulting not only from powerlessness but also from acquiescence: he is at fault in knuckling under, in not rebelling in an attempt to regain his dignity as a man, in offering himself — in the Prologue — to the up-and-coming middle class in the same capacity as to the feudal order — as 'ein dienender Geist'. Thus Läuffer is throughout a butt of Brecht's criticism; although driven into a corner by class differences he identifies himself at heart (through cowardice, convenience, lack of insight) with the social structure that precipitates his problem, and he plays according to its rules. That Brecht intended the responsibility for Läuffer's quandary to rest largely with him is amply borne out by comments in rehearsal.[23]

Not unexpectedly, the motif of economic advantage or necessity is given some prominence by Brecht. Already in the original Läuffer soliloquizes in the opening lines of the play on the factors that have made of him a private tutor:

Mein Vater sagt, ich sei nicht tauglich zum Adjunkt. Ich glaube, der Fehler liegt in seinem Beutel; er will keinen bezahlen.

Brecht, however, blames the meagre salary of Läuffer's father rather than his reluctance to pay, when the Geheimer Rat is explaining to the Major who this private tutor is:

Sein Vater hat mir das Haus eingerannt für ihn. Wollt eine Stell an der Stadtschule. Da ist er nicht studiert genug. Seines Vaters Beutel hat für die Schlußexamina nicht gelangt.[24]

Throughout, the Major is intent on squeezing as much as he can out of Läuffer as cheaply as possible, and imposes on him an extra task:

Er soll meiner Tochter auch zeichnen lehren. — Mein Beutel erlaubts nicht, daß ich ein ganzes Bataillon sündhaft teurer Hofmeister in Sold setz.[25]

The seduction of his daughter can be attributed directly to this stinginess which throws the two together, and Läuffer is quick to point out to Gustchen that if he had been paid adequately he could have hired a horse and got to Königsberg to indulge his sexual needs:

An allem war von Anfang nur dein Vater schuld. Mußt er einen Präzeptor für dich sparen wollen? Im selben Atem seines Geizes kürzte er mich.[26]

But the fortuitous avarice of one character would be very weak motivation for the 'tragedy' in this play, and Brecht typically makes the Major's tight-fistedness a resultant of political and economic forces at work in that particular state at that time. To achieve this he introduces the entirely new motif of the Seven Years War which has just been concluded by Frederick II, victoriously, it is true, yet leaving Prussia exhausted and with outstanding debts. Thus, the Major brushes aside his brother's cautions concerning Läuffer:

MAJOR: Ich weiß nur, er überfordert nicht. Und mit dem Krieg und der Teuerung . . .
GEHEIMER RAT: Ich mag nicht, was wohlfeil. Drum schick ich meinen Fritz auf die Universität nach Halle.[27]

The Major had in fact opened the conversation (and, indeed, the play) by voicing his anxiety about the ruinous effects of the war, especially on his own farming:

Mit der Ökonomie geht es nicht zum Besten, Wilhelm; keine Gäule aufzutreiben, selbst fürs Geld. Potz hundert, die sieben Jahre Krieg sind noch nicht verwunden im Land.[28]

This remark is later turned to advantage by the Geheimer Rat in a parting shot to Läuffer:

Mein Bruder bekommt für seine Ökonomie nicht Ackergäule, und da will Er von ihm einen Gaul für Seine Ausschweifungen![29]

In Scene 11 the Major's wife complains of being neglected, telling Graf Wermuth that her husband 'kennt seit dem Krieg nichts mehr außer seiner leidigen Ökonomie', to which her husband later retorts: 'Meiner Treu, du vergißt, Frau, daß ein Krieg bezahlt sein muß.' On the other hand, the Major is too involved in supporting the status quo as one of the privileged class to look in a detached way at the causes of his financial predicament; Frederick the Great, who exploited the war for the consolidation of earlier conquests, nevertheless disposes of the Major's blind loyalty, and the latter angrily taxes Läuffer with insufficient glorification of the 'soldier king' in teaching Leopold:

Der Aufsatz über den Heldenkönig, den ich da lese, ist schlampig, daß ichs nur sag. Bei der Aufzählung der Feinde, die Er auf sich genommen hat, ist vergessen, daß Er nicht nur die Sachsen, die Österreicher, die Franzosen und die Russen heraus- gefordert hat, sondern daß Er auch noch mit den Briten eine deutliche Sprache gesprochen hat. Es kommt so nicht heraus, wie Er vor dem Untergang gestanden ist — und so nichts von der Glorie.[30]

In this way even the minor character of the Major is conditioned dialectically in the adaptation: like the rest of his class, he is damaged by the very social structure which he helps perpetuate and he lacks the discernment to see his own position — this is left to the observation and reasoning powers of the modern audience.

The recent war naturally affects other characters as well: Frau Blitzer, the students' landlady, reproves Pätus for continually failing his examinations and being a burden on his mother:

Seine Mutter kann einem leid tun, und eine Witwe dazu. Und die Witwen- und Waisenpensionen gekürzt wegen dem siegreichen Krieg.[31]

Even Wenzeslaus, in one of his less idealistic moments, as he prepares a calculated exploitation of Läuffer as a dog's-body, paints a gloomy prospect for the tutor who has forfeited his post by seducing his employer's daughter:

Mit dem Hofmeisterspielen ist es ja nun wohl aus, junger Herr, so ohne Zeugnis. Und auf eine Stelle in der Dorfschule kann Er da auch nicht hoffen, wo jetzo der König doch nach seinem Krieg die invaliden Unteroffiziers zu Lehrern anstellt, ja, ja.[32]

It is quite explicitly the fear of unemployment that dictates Läuffer's self- destructive deed ('Sorgen um meinen Beruf' supplanting the vagueness of 'Verzweiflung' in the original) which in turn enables him to beg a testimonial of the Major:

. . . Zwischen Scylla und Charybdis von Natur und Beruf habe ich mich für den Beruf entschieden und hoffe ich, Sie werden mir ein Zeugnis gnädigst nicht versagen, damit ich meinen Beruf wieder ausüben kann . . .
WENZESLAUS: Hochherziger Dulder, jede Lehrerstelle, ich bins sicher, jede Lehrer- stelle im Kreis steht Ihm jetzt offen.[33]

Lenz had motivated Läuffer's self-castration with his remorse at having fathered a child on Gustchen, and extracted only (tragi-)comic elements from the quite separate episode of his subsequent desire to marry Wenzeslaus's ward, Lise; Brecht integrally connects the two by placing Läuffer's meeting with and carnal desire for Lise immediately *before* his self-castration which is thus prompted by his fear of yielding to these sensual stirrings, and, consequently, of losing his wretched job as assistant to Wenzeslaus. On surprising Läuffer in the act of kissing Lise, the schoolmaster had at once expressed the realities of the situation:

WENZESLAUS: Und wie wollt Ihr sie ernähren, Habenichts?
LÄUFFER: Ich habs ihr gesagt.
WENZESLAUS: Und wird das sie satt machen?... Was habt Ihr aus Eurem Stand gemacht? Wo sind Eure Zeugnisse? Wo könnt Ihr Euch noch blicken lassen?[34]

As a result, Läuffer breaks the deadlock in the most unproductive and negative way: his self-castration will eminently fit him for an employment by which he will be able to maintain a wife that his action prevents him from being a proper husband to. This is the irony in the closing lines of the adaptation:

LÄUFFER: Und ich bins gewiß, die Herrn zu Insterburg werden mir, so wie ich vor ihnen stehe, eine gute Stell verschaffen, so daß ich mein Eheweib ernähren kann.[35]

Brecht neatly parallels Läuffer's decision with the course taken by Pätus in another segment of society when he prostitutes his idealism to economic interest:

FRITZ: Ich denk, du hast dem Kant abgeschworen?
PÄTUS: Nur öffentlich. Wie hätte ich ansonsten eine Lehrerstelle gekriegt? Und ohne Lehrerstelle, wie hätte ich meine Karoline ... ehelichen können?... Beiläufig, sie ist des Rektors Tochter.[36]

The themes of economic necessity and social ranking, already expressed by Lenz and brought into prominence by Brecht, are environmental factors, produced by class distinction, which determine the actions of the personages in this play. But their behaviour is also governed by a complementary force, the sexual urge, that overrides the rigidity of class boundaries and yet, even in the postulated absence of these, would have to come to terms with some sort of social convention. Thus the existence of upper and lower classes is complicated by the problem of individual freedom within a community. Lenz provided sufficient indication of the essential physiological needs that led Läuffer to do himself violence, in the mention of the horse he had been promised, his involvement with two girls (one of them after his deed), and his words in the opening soliloquy: 'Zum Pfaffen bin ich auch zu jung, zu gut gewachsen, habe zu viel Welt gesehen ...'. *Die Soldaten*, Lenz's companion piece to *Der Hofmeister*, deals even more centrally with the same social problem: in this case the soldiers, who have sworn to serve their monarch and whose way of life does not permit settled marriage, inevitably seduce the women in the towns where they are quartered. The fault does not lie entirely with the military (especially as there is the added hazard of the women parading their sex) and the Colonel makes specific suggestions at the end of the play for solving the problem. Though *Der Hofmeister* demands a similar solution, none comes. Brecht expands the theme by continually channelling attention on to the inordinate sexual stirrings not only of Läuffer but also of several other characters; in this way he counterpoints the social theme. As might be expected, Brecht makes more conspicuous the licentious possibilities latent in this aspect of the play; there is an undertow of near-obscenity in the adaptation that Lenz himself might have been tempted to bring out had he not been hampered by the more prudish public conventions of his time. Though the tutor shows excesses in his behaviour, it is in the mouth of the Geheimer Rat that Brecht formulates the grosser remarks that clearly define the situation for the audience; by this means he suggests formally the physical coarseness lying beneath the surface of eighteenth-century elegance and also the fortuitous nature of the Geheimer Rat's superiority. The latter, unlike his brother, recognizes at once why Läuffer wants the periodic loan of a horse:

GEHEIMER RAT: Was will Er denn in Königsberg?
LÄUFFER: Gnädiger Herr Rat, in die Bibliotheken.
GEHEIMER RAT: Ich dacht, in die Bordelle. Ihn sticht wohl der Hafer?[37]

With ironical profanity he agrees, after Läuffer's self-mutilation, to provide him with an attestation: 'Du sollst dem Ochsen, der da drischet, haha, dem Ochsen! — nicht das Maul verbinden!', which evokes a disgusted 'Pfui!' from the Majorin. In fact, the motif of the horse, with its connotations of unrestrained and uncontrollable sexual power, though mentioned parenthetically in the original play, is set in key by the Geheimer Rat in Scene 2 when he finds Fritz and Gustchen in an embrace and sharply reprimands his son for not showing more self-restraint:

Und [daß du] die wahre Freiheit kapierst! Als welche die Menschen von den Tieren unterscheidet. Die Hengste und Stuten müssens, aber die Menschen sind frei, es nicht zu tun.[38]

Indeed, animal imagery is constantly brought into play to allude to Läuffer's needs and impulses: as a prelude to his storming of Gustchen, Läuffer, 'unter zunehmendem Geschlechtshunger leidend, produziert sich hahnengleich auf dem Schlittschuhplatz vor den jungen Mädchen'[39] while they gossip about his lecherous propensities:

JUNGFER MÜLLER: Er ist bald stadtbekannt wie ein gelber Hund.
JUNGFER WATTEN: Wobei?
JUNGFER MÜLLER: Er ist am letzten Sonntag sogar hinter der Beckschen hergegangen. Sie hat ihn nicht angenommen und ist nicht etepetete, wahrhaftig nicht, das lüderliche Mensch . . .
JUNGFER RABENJUNG: Aber was soll er machen, wenn keine Ordentliche mit ihm geht?
JUNGFER WATTEN: Wenn eine von uns sich mit ihm zeigt, weiß mans zu gut, bei dem wärs nicht nur zum Spaß.[40]

Brecht described Läuffer in this scene as ' "der Hahn im Korb", der als "Hecht im Karpfenteich" behandelt wird'.[41] Two scenes later, on Läuffer's next appearance in feminine company (this time with Gustchen who has been imposed on him as an extra pupil), the notes again refer to him as 'einen Hecht im Karpfenteich, freilich einen Hecht, der sein eigener Dompteur ist'.[42] He reverts to the mechanical artificial movements characteristic of his earlier encounters with his employers, and while Gustchen is exerting on him the combined powers of her physical bloom and social superiority, the tension builds up in her tutor between sexual excitation and the attempt to control it:

Er macht unruhig gequälte Schritte hin und her, dreht sich wie auf dem Eislaufplatz spindelförmig, bleibt jäh stehen, den Tatzenstock am Rücken zwischen den Ellbögen verkrampft, als fessele er sich selbst. Sie betrachtet ihn wie ein interessantes Insekt, ist einmal beinahe gerührt . . .[43]

The Graf, too, had examined Läuffer like an insect through his lorgnette, but Gustchen also pricks him with a needle. This scene opens as Läuffer prompts Gustchen in her stumbling recital of the catechism, in which the stress is entirely on the body:

LÄUFFER: Ich glaube, daß mich Gott geschaffen hat . . .
GUSTCHEN: Samt allen Kreaturen . . .
LÄUFFER: Mir Leib . . .
GUSTCHEN: Mir Leib und Seele . . .
LÄUFFER: Auch Leib . . .
GUSTCHEN: Augen, Ohren und alle Glieder, Vernunft und alle Sinne gegeben hat . . .
LÄUFFER: Mit aller Notdurft und . . .
GUSTCHEN: Nahrung . . .
LÄUFFER: Des Leibs . . .
GUSTCHEN: Und Lebens . . .
LÄUFFER: Leiblich und täglich . . .[44]

Throughout the scene Läuffer tries to control his excitement by his agitated handling of the ruler — emblem of his profession — even rapping himself with it, 'sich für die sexuelle Gier bestrafend',[45] perhaps getting from this surrogate a perverted satisfaction. Earlier his social humiliation had centred on visual situations and objects on the stage such as the fern, the box-tree, the minuet; now his sexual humiliation and constraint have to be administered by himself, as we see later when he makes a last attempt to coerce his bodily cravings by bolting the door against Lise and chastising himself with the ruler: 'In der vierzehnten Szene wird das Tatzengeben dem Zuschauer ankündigen, daß sich sein Geschlecht wieder gegen ihn erhoben hat!'[46]

Läuffer's struggle to dominate his instincts is counterpointed by the metaphor of the capon which has functional significance both before and after the castration. Lenz had himself used this image for Läuffer at the end of the play, and Brecht adds to this Pätus's comment on his craven Professor Wolff (presumably an allusion by Brecht to the Halle philosopher Christian Wolff, who had died, however, in 1754): 'Wer ist Wolffen! Die Kreatur haßt die Kantschen Freiheitsschriften wie der Kapaun das Hahnenkrähn!'[47] Within the associative complex of the same image Läuffer justifies without a scruple his seduction of Gustchen, while they are still lying in bed:

Soll ich mir da ein Gewissen daraus machen, daß ich mich nicht bezähmt? Sicherlich, ich werde zu üppig verköstigt für einen Sklaven. Der Sellerie, die Truthähne, die Schokolade — Ein so gepäppelter Korpus soll nicht sündig werden?[48]

Over-indulgence (here in food that is often believed to have aphrodisiac properties) leads to a weakening of the will, and the 'pampered body' ironically evokes the 'capon' that, rendered sexless, loses its own will and function, and is fattened solely to satisfy the appetites of the rich. The restraining of this coddled body is undertaken unsuccessfully first with the ruler, then the door-bolt. There is a deadlock that can only be resolved by a desperate measure, castration, already anticipated in the other significant addition to the seduction scene by Brecht — Läuffer's request that Gustchen should recount the story of Abelard and Heloise that she has read. Abelard had, of course, been caught and castrated by henchmen of Heloise's uncle. Immediately preceding his self-humiliation Läuffer admits to abusing Wenzeslaus's trust in him with regard to Lise: 'Nur, kann man solchen Reizungen widerstehen? Wenn man mir nicht das Herz aus dem Leibe reißt —',[49] and follows this up in the monologue that decides on his suicidally violent deed with a clear indication of what he is about to do: 'Die Roßknechte dürfen Männer sein, ich darf es nicht. Soll ich mirs ausreißen, das Aug, das mich ärgert?'[50]

The subjection of Läuffer to the class in power is repeated by Brecht in the role of Bollwerk, whose significance is far greater in the adaptation (though he appears no more often) than in the original. Bollwerk is a student with little money who intends to become a private tutor, and so, acquiescing in the status quo, he quite deliberately and unscrupulously determines to have his fling before his wings are clipped; thus he brusquely retorts to Fritz's enquiry as to whether he is interested in the polemic between Professor Wolff and Kant: 'Nein, ich werd Hofmeister, da gehts in die Klausur in einem abgelegenen Nest, ich muß mich bevor weidlich ausslieben.'[51] Brecht transfers to Bollwerk the aggressiveness and sexual enterprise that had belonged to Pätus in the original, thus leaving the latter free to get caught up in the dialectic of idealistic Kantian ethics and realistic action for survival. Bollwerk now seduces the lute-teacher's daughter in place of Pätus, but Pätus has to find the money for the abortion. Bollwerk behaves from a purely pragmatic attitude to reality that deserves censure for its deliberate selfishness; he is fully aware of the workings of the existent order but opts out of any responsibility of altering it, concerned as he is with himself alone. With Bollwerk, as with Läuffer, Brecht breaks the illusion of what the audience might conventionally expect of them as representatives or types: the scholar, scientist or teacher exists in popular belief as a pale, intellectual, impotent figure,[52] but in Brecht's adaptation these tutors are given to sexual excess. The burden of Bollwerk's conversation is sex and he misses no opportunity for a suggestive remark:

Der Herr aus Insterburg scheinen seine Physiologie zu vergessen. Man will nicht schlafen, weil man liebt; man liebt, weil man schlafen will. Wart Er nur auf den Märzen!... Bei den Mädchen ists nicht unser Rock, sondern unser — ... Ich lehr Ihm: Sag mir, von welcher du träumst, und ich sag dir, mit welcher du nicht geschlafen hast.[53]

and

FRITZ: Ich will mich auch auf die Philosophie werfen.
BOLLWERK: Herr von Berg, ich kann nur hoffen, sie verträgts. Man wirft sich auf sie allenthalben.[54]

The significance of Bollwerk is that his opportunist lechery is a pattern of social behaviour prefiguring the ultimate submission of apparently 'purer' minds on similar grounds of expediency. Already when reading Gustchen's letter aloud in Scene 9 Fritz confesses his fear that he may succumb to passion if he travels to see her. And later in the play the news of Gustchen's seduction draws from Pätus a coarse comment that could only have come from Bollwerk's arsenal:

... sie wird schon nicht ganz so in Unschuld es getan haben. Frauenzimmer! Man kennt das! Sie wollens nicht, aber sie tuns. Wenn es sie juckt, denken sie an nichts anderes mehr, als daß einer sie kratzt.[55]

Noticeably, in this scene Pätus appears in a state of total capitulation; he has abandoned his idealism, submitted to the Professor and even married the Rector's daughter. That is why he is now suspicious and wary of his former crony, Bollwerk, and realizes the danger emanating from that quarter. Pätus has been bitten once — over the seduction of Jungfer Rehhaar — and now that he has come down to Bollwerk's opportunist level, he is going to forestall even the possibility of the latter's acting as his stand-in with his wife.

It is in connexion with Pätus in particular that a wholly fresh theme was incorporated by Brecht in his adaptation: on the one hand he simplified the plot of Lenz's play by excising many subsidiary aspects, on the other he made the action far more complex by thematic additions such as the one now to be discussed. Brecht seized on the opportunity offered by the epoch of the play and its student characters to put in the dock not so much classical German philosophy as the enthusiasm which greeted its idealistic postulates and the bad faith that abandoned them in the interests of expediency. In order to introduce the philosophy of Kant Brecht resorted to a technique familiar to him, that of telescoping certain historical data: he places the action of the play soon after the conclusion of the Seven Years War (1756–63) — all the references are to immediate effects of the war that a few years at most would erase — yet he uses quotations from writings of Kant that were not published until a decade after Lenz's play and a score and more years after the end of the War (e.g. *Grundlegung zur Metaphysik der Sitten*, 1785; *Vom ewigen Frieden*, 1795). The dramatic licence that Brecht arrogates to himself in this respect has perhaps some historical justification in that, through Leibniz, the Aufklärung and the Encyclopédistes, the accumulated thought and sensibility of the eighteenth century was inexorably leading up to the grand philosophical structure erected by Kant. Thus Pätus becomes the focal point of Brecht's criticism of the Kantian ethics that play a dominant role in his behaviour. The point is made more forceful and, indeed, aesthetically satisfying, since Pätus (and Läuffer as well) arrives at his ultimate position by a process of dialectic based on the antinomies dear to Kant, yet in doing so he paradoxically has to deny his master. Pätus starts off as the inflexible idealist dedicated to supporting Kant's progressive writings through thick and thin. Bollwerk disparages the Königsberg philosopher for his muddle-headedness and comments with scornful realism on his pacifist pamphlet:

Schon der Titel 'Zum ewigen Frieden!' Wenn wir beide hier einen Tag aufhörten, mit der Blitzer Krieg zu führen, bestünde ihr Kaffee nur noch aus Gerste.[56]

But Pätus at first adamantly refuses to deny his Kantian adherence merely in order to pass his examination:

... Und dies Nein gilt gleichermaßen der ganzen teutschen Untertänigkeit, indem sie doch nur selig sind, wenn sie Knechte sein können, am liebsten Kriegsknechte, als welche sie sich für irgendein Oberhaupt aufopfern![57]

He is thus initially established as a figure of principles and probity, so as to make his somersault from idealism to pragmatism all the more marked. In the course of the play, while Läuffer is obeying the whip of his masters, Pätus is quietly preparing his volte-face and, for the audience, his capitulation with its ironic betrayal of Kant follows hard on the heels of Läuffer's. While the horse, the ruler, the capon are the objects and images attending Läuffer's surrender, the submission of Pätus is reflected in the narrow, philistine middle-class world he has elected to fit into; he appears with pipe and slippers and his last words are a cowardly withdrawal from Fritz's troubles: 'Traurig. — Aber unsere Sorgen sinds nicht. Komm an den wärmenden Ofen, Karoline!'[58] This closing remark by Pätus, which shows up his deliberate surrender of responsibility and his ensnarement in a trap of his own choosing, was described by Brecht in rehearsal notes as 'nur noch der Nagel zu dem Sarg des Sturm und Drangs, mit dem einst die Laufbahn Pätus' begann. Der ehemalige moralische Riese und spätere Verräter zieht sich in das bürgerliche Heldenleben zurück'.[59] Throughout this scene Pätus was to be shown as fully conscious of his betrayal, especially in his evasive answer to Fritz's 'Worüber schriebst du im Examen?' The humiliation of his self-imposed constriction is made graphic in the brief appearance of Karoline with its crippling effect on any sort of initiative and thinking:

Die Schritte Karolinens lassen Pätus zusammenfahren. Hastig verbirgt er den Kant in einem Tabaktopf. Der lange Arm der Obrigkeit reicht bis ins Familienschlafzimmer. Man sieht die Nachteile der Vernunftehe.

Von größter Wichtigkeit ist die Figur der Karoline Pätus. Zopf, Biedermeier und Jugendstil kommen in einer Person zur Tür herein. Eine lähmende Kaffeetopf-Atmosphäre breitet sich aus. Es bleibt gar keine andere Möglichkeit: die wilden Tage haben hier ein Ende.[60]

Nothing but dismay can be engendered by her meaningless reflex reaction to Fritz's trouble: 'Ach, so schwarz wird das Unglück nicht sein, als daß nicht eine schöne Tasse Kaffee —',[61] words that evoke the stifling dullness of mind which is now Pätus's lot. It is the dullness of mediocrity that takes refuge in trivial, deadening cosiness and spreads miasmatically into the twentieth century.

However, the involvement of Kant in Brecht's adaptation does not end with Pätus landing on his slippered feet by the reassuring fire: dialectical links are established between Pätus, Fritz and Läuffer that illuminate their respective attitudes and help enmesh the eighteenth-century philosopher inextricably in the conceptual structure of the play. The relationship between Bollwerk and Pätus echoes that of Läuffer and Fritz except in the outcome, when Pätus has learnt to suppress his ideals while Fritz acts according to them (in accepting as his own Läuffer's bastard child) and emerges as a ridiculous cuckold but with more moral worth. Yet even this difference in behaviour must be measured in its social context: Pätus's career depends on his viewing his situation realistically while Fritz can afford his ideals. On his very first appearance in Scene 2 Fritz sweeps Gustchen along on his enthusiasm — they inflame their passions by declaiming Klopstock's odes and promise to be faithful ('im Geiste zusammenbleiben') when separated. The Geheimer Rat then irrupts into these idealistic sentiments and his mouthings on the voluntary acceptance of necessity make a mockery of the pseudo-Kantian terms he voices:

Deshalb will ich, daß ihr eure Separation aus Notwendigkeit selber wissentlich vollzieht, ohn Zwang, aus Einsicht, freiwillig . . . Der Gedank ist frei, aber Geschriebenes wird zensuriert! Jetzo nehmt Abschied, in meiner Gegenwart — und, aus eigenem Antrieb, nichts, was nicht in Gegenwart von Zeugen stattfinden kann! . . . Ja, meine Lieben, die Vernunft ist eine gestrenge Herrin.[62]

And after it has turned out that he had been mistaken, that human beings have animal instincts as well as mind, the Geheimer Rat still relies on a specious appeal to logic to save the situation and persuade Fritz to accept Gustchen's bastard child:

Mein Sohn, Er hat die Ursach sanktioniert, nun fahr Er gefälligst nicht zurück vor der Folge. Einen hohen Wipfel erklommen und dann zurückgeklettert, den windverwehten Hut zu holen? Wozu hat Er seine Logik studieret?[63]

The dialectic between Pätus and Fritz becomes dramatically significant in the entirely new Scene 9 of the adaptation which opens with Fritz reading to Pätus the lines from Klopstock that Gustchen has written him, thus establishing the link with her protestations of fidelity in Scene 2. But Pätus has other things on his mind, forlornly hoping that philosophy will provide a comforting answer to the problem of a woman loving one man in her mind but satisfying her body with another. Before his head can assemble a specious logic to convince his heart Pätus bursts into tears, revealing that Bollwerk has seduced Jungfer Rehhaar in his stead and admitting the inadequacies of a philosophically reasoned argument to assuage his own feelings. Yet he is still at his idealistic stage of believing that she had only him in mind during the act and so feels it his duty to procure the necessary money for an abortion — money that he does not possess because his championing of Kant had failed him in his examinations. Pätus's idealism hinders him from carrying that idealism into effect. Fritz comes to his rescue and solves the 'antinomy' in a practical way that has the dramatic effect (in the following scene) of entangling him in the very dilemma he resolves for Pätus: to pay for Jungfer Rehhaar's abortion he magnanimously offers Pätus the money with which he was going to visit Gustchen during the vacation. His generous action is partly motivated by the apprehension of finding 'eine kühnere Julie' in Gustchen now that he himself is no longer 'der alte keusche Joseph'. So Pätus takes the money and quotes Kant's categorical imperative in praise of Fritz. The circle is completed: Fritz is afraid of his own body and drives Gustchen into Läuffer's arms by staying away; both he and Pätus abdicate in favour of substitutes, and at heart prefer to be seditious in thought only, not in deed. Fritz leaves Insterburg in order to become worthy of Gustchen, and by his action causes her to become unworthy of him; the story of Hermann and Thusnelda turns into that of Abelard and Heloise. Whereas Pätus soon renounces his ideals from self-interest Fritz remains with his to the very end, when he justifies Gustchen's behaviour (she presents him with Läuffer's child) in terms of the Jungfer Rehhaar incident. Thus Fritz sticks by the categorical imperative while Pätus chooses to act on the dictate of a hypothetical one.

Though for Gustchen Läuffer is merely a surrogate for the absent Fritz, she represents more in *his* life than a chance medium for sexual satisfaction. Furthermore, the Kantian ethical arguments introduced by Brecht to give pith and direction to the roles of the students in Halle are also implicitly involved — although not always directly adduced — in the dominant crises the Hofmeister undergoes. Pätus's citing of the Kantian passage concerning 'Das Eherecht' has as much bearing on the relationship of Läuffer to Gustchen as of himself to Karoline; a further paragraph on 'Das Eherecht' underlines the contractual nature (for Kant) of matrimony:

Der Ehe-Vertrag wird nur *durch eheliche Beiwohnung* (copula carnalis) vollzogen . . .

Die *Erwerbung* einer Gattin oder eines Gatten geschieht also nicht facto (durch die Beiwohnung) ohne vorhergehenden Vertrag, auch nicht pacto (durch den bloßen ehelichen Vertrag, ohne nachfolgende Beiwohnung), sondern nur lege: d.i. als rechtliche Folge aus der Verbindlichkeit, in eine Geschlechtsverbindung nicht anders, als vermittelst des wechselseitigen *Besitzes* der Personen, als welcher nur durch den gleichfalls wechselseitigen Gebrauch ihrer Geschlechtseigenthümlichkeiten seine Wirklichkeit erhält, zu treten.[64]

Thus matrimony (and sexual relationships) are seen in a social framework, and it is this that prompted Brecht to guy the Kantian analysis in one of the *Studien* sonnets, 'Über Kants Definition der Ehe in der *Metaphysik der Sitten*'. In the actual situation of *Der Hofmeister* certain questions are unavoidable: why can Läuffer not marry Gustchen after he has damaged her honour? why does he settle for Lise when he has rendered himself unsuitable (in the Kantian definition) as a husband? The answers lie in the social differences between these persons: to marry Gustchen it would have been necessary for Läuffer to be inducted into the nobility by the Major's purchase of a title for him, and without this the only matrimonial course open to him is to marry 'lower' than himself, after his self-castration has nullified the 'advantage' of his superior social position over Lise. In all essentials, this aspect of Läuffer's position already exists in the original play; Brecht's adaptation, permeated as it is with the parodied spirit of Kant, helps to bring to the surface a crucial motivation of these events.

The private tutor's other crushing experience, his self-mutilation, which is partly the consequence of his social blunder with Gustchen, has no overt connexion with Kant, yet it is again *Die Metaphysik der Sitten* that illuminates his desperate act. Kant defined man's first duty, 'in his quality as an animal', as self-preservation; its counterpart is the intentional destruction of oneself, total in suicide, partial in self-mutilation. He goes on to discuss cases of 'partial suicide' and concludes that only the removal of a decaying organ that threatens the survival of the whole body is justified. Among the 'Casuistische Fragen' in this connexion Kant describes the hypothetical problem of the man who took his own life knowing he had hydrophobia. A similar question can be put of Läuffer: realizing he cannot control the raging sexual storms inside him he castrates himself in order not to harm Lise. Again, the Kantian argument can be adapted to Läuffer's position, and again in a purely social context. In his second monologue following Lise's appearance Läuffer has to choose between the temptations of his sexual potency and survival as a harmless, and therefore accepted, member of society:

Du kannst sie vernichten, aber nicht nähren. Und doch, ist es etwas so Fluchwürdiges, Mensch sein? Sind diese Gefühle, fleischlich wie sie sein mögen, so unnatürlich? Verfluche eine Natur, die dich nicht zum Stein gemacht hat, vor dem, was sie geschaffen![65]

Läuffer's sexuality is not in itself bad, but in his particular social situation it is a Kantian 'dem Leben nachtheiliges Organ', and so he opts for survival; quite soberly and wittingly he reports his submission to the class structure in his letter to Gustchen's father:

Zwischen Scylla und Charybdis von Natur und Beruf habe ich mich für den Beruf entschieden und hoffe ich, Sie werden mir ein Zeugnis gnädigst nicht versagen, damit ich meinen Beruf wieder ausüben kann. Um so mehr, gnädigster Herr Major, als ich auch im übrigen mich pflichtschuldigst bemühen werde, in allem, ich schreibe in allem, immer das zu tun und zu lehren, was gewünscht wird, zu meinem und aller Besten . . .[66]

At the same time, Wenzeslaus, inverting the Kantian 'duty' and so emptying it of meaning, welcomes Läuffer's deed as the start to a blossoming existence:

Habt Ihr nicht die Aufsässigkeit in Euch für ewig vernichtet, der Pflicht alles untergeordnet? Kein Privatleben kann Euch fürder abhalten, Menschen zu formen nach Eurem Ebenbilde.[67]

The village schoolmaster's almost total misunderstanding of the real situation becomes thus the ironical correlate of his historical ineffectualness.

By different routes both Läuffer and Pätus are seen to arrive at the same ignominious end: capitulation to the faulty existing order, the one in body, the other in mind. Brecht even went to the trouble of emphasizing a certain physical similarity between them — a slight paunchiness — after they have surrendered the initiative to a life of comfort. Both, without being aware of it, expose the discrepancies in the social organism they form part of; this organism or structure is shown to be circumscribed in its time and its assumptions, and certain basic idealist Kantian attitudes of that time are adduced to lay bare the flaws that, for Brecht, these very attitudes perpetuate. In order to spotlight these defects Brecht here makes use of the procedure of central alienation most typical of all his plays, namely that of the 'split' character, as in *Leben des Galilei, Der gute Mensch von Sezuan*, etc. Because of this, Bollwerk and Pätus fulfil different functions from those given them by Lenz and become, with Läuffer, related variants of the same figure. Bollwerk is consistently realist, Pätus deserts his idealism for pragmatic action, Läuffer is centrally implicated in a real, irreversible situation in which, unconsciously and through his senses, he tries to establish a sexual relationship which cuts across class barriers but, failing in the attempt, relapses into the pragmatism of Bollwerk and Pätus. They all three share an inability to face up to their social reality and, in terms of the play at least, take refuge from an abject paralysis of action in submission to the 'inevitability' of their powerlessness. The different aspects of the German student and future teacher thus thrown into relief are not only individually contradictory but also mutually illuminating (through their reciprocal alienation) within the action of the drama, and converge to a focal point in Läuffer.

The resultant of the interaction of the play's major forces (social position, economic necessity, individual desire, idealism) is expressed in the dialectic of Läuffer's self-castration, which generates the dramatic energy. His negative physical act is the necessary counterpart of his social surrender and, while paralleling Pätus's symbolic castration in the events of the play, it simultaneously echoes and reinforces the latter formally by being worked out on the pattern of Kantian antinomies. The dialectic rests on the view of the individual, Läuffer, as an element in society: it is 'wrong' for him to castrate himself in order to live more comfortably (the Kantian model is the singer who submits to castration in order to sing better and earn more) — *instead of attempting to alter the conditions* that bring him to this pass, but 'right' to remove any organ that threatens to upset society and his place in it (Kant's 'dem Leben nachtheiliges Organ'). Since Brecht viewed the individual and society as interdependent and both equally open to change, it follows that the necessity and concatenation of events leading to Läuffer's deed indicate the wrongness of that society and its indictment. Läuffer's dereliction of duty is dialectical in that he is doing society a service at the expense of his quality as a man; and here Brecht's concept of society as relative clashes with the Kantian absolutes in so far as a refusal to accept categorical imperatives would obviate the problem. It is possible to analyse the salient situation in *Der Hofmeister* from many angles, but no abstraction is equal to Brecht's own compressed formulation of Läuffer's dialectical see-saw in his sonnet on Lenz's play:

> Nun er gewahrt, daß sich mit seinem Glied
> Zugleich sein Brotkorb in die Höhe zieht.

Läuffer's sacrifice of himself, knowing he has a 'disease', is a blurred idealism carried out in reality; Mayer's term 'die Selbstentmannung der deutschen Intellektuellen' is for Brecht a real historical fact, here embodied symbolically. Läuffer's social position hinders him while he has the full capacity to marry; castration enables him to support a wife, through his very inability to consummate a marriage in a true sense. His deed renders him no longer a danger to upper class girls, but also no longer of use to Lise (who wants to marry him) except in so far as he becomes economically viable now that he can be tolerated.

The varied responses of Läuffer, Bollwerk and Pätus to situations that are essentially similar can be seen as an application of a cardinal element of the Hegelian dialectic, that 'the same thing twice is not the same thing'. A second Hegelian principle, dear to Brecht and pivotal in his dramatic work, is that to which he attached the technical appellation 'Fixieren des Nicht — Sondern'. A detailed description of how the actor should accomplish this effect first appeared, perhaps not fortuitously (though written in 1940), in the same volume of *Versuche* as the adaptation of *Der Hofmeister*:

Geht er auf die Bühne, so wird er bei allen wesentlichen Stellen zu dem, was er macht, noch etwas ausfindig, namhaft und ahnbar machen, was er nicht macht; das heißt, er spielt so, daß man die Alternative möglichst deutlich sieht, so, daß sein Spiel noch die anderen Möglichkeiten ahnen läßt, nur eine der möglichen Varianten darstellt ... Das, was er *nicht* macht, muß in dem enthalten und aufgehoben sein, was er macht.[68]

Though this advice refers specifically to the actor, the interpreter of a personage, there is little doubt that Brecht structured the roles he created with the same end in view: there is a unity of intent throughout his work in text, acting and staging that entails a consistency between method of acting and part played. Pätus, for instance, renouncing Kant in order to get a job and a wife, emerges as fully conscious of his decision as a *choice* and not a coercion, and bears, as a character in the play, the historical responsibility for his behaviour.[69] The apparent inconsistency that has been noted in Brecht's presentation of Pätus is essentially reducible to the question of determinism and free will; but because Brecht refuses to handle this as an abstract philosophical speculation, implanting it instead in a socio-historical context, the seeming contradictions dissolve in the dialectic of real living. Like his fellow-characters, Pätus is not just a pawn of events, he helps determine those events. The actor's task is to bring home to the audience this choice (and the possibilities that it necessarily excludes) in the most differentiated and immediate way: through voice, gesture, visual impact. The dialectic contained in the technique of 'Not — But' is the inevitable corollary of alienation and as such underlies the whole theory and practice of epic theatre in which the actor is urged to present events as historical occurrences in order to inculcate a critical attitude towards them in the audience. The insertion of this process of 'historicizing' has a dual result in the case of an adaptation as it facilitates critical reflection on the play itself and on the original author's standpoint.

As mentioned earlier, the Prologue in *Der Hofmeister* is an important functional innovation complemented by the even more significant Epilogue which, by its very nature, enjoys the advantage of referring to and summing up precise happenings that the audience has just witnessed. Together they create a frame that orientates the spectator's reception of the picture inside; yet the frame itself is integrally related to the picture since it is presented by the chief protagonist. However, while the Prologue prepares the ground for the events to come by inducing in the audience a very specific image of the Hofmeister (as an obsequious, mechanical, will-less figure) the Epilogue is differentiated from it in several ways: in place of the promise of events we are given a résumé of the action followed by a conclusion drawn from this. Naturally, the present tense in the Prologue gives way to the past tense in the Epilogue and — a more significant change — the first person yields to the third, for at the end the Hofmeister steps forward as the mouthpiece of the dramatist (i.e. the adaptor). The concluding couplet of the Prologue ('Wills euch verraten, was ich lehre: | Das ABC der Teutschen Misere!') is not essentially didactic, being merely the announcement of the depiction to come. But in the Epilogue the Hofmeister is to be identified with the author, hence the necessary use of the third person to detach himself from his role, and launches his message concerning 'der deutsche Schulmeister' directly at the audience:

> Schüler und Lehrer einer neuen Zeit
> Betrachtet seine Knechtseligkeit
> Damit ihr euch davon befreit!

In one unpublished version the final couplet ran: 'Beseht euer Erbe mit Heiterkeit | Damit ihr euch davon befreit', which indicates the theme's topicality for Brecht at least, for earlier in the Epilogue 'die Misere im deutschen Land' is defined as existing:

> Vor hundert Jahr und vor zehn Jahr
> Und vielerorts ists auch heut noch wahr.

Brecht's didacticism aims first of all to convey information but is incomplete without the active application of that knowledge in his own life by the spectator, who is called on to meditate further on the moral, not just take it in.

In terms of dramatic structure there is, of course, nothing new in the use of prologue and epilogue; it reaches back through a long tradition to the parabasis of the Attic Old Comedy in which, just before the middle of the play, the actors would remove their masks and address the audience directly in the name of the author, often using the moment to inveigh against some social abuse or an aversion that aroused his wrath. The difference in Brecht is that the actor does not remove his mask and step *entirely* out of his role: the Hofmeister *is* himself in the situation of the play and *comments* on himself in that situation in the Prologue and Epilogue. He is the link between depiction and meaning, the play and the message, and furthermore, since the situations and themes of the play are structured in dialectical terms, there is in substance no division between play and epilogue, each performing the same function through differing formal means. The effect of parabasis is achieved at the outset when the Hofmeister introduces himself to the audience in front of the curtain, and is sustained throughout the play in the dialectical polarity of events and characters.

This peculiarly Brechtian form of parabasis is closely connected with the species of drama to which *Der Hofmeister* belongs. The retention of Lenz's appellation 'Eine Komödie' by no means implies an invitation to laughter, for the Hofmeister opens the Epilogue with an immediate limitation if not a rescission of the term:

> Und das war nun der Komödie Schluß:
> Wir hoffen, ihr saht ihn nicht ohne Verdruß
> Denn ihr saht die Misere im deutschen Land . . .

And the final couplet of the discarded earlier version hinted at the serious function that comedy has for Brecht, namely the inducement of a state of calm serenity in the spectator which allows him to take in the events unfolding before him with *both* sympathetic enjoyment (aesthetic appreciation) *and* detached clarity of judgement. If George Meredith was right in his assertion that comedy appeals not so much to the emotions as to the intellect and is concerned with the social group rather than the individual, then, seen against the background of Lenz's play, Brecht's adaptation (with its peculiar application of parabasis and dialectic) produces a stereoscopic effect fitting into a heritage of social comedy that merges entertainment and critical thought. This is not to say that Lenz's play is not in some measure a responsible analysis of the structure of the society of his time; for him comedy was a serious genre. In *Rezension des neuen Menoza* he attempted to differentiate it from tragedy, and suggested that in comedy the characters were subservient to plot. However, it would be wrong to infer that Lenz believed comedy should be merely a matter of hanging a theme on the actions of schematic characters; he was imbued with the spirit of the Sturm und Drang and shared the typical enthusiasm of that movement for the richness and variety of life. He was well aware that any simplification of the diversity of life would in fact tend, not to

4

an idealization, but to a caricaturistic overemphasis of distinctive individual characteristics.

It is in this respect that Brecht's adaptation diverges significantly from the original: in place of Lenz's diffuse, rambling, eccentric, only implicitly critical structure of human relations Brecht offers a highly conscious paradigm of a certain socio-historical configuration. It is a commonplace of Lenz criticism that in asserting the dramatic value of idiosyncratic human action he virtually created a new and personal aesthetic in the drama of disconnected scenes. His is the unity of disjointedness. Brecht's unity is of a very different kind; while accepting the validity of Lenz's depiction of arbitrary individual behaviour he at the same time imposes reason on it. The result is the enormous qualitative difference between description and analysis, since Brecht wanted primarily to present not the troubles of an oppressed private tutor but an examination of how they had arisen.[70] This is accomplished through a bifocal treatment of the characters; while retaining their personal characteristics they are at the same time de-individualized to represent particular and well-defined social positions. By typifying towards caricature (brutal Geheimer Rat, mincing Graf, obsequious Hofmeister, etc.) Brecht puts the *group* to which the individual belongs in the centre of attention; the social satire this generates is quite different from that of, say, Molière, who exposed in one individual failings or vices that anyone might have. The factor that essentially differentiates Brecht's satire derives from his belief that individual behaviour is largely explicable in terms of social motivation and can be altered in proportion to the mutation or elimination of given conditions. What is left over of tragedy from Lenz's 'Lust- und Trauerspiel' is a tragicomedy, not as a mingling of comic and tragic elements, but, seen now a century and a half later, as a serious depiction of a society whose 'tragedy' is measured in direct ratio to the unquestioning acquiescence of the rising middle classes in the feudal domination on which they would in due course have to encroach. The encouragement of the spectator to 'serenity' prevents the intrusion of tragedy in any accepted sense, as this serenity is itself intimately bound up with and dependent on the distancing effect of a historical perspective fully aware of intervening events.

In his sonnet on Lenz's *Hofmeister*, as we saw earlier, Brecht had described Läuffer as 'Figaro diesseits des Rheins' and hinted at the contrasting style of drama in France resulting from the breakthrough of the 'rabble' to power: 'So wirds ein Lustspiel drüben und hier keins'. On the same terms Lenz was involved in the near-tragic vicissitudes of his hero: 'Des Dichters Stimme bricht, wenn er's erzählt'. These two comments are the measure of Brecht's considered detachment from Lenz; the adaptation is not only a historical drama, it is also altered in nature by the added dimension of events between then and now. The supersession of feudalism in Europe enabled Brecht to turn this into a comedy of the serious sort that prompts to thought. If there is anything didactic in the adaptation it is teaching of a different sort from that contained in a contemporary theme with its attack and call to action.[71]

The essence of the adaptation is *reflection* and it is of the same nature as the study of history, which is ultimately nothing less than the consideration of unique happenings in the light of what they theoretically might have been in other conditions. The historian presupposes the excluded possibilities (as manifold complements to the actual events), otherwise he would have no call to meditate on these events. The historical sense that Brecht tried so keenly and assiduously to cultivate in the theatre-going public is exactly the dialectical perspective of the historian, a prerequisite for analysis and understanding. Brecht's practice of adaptation parallels the activity of the historian, and is as valid a way of coming to grips with the past; a difference in quality arises from Brecht's approach being made through the aesthetic medium of the theatre, instead of through scholarship. In *Der Hofmeister* he proceeds by a dialectical method which establishes a significant contrast and cross-fertilization between original and adaptation, *both* of which are thus altered for the spectator. Brecht's *Hofmeister* is a modest example of Goethe's celebrated remark 'nur durch Aneignung fremder Schätze entsteht Großes'; the constructive and inventive plagiarism of his dialogue with Lenz not only provokes a potential energy in the lively interrelation of the two plays but also promotes the continued vigour of a literary tradition.

NOTES

1 *GW*, 17/1221.
2 *GW*, 17/1250.
3 Mayer, op. cit., p. 56.
4 Ibid., pp. 56 f.
5 *GW*, 6/2375; compare *Th*, 75: 'Erschüttert zieht der Major seine Tochter aus dem Dorf-teich, in den sie, seines Eingreifens sicher, watete.' The enormous rift between original and adaptation at this point is well illustrated by H. O. Burger's comments in *Das deutsche Lustspiel*, 2 vols, edited by H. Steffen (Göttingen, 1968), I, pp. 62 f.: 'Das ist wohl die berühmteste Stelle im *Hofmeister*, von Heinrich Leopold Wagner in *Reue nach der Tat* und Schiller in *Kabale und Liebe* nachgeahmt . . . Brecht ließ die Szene am Teich komödienhaft ausspielen und machte sie damit zur Posse . . . Die Regieanweisung ist für uns als Publikum Brechts nicht sehr schmeichelhaft, was müssen wir dickhäutig und hämisch geworden sein!'
6 According to a collaborator Brecht reversed the order of his final two scenes only at the last minute; compare Egon Monk, BBA 2062/9: 'Bis zur Hauptprobe blieb die Frage offen, ob nach dem Abschluß der Pätushandlung die Rückkehr Fritzens nach Inster-burg und seine Versöhnung mit Gustchen, oder die Verlobung des kastrierten Läuffer mit der Tochter des Schulmeisters den Stückschluß bilden sollte. Bis dahin war es die falsche Idylle des Familienfestes bei dem Major von Berg, mit Punsch und Tränen der Rührung über die glückliche Wendung durch Gottes Fügung, die am Schluß gestanden hatte. Erst nach der Hauptprobe entschieden wir uns, das Stück mit Läuffer abzu-schließen. Der Hofmeister ist es, dessen Glanz und Elend das Stück erzählt, und der für den Abend Anlaß war, den Ursachen der deutschen Misere nachzugehen.'
7 *GW*, 17/1238.
8 *GW*, 17/1248.
9 *GW*, 6/2390.
10 H. O Burger, op. cit., p. 66.
11 G. Mattenklott, *Melancholie in der Dramatik des Sturm und Drang* (Stuttgart, 1968), p. 146.
12 P. Böckmann, *Formgeschichte der deutschen Dichtung*, 2 vols (Hamburg, 1949), I, pp. 661–8, analyses the impact of feeling on *Der Hofmeister*; the parallel with the Prodigal Son parable is developed by A. Schöne, *Säkularisation als sprachbildende Kraft*.

Studien zur Dichtung deutscher Pfarrersöhne (Göttingen, 1958); and G. Mattenklott, op. cit., traces the implications of melancholy.

13 See W. Hinck, *Die Dramaturgie des späten Brecht* (Göttingen, 1960) pp. 30 ff., for an analysis of the functional difference between the Hofmeister in the Prologue and in the play.

14 See Paul Rilla, *Th*, 81: 'Wo Lenz in seiner reformerischen Enge befangen bleibt, tritt in der Bearbeitung der wirkliche gesellschaftliche Konflikt zutage. Nicht die Nachteile der Privaterziehung, sondern die Verrottung eines Erziehungssystems, das auf einer mumifizierten ständischen Ordnung beruht. Nicht der Hofmeister, sondern der historische deutsche Schulmeister.'

15 See BBA 1561/02; an earlier version of the last lines ran:
> Das hat seine Vorteile und ist bequem.
> Sodaß man mirs übersehen kann
> Was mir doch fehlt: ich bin kein Mann!

This is much inferior to the later version as it remains caught up in the individual experience of Läuffer and does not reach out to connect with the social situation.

16 *GW*, 6/2335.
17 *GW*, 6/2339.
18 *GW*, 17/1249 f.
19 *GW*, 6/2341.
20 *GW*, 6/2343.
21 *GW*, 6/2346.
22 *GW*, 17/1230.
23 See BBA 547/98 for a note by Caspar Neher on Läuffer's soliloquizing in Scene 14a after Lise has gone to prepare coffee: 'Jetzt Läuffers Monolog: Mir scheint der bisherige Ton echt tragisch. Der Monolog ist aber die günstigste Gelegenheit, die Fähigkeit zur Kastration zu motivieren. Der Ton müßte sein: Der Führer der Deutschen spricht mit sich selbst und macht aus der Mücke einen Elefanten — solche Leute sind zu allem fähig — das ist die deutsche Misère.
Ich weiß nicht ein, wieso man Läuffer durchweg damit verteidigen soll, daß er gezwungen wird, was er tut.'
Neher pencilled a further note, BBA 547/99: 'Monolog-Sätze, die das Komische zeigen: "Wohin gehen wir mit den *Orkanen* in der Brust?" Welche Allüren!? Läuffer hat die Formen der Herrschaft angenommen, und: "von einem *verzweifelten Vater* aus dem Teich gefischt, von mir *hineingestoßen*".'
24 *GW*, 6/2335.
25 *GW*, 6/2347.
26 *GW*, 6/2362.
27 *GW*, 6/2336.
28 *GW*, 6/2335.
29 *GW*, 6/2357.
30 *GW*, 6/2344. Towards the close of the play Läuffer adds an abject postscript to the grovelling letter in which he asks for a job: 'Und ich verspreche auch, unseres Heldenkönigs Martyrium immer ohne Weglassung zu lehren' (ibid., 2383). A further example of his surrendering of principles to expediency.
31 *GW*, 6/2350.
32 *GW*, 6/2372.
33 *GW*, 6/2383.
34 *GW*, 6/2380.
35 *GW*, 6/2393.
36 *GW*, 6/2384 f.
37 *GW*, 6/2357. The Graf, expressing a similar sentiment, characteristically takes refuge from crudeness in affectation: 'Unter uns, Major, ich habe immer gedacht, ein kleiner Abstecher hin und wieder nach Sodom frischt das Blut auf.' (ibid., 2367).
38 *GW*, 6/2338.
39 *Th*, 102.
40 *GW*, 6/2343. See also *Th*, 108, where Lise is described as 'Läuffers Opferlamm', and 'Der ausgehungerte Tiger stürzt sich noch auf ein Gänseblümchen'.
41 *GW*, 17/1242.
42 *GW*, 17/1228.
43 *GW*, 17/1229.

44 *GW*, 6/2353 f.
45 *GW*, 17/1243 f.
46 *GW*, 17/1244.
47 *GW*, 6/2351.
48 *GW*, 6/2362.
49 *GW*, 6/2380.
50 *GW*, 6/2381.
51 *GW*, 6/2352.
52 Brecht had already drawn attention to this phenomenon when creating the figure of Galilei; see *GW*, 17/1106 f.: 'Für Jahrhunderte und ganz über Europa erwies ihm das Volk in der Galilei-Legende die Ehre, nicht an seinen Widerruf zu glauben, als es schon lange die Wissenschaftler als einseitige, unpraktische und eunuchenhafte Käuze verlachte. Schon dem Wort "Der Gelehrte" haftet etwas Lächerliches an; es hat etwas vom "Abgerichteten", etwas Passives ... Es gab die "Gelehrtenwelt", und sie war eine andere Welt. Der "Gelehrte" war eine impotente, blutleere, verschrobene Figur, "eingebildet" und nicht sehr lebensfähig.'
53 *GW*, 6/2348 f.
54 *GW*, 6/2353.
55 *GW*, 6/2386 f.
56 *GW*, 6/2351.
57 Ibid.
58 *GW*, 6/2387.
59 *Th*, 92.
60 Ibid.
61 *GW*, 6/2387.
62 *GW*, 6/2338 f.
63 *GW*, 6/2390.
64 I. Kant, *Metaphysik der Sitten*, I. Teil, § 27.
65 *GW*, 6/2381.
66 *GW*, 6/2383.
67 *GW*, 6/2382 f.
68 *GW*, 15/343.
69 G. Löfdahl, 'Moral und Dialektik — Über die Pätus-Figur im *Hofmeister*', *Orbis Litterarum*, 20 (1965), 23, draws particular attention to the difference of awareness between Pätus and Läuffer in Brecht's adaptation: 'Die Haltung gegenüber Pätus wird ambivalent, einerseits wird gezeigt, wie seine Handlungen durch äußere Bedingungen determiniert sind, andererseits wird ihm ein freies, d.h. persönliches und vom äußeren Mechanismus unabhängiges Handeln abverlangt ... Es ist gänzlich unfruchtbar, ihn [i.e. Läuffer] aus moralischen Gründen zu verurteilen, was natürlich nicht bedeutet, daß man ihn nicht kritisch sehen kann; gleiches sollte eigentlich auch für Pätus gelten, aber von ihm postuliert Brecht ganz einfach Moral. Im Unterschied zu Läuffer weiß Pätus, was er macht, zu welchen Folgen sein egoistischer Verrat führt, er weiß, daß er nicht nur sich selbst sondern auch seine Aufgabe in der Gesellschaft verraten hat.' The sharp formal difference between Läuffer in the play and in Prologue and Epilogue does, however, enable Brecht to pin responsibility on him while seeming to leave him entirely at the mercy of forces he cannot control.
70 Mattenklott, *Melancholie*, p. 165, discusses the view that sees Lenz's play 'als Lehrstück im Sinne der Aufklärung', and quotes a *Tagebuchnotiz* by Hebbel that contradicts it: 'Es mag in der Hofmeister-Zeit manchen Lump der Art gegeben haben, aber der Grund davon liegt in der Natur dieser Lumpe, nicht in der Natur ihrer Situation.' But Mattenklott does add a rider to Hebbel's uncompromising 'classical' view of the hero: 'Es wäre zu modifizieren, daß wohl die Natur der Situation, nicht aber die des Hofmeister-*standes* den Konflikt verursacht.'
71 The difference in Brecht's drama between historical and topical material, the impulse to study or to decision, emerges from a comparison of the epilogues to *Der Hofmeister* and *Der gute Mensch von Sezuan*: where in the former the author hopes the spectators have witnessed the end of the comedy 'nicht ohne Verdruß', he has to plead for their indulgence in the latter: 'Verehrtes Publikum, jetzt kein Verdruß: | Wir wissen wohl, das ist kein rechter Schluß'. A historical and actual situation provides its own conclusion or 'correction' whereas a parable or contemporary theme thrusts the onus of conclusion on to the audience: 'Verehrtes Publikum, los, such dir selbst den Schluß.'

CHAPTER III

DER BIBERPELZ AND DER ROTE HAHN

Although Brecht dissociated himself from the artistic tendencies of Naturalism he did see some positive elements in the period, one of them being the beginnings of epic drama in Europe, derived from the middle-class novel of Zola and Dostoevsky. Yet the apparently revolutionary metamorphosis of the theatre was nothing more than 'eine leichte und im Grunde folgenlose, also unverbindliche Beeinflussung des Dramas durch den internationalen bürgerlichen Roman';[1] and this theatrical style had now again become indistinguishable from the conventions of that fortress of tradition, the Vienna Burgtheater, although the crude and shallow realism of the Naturalists was for Brecht a great advance on the Wagnerianism that dominated the theatre before, during and after it. His criticism hinges on the inability and unwillingness of Naturalism to realize what it was doing: it had incorporated some epic elements into drama, but:

Die Vorwürfe, die sich gerade dagegen (daß er 'undramatisch', 'bühnenunwirksam', 'schwach in der Spannung' und so weiter war) richteten, haben ihn rasch dazu gebracht, seine eigentlichen Tendenzen zu verraten und aufzugeben.[2]

The dramatists dropped their themes as they discarded their form and the movement came to a standstill. Thus Brecht could be cuttingly contemptuous of the dramatists who failed to stand by their initial impulses and carry them out consistently, accusing them of betraying their tenets and spending the rest of their lives putting their aesthetics in order. Yet as late as 1953, in a conversation on the production of Strittmatter's *Katzgraben*, Brecht was able to acknowledge the contribution, however limited, of Naturalism to a realistic theatre; he saw it, despite all its drawbacks, as the breakthrough of realism in modern literature.

Despite his fluctuating attitude Brecht was aware of some valuable social impulses emanating from Naturalism, though he thought the positive value of these was diminished by their limited efficacy in bringing about actual reforms. As is to be expected, Brecht found the source of the *political* ineffectualness of naturalistic theatre in the essentially unaltered perspective of the dramatists themselves:

Es lehrte die Welt so anzuschauen, wie die herrschenden Klassen sie angeschaut haben wollten. Insofern diese Klassen unter sich uneinig waren, gab sich auch der Aspekt der Welt auf dem Theater unterschiedlich. Das Theater der Ibsen, Antoine, Brahm, Hauptmann wurde durchaus als Politikum empfunden. Jedoch ging der Funktionswandel des Theaters nicht in die Tiefe, da von diesen Leuten nicht die

Grundlagen der Gesellschaft in Frage gestellt wurden, sondern nur Modifikationen ins Auge gefaßt wurden.[3]

Thus the ruling classes have 'particular preferences regarding the choice of subject-matter and its artistic presentation' (as an example Brecht describes *Fuhrmann Henschel* as presupposing certain 'bourgeois notions of property', so that its tragic action is geared to these assumptions). For Brecht it is by no means enough that a dramatist makes a show of feeling and sympathy — it is his *opinions* that must be subjected to the closest scrutiny. When he applied this criterion to the framework of attitudes within which he claimed the Naturalists always operated, Brecht equated them in quite virulent terms with the essential notions of the ruling classes, going so far as to call them criminal:

Die bei uns bestehenden Verhältnisse zwischen den Menschen als natürliche hinzustellen, wobei der Mensch als ein Stück Natur, also als unfähig, diese Verhältnisse zu ändern, betrachtet wird, ist eben verbrecherisch. Eine ganz bestimmte Schicht versucht hier unter dem Deckmantel des Mitleids mit den Benachteiligten die Benachteiligung als natürliche Kategorie menschlicher Schicksale zu sichern. Es ist die Geschichte der Benachteiliger.[4]

In several critical pronouncements Brecht defined the socio-philosophical attitude of Naturalist drama as identical with that current in all middle-class thought, intent on depicting an eternal and immutable universe resulting in a clumsy and superficial realism which failed to uncover the underlying relationships. This is the burden of Brecht's criticism: that Naturalist drama did not deviate in any essential from the established bourgeois view of man and society, a view that possessed an invalid aesthetic of the tragic hero unless one accepted the inevitability of his fate in a social dimension. This leads to a passive theatre with passive heroes, and Brecht alleges that the 'activist atmosphere' associated with Naturalist drama is created by stage effects only and is therefore not merely pseudo-revolutionary, but anti-revolutionary. The core of Naturalist drama that Brecht rejects is thus the concept of man subjected to *social* forces outside his control as *zoon politikon*, a condition of Naturalism that places it in the long tradition of bourgeois theatre:

Wir finden im alten Theater eine ausgebildete Technik vor, die es gestattet, den passiven Menschen zu beschreiben. Sein Charakter wird aufgebaut, indem gezeigt wird, wie er seelisch auf das reagiert, was ihm geschieht ... Wallenstein antwortet auf die Versuchung, dem Kaiser untreu zu werden, Faust auf die des Mephisto, zu leben. Die Weber antworten auf die Unterdrückung durch den Fabrikanten Dreißiger, Nora auf die durch den Ehemann. Die Frage wird durch 'das Schicksal' gestellt ... es hat nur auslösenden Charakter, es untersteht nicht der menschlichen Tätigkeit, es ist eine 'ewige' Frage, sie wird immerfort, immer aufs neue auftauchen, durch kein Handeln je verschwinden, sie ist selber nicht menschlich, nicht als menschliche Tätigkeit kennbar gemacht. Die Menschen handeln zwangsmäßig, ihrem 'Charakter' entsprechend, ihr Charakter ist 'ewig', unbeeinflußbar, er kann sich nur zeigen, er hat keine den Menschen erreichbare Ursache. Es findet eine Meisterung des Schicksals statt, aber es ist die der Anpassung; die 'Unbill' wird ertragen, das ist die Meisterung. Die Menschen strecken sich nach der Decke, es wird nicht die Decke gestreckt.[5]

The inertia of this approach is manifested in the well-known 'Zustands-schilderungen' of Naturalism, which for Brecht are socially critical only to the extent that they show something, but do not suggest in their structure a possible course of action to *eliminate* what they describe. He puts his finger on what for him is an essential question:

Die Frage ist, ob das Theater dem Publikum die Menschen so zeigen soll, daß es sie interpretieren kann, oder so, daß es sie verändern kann. Im zweiten Fall muß das Publikum sozusagen ganz anderes Material bekommen, eben nach dem Gesichtspunkt zusammengestelltes Material, daß die jeweiligen, komplizierten, vielfältigen und widerspruchsvollen Beziehungen zwischen Individuum und Gesellschaft eingesehen werden können (zum Teil auch eingefühlt werden können).[6]

This allusion to the last of Marx's *Theses on Feuerbach*, that the function of philosophy is to change the world, not interpret it, best defines Brecht's rejection of Naturalism, for he sees the necessity of a different *form* of drama (i.e. an *epic* form) if it is to perform a different function. The true realm of Naturalism, in Brecht's eyes, was 'the eternally human' in the depicted milieu. When it attempted to fulfil an *active* critical purpose Naturalist drama disintegrated in artistic failure.

Because he is convinced that the socio-philosophical ethos determines the aesthetic nature of a play Brecht devotes most of his attention to defining the differences between Naturalist and truly realist drama, dismissing in no uncertain terms the total illusion of reality of the former. It was probably this Naturalist desire to create as exact a replica of reality as possible that prompted Brecht a year before his death to talk of it as 'the poorest manifestation of formalism'. The illusion achieved by Naturalism is that which allows the spectator to feel the same as the personages in the play. Repeatedly, Brecht bores away at this feature of Naturalism; we, the audience, do not see or feel beyond the experiences of the characters, even in such plays as Ibsen's *Ghosts* or Hauptmann's *Die Weber*, where, though the milieu is depicted as problematic, the sensations, insights and impulses of the chief personages are forced upon us, as a result of which we are given no deeper awareness of society than the milieu provides. The marshalling on the stage of a highly differentiated group of individual people would lead paradoxically to a blunting of insight and discernment in the audience, and we would have nothing more than a naturalistic presentation.

It is in the aesthetic dialogue *Der Messingkauf* that Brecht opposes the theoretical analyses of Naturalism and realism most directly. Here the Actor calls in question even the accepted view that Naturalism aims at a photographic reproduction of reality, though the end result of the simulation practised is the same. He defines Naturalism as 'unnatural naturalism' and claims,

daß der Naturalismus niemals eine genaue Wiedergabe vornahm, sondern eine genaue Wiedergabe vortäuschte. Es ging mit den Naturalisten so: In ihre Vorstellungen kommend, glaubte man in eine Fabrik oder in einen Gutsgarten zu kommen. Man sah von der Wirklichkeit so viel (und fühlte auch ebensoviel), als man am Ort selbst sah (und fühlte), also sehr wenig.[7]

The common thread in all these pronouncements on Naturalism is a condemnation of the basic failure to tell the audience more about the world than it already knows, so that Naturalism is blunt and ineffectual criticism. The synapse at which naturalistic is transformed into realistic drama lies in its purpose: where the depiction of reality is absorbed by the intention in doing so, that intention being an added dynamic factor, namely the mastering of reality, as the Philosopher argues. Mastering reality can mean finding fault with, controlling and setting to rights and, if this is the primary aim of Brecht's realist drama, then the drama itself will undergo drastic formal changes in keeping with this functional reorientation. The first step to this end is the discarding of the 'photographic' reproduction of reality, as the Dramaturg explains in defining a truly realist approach:

Der Realismus gibt keine ganz und gar exakten Abbilder der Realität, das heißt, er vermeidet ungekürzte Wiedergabe von Dialogen, die in der Wirklichkeit stattfinden, und legt weniger Gewicht darauf, mit dem Leben ohne weiteres verwechselt zu werden. Dafür will er die Realität tiefer fassen.[8]

The formal change that would most immediately and incisively transform the static of naturalist into the dynamic of realist drama was early seen by Brecht to be the resolution of a situation into its component elements, that is, the depiction of the process that had brought it about:

Die dialektische Dramatik setzte ein mit vornehmlich formalen, nicht stofflichen Versuchen. Sie arbeitete ohne Psychologie, ohne Individuum und löste, betont episch, die *Zustände* in *Prozesse* auf ... So sollte das Hauptaugenmerk auf die Zusammenhänge der Handlungen, auf die Prozesse innerhalb bestimmter Gruppen hingelenkt werden ... Nicht weniger als ein *Funktionswechsel des Theaters* als gesellschaftliche Einrichtung wurde verlangt.[9]

This essential difference between states and processes is pithily summed up as a divergent way of looking at things in Brecht's image of the tree: 'Die Naturalisten nun zeigen Menschen, als zeigten sie einen Baum einem Spaziergänger. Die Realisten zeigen Menschen, wie man einen Baum einem Gärtner zeigt.'[10] Again the Philosopher in *Der Messingkauf* indicates the active extension to the *depiction* of the processes of reality, namely the understanding of them:

Es müssen die Gesetze sichtbar werden, welche den Ablauf der Prozesse des Lebens beherrschen. Diese Gesetze sind nicht auf Photographien sichtbar. Sie sind aber auch nicht sichtbar, wenn der Zuschauer nur das Auge oder das Herz einer in diese Prozesse verwickelten Person borgt.[11]

An earlier and franker articulation of the same conviction appears in unambiguous terms in the essay *Volkstümlichkeit und Realismus*. This important statement runs:

Realistisch heißt: den gesellschaftlichen Kausalkomplex aufdeckend/die herrschenden Gesichtspunkte als die Gesichtspunkte der Herrschenden entlarvend/vom

Standpunkt der Klasse aus schreibend, welche für die dringendsten Schwierigkeiten, in denen die menschliche Gesellschaft steckt, die breitesten Lösungen bereit hält/ das Moment der Entwicklung betonend/konkret und das Abstrahieren ermöglichend.[12]

Thus the initial impulse of Naturalist drama towards a realist theatre trickled away, for Brecht, in an essentially meaningless portrayal of 'reality' and had to be re-charged by a type of drama that in its form and structure aimed at revealing the workings of society with a view to active intervention in this reality by the theatre audience. The unnatural naturalism of a realistic theatre is an ineluctable necessity, 'weil man das Wesentliche nur herausarbeiten kann aus der Fülle des Wesentlichen und Unwesentlichen, als die sich uns das Leben darstellt'.[13]

Any consideration of Naturalist literature must inevitably come to grips at some point or other with the social and socialist interests of Naturalism. This was the magnet that drew Brecht to Hauptmann's plays. But the socio-economic concern demanded in its turn a clarification of the nature of Naturalist 'realism' which seems so close to true realism. Despite many discrepancies and nuances, Naturalism is generally equated with a strong involvement in topical social problems, and politically with socialism: 'Aber doch ist wieder das soziale Gefühl das Grundgefühl, die Grundstimmung der naturalistischen Dichtung gewesen.'[14] From his experience of it at close quarters, Soergel, a representative critic, firmly established Naturalism as the artistic correlate of the social feeling of the time:

Denn der Sozialismus — das Wort aller Parteienge entzogen — ist das weltanschaulich Neue, das in diesen Jahrzehnten in das Massenbewußtsein dringt, der Naturalismus ist der erste rohe Versuch, dies Neue für die Dichtung zu gewinnen...[15]

Hauptmann, far outstripping his contemporaries in creative ability, is often inaccurately seen as the representative and therefore spokesman of active political attitudes that are *attributed* to rather than demonstrably inherent in the movement of Naturalism. Georg Lukács, however, does take pains to make a detailed distinction between the 'instinctive democratic feeling' of the writers of the time and a genuine socialist philosophy and activity under the pressure of Bismarck's *Sozialistengesetz*:

In seinem *Emanuel Quint* beschreibt Gerhart Hauptmann diese Geistesverfassung:
    'Man rechnete allen Ernstes mit einem gewaltigen, allgemeinen gesellschaftlichen Zusammenbruch, der spätestens um das Jahr Neunzehnhundert eintreten und die Welt erneuern sollte... so und nicht anders hofften die sozialistischen Kreise und diejenigen jugendlichen Intelligenzen, die ihrer Gesinnung nahestanden, auf die Verwirklichung des sozialistischen, sozialen und also idealen Zukunftsstaates...'
    Aus solchen Gesinnungen erwächst auch der 'Sozialismus' der jungen Schriftstellergeneration... Erneuerung der Literatur ist in ihren Augen nur ein Teil der vollen Erneuerung des menschlichen Lebens. Darin liegt die allgemeine Bedeutung dieser literarischen Bewegung als Widerspiegelung der generellen Wirrnis und

Unklarheit. Ihr 'Sozialismus' ist nicht nur verschwommen, ethisch und religiös-messianisch, sondern vermischt sich ununterbrochen mit allerhand anderen unklar gärenden, vorwiegend reaktionären Tendenzen, die den Übergang des deutschen Kapitalismus zur imperialistischen Periode vorbereiten.[16]

Lukács justifiably singles out Hauptmann as the prime example of a sincerely socialist writer in his early plays. But because Hauptmann confined himself essentially to his *individual* sensitivity and reaction to situations that needed to be seen in a wider, *objective* social context, he (and his fellow-writers) abruptly altered course:

Und seine weltanschauliche Vertiefung treibt einerseits ins bloß Privat-Individuelle hinein, andererseits und zugleich in einen luftleeren Raum der bloßen Abstraktion . . .
    Hauptmanns Schicksal wirft ein Licht auf die ganze literarische Bewegung. In ihm drückt sich eine allgemeine Tendenz, das Schicksal vieler Schriftsteller seiner Generation aus. Die Sympathie mit dem Sozialismus war für sie alle nur eine Episode, ein Übergang. Nach der vergeblichen Revolte der 'Jungen' ist die 'sozialistische Welle' in der Literatur vorbei . . .[17]

A less partisan explanation of the ambiguous relationship of the cultured middle class to purposeful political activity is found in F. Naumann's historical analysis of the impotence of 'liberal' attitudes in Bismarck's time. The liberals, he points out, had lost the confidence of independent judgement and succumbed to the pressure of Bismarck's success:

Sie glaubten an die Größe und Kraft des einen großen Mannes und verloren damit allen Sinn für eigene politische Einzelarbeit. Die Verachtung, mit der Bismarck gelegentlich die Berufsparlamentarier behandelte, wurde übernommen, als sei sie ein ewiges und allgemeingültiges Werturteil. Und als nun Bismarck außer Dienst gestellt wurde und als er dann starb, da übertrug sich das Verhältnis zu ihm nicht einfach auf Wilhelm II., sondern es blieb eine leere Stelle im Gedankenschatz des gebildeten Deutschen. Er hatte sich abgewöhnt, selber ein Herrschaftsfaktor sein zu wollen, und fand den Rückweg nicht zum politischen Wollen.[18]

This is the most convincing assessment of the role of the articulate middle classes as theorists and talkers rather than initiators or supporters of effective political action; the roots of their subjugation reach back to the abortive first German parliament at Frankfurt in 1848 when the middle class showed itself incapable of retaining and wielding power. The Social Democratic party, formed by the fusion of several Socialist groups in 1875, leaned heavily on the trade union and co-operative movements — intellectuals were largely side-line sympathizers. Well-known figures like Hauptmann understandably denied direct association with political activities: 'Wir waren Wissenschaftler und Dichter. Politische Agitatoren in irgendwelchem Sinne waren wir nicht.'[19] Only a few contemporary writers like Bruno Wille were prepared to take the drastic and decisive step from theoretical to practical politics: 'Ich wollte aus einem "Romantiker" ein "Realist", einem Ästhetiker ein Ethiker, einem Individualisten ein Sozialist, einem Einsiedler ein Genosse werden.'[20] Hauptmann himself owed his notoriety as an agitator to the official reception of some of his plays in the prevailing political climate rather than to any innate subversiveness in the plays themselves. Thus Wilhelm II gave up his box in the Deutsches Theater when valid grounds could no longer be found for banning *Die Weber*, and *Vor Sonnenaufgang* had brought on Hauptmann's head unjustified suspicions that it took him a long time to shake off.[21] In the wake of the *Sozialistengesetz* Hauptmann was subjected to interrogations concerning the socialist activities of Breslau acquaintances but he was never one to commit himself to more than a *personal* attitude. Half a century later and with all the lability of recollection, Hauptmann defined his rebelliously individualistic standpoint in *Das Abenteuer meiner Jugend*:

Von früh aus in Opposition gedrängt, war ich ihr freilich auch heut noch verfallen. Ein ruhiger Bürger war ich und war ich nicht. Was ich dachte, war Neuerung. In keiner erlaubten noch unerlaubten Rubrik ließ es sich unterbringen. Stand ich dem Sozialismus nahe, so fühlte ich mich doch nicht als Sozialisten. Die Einzigkeit meines Wesens war es, auf der ich bestand und die ich gegen alles mit verzweifeltem Mut verteidigte.[22]

The months he spent at his brother's home in Zürich in 1888 remained in his memory a time of privileged safety notwithstanding the harsh impact on his *feelings* of the human misery that Auguste Forel revealed to him in the Burghölzli mental institution. His retrospective irony casts a sad light on his earlier 'convictions':

Wie gesagt: die Woge des Elends [especially referring to the Burghölzli], die immergegenwärtige Brandung des Jammers warf trotzdem damals nur leuchtenden Schaum an unseren Strand, den die Sonne vergoldet hatte. Aber wir waren ja auch Soldaten, die sich überzeugt hielten, wider Elend und Jammer der Menschheit ins Feld zu ziehen! Sollte ja damals doch das Paradies aus dem Jenseits ins Diesseits verlegt werden![23]

Hauptmann shared with those who did *not* work in factories and face unemployment the common belief in an easily attainable, inevitable progress, a belief that the millennium would arrive of its own accord by a natural and mysterious process of evolution. They were revolutionaries in feeling, not analysis and action, with what seems in retrospect a fervent but somewhat pathetic Fabian optimism:

Glaubten, liebten und hofften wir doch aus Herzensgrund! Eines Tages würde das letzte Verbrechen mit dem letzten Verbrecher ausgestorben sein wie gewisse Epidemien infolge der Hygiene und sonstiger Prophylaxe der medizinischen Wissenschaft.[24]

Like his fellow-writers Hauptmann stopped short of intervention and his plays of this period display in consequence formal characteristics that are the aesthetic correlate of his ethical position. Their content and the expression of this content are an uneasy compromise between status quo and revolt; socially, an inadequate attempt to pour new wine into old bottles.

In terms of the linguistic counters glibly used to distinguish personality types Hauptmann was a *Gefühlsmensch*, not a *Verstandesmensch*. He was involved in creating dramatic personages equivalent to those one might meet in reality; an analysis of the complex forces (social, economic, psychological, etc.) that prompt his many-sided characters to act as they do is never more than implied. Thus it is not totally to Hauptmann's detriment when Lukács attempts to establish the limits of his achievement:

Erstaunlich ist die artistische Reife des jungen Hauptmann, sein dichterischer Takt der Begrenzung in diesen beiden Werken: einerseits eine Revolte der Sehnsucht ohne klare Ziele (Weberaufstand der vierziger Jahre), andererseits die Guerilla der Unteren gegen das veraltete und korrumpierte Oben [*Der Biberpelz*]. Die Begrenzung liegt aber letzten Endes in seiner Zeit, im damaligen Deutschland; sein dichterischer Takt bestand darin, daß er das innerhalb dieses Rahmens irgend Mögliche geschaffen hat. Sobald er höher hinaufstrebt, muß er versagen. *Florian Geyer*: Eine Bewegung von welthistorischer Tragik, das Scheitern Deutschlands an der Schwelle des Übergangs vom Mittelalter zur Neuzeit. Die tiefe historische Dialektik seines Stoffes hat Hauptmann nicht erfaßt. Er ist dichterisch groß nur im Milieu und in der rein menschlichen Größe der Stimmung des tragischen Untergangs eines Menschen, der das Reine will. Und die Ausdehnung des Kleinkriegs von unten und oben zu einem dauernden und latenten Kampf auf der ganzen Linie ... scheitert ebenfalls im *Roten Hahn*.[25]

Thus the premisses are set for Brecht's adaptation of *Biberpelz* and *Roter Hahn*; Hauptmann's limitations were those of his time, that in its thinking did not operate in terms of the historical dialectic. Instead Hauptmann provides a well-nigh perfect milieu packed with subtle details of real observation which Brecht interferes with only for the purpose of revealing the underlying social forces at work; his admiration for Hauptmann's perceptiveness in an abundance of *isolated* particulars increased with his familiarity with the text. Brecht finds the experiential events almost all present: he adds to them or takes away in order to strengthen the links between cause and situation, motive and action, to produce a perfect congruence of event and meaning. In this is his tendentiousness.

Hauptmann was an observer, not a commentator; Soergel expresses the typical reaction to Hauptmann's creations in *Der Biberpelz*: 'Hier ist keine Person nur skizziert, alle haben die große greifbare Lebensnähe der Hauptmannschen Menschen. Sie gruppieren sich um einen aufgeblasenen, eitlen, streberhaften, immer Demagogen witternden Amtsvorsteher und eine von ihm protegierte derbe, schlaue Diebin, die Mutter Wolffen.'[26] And the dramatist himself later described the living prototype of von Wehrhahn as a witch-hunting official in Erkner where he registered the births of his sons. That Hauptmann was a 'natural' for the theatre is beyond dispute; discussion and theoretical argument were not to his taste and he opted out of profound explanations. Brecht's adaptation of *Der Biberpelz* is the measure of the gap between his proneness to analysis and Hauptmann's aversion to it. Hauptmann is certainly not an explicit commentator but he does go some way towards indicating the causes of the situations he depicts. Alfred Kerr saw this, especially in connexion with *Der rote Hahn*:

Mit demselben Blick sieht Hauptmann politisch radikale Gestalten. Die Weber-zeiten sind vorüber. Dieser Ede, Schmiedegesell, prachtvoll gezeichnet, ist gutmütig, betulich, willig, pfiffig, mit dem Mund vorneweg; aber mit leisen Sklaveninstinkten. Oder der Schmied selbst, eine Meistergestalt . . . Nirgends sind die Unterströmungen des sozialen Lebens so dargestellt . . .[27]

Indeed, in this review of the play, Kerr sums up the relationship of Haupt-mann to his public very succinctly:

Er will die Zuschauer gewöhnen, anders zu betrachten; auf andre Art die Ohren zu spitzen. Man sagt: in diesem Stück liegt viel, aber es kommt nicht heraus! Er sagt: es liegt viel drin, warum hört ihr's noch nicht heraus! Welche Partei wird siegen? Es steht fest, daß auf uns alle die Wirkung dieser bedeutsamen Tragikomödie gering war. Es steht mir nicht fest, daß sie es immer sein muß.[28]

This would be the typical reaction of Hauptmann to questions prying and probing beneath the moving surface of his plays: a depth is there, but, because he fights shy of logical analysis, he is incapable of formulating it in any but the ambiguous terms of the movement itself. This gives rise to the tendency of critics to search for symbolic meaning in Hauptmann's dramas and to the constant danger that they have to bury their quarry before they can uncover it. The quandary lies in the implied attitude in Hauptmann's social plays, when all the apparatus of modern publicity urges the dramatist to define his position explicitly. Hence arise Hauptmann's twistings in brief oracular statements that explain and at the same time obscure his way of going about things: 'Was liegt tiefer, der Grundernst eines Dichters oder der Humor? Zu einem von beiden oder gar zu beiden durchzudringen, ist schwierig.'[29] Or his reluctance to surrender the multiplicity of life: 'Man kann ein und dieselbe Sache in so vielen Gestalten richtig darstellen, daß es schmerzt, sich für eine allein entscheiden zu müssen.'[30] And he makes an apparently unequivocal stand for not taking sides: 'Ein Drama steht um so höher, je parteiloser es ist.'[31]

Explanations for Hauptmann's non-commitment are sought in a philosophy of life frequently expounded by commentatory figures in the plays which is then adduced as that of the playwright. This procedure of Hauptmann's is based on a double perspective derived from a mode of thinking that is aware of the wrongs in a situation yet accepts them as an inevitable part of a wider context. This all-embracing view (that can easily slip into smugness and self-righteousness) encompasses the 'criminality' of a character's behaviour within the narrow ambit of a particular social situation in which men apply certain standards of right and wrong (if only for the smooth working of society), and it simultaneously sees this reprehensibility as part of the ultimate helplessness of all human beings. Emrich argues that Hauptmann, taking the tragic and pessimistic view of man, creates a new type of tragedy from the polarity immanent in a situation where human beings live in constant struggle with each other. In fact, he sees Hauptmann's early naturalist dramas:

— als sozialkritische Tragödien, in denen die tragischen Antinomien der Klassen
... oder der bürgerlichen Familie ... in Erscheinung treten ... Offenbar liegt
hinter der sozialkritischen Thematik der Frühzeit eine umfassendere Problematik,
die Frage nach der Überwindung der irdischen Antagonismen selbst und zugleich
das tragische Bewußtsein der Ausweglosigkeit eines solchen Versuchs. Noch in
der naturalistischen Tragikomödie *Der rote Hahn* wird diese Problematik in der
Schlußszene außerordentlich eindrucksvoll sichtbar.[32]

This view of necessity attributes to Hauptmann a naturalistic *Weltanschauung*
which can be reduced to the simple dialectic: it is good and proper to feel
strongly about social and individual injustice, but since all values are relative
when measured against the ultimate helplessness of humanity, there must be a
reservation to moral indignation that stops short of making it absolute.
Emrich is not alone in this opinion; indeed, Hauptmann's 'ethical neutrality'
is almost a commonplace of criticism.

Interpreted thus, Hauptmann must undoubtedly be seen to hold a view of
life that essentially leaves the question of man's free will unanswered, since
his individual actions are viewed in a much wider context. One critic, H. W.
Reichert, in contrasting Frau Wolff and Brecht's Mutter Courage, asserts
that as a result of Brecht's merging the respective characterizations of the
heroine in *Der Biberpelz* and *Der rote Hahn* 'we get a character that closely
approximates to Mutter Courage, but differs from her in one fundamental
respect; even the composite Frau Wolff does not have free will'. Reichert
lists some of the aspects of Mutter Courage that expressed her free will,
especially that she had freedom to choose a way of life and made a wrong
choice in supporting war:

Frau Wolff had no such freedom. The unfortunate product of harsh circumstances,
she follows the proddings of an unkind fate. In *Biberpelz* her acts are motivated
either by necessity or by her erroneous idealization of bourgeois standards. In
Der rote Hahn she at first appears to have greater freedom of action, but on closer
consideration it is evident that she is an integral and unfree part of her society.
She thinks and acts exactly like her fellows ... The generally immoral tenor of her
thought is symptomatic of an entire social class ... Thus, since she is created by her
author as a product of her times and of her environment. She is shown to be un-
sympathetic, even detestable, but never morally responsible. Considerable credence
must be lent to her words in the scene that took place shortly before her death, in
which she told Rauchhaupt, the imbecile's father, that her hard life had caused her
to act as she had.[33]

With some justice, Reichert too emphasizes the ambivalence of Hauptmann's
outlook:

Frau Wolff is a superb expression of Hauptmann's belief, colored by his curious and
gloomy admixture of determinism and mysticism, that man was unfree and that the
world had to proceed on its tragic course. Mutter Courage brings into sharp focus
Brecht's Marxist conviction that men should be led to believe that it lies within their
power to make a choice between the decadent bourgeois society that spawns war
and the brave new socialist world.[34]

It is unnecessary to go as far afield as Mutter Courage to find a counterpart to Frau Wolff — she is created, or rather remodelled, by Brecht out of Hauptmann's own heroine: Brecht's adaptation hinges on his rejection of inescapable fate lying like a trap in the very nature of things, his refusal to apply Hauptmann's putative ethical neutrality. It is the final scene of *Der rote Hahn*, cited by so many critics in illustration of Hauptmann's philosophy, that Brecht makes the cardinal point of his adaptation: 'Die Wolffen, die von ihrer allgemeinen Beliebtheit gelebt hat, ... stirbt an ihrer Unbeliebtheit. Der Tod der Wolffen erregt wenig Mitleid ... Das "Ma langt ... Ma langt nach was!" der Sterbenden klingt hohl.'[35] To this comment one critic appends his own:

Was bei Brecht hohl klingt, klingt bei Hauptmann erschütternd. Wohl sah er das Unrecht, das seine Frau Fielitz vor allem durch die Denunziation eines unschuldigen, geistesschwachen Jungen begeht, mit aller Schärfe. Vor allem aber sah Gerhart Hauptmann das auch durch Gesellschaftsreformen und Revolutionen nicht zu beseitigende Elend der menschlichen Existenz.[36]

Discussion of such conflicting opinions pivots on the meaning given to 'Elend': if this is immanent and deeper than social and material misery, if it is, in short, existential, then, one can ask, why so much indignation about the injustice of man to man? (Yet in Hauptmann too there are substantial differences in the emphasis placed on different aspects of social structure: in plays like *Die Weber* socio-economic features of the group are important while in *Einsame Menschen* more personal relationships are stressed.) Hauptmann has the essential paradox of all Naturalists: powerful tendencies to social criticism and reform are retracted in the face of pessimistic despair about the existential wretchedness of being human. In Hauptmann's work the paradox is carried almost entirely in emotional terms. Brecht cannot accept the paradox; in his view, man bears *responsibility* for his actions, and the motives prompting these actions (especially where they impinge on his fellow-men) can and must be analysed. Brecht is an idealist as he operates with the concepts of right and wrong as absolute measures in the social context, the community, outside of which, in his view, human values are non-existent.

If *Der Biberpelz* and *Der rote Hahn* are closely concerned with their author's attitudes on criminality and the human condition, the double scale of morality that seems to be at work in them must also be subjected to scrutiny. The following is a typical reaction of both critics and public to *Der Biberpelz*:

Das Unwahrscheinliche tritt ein: obwohl Frau Wolff stiehlt wie ein Rabe, wird sie niemals unsympathisch. Der Gedanke 'Verbrechen' kommt nirgends auch nur einen Augenblick auf — es ist ein voller Triumph der Bühne über die Wirklichkeit, und dies seinerseits der tiefere Grund für die Beliebtheit des Stückchens.[37]

A true and honest appraisal of what Hauptmann is really offering is totally lacking, as is further indicated by the same critic's comment on *Der rote Hahn* that it lacks a dramatic core. Yet *Der rote Hahn* undoubtedly contains more serious and more cogent social comment than *Der Biberpelz*; and disturbing questions do arise from the ethos so inoffensively expressed in the above quotation: when do the haves tolerate the crimes of the have-nots? when no one is harmed by the theft? only in the theatre as an audience intent on entertainment? when it is not their own firewood or fur coat that is stolen? when the crime is accompanied by a witty tongue? We must remember that even a small theft could be heavily punished in Hauptmann's day. Walter Müller-Seidel comes closer to defining the insidious double morality that cannot be ignored in *Der Biberpelz*:

Wie sie [Mutter Wolff] robust, aber niemals brutal über die Ihren herrscht und die Vornehmen ein wenig hintergeht, nötigt uns einen Respekt ab, den es so nur in der Komödie gibt; denn natürlich gilt der Respekt nicht unbedingt, sondern mit den Vorbehalten, die wir dem Bürgerlichen Gesetzbuch schuldig sind. Die Mutter Wolff ist ihrerseits eine zwielichtige Gestalt. Aber sie ist es auf seltsam sympathische Weise. ... Wir sehen, wie die Mutter Wolffen, ein wenig lächelnd über die Moral hinweg, ohne ihr darum die Gefolgschaft zu verweigern. Wir sehen uns damit einer doppelten Moral gegenüber.[38]

Elise Dosenheimer, too, sees the justification for this double standard of morality in the nature and function of comedy which in Schillerian terms compensates for an affront to our moral feelings by delighting our intellect:

Die scheinbare Unzulänglichkeit des Ausgangs im *Biberpelz* erregt nicht nur, im Gegensatz zu unserm moralischen Unbehagen, unsere ästhetische Befriedigung, sondern sie ist auch eine Symbolisierung der Irrationalität des Weltlaufs, jener — um mit Kleist zu reden — 'Gebrechlichkeit der Welt', die uns ewig aufgegeben ist...[39]

But this critic clearly distinguishes the altered moral reaction to Mutter Wolff when she turns into Frau Fielitz in *Der rote Hahn*:

Das was uns trotz allem an ihr einnahm, ist gewichen, wir können die ästhetische Freude an ihr nicht mehr haben. Konnten wir dort [Mutter Wolff in *Der Biberpelz*] das Gelingen ihrer genialen Streiche in jenem Sinne genießen, so überwiegt jetzt das Unbehagen über ihre Unverfrorenheit und vor allem Gewissenlosigkeit, einen Unschuldigen büßen zu lassen, im Gegensatz zum *Biberpelz*, wo nichts entdeckt, aber auch niemand zu Unrecht verurteilt wurde. Die Verletzung unseres moralischen Gefühls geht hier nicht in 'uninteressiertem Wohlgefallen' auf.[40]

When Hauptmann wrote *Der Biberpelz* he presumably had no idea that eight years later he would cap this comedy with a tragicomedy involving the same characters. One may argue that each play is self-contained and can be performed and witnessed with no thought for the other, but the fact remains that we have two plays that belong together integrally and gain by being seen as functionally reciprocal. Over more than half a century *Der Biberpelz* has gained a reputation as one of a handful of successful German comedies, while *Der rote Hahn* is known only to the specialist literary historian and even then merely as a lame appendage to its predecessor to which all fame has accrued. When Brecht came to meditate his adaptation the simplest and at the same time most radical intervention he made was to telescope the two plays into one to be *performed* as a single entity in one evening. With his sense for realities Brecht was fully aware of what he was about:

Auf die lustigen Diebereien folgen die Verbrechen. Der *Rote Hahn* zeigt das dicke Ende des individualistisch geführten Existenzkampfes der Wolffen. Beide Stücke behalten ihre Essenz (vielleicht ist im ersten die Komik, im zweiten die Tragik etwas verstärkt), jedoch sind sie einzeln nicht mehr aufzuführen.[41]

In his adaptation, consequently, Brecht condensed the four acts of each of Hauptmann's plays into three and inserted a *Zwischenspruch* to make it quite clear to the audience that twelve years have elapsed between the two halves, thus immediately ensuring an epic quality in the external structure itself. In addition, Brecht either intensified or introduced certain social and political motifs that very emphatically — if slyly — determine the actions of the characters and condition the reaction of an audience. Finally, in the deployment and structuring of the elements he juxtaposed or interwove, Brecht aimed at a continuous feedback between the two parts that, without altering a great deal of Hauptmann's *text*, nevertheless reorientates the meaning of the plays.

In an analysis of the adaptation Heinz Lüdecke seeks to justify Brecht's action in changing the inherent character of Frau Wolff 'und mit ihr den ideologischen Charakter des Ganzen'. He first of all poses the theoretical question:

Soll und darf man aber so weit gehen, daß man gleichsam die Gedanken großer Dramatiker früherer Epochen weiterdenkt, daß man sie über den Grad der Kenntnis und des Bewußtseins hinausführt, den die Autoren erreicht hatten, als sie ihre Texte veröffentlichten?[42]

Then Lüdecke attempts to show how Brecht (in collaboration, of course, with his company) thinks Hauptmann's unexpressed political thought to a logical end for him, with Rauert embodying the historical role of the proletariat:

Rauerts politische Analyse am Schluß stimmt mit der Meinung überein, die sich ein ideologisch geschulter Zuschauer von heute bilden muß, wenn er Frau Wolff-Fielitz und Herrn von Wehrhahn nach den geschichtlichen Folgen ihres Verhaltens beurteilt.[43]

The figure of the worker Rauert thus serves to bridge the gap between stage and audience. Lüdecke considers the changes made by Brecht desirable because the adaptation instructs where Hauptmann depicts. This sounds a presumptuous claim but it does essentially describe the procedure Brecht followed in adapting Hauptmann's work: he was prepared to trust Hauptmann's eye for realistic detail, but not so much his understanding of what was historically (i.e. socio-politically) significant:

Wir mußten also die Arbeiterbewegung (Sozialdemokratie) in Sicht bringen, welche Hauptmann nahezu völlig übersieht. Den Vertreter des liberalen Bürgertums, Dr. Fleischer, beließen wir natürlich, setzten aber seinen Liberalismus gegen die radikaleren Forderungen der Arbeiterbewegung ab, das heißt gaben ihm einen leise komischen Anstrich. Im *Roten Hahn* führten wir an stelle des Rauchhaupt den sozialdemokratischen Arbeiter Rauert ein.[44]

To these two changes may be added the political blackmail of Frau Wolff by Motes in Act I; the expansion of the theme of the Navy Day (as a yardstick of German imperialist desires); the attribution by the authorities to the unemployed and class-conscious Rauert of arson as an act of political revenge; and the intensification of the atmosphere of the *Gründerjahre*, when every individual tries to jump on the bandwagon of the national building boom at the expense of morality and the good of the community.

Unlike most other adaptations this one has never been published as an integral and independent text (although some sections appear in *Theater-arbeit*). This is partly due to the rejection of this bowdlerized version by Frau Margarete Hauptmann, the author's widow and copyright-holder. A schematic synopsis of the adaptation may be the clearest way to indicate what Brecht and his collaborators did:

Bearbeitung

Act 1 = *Biberpelz*, Act I (Motive for Motes's extortion of bread and eggs from Mutter Wolff no longer suspicion of her poaching but her daughter Leontine's association with the socialist type-setter. — Linked with this is her reprimand of Leontine on this matter).

Act 2 = *Biberpelz*, Act II and Act IV (Whole act now in Wehrhahn's office; theft of coat takes place on stage; Fleischer represents weakness of Nationalliberalen).

Act 3 = *Biberpelz*, Act III (Krüger and Fleischer visit Mutter Wolff. Former apologizes for suspicions cast on her).

Zwischenspruch — spoken by Leontine before curtain.

Act 4 = *Der Rote Hahn*, Act I (Motif of Flottentag more prominent). (*Der Rote Hahn*, Act II totally excised: with it Dr Boxer).

Act 5 = *Der Rote Hahn*, Act III (Unemployed socialist Rauert replaces Rauchhaupt; accused of arson for political reasons; crowd scene in Wehrhahn's office).

Act 6 = *Der Rote Hahn*, Act IV (Intense *political* argument between Frau Fielitz and Rauert; Wehrhahn visits Frau Fielitz to assure her of support of authorities).

The immediate effect of telescoping the two plays into one is to *historicize* the situations originally appearing as separate entities. In this way the preponderantly Aristotelian assumptions of the originals (interest of the audience in the immediate events acted out on the stage, empathy into the feelings and problems of Frau Wolff-Fielitz, etc.) yield to a detached examination of the processes that lead up to these situations and further developments that emerge from them. Brecht turns the essential depiction of situation into open-ended *epic* theatre where the audience is given information that must lead it to incorporate actual historical processes in its appraisal of the play; that is, the socio-political context of Germany during and after Bismarck's hegemony becomes an indispensable premise of the action. Thus the adaptation becomes the re-enacting of historical circumstances which confronts the audience with the challenge to take up an attitude towards these circumstances that have helped determine the present. In order that it may stand back, weigh up and reach an understanding the audience must be detached from the situations being developed by means of the most radical technical resource of epic theatre, namely the interruption of the action to produce a maximum impact of 'gesture'. This interruption is not necessarily a literal suspension of the flow of actions on the stage (as happens when a commentary song or speech is inserted); instead, by enacting Frau Wolff-Fielitz's two 'crimes' within one play Brecht inexorably fractures and opens up her character, since the crimes now stand as mutually enlightening comments. Each delimits the other and each thus stands silhouetted — alienated — as a social 'gesture' with its motivation laid bare and leaving inferences to be drawn.

Apart from this confrontation of the heroine's two important acts (fundamental to the re-ordered conception of her character and resulting in a shift in its dramatic function) Brecht seized on the opportunity presented by amalgamating two dramas to insert a *Zwischenspruch* centrally between *Der Biberpelz* and *Der rote Hahn*. This *Zwischenspruch* or *Zwischenspiel*, like prologue and epilogue, was a favourite device (used, for example, in *Der gute Mensch von Sezuan, Schweyk im Zweiten Weltkrieg, Pauken und Trompeten*, etc.) and here serves to inform the audience without further ado of the historical context in which the remaining three acts are embedded. Mutter Wolff's unmarried daughter, Leontine, recites the lines:

> Zwölf Jahre sind verjangen, wehrte Höra
> und Wulkow Biberpelz is nu och längst Verjangenhet
> wie's jeht, wenn's jeht, is jänzlich Nebensache
> Hauptsache: det et imma unaufhaltsam aufwärts jeht.
>
> Pappa liecht ja nun untern jrünen Rasen
> und Mamma, hat, wir warn alle platt
> und Mamma mit ihrn alten Mumm, hat neu jeheirat
> Die Leute sag'n, det Mamma sich verbessert hat.
>
> Auch Adelheid hat et, weiß Jott, vamoos jetroffen
> ick seh se selten, wat ick, unter uns, nich sehr bedaure.
> Mit mir is det ja nich so jut jejangen,
> ich sitz bei meine Nähmaschine und versaure.
>
> Wat unse Zukunft anjeht, ham wa jetz nen jungen Kaisa
> dem wit's mit Jott und mit ner starken Flotte, heeßt's jelingen
> dem Ausland nu die Flötentöne bei zu bringen:
> Der deutsche Aar spannt, heeßt et, mächtig seine Schwingen.
>
> Schmarowski sagt (Schmarowski ist mein Schwager)
> et soll nu och an unsern deutschen Wesen
> die janze Welt, ob se will oder nich
> un des do schlimmer für se, wenn se nich will, ja jenesen.[45]

Leontine uses no extravagance: she delivers information about menacing military preparations soberly and factually.[46] Each of the first three stanzas ends with an economic or social fact; the last two describe the intensified political background against which *Der rote Hahn* will be played out. Brecht and his collaborators seized on the figure of Leontine to demonstrate through *her* reactions the implications of her mother's behaviour without actually destroying the positive characteristics of Mutter Wolff so carefully built up by Hauptmann to vindicate her actions:

Es mußte ein Weg gefunden werden, den Zuschauer der Wolffen gegenüber kritisch zu stimmen. Das Verhalten anderer Figuren mußte das schädliche Verhalten der Wolff-Fielitz aufdecken. Das waren Rauert und Leontine, die ältere Tochter der Wolffen . . . Unsere Bearbeitung erforderte eine andere Leontine. Wir wollten an Stelle der Dulderin, die Gegnerin der Praktiken ihrer Mutter setzen. Wir zeigten einmal, wie sie versucht, sich gegen die Mutter durchzusetzen ('ick laß mir von dir nich mein Lebensglück vermasseln', 1. Akt). Die Mutter ist schuldig geworden an ihr. Man wird ihre Entwicklung nun mit anderen Augen verfolgen.[47]

In the adaptation Leontine thus becomes virtually a victim: her mother, bent on bettering her lot through selfish, even criminal acts, ironically misuses to this end the very person whom a betterment might ultimately have benefited.[48] In Act I, when she runs away from her employers, the Krügers, her mother will not listen to her complaints:

LEONTINE: Die ham ooch noch nischt vom Zehnstundentag jehört.
FRAU WOLFF: Vom zehn . . . wat?[49]

In Act IV, she appears on hearing the altercation between Frau Fielitz and her husband, but she is curtly given her orders for the next morning (when Frau Fielitz has planned to burn down her house in order to collect the insurance on it):

LEONTINE *In der Kammertür:* Was is'n nu los?
FRAU FIELITZ: Nischt. — Du fährst morgen früh nach Fürstenwalde das Kernleder holen.
LEONTINE: Die ham doch gesagt morgen oder übermorgen. Da fahr ich doch besser übermorgen.
FRAU FIELITZ: Du fährst morgen, basta. *Leontine maulend ab.*

Nor do her servile position in relation to her younger, successfully married sister and the amorous attentions of the boorish smith Langheinrich contribute to sweeten her mood in the final act. On the day of the festivities she has to toil away at a dress for Adelheid:

LEONTINE: Jnädige Frau! Nich mal Dankeschön kann sie sagen. 'Der Ärmel sitzt nich'.
FRAU FIELITZ: I laß gutt sein. Dem Schmarowski hab'n wir's zu verdanken, daß der Wehrhahn persönlich hier nuff gekommen is und hat mer gratuliert zu meim Hause. Das wird viele beese Mäuler stoppen. Nu tummel dich ock, daß der Langheinrich ni warten muß.

LEONTINE: Laß ma in Ruhe mit dein'n Langheinrich. Der wird ma jenau so schinden, wie er seine erste Frau jeschunden hat. Die hat immer weiter nähn jemußt und verdienen, trotz daß se'n so ville injebracht hat. *Ab in die Kammer.*

Small wonder, then, that Brecht dispassionately allows Frau Fielitz to die in her chair alone, while Leontine with the unemployed Rauert stands at the window with her back turned and watches the firework display. Her last words are a peevish complaint when her mother suddenly collapses: 'Du mußt ooch immer wat ham, wenn ick mal weg will.'[50]

Throughout the adaptation Leontine's speech is curt and sour for she has little to thank her mother for (she labours away at her sewing-machine the whole time and even her savings book is sacrificed to Schmarowski's speculations unbeknown to her). But the most evil deed she has to suffer from is the ruining of her marriage prospects, a motif added in the adaptation, where she flares up at her mother who tries to pacify her: 'Du hast se mir doch alle verjrault. Es war dir keener jebildet jenuch. Der Einzige, for den ick mir vielleicht interessiert hätte, den haste Sozi geschimpft.' By this means even the mother–daughter relationship now interacts directly with the preponderantly political theme. In Act I the dark hints concerning poachers by which the informer couple Motes extort eggs and bread from Mutter Wolff are replaced by their threats to divulge to von Wehrhahn Leontine's association with the Social-Democrat typesetter, Henschke:

MOTES: ... Der junge Mann, mit dem wir Ihr Fräulein Tochter gesehen haben, is'n gewisser Henschke, Setzer und strammer Sozi! Vielleicht sagt Ihn'n das was.

FRAU MOTES: Wenn sie unter so'nen Einfluß, sozusagen aus politischen Gründen, die Arbeit hingeschmissen hätte, das wär' nich hübsch, was, Männe?

MOTES: Die Herren Jenossen sind ja jrade jetzt nich besonders beliebt bei die Behörden, wo sie gegen Bismarcks Große Militärvorlage wühlen.

FRAU MOTES: Sie waschen schließlich bei Amtsvorsteher Wehrhahns.

MOTES: Vaterlandslose Jesellen, diese Henschkes, die uns dem bis an die Zähne jerüsteten Erbfeind wehrlos ausliefern wollen!

FRAU MOTES: Werd' nich politisch, Männe! Frau Wolffen, haben Sie 'n paar frische Eier?

FRAU WOLFF: Jetzt mitten im Winter? Die sind rar.

MOTES: Die Behörden greifen ja noch lange nich scharf genug durch. Die Hunde müssen noch ganz anders gezwiebelt werden. Und die ganze Sippschaft, die mit so'ner Kanaille in Verbindung steht, dazu. Mitjefangen, mitjehangen. Alles soll sich jetzt mal vorseh'n, was staatsfeindlichen Elementen Vorschub leistet.[51]

Soon after this Mutter Wolff gives her daughter a dressing-down as she *simultaneously* makes her preparations for the expedition to steal Krüger's firewood:

FRAU WOLFF: Adelheid, du geh ruff. *Zu Leontine.* Was hast de mit dem Henschke?

LEONTINE: Jar nischt. Wo hast'n det wieder her?

FRAU WOLFF: Ich sag' dir, des heert uff am Beginne.

LEONTINE: Und det hört nich uff, ja nich! Ick laß' mir von dir nich allet vermasseln. Mein Lebensjlück is mir wichtiger als det Gerede von die Leute.

FRAU WOLFF: Wie oft hast'n getroffen?

LEONTINE: Zweemal. Und überhaupt war Emilie mit bei. Er is'n anständjer Mensch.
FRAU WOLFF: Anständjer Mensch! Een Sozi is er! Wer gegen die Obrigkeit is, der stiehlt oock und zind't Häuser an. Mach mi ooch nich ticksch, du! Wenn du mir so anfängst und schwiemelst mit die Sozi rum, dann hau' ich dich, daß de schon gar ni mehr uffstehst ... Nu weeß ick oock, warum de so frech bist und von die scheene Stelle so mir nischt dir nischt wegloofen tust und läßt das gutte Holz liegen, als wärsch nischte. Haste denn gar keen Verantwortungsgefiehl mehr?! ... Aber das is der neue Umgang. Bei uns haste sowas nie gelernt. Du bist aus'm anständjen Hause, und Wörter wie Zehnstundentag, ich hau' se der um die Ohren. Wenn ich und dein Papa so dumm quatschen wirden von a Zehnstundentag, dann hättste keene Schuhe ni gehabt zur Konfirmation. Jetzt gehn mir noch raus, jetzt, und jetzt is't elfe ... Hat er dir's Bier bezahlt?
LEONTINE: Habe ick selber.
FRAU WOLFF: Dann kannste ohne weiteres Schluß machen, und merk dir: Pollitik is nich fer arme Leute.[52]

The importance of political affiliations does not end here: where Hauptmann touches only lightly on the theme of socialism in order to strengthen his caricature of the clumsy, blinkered, sedition-hunting official in von Wehrhahn, Brecht uses it to convey both the historical significance of a von Wehrhahn and to define the social impact of Frau Wolff-Fielitz's crimes. Laughter evoked by the ham-fisted official is abruptly curtailed in the adaptation by his vicious dedication to persecution; he is in deadly earnest and fully conscious of the scale of operation of the oppressive and aggressive state authority he represents. Brecht expressly introduces the subject of the army bill and a pamphlet denouncing it reaches von Wehrhahn:

WEHRHAHN: Ja richtig! Glasenapp, lang'n Se mir mal die Akten runter, mit dem sozialdemokratischen Flugblatt, dem Wisch da gegen die Militärvorlage.
GLASENAPP: *geht zu den Akten.* Unter 'Unerledigt'. *Blickt in die Akte.* 'Beschlagnahmt am 2. Dezember im Wartesaal 4. Klasse des hiesigen Bahnhofs. "Arbeiter! Keinen Mann keinen Groschen für Bismarck! Nieder mit der Militärvorlage!"'.[53]

Wehrhahn then tries to foist authorship of the leaflet on the liberal-minded Dr Fleischer but the latter vehemently denies any connexion with the Socialists. Brecht deliberately turns this independent into the mouthpiece of the acquiescent National Liberal party line that half-heartedly allowed Bismarck to have his way for fear of a foreign threat to German sovereignty and pride:

WEHRHAHN *In beiläufigem Ton*: Sagen Sie mal, Mann, wie stehen Sie eigentlich zur Militärvorlage?
FLEISCHER: Auch das will ich nur zu gern klarstellen. Den Standpunkt der Krone darf ich hier wohl als bekannt voraussetzen. Die Krone verlangt eine nicht unbeträchtliche Erhöhung des Militäretats für sage und schreibe sieben Jahr. Als geistiger Mensch stehe ich dem Militarismus natürlich ablehnend gegenüber.
WEHRHAHN: So hab' ich's mir auch ungefähr vorgestellt. *Sieht in das vor ihm liegende Flugblatt.* Nieder mit der Militärvorlage!

FLEISCHER: Ausgezeichnet.

WEHRHAHN: Glasenapp! Legen Se mal 'nen Akt an ... *diktiert.* Kopf wie üblich, Datum: das heutige etcetera pp. Amtsvorsteher von Wehrhahn zitiert dem Fleischer etcpp. aus illegal gedrucktem Flugblatt etcpp.: 'Nieder mit der Militärvorlage'. Fleischer Doppelpunkt. Ausgezeichnet.

FLEISCHER: Jawohl. Eure Militärvorlage ist nichts als der Versuch, Deutschland vollends ganz unter den Kürassierstiefel zu zwingen.

WEHRHAHN *triumphierend*: Gewiß, gewiß! 'Keinen Mann und keinen Groschen für Bismarck!'. *Überreicht Fleischer das Flugblatt.* Wie es denn hier auch zu lesen ist, wie, Herr Doktor Fleischer?

FLEISCHER *sofort*: Das ist nicht meine Sprache, Herr von Wehrhahn. Das ist eines dieser sozialdemokratischen Machwerke! Ich distanziere mich aufs schärfste von derlei rüden und im Grund primitiven Forderungen der Tagespolitik. Meine Stellungnahme gegen die Militärvorlage entspricht doch etwas komplizierteren Gedankengängen.

WEHRHAHN: Da sind wir ja gespannt. Kommen Sie mit, Glasenapp?

FLEISCHER: Ich lege Wert darauf, daß meine Antwort auf diese Frage ordnungsgemäß protokolliert wird. Da in der Realität, in der wir nun einmal leben, der Schutzlose nur allzuleicht das Opfer der brutalen, aber besser gerüsteten Nachbarn wird ...

WEHRHAHN: Nanu? ...

FLEISCHER: Leider ... *diktiert Glasenapp*: Auf Grund dieser Erwägungen schließe ich mich, *zu Wehrhahn*, wenn Sie es absolut wissen wollen ... *diktiert weiter* ... am ehesten noch etwa dem Standpunkt, sagen wir, der Nationalliberalen Partei im Reichstag an.

WEHRHAHN *beunruhigt*: Moment mal, Mann!

FLEISCHER: Diese Partei verwirft die von Bismarck geforderten sieben Jahre des erhöhten Militäretats aufs entschiedenste und spricht sich für drei Jahre aus ... Jawohl, auch nach meiner Meinung sind drei Jahre völlig ausreichend, und diese meine Meinung werde ich gegen jeden Einspruch der Gewalt, woher er auch komme, laut und deutlich geltend machen.

KRÜGER *Geste zu Mitteldorf, daß sein Pelz verschwunden ist.*

WEHRHAHN *bricht los und erhebt sich*: Ihre Meinung! Herrn Doktor Fleischers Meinung gegen die Meinung unseres allverehrten Kanzlers, Fürst Otto von Bismarck!

FLEISCHER: Ich erhebe schärfsten Protest dagegen, daß hier versucht wird, mit Hilfe feudaler Namen die Meinungsfreiheit zu beschneiden.

WEHRHAHN: Zuerst müßten Sie mal mannhaft Ihre Meinung bekennen, Herr Doktor Fleischer, bevor ich sie beschneiden kann! Aber dazu fehlt Ihnen die Zivilcourage!

FLEISCHER: Zivilcourage!

WEHRHAHN: Sagen Se mal, schämen Sie sich nicht, sich hinter so 'ner ooch reichlich anrüchigen Partei zu verschanzen? Warum sagen Sie nicht wie'n Mann, ich habe dieses Flugblatt verfaßt? Basta! ... Ob Sozi, ob Liberaler, ob Fortschrittler, ich mache da keinen Unterschied. Für mich ist alles ganz einfach Schlappmacherei und Insubordination.

FLEISCHER: Ich stehe hier für das gesamte deutsche Bürgertum. *Zu Krüger*: Lassen Sie uns doch endlich mit Ihrem verwünschten Pelz zufrieden, Krüger, ich kämpfe hier um meine Weltanschauung ... Ich verbitte mir hier endgültig, in einen Topf mit irgendwelchen Sozialdemokraten geworfen zu werden.[54]

Less chimerical (for both Fleischer and Wehrhahn) than foreign power was the 'red' menace; while investigating the arson to Frau Fielitz's house Wehrhahn had already made up his mind in advance ('Ich habe auch meinen Verdacht schon gefaßt') that it is a political act, not that of a mentally handicapped boy, for he bursts out: 'Die Roten schießen ja neuerdings aus'm Boden wie Pilze nach'm Regen. Landplage!' Hauptmann's title *Der rote Hahn* is given added depth by Brecht and integrated significantly into the political theme: the idiomatic sense of 'fire' in the original is made more ironical by Brecht, who has Ede and Langheinrich bring an already painted red weathercock to fix on the roof of Frau Fielitz's new house. This leads to an altercation that hinges on the implicit knowledge that the red cock is an emblem of socialism as well as fire.

Brecht achieves seriousness in the figure of Wehrhahn by transforming his quarry from the harmlessly ineffectual, pensioned-off Prussian constable Rauchhaupt into the politically aware, card-holding, jobless metal-turner Rauert, who first appears with the cross for the grave of Frau Fielitz's first husband, Julian. He is employed as casual labour by Langheinrich and it is quite clear that it is his political views that prevent him from getting a job:

LANGHEINRICH: Der Rauert hat sein Kreuz mit dem Jungen.
FIELITZ: Det is seine eigene Schuld. Wenn er nich'n Roter wäre, und eener von die Radikalsten, denn könnt'er heute noch seine schöne Arbeet haben und den Jungen Pfleje anjedeihen lassen.

Later, Wehrhahn bursts out with 'Vater strammer Sozialdemokrat' on hearing that Gustav had been seen with a box of matches; and when he upbraids Gustav he no longer talks in terms of a decline in morals resulting from a lack of religion: 'Da haben wir nun den typischen Fall eines Jugendlichen, der mir nichts, dir nichts, das Hab und Gut ehrlicher Leute ansteckt. Sowas wächst auf in einer durch und durch vergifteten Atmosphäre. Tja, ohne Zucht, ohne Jlauben, ohne Halt und vermutlich mit nichts als politischer Hetze gespeist.' Hauptmann had concluded this act with an interrogation that disclosed Rauchhaupt's powerless reliance on irony and his service medals. He made a desperate appeal to Frau Fielitz's conscience: 'Fielitzen! Fielitzen! Kannst du mir ankieken?'; and, after a stage direction (*Er sinkt dumpf in sich zusammen*), a helpless final threat: 'Ick decke dir uff!' Brecht replaces the whole of this emotional scene with the cross-examination of Rauert, who stands up to the political pryings of Wehrhahn with perfect composure, realizing he must meet irrational threats with clarity and logic:

RAUERT: Moment, Herr Vorsteher. Ick habe det Recht, mit meinem Jungen unter vier Augen zu sprechen, bevor er abjeführt wird. Ick will jetzt wissen, wat eijentlich passiert is. Außer mir versteht ihn doch keener . . .Ach so! Wer an dem Brand schuld is, det is Ihn'n janz egal. Für Sie is det bloß 'ne jünst'je Jelegenheit, det Sie politisches Kapital draus schlagen. Det is doch keene Untersuchung. Von mir zum Beispiel wollten Sie bloß wissen, ob ick Sozialdemokrat bin. Hab'n Sie Frau Fielitz gefragt, wie hoch sie versichert war? . . .

zu Fielitz: Fielitz, ick weeß, wat du bist. Aber bis zum Mord hat es jetzt nich gelangt. Ihr beede könnt den Jungen ebensojut gleich mit'm Beil vorn Kopp schlagen wie nach Dalldorf schicken. Det is 'ne staatliche Anstalt, und wie die sind, det weeß doch jeder. *Scharf*: Kiek mir an, Fielitz! . . . Kiek mir mal in die Oogen, Fielitz!
FRAU FIELITZ: Lassen Se uns zufriede, wir könn'n Ihn' ansehn. Ich kann Ihn'n drei Tage und Nächte ansehn, und da seh'ich bloß, daß Sie a Roter sind.
WEHRHAHN: Und damit ist das Wort endlich gefallen. Sie haben sich nicht entblödet, Ihren jeistig minderbemittelten Sprößling zur Befriedigung Ihrer politischen Rachejelüste zu mißbrauchen.[55]

Further, while Hauptmann limits his crowd to a collective murmuring, chattering and laughing, Brecht particularizes his onlookers in typical fashion and allows them a running commentary that punctuates the verbal tussle between autocratic authority and the repressed rights of the individual. This serves not merely to enliven the scene but also a clear-cut dramatic purpose: these common folk use their heads and past experience to weigh up what they hear, and react to force and injustice with mockery and bitterness. Indistinct muttering becomes articulate judgement.[56] The scene ends with a general condemnation of the Fielitz couple:

JUNGE FRAU: Das sieht doch 'n Idiot, warum hier Häuser abbrennen.
ÄLTERE FRAU: Jetzt schieben sie's auf einen Unschuldigen.
MANN: Rauert ham se schon lange auf'm Kieker!
ZWEITER MANN: Ein Sozi ist doch kein Verbrecher!
JUNGE FRAU: Der Fielitzen sollte man's mal zeigen, die gehört ins Zuchthaus! Da is ja keen Mensch mehr sicher.
Draußen vor dem Amtszimmer
ERSTER MANN: Fielitzen, wann holst du denn das Jeld ab?
ZWEITER MANN: Fielitzen, paß mal uff, det de nich uff de Fresse fällst dabei!
ÄLTERE FRAU: Spitzel!
JUNGE FRAU: Fielitzen, was kriegt denn Wehrhahn ab?
WEHRHAHN: Wo werden Sie denn unterkommen?
FRAU FIELITZ: Ich denke, wir gehn jetzt erscht ma bei Adelheid. Die Leute sind ja so feindlich!
WEHRHAHN: Nickel, begleiten Se mal Herrn und Frau Fielitz, und sehn Se zu, daß se nicht belästigt werden.[57]

The next and final act also ends with the assertion of Rauert's trained political awareness in place of Rauchhaupt's fumbling, snuffling mawkishness that Frau Fielitz manipulates at will. With Rauchhaupt she takes the initiative by accusing him of ingratitude, and drives him to the maudlin admission 'ick bin 'n verträglicher Mensch' by appealing to his sympathy for a feeble old woman; and as he wipes his eyes and takes her wine she makes an offer to buy his land. An entirely different situation is created when Rauert replaces Rauchhaupt in the adaptation and aggressively enters Frau Fielitz's room with his accusations, having passed the brass hats on the stairs:

RAUERT: Ja, ick hab' se jehn sehn, und ick wees ooch, wohin die jehn! Een' kleen' Weltbrand anstiften. Mit Musike! Von Köpenick bis Kamerun — immer feste druff, und det wird jenau so 'ne Pleite, wie bei Ihnen, Frau Fielitz.

FRAU FIELITZ: Bis jetzt hab' ich noch immer mei guttes Auskomm', ich kann ni klagen.

RAUERT: Ick bin unten bei Grabow'n jewesen, da sitzt Langheinrich, die stärken sich für die Klettertour. Er hat ausjepackt, Frau Fielitz.[58]

Frau Fielitz is put entirely on the defensive; her efforts to bribe his silence and her last desperate throw at his fellow-feeling for the 'poor' only provoke from him a trenchant assessment of the political implications of her actions:

RAUERT: Frau Fielitz, ick versteh' janz jut, warum Sie die olle Bude anjesteckt ham: Sie wollten ma' anständig wohnen, det woll'n wa alle! Bloß mit Anstecken is det nich jemacht. Und Gustav muß raus aus Dalldorf.

FRAU FIELITZ: Ich zahl'! Ich zahl'! Ich zahl' ihm a Platz in ee'm Privatheim. Warten Sie oock noch een, zwee Wochen, ich bin in ee'm Geschäft mit Grundsticken.

RAUERT: Ich will Ihr Geld nich. Auch een Privatheim nützt jar nischt.

FRAU FIELITZ *fieberhaft*: Ja, ich weeß schon, Gustav muß raus. Was aus meine Kinder wird, is Ihn' alles egal. Bloß damit so a Kranker frei rumloofen tutt. Was wird Gustav schon tun? Im Graben sitzen und uff die Glocken uffpassen!

RAUERT: Ooch das; soll er.

FRAU FIELITZ: Rauert, ich weeß, wie eens da zumute is. Ich verstehe Sie, bloß es geht ni. Rauert, Sie sind a Roter, nich? Se missen doch a Mitgefiehl haben mit die armen Leute. *Pause*: Eene neie Untersuchung wird' ich ni aushalten, ni mit meinem Herze.

RAUERT: Wat Sie sich injebrockt ham, det missen Se schon auslöffeln. Ick kann Ihn' nich helfen. Sie wollten ruff, alleene, kost' wat kost'. Det heeßt: nich, wat et Sie kost', sondern wat et uns kost'! Sie sind jenau wie die andern, die jetzt da drüben Brand legen in jroßem Maßstab und jleichzeitig rufen, die Roten legen Brand. Sie ham's jegloobt, Se könn' sich jesundstoßen, wenn Sie Brand lejen, Sie ham's nicht jeschafft, und die andern, die Jroßen, werden's ooch nich schaffen. Sie werden nur alles zugrunde richten. Sie sind aus Peterswalde, Sie sind die Tochter von 'nem Weber, Frau Fielitz. Et jibt sowat wie 'ne Arbeiterbewejung, davon müssen Se jehört haben, Sie sind 'nen andern Weg jejangen, Ihren eigenen, nich mit Ihrer Klasse! Jetzt, wo Se bis zum Halse im Dreck stecken, woll'n Se vons uns Mitgefühl. Nee, det is nich.[59]

He follows this up by forestalling her incipient attempt to soften him with a drink:

FRAU FIELITZ: . . . Se könn' ma dorte die Flasche uffmachen. *Rauert öffnet die Flasche und reicht ihr ein Glas.* Nicht vor dem Mädel. Wir werd'n uns doch nich zerfleischen am End'. Nehmen Se sich ooch een Glas. Warum soll'n wir keen Tröppel ni trinken mit'samm'.

RAUERT: Machen Se sich da keene falschen Hoffnungen, Frau Fielitz.[60]

By introducing Rauert Brecht adds a new historical feature to the play and, indeed, does not leave it at the external relationship of present audience to past situations, but builds the dialectic into the adaptation by means of this figure. It is evident that Rauert is not a typical worker of the Wilhelmine era, but disposes of a sharp and perceptive insight into the socio-political forces of the time, and into what was to be their outcome, that in reality can only be fairly ascribed to hindsight on the part of the adaptor. A similar phenomenon occurs in Heinrich Mann's novel *Der Untertan*, which appeared during the First World War but described the same era as Hauptmann's two plays. Napoleon Fischer, like Rauert, is ahead of his time in his awareness of significant political configurations, but he 'betrays' his class by his willingness to engage in shady dealings with his opponents. Brecht makes unashamed use of the fact that half a century of pertinent history has elapsed between original and adaptation in order to enrich Hauptmann's plays by re-shaping them so that the full impact of their latent dialectic emerges. It would be as otiose to accuse Hauptmann of blindness as to praise Brecht's vision.

Rauert is thus rendered vital to the essential function of Brecht's adaptation; and because he is necessary for the historical dialectic to be adequately deployed, the figure of Dr Boxer can, and indeed has to be excised. In *Der rote Hahn* Dr Boxer had represented a favourite device of Hauptmann's (and of other Naturalist dramatists): he is a doctor, required to attend to one of the most primitive and imperative human needs, with access (like priests) to all levels of society, and observing human misery from a slightly detached vantage-point.[61] Like Der alte Kopelke (*Die Familie Selicke*), Dr Schimmelpfennig (*Vor Sonnenaufgang*), Dr Wachler (*Hanneles Himmelfahrt*), Sanitätsrat Steynitz (*Vor Sonnenuntergang*), Dr Boxer fills an individual role in the play (insofar as he is among the dramatis personae) but at the same time voices comments that could be taken as the 'private' opinions of the dramatist himself. Brecht realized the implications of such a commentating role when, in *Der Messingkauf*, he defined the limitations of Naturalism to the reality of what was seen and felt: 'Darum fügten die Naturalisten dann meist einen sogenannten Raisoneur ein, eine Person, die die Ansichten des Dramatikers aussprach. Der Raisoneur war ein verhüllter, naturalisierter Chor.'[62] The *raisonneur* was for Hauptmann a medium for making external comments and is an epic device in one sense since he is not entirely incorporated into the dramatic structure of the play. Brecht transforms the play into epic theatre through the historical dimension that enters with the introduction of Rauert and can thus dispense with Dr Boxer, his essential aloofness from the action, his 'Sehnsucht' that will not allow him to participate in the corrupt morality around him ('Aber mitthun — nee!') and his readiness to opt out of this society by emigration.

The effect of Brecht's elaboration of Hauptmann's two plays culminates in his final Act VI which corresponds to the last act of *Der rote Hahn* but incorporates only about four-fifths of the original text. Here various threads are brought together to present the ageing Frau Fielitz as a pillar of society, speculating in tacit collusion with others of her kind under cover of such catchwords as patriotism, national prestige, home and fatherland.

The motif of sentimental attachment to one's own home, however modest, is inserted by Brecht early, on Wehrhahn's visit to Frau Fielitz to collect his repaired boots:

WEHRHAHN *blickt sich um*: Janz hübsches Häuseken!
FIELITZ: Da hab' ick och 'n hübschen Batzen rinjesteckt.
WEHRHAHN: Der Mensch muß was haben, wo er Wurzeln schlagen kann. Die Liebe zum Vaterland jründet sich auf die Liebe zum eigenen Heim!
FRAU FIELITZ: Der Herr Amtsvorsteher weeß eben, wie's a kleenen Leuten um's Herze is. Ohne den alen Korbstuhl und ohne die Blumenteppe wißt ich reene gar ni, wie ich wollte weiterleben.
WEHRHAHN: Wie im Kleinen, so auch im Jroßen. Von der Etsch bis an den Belt!

Ede, the blacksmith's assistant, is made to add one or two sly comments later in Act v after the burning down of Frau Fielitz's house: 'Wohltätig ist des Feuers Macht', and of her tears he says 'Det sind wohl Freudentränen'. He retorts tartly to her pretence of perplexity as to the cause of the fire: 'Na, vielleicht war's 'n Glühwürmchen.' His sarcasm ensures that we see through the mask that conceals the insurance swindle:

WEHRHAHN: Sind Sie wenigstens versichert?
FRAU FIELITZ *Nickt schluchzend*: Aber man hängt doch an sein'm Gewese'.

From this it is an easy step to property speculation, and Brecht intensifies the speculative scramble already outlined by Hauptmann in the last act by making precise the field of investment for which Schmarowski is pressing his mother-in-law to disburse every penny of cash:

SCHMAROWSKI: Also klappt det nu mit Ihnen oder nich? Aber darüber mußt de Dir dann klar sein, liebe Schwiegermutter, wenn 'ne Bank einsteigt, sind wir beede Neese.
FRAU FIELITZ: Lassen S'es man gut sein. Ich werd's schon machen.
SCHMAROWSKI: Jut. Also nu is noch 'ne andre Sache. Es is nämlich 'ne neue Kiste im Jang. Nationale Sache! Kasernenbau! Riesenjeschäft! Natürlich sind Sie mit drin. Wir möchten an Mulickes Jrundstück ran. Der kann doch nicht mehr hinten hoch mit seine Järtnerei. Det können wir jetzt noch jegen bar spottbillig kaufen. Wenn wir das janz, nich jeteilt in die Hand kriejen, und es an Vater Staat verkaufen, denn springt 'ne Million' und mehr bei raus. Vater Staat knausert nich, Mutter Fielitzen.

Thus the political and the commercial interests merge: the themes of military and naval power, colonial expansion and national self-importance, together with the crushing of free thought and left-wing opposition, all engrossing von Wehrhahn in the course of the play, are brought together in the grand final scene and shown to be in symbiosis with the self-interested aggrandizement of a Frau Fielitz. Brecht has von Wehrhahn utter a resounding promise to Mutter Wolffen just before her metamorphosis into Frau Fielitz: 'Danken Sie ihrem Herrgott, daß ich hier stehe und wache! . . . Durch Nacht zum Licht! In zehn Jahren von heute, das garantiere ich Ihnen, der Wehrhahn, hat Deutschland seinen Platz an der Sonne, Wolffen und Sie auch'. The place in the sun for Germany includes a colonial empire,[63] and in Act IV von Wehrhahn adds to this announcement of the 'Jründungsversammlung der hiesigen Ortsgruppe des Flottenvereins' the rider to Frau Fielitz: 'Sie erwähnten da vorhin den Heimatgedanken, in jewissem Sinne is heute auch schon das ferne Kamerun des Deutschen Heimat.' The German dream in von Wehrhahn's mind is seen pictured on the wall of his office at the beginning of Act v: *In protzigem Goldrahmen hängt auffällig ein Bild des Jungen Kaisers Wilhelm II. an der Wand. Außerdem der Öldruck eines Schlachtschiffes.* It culminates in the symbolic and deliberate choice of the Navy Day for the inauguration of Frau Fielitz's new house: *Es ist Flottentag. Man hört während des ganzen Aktes immer wieder von außen Geschrei, Blechmusik anziehender Militärkapellen, Gesang usw.*[64] To the sound of this music von Wehrhahn pays a ceremonial visit to the infirm Frau Fielitz in her poky temporary quarters and sets the seal on the implicit concurrence of their motives and aims:

Es klopft. Hereingeführt von Glasenapp, tritt Amtsvorsteher von Wehrhahn in der Uniform eines Reserveleutnants — Gehrock, mit Ordensbändchen — herein. Frau Fielitz will aus ihrem Sessel aufstehen.

WEHRHAHN *winkt ab*: Keene Umstände, Fielitzen, habe jehört, sind leidend. Dachte, spritze mal rauf, gratulieren.

FRAU FIELITZ: Zuviel Ehre, Herr Amtsvorsteher, daß Se wegen mir alten Frau hier ruffgeklettert komm', wo Se doch schon so gietig sind und weihn unser neues Haus ein. Und alles grade heute, wo Se doch so schon genug am Koppe hab'n.

WEHRHAHN: Ehre, wem Ehre jebührt. Jehört schon irgendwie zusammen! Ihr Neubau und die Kiellegung unserer jungen Flotte.

Adelheid tritt in Festrobe aus der Kammer. Hinter ihr Leontine. Adelheid tut, als überraschte sie Wehrhahns Anwesenheit.

ADELHEID: Ach, der Herr Baron ...

SCHMAROWSKI: Gratuliert Mama, liebe Adelheid.

WEHRHAHN: Fabelhaft elejant, jnäd'je Frau. Wir brauchen Paris nicht mehr. Unser Schmarowski bringt Jeld unter die Leute. Trägt auf seine Weise als deutscher Kaufmann zur jroßen Sache bei.

FRAU FIELITZ *zu Leontine*: Leontine, hol' mal die Gläser, daß mer kenn'n anstoßen.

Leontine bringt Gläser.

WEHRHAHN *erhebt sein Glas*: Wer immer strebend sich bemüht, wie schon Joethe jedichtet hat. Frau Fielitz, auf Ihr neues Heim! Das steht da, das ist real. Meckerei jibt's immer! Speziell bei Erfolg. Und straucheln kann jeder mal. Aber wir wissen genau, wer gegen uns is, und wer zu uns steht, zu dem stehn wir auch durch dick und dünn. — Jnäd'je Frau, meine Herren! Ach, Kinder, habt ihr schon mal so'n Ding, so'n Schlachtschiff schwimmen jesehn ... wie sich die Jeschütze einstellen ... und dann 'ne Breitseite ... Deutschland jreift aus! Machen Se's jut, Fielitzen.

Er schüttelt Frau Fielitz die Hand, bietet Adelheid seinen Arm und geht ab, gefolgt von Schmarowski und Glasenapp.[65]

The scene marks the symbolic confluence of economic and political power in capitalist aggression; the *Gründerjahre* generated bottled-up energies in industry that strove for and eventually found an outlet in political action.

Brecht was fully alive to the dangers of allowing von Wehrhahn an operatic entrance in his uniform;[66] and his speech itself had to be deepened with anticipatory historical allusions in order to maintain the same tenor of response in the audience. Brecht asserted that von Wehrhahn's Navy speech represented such a marked relapse into the comic and satirical vein that it might prejudice the threatening close to the adaptation which held the omen of two future world wars:

In dieser letzten Szene mußte die Gefährlichkeit des Typs Wehrhahn gezeigt werden . . .
Wehrhahn läßt durchblicken, daß er die Wahrheit weiß oder mindestens ahnt. Er steht nach wie vor zur Wolffen, die für ihn das Volk darstellt, wie er es braucht. Er wird zu ihren Komplicen. Der Staat und sein Untertan haben ein Gentleman-Agreement geschlossen. Das große Geschäft kann beginnen.[67]

This scene, in which those in power close their ranks (as at the end of *Pauken und Trompeten* or the *Dreigroschenoper*), is intended as a historic moment and cannot be allowed to slip into the ludicrously satirical:

Aber mit dieser Uniform tritt die ganze deutsche Heeresmacht in die enge Dach-kammer, sie hält die Wacht am Rhein, und sie wird auch die Wacht an Frau Fie-litzens Phönixhaus halten. Es gibt Handdrücke, die tiefere Bedeutung haben, verpflichtende Handdrücke, und Frau Fielitz und der Herr Reviervorsteher tauschen einen solchen . . . Die Herren verbeugen sich, es entsteht der Eindruck einer Staats-aktion, die ja auch vor sich geht.[68]

The essential difference between Hauptmann and Brecht emerges once again in their divergent attitudes to the death of Frau Fielitz. Karl S. Guthke sees three structural principles of tragi-comedy at work in Hauptmann's play: 1. The embodiment of 'die beiden entgegengesetzten Perspektiven in zwei Gestalten mit kommentatorischer Funktion'. 2. The dichotomy of 'Schein' and 'Sein' in the main character ('der unüberwindliche Kontrast in der Persönlichkeit des Helden', 'der Widerstreit von Maske und Sein'): 'Frau Fielitz ist gerade so schlecht, daß der Zuschauer das Komische ihrer Un-schuldsrolle erfaßt, und gerade so gut, daß er für ihre Entlarvung fürchtet. Da nun immer beides zusammen in ihr wirksam ist: die Pose des entrüsteten guten Gewissens und die Angst des schlechten Gewissens, da beides sich bedingt, entsteht der einheitliche tragikomische Gesamteindruck'. 3. The disintegration of the moral atmosphere ('des ethischen Ordnungsbewußt-seins'): '*die Konfusion der Werte*, die das oberste zuunterst stellt: Komik wird also durch genau das hervorgerufen, was bei tieferer Erfassung das Tragische in dieser Welt der Fielitz und ihrer Kumpanen ist'.[69] Guthke maintains that Hauptmann stops short of pure satire by endowing his characters with 'wertvolles, substantielles Menschentum'. Brecht removed these props by doing away with Dr Boxer, by illuminating Frau Fielitz's 'Sein' in a social context, and by emphasizing the serious effects of a confusion of values. Hauptmann had typically enlisted the sympathy of the audience for his heroine by showing her at the point of death to be a poor, miserable, erring but striving mortal like the rest of humanity, caught in the grip of a common fate greater than herself. A sort of expiation is perhaps intended in the call to her late husband when she throws up her hands 'wie vor Freude,

in die Luft und ruft, halb selig, halb erschrocken ausatmend: "Julian!".'
It is certainly meant to catch at our heart-strings in a blur of emotion. Brecht,
on the other hand, went confessedly all-out to re-orientate the function of the
play: his withdrawal of sympathy from Frau Fielitz retroacts on the putative
comedy of Mutter Wolff (now that the two plays are fused) and throws into
harsh relief the ultimate consequences of even her early actions. Hauptmann's conciliatory end — Frau Fielitz's death on-stage accompanied by
Dr Boxer's final remark: 'Und von jetzt ab schweigt sie sich aus.' — yields
to the noisy activity of those who go on living, with the threatening shape of a
vast eagle flickering above them:

Leontine und Rauert stehen am Fenster und sehen dem Feuerwerk zu. Man hört Schritte
die Treppe heraufkommen und Fielitzens Stimme. Fielitz singt:
>Stolz weht die Flagge Schwarz–Weiß–Rot
>An unsres Schiffes Mast,
>Dem Feinde Tod,
>Der sie bedroht,
>Der diese Farben haßt!

Marschmusik und Geräusche sind nahezu verstummt, und anscheinend hat von
Wehrhahn ein Hoch auf irgend etwas ausgebracht, man hört ein hundertfältiges
'. . . rra . . . rra . . . rra'.[70]

Frau Fielitz's death is in this way absorbed into a wider situation which fills
the end and spills over into the future; the life and death of this woman
become symptoms of a temporal and social context that illuminates more than
itself and is conscious of subsequent events. The circumstances attendant on
Frau Fielitz's death historicize her career in a truly 'epic' manner: her husband's martial song links with the drunken lines of Amtsdiener Mitteldorf
at the close of Act I in *Der Biberpelz*:

>Heute noch auf stolzen Rossen
>Morgen in die Brust geschossen,
>Übermorgen in das kühle kühle Grab.[71]

and the recitation in that same act by the schoolgirl Adelheid of Ernst von
Wildenbruch's mawkishly sentimental *Des Toten Kaisers Roß*. Frau Wolff-
Fielitz's life is put into perspective as a paradigm of Prussian Germany's
bellicose ambitions in the direction of imperial and economic aggrandizement.
In the adaptation, therefore, we cannot view Frau Wolff-Fielitz as an autonomous creation existing in and on her own terms; the epic structure of the
adaptation throws up the dialectic of her actions and their consequences, and
this dialectic is the root of the altered function of the plays. The *Programmheft*
itself was, according to Brecht, to condition the attitude of the audience even
before the curtain rose:

Das Programmheft will — wie die Bearbeitung — hauptsächlich das Stück
politisch stützen. Der Zuschauer soll schon vor Aufgehen des Vorhangs umwerten.
Er wird vorbereitet nicht mehr nur auf eine im Grunde unverbindlich gewordene,
sozial entschärfte Diebskomödie, sondern auf ein politisches theatralisches Ereignis,
das auch bei ihm eine politische Haltung provoziert.[72]

Thus the categories around which much discussion of Hauptmann's two plays revolves — comedy, tragedy, tragicomedy — are, as usual, inapplicable in a consideration of the adaptation. Brecht and his collaborators took Hauptmann's plays as lively documents of social history and re-aligned their elements and information in order to release the maximum of social implication and comment. The historical attitude that is at work dialectically in the adaptation can only operate in terms of epic theatre, not in the traditional modes of drama — history is neither comic nor tragic. The aesthetic *raison d'être* of the adaptation is that it pursues its intellectual aim by means of the intense visual and verbal stimulus of dramatic presentation.

NOTES

1   *GW*, 15/139.
2   *GW*, 15/201.
3   *GW*, 15/358.
4   *GW*, 15/207. Brecht is here deliberately taking the word 'naturalism' more literally than its literary use justifies.
5   *GW*, 15/332 f.
6   *GW*, 16/922.
7   *GW*, 16/518 f.
8   Ibid.
9   *GW*, 15/220.
10 *GW*, 16/797.
11 *GW*, 16/520.
12 *GW*, 19/326.
13 *GW*, 16/852.
14 A. Soergel, *Dichtung und Dichter der Zeit* (Leipzig, 1911), p. 215.
15 Ibid., p. 216.
16 G. Lukács, *Skizze*, pp. 147 f.
17 Ibid., pp. 158 f.
18 F. Naumann, 'Die politische Mattigkeit der Gebildeten' (1904), in *Ausgewählte Schriften*, (Frankfurt, 1949), p. 191.
19 *Das Abenteuer meiner Jugend*, 2 vols (Berlin, 1937), II, p. 418.
20 Quoted by Soergel, op. cit., p. 591.
21 See ibid., p. 202, for the reaction to *Vor Sonnenaufgang*: 'Im preußischen Abgeordnetenhaus nannte im April 1890 ein Abgeordneter das moderne Theater ein intellektuelles Bordell, und vom Berliner Polizeipräsidenten, dem Freiherrn von Richthofen, wußte man die Äußerung zu verbreiten: "Es muß mit der ganzen Richtung aufgeräumt werden".'
22 Op. cit., p. 398 f.
23 Ibid., p. 423.
24 Ibid., p. 433.
25 Lukács, *Skizze*, pp. 157 f.
26 Soergel, op. cit., p. 326.
27 '*Die Welt im Drama I*', in *Das neue Drama* (Berlin, 1917), p. 95.
28 Ibid., p. 100.
29 *Das gesammelte Werk*, 1. Abt., XVII (Berlin, 1942), p. 419.
30 Ibid., p. 418.
31 Ibid., p. 270.
32 W. Emrich, 'Der Tragödientypus Gerhart Hauptmanns', in *Protest und Verheißung* (Frankfurt, 1960), p. 194.
33 H. W. Reichert, 'Hauptmann's Frau Wolff and Brecht's Mutter Courage', *German Quarterly*, 34 (1961), 447.
34 Ibid., p. 448.
35 *GW*, 17/1272 f.
36 K.-L. Tank, Nachwort to edition of *Der rote Hahn* (Berlin, 1959), p. 76.

37 J. Gregor, *Gerhart Hauptmann. Das Werk und unsere Zeit* (Wien, 1944), pp. 277 f.
38 W. Müller-Seidel, *Klassische Deutsche Dichtung*, Bd. 17: *Lustspiele* (Freiburg, 1962), pp. 731 f.
39 Elise Dosenheimer, *Das deutsche soziale Drama von Lessing bis Sternheim* (Konstanz, 1949), p. 147.
40 Ibid., p. 149.
41 *GW*, 17/1270.
42 *Th*, 196.
43 Ibid., p. 197.
44 *GW*, 17/1269.
45 BBA 1595/79. The following 'prologue', spoken by Leontine's sister, Adelheid, was to be inserted here, but was excised by Brecht (cf. BBA 1595/80):

> Zehn Jahr' vergingen, liebes Publikum, indessen.
> Wo sie verblieben, weiß man nie.
> Drum laßt sie mich noch einmal schnell durchmessen
> Und folget mir im Flug der Phantasie.
>
> Der alte Heldenkaiser ging von dannen,
> Ritt nach Walhall rauf hoch und hehr,
> Des deutschen Volkes bittre Zähren rannen,
> Es war als hätten wir kein'n Vater mehr.
> Bei uns ist es tatsächlich so gekommen,
> Auch Julius Wolffen's Leben hatte sich erfüllt.
> Da sind wir nicht in Tränen weggeschwommen,
> Denn Vater war für uns zu ungebild't.
> Es folgt ein junger Hohenzollernsprosse
> Nach neunundneunzig Tagen hinterdrein,
> Und in dem schönen alten Kaiserschlosse
> Kam wieder Zug in die Kolonne rein.
> Auch Mutter bracht's zu neuem Eheglücke.
> Wir sang'n: Wir winden dir den Jungfernkranz,
> Doch tauschten wir dabei verschmitzte Blicke,
> Wir wußten ja, es stimmt damit nicht ganz.
> Der deutsche Aar spannt nun die Schwingen dreister,
> Und von des Nordmeers steilem Felsenriff
> Verjagte er die brit'schen Krämergeister,
> Nahm Helgoland in seiner Krallen Griff.
> Jetzt hab'n wir einen Aufschwung ohnegleichen,
> Selbst unser Kaiser fährt schon mit Benzin,
> Drum mußte Bismarck auch Caprivi weichen
> Und Zeppelin erfand den Zeppelin.
> Man redet viel jetzt von soziale Lage,
> Elfstundentag für Frau'n ist durchgebracht,
> Für mich kommt sowas sowie so ja nicht in Frage,
> Ich habe nämlich 'ne Partie gemacht.
>
> Die Zukunft liegt im dunklen Schoß der Zeiten,
> Jedoch für uns wird's eine lichte sein.
> Stets soll als Wahrspruch unser Tun begleiten:
>
> FEST STEHT UND TREU DIE WACHT AM RHEIN!

Brecht possibly excluded this from the adaptation as its grotesque rhetoric, though satirically ridiculing the military and colonial aspirations of the time, nevertheless lessens the impact of the message: mockery and derision divert attention from the dangerous earnestness of such hopes. For the same reason von Wehrhahn had to be shown to be a serious threat, not just a political buffoon, compare BBA 1505/12: 'Der letzte Akt ist keine Satire. Grau große Darstellung; man muß 1914 bis 1933 voraussehen . . . Wehrhahn muß bei diesem Auftritt etwas fahles, unheimliches haben. Die Uniform muß sein, wie ein Bild aus dem Simplizissimus oder von Daumier. Er ist bereit Frau Fielitz als Komplice zu decken.' Compare also the suggestions arising in rehearsal, BBA 1505/67: 'Der politische Hintergrund von Wehrhahn im 6. Akt hauptsächlich kommt nicht genug heraus, er wirkt zu komisch, der Vorfahr von dem SS-Mann wird nicht klar.' In the same way, the actor had to guard against a grotesque interpretation of Rentier Krüger, ibid.: 'Die Rolle des Krüger muß echte Komik haben, der Choleriker von Männerstolz erfüllt und sein Eigentum verteidigt. Sie darf nicht ins Groteske gehen.'

46 See *Th*, 203: 'Leontine spricht auch den Zwischenspruch vor dem vierten Akt. Wir benutzen die Gelegenheit, etwas von der weiteren Entwicklung der Leontine zu zeigen. Sie berichtet von dem Aufschwung, den sowohl Deutschland als auch die Familie Wolff-Fielitz genommen hat, mit einem bitteren Unterton, der erkennen läßt, daß sie selbst nicht daran teilgenommen hat.'

47 Ibid., 202 f.

48 See ibid., 203: 'Sie will sich das Geschäft bei Krügers nicht verderben, dafür muß die Tochter schuften und darf nicht mucksen. Das wichtigste Kapital der Wolffen ist ihr guter Leumund, mit dem sie in Ruhe ihr Schmuggelgeschäft betreibt. Leontine nickt dazu verstehend mit dem Kopf. Sie wird benutzt, sie zu decken.'

49 This and subsequent quotations from the adaptation are taken from BBA, Mappe 1595, which appears to contain the final Bühnenfassung; or, if indicated, the text used is that of the excerpts published in *Theaterarbeit*.

50 *Th*, 194.

51 Ibid., 179 f.

52 Ibid., 180 f.

53 Brecht's apparently arbitrary expansion of the political theme may be justified by the fact that Hauptmann took the trouble to give the time of his plays as 'Septennatskampf gegen Ende der achtziger Jahre' (*Der Biberpelz*) and 'Kampf um die Lex Heinze' (*Der rote Hahn*). The Septennat referred to the army estimates introduced by Bismarck (the first of them in 1874) seeking public moneys every seven years to increase the armed strength of the nation in peace time; they were bitterly opposed by the Social Democrats. The Lex Heinze was an Obscenity Act of 1899 that aroused violent opposition in artistic and literary circles.

54 *Th*, 182 ff.

55 *Th*, 189 ff.

56 See ibid., 204: 'Um zu zeigen, daß das Verbrechen der Wolff-Fielitz auch verurteilt wird, ließen wir einen Teil von ihnen Rauerts Partei nehmen. Dem Aussehen nach ältere Arbeiter, Arbeitslose und Frauen von Arbeitern.'

57 Ibid., 191 f.

58 Ibid., 193.

59 Ibid., 193 f.

60 Ibid., 194.

61 See H. Barnstorff, *Die soziale, politische und wirtschaftliche Zeitkritik im Werke Gerhart Hauptmanns* (Jena, 1938), p. 56: 'Der Arzt ist ein Charakter in den Hauptmannschen Werken, der für die menschlichen Verhältnisse das meiste Verständnis besitzt.'

62 *GW*, 16/519.

63 The later Reichskanzler von Bülow declared to the Reichstag on the acquisition of the Chinese colony Tsingtan in 1897: 'Wir wollen niemand in den Schatten stellen, aber wir verlangen auch unseren Platz an der Sonne.'

64 Compare *Th*, 223: 'Diesen Flottentag zu illustrieren, dem zuliebe Schwiegersohn Schmarowski, auch Spekulant in Patriotismus, das Richtfest der Fielitzschen Mietskaserne vorverlegt hat, ließen wir den ganzen Akt hindurch Marschmusik spielen: den Königgrätzer, den Präsentiermarsch, den Einzug der Gladiatoren, den Abschied der Gladiatoren, der Pariser Einzugsmarsch usw ... Zeitweilig ließen wir auch zwei Marschplatten zugleich laufen, beim Auftritt Wehrhahns zum Beispiel, was akustisch bewirkte, daß der nationale Rummel sich sofort in einen wirklichen Rummel verkehrte und dadurch auch die Lächerlichkeit dieses "Feiertages" der Nation entlarvte.'

65 Ibid., 192.

66 See ibid., 223: 'Andererseits lag die Gefahr nahe, daß das Auftreten Wehrhahns im wirklich noch 'bunten Rock' der damaligen Zeit diesem ernstesten und finstersten Akt des ganzen Stückes eine entscheidende Wendung zurück ins Komisch-satirische gab ... Was wir wollten, nämlich die Darstellung des Kriegerischen des Flottentages, die Vorwegnahme der folgenden zwei Weltkriege, hätten wohl nur der Stahlhelm und das feldgraue Tuch hergeben können, die Uniform, die es damals noch nicht gab.'

67 Ibid., 205.

68 *GW*, 17/1273.

74

69 K. S. Guthke, *Geschichte und Poetik der deutschen Tragikomödie* (Göttingen, 1961), pp. 253–60.
70 *Th*, 195.
71 A slight but significant variation of Wilhelm Hauff's 'Reiters Morgenlied':
        Gestern noch auf stolzen Rossen,
        Heute durch die Brust geschossen,
        Morgen in das kühle Grab!
72 *Th*, 225.

CHAPTER IV
DON JUAN

When Brecht set about adapting Molière's comedy *Dom Juan* — the first adaptation of a major foreign play (*Antigone* had been filtered through Hölderlin's translation) and the only French one — he was linking on to a European tradition that started in the seventeenth century and had undergone a variety of changes.[1] Molière's *Dom Juan* appeared early on the scene in 1665, little more than a generation after the Spaniard Tirso de Molina's *El Burlador de Sevilla y convidado de piedra* had set the ball rolling. The subject had become fashionable in the Parisian theatre, the Italian version by Cicognini was made popular by a *commedia dell'arte* troupe, and two French attempts by Dorimon and Villiers preceded Molière. Fundamental shifts in interpretation were already evident and Molière invested his hero, supposedly a Sicilian sensualist, with the quite distinct ethos of Parisian aristocrats; the other characters, too, are recognizably of Molière's time. Over a hundred years later Mozart's *Don Giovanni* incorporated the eighteenth-century view of the deceiver and led on to the narcissistic Romantic vision of Don Juan as a restless demonic spirit, a composite of *l'homme révolté* and *l'homme fatal*, acquiring metaphysical significance in his search for happiness, perfection, paradise. Perhaps E. T. A. Hoffmann, being transported by Mozart's opera and consequently idealizing its hero, was most influential in establishing this conception; in his story *Don Juan* (1813) he muses on the superhuman aspirations that induce the transgressions of the seducer. Although Hoffmann extrapolates this aspect from his enthusiasm for Mozart's music (which he described in a letter to Hippel in 1795) it is the interpretation of Don Juan that has predominated from the Romantics onwards,[2] more particularly perhaps in Germany where, consciously and unconsciously, his demonic striving has assimilated many Faustian elements. It is this detaching of the hero from the realities of society and his elevation into an absolute sphere that Brecht sets out to counter.

In his notes to Besson's production of the adaptation for the Berliner Ensemble Brecht rails at the tradition of the bourgeois theatre that draws the sting of Molière and makes of Don Juan a tragic, superhuman hero:

Mit dem Molière wurde die bürgerliche deutsche Bühne fertig, ohne die Texte zu demolieren, sie kriegte ihn unter, indem sie ihn 'tiefer auffaßte', 'vermenschlichte', 'dämonisierte' . . . Don Juan wurde der 'vielleicht sogar tragische Wüstling', der 'nie zu sättigende Sucher und Begehrer'.

Nichts in dem Text, der vorliegt, ermuntert eine solche Auffassung, die auch von einer völligen Unkenntnis der Zeit zeugt, in der Molière lebte, und der Stellung, die er zu ihr einnahm.[3]

A comment made during a discussion about *Don Juan* with his collaborators on 23 September 1953 also testifies to Brecht's realization that he was swimming against the tide in reinstating a comic Don Juan (although it goes without saying that Brecht's comedy, like Molière's, would be eminently serious):

Bei Molière tritt Don Juan offen und schamlos auf, dafür ist er bei den Spaniern tragisch. Mehr und mehr wurde dieser Don Juan tragisch gespielt in den folgenden Jahrhunderten mit zunehmendem bürgerlichem Einfluß, sodaß wir jetzt, als wir es mit Ausländern besprachen — Volksbühnenkonferenz — , auf großes Erstaunen stießen, daß wir es komisch spielen.[4]

If the theme tackled by Brecht in this adaptation was common, almost legendary, European property, the actual prototype he worked over was the unmistakable expression of a particular cultural and historical situation in France. For this reason, Brecht's procedure of studying minutely Molière's time and his attitude to it and setting about the adaptation with the insights thus gained in mind, inevitably had to be of a different nature from the similar method applied to the German dramatists Lenz and Hauptmann. Whereas the German plays were embedded in the more or less recent historical heritage of both Brecht and his public and presupposed all the subtle differentiation of fibres connecting the past and present of a nation in a living tissue, he was in the case of Molière approaching from outside, making a cooler and less involved appraisal, yet one that blunted or distorted many delicate and discriminating finesses in Molière's play. The overall ethos of *le Grand Siècle*, Molière's satire on medicine and hypocrisy, the ferreting activities of the Compagnie du Saint-Sacrement, the *dévots* and their subterranean campaign that led to the banning of *Tartuffe* in 1664 (a year before *Dom Juan* had its brief fifteen performances), the *libertinage* of thought that was spreading so quickly were all topical for Molière and the Parisians. In adapting the play almost three hundred years later for a different language and culture Brecht had to reduce or exclude altogether some of these aspects (e.g. the attack on the medical profession is now vestigial) and switch the function of others to fit his own total assessment and image of Molière's age and intent. It is thus difficult to accept at its face value Brecht's assertion that his avowed Marxist attitude would allow the 'pure' viewpoint of Molière to emerge unalloyed, where it had been distorted by persistent bourgeois attempts to 'interpret'. Many would claim that cunning interpretation is a cardinal *modus operandi* in Brecht's adaptations, and he demonstrably imposes later points of view on those of the original author. This is not necessarily to be condemned; it is perhaps desirable that Brecht should have rethought the terms of *Dom Juan*. In any age the production of a play (classic or not) is a doubtful boon if the presentation is devoid of ideas that make the drama relevant to that age.

To establish the relationship of Brecht to Molière and his time in the proper perspective we must take into account the broad picture of the social history of the seventeenth century in France and in particular Brecht's interpretation of it. Central to this age (later dubbed *le Grand Siècle*) is of course the court culture pivoting on the power of Louis XIV, the prime example of an absolute monarch and one who used the energies of the middle classes to bolster his dominion, yet sat enthroned at the summit of a feudal pyramid that effectively crushed any attempt from below to alter the ossified social structure. The programme accompanying the Berliner Ensemble production of *Don Juan* carries a score of pages of documentary material indicating quite clearly the political and economic background to Molière's play; it contains descriptions of the wars waged by Louis XIV, the elaborate ceremonial of his *levée*, his lavish spending on palaces, pyrotechnics and prostitutes, the wretched lot of the submerged nine-tenths in their stinking misery, the organizing ability of Colbert, the draper's son who ruthlessly created the economic premises for the King's splendour. Brecht and his collaborators analysed the royal exploitation of both nobility and middle class as they tussled for the King's favour. The middle classes, though instrumental in creating the trade and industry of a powerful France, were not conscious of their ability to act in unison and shape the society they formed part of. They were overawed by the dazzling apparatus of aristocracy surrounding the King and most often set the limit of their ambition in the aping of its manners — hence the cutting satire of Molière's *Le Bourgeois Gentilhomme*.[5] During the discussion held in 1953 in which he was seeking to define the terms of the 'comedy' in *Don Juan* Brecht indicated that both these classes were 'komisch' either through situation or through aspiration:

Für Molière war maßgebend, daß durch dieses Vordringen des Bürgertums bestimmte adelige Gewohnheiten, Sitten, Ideen komisch wurden. Da stand er im Bunde mit dem Hofe. Der Hof zog die Bürgerlichen her, die Einfluß bekamen. Gleichzeitig komisch waren die eingefleischten Adligen, die als Höflinge Macht und Geld bekamen, sich aber ducken mußten. Zu gleicher Zeit war das Bürgertum komisch, das die abgewirtschafteten Höflinge nachzuahmen versuchte (Emporkömmlinge).[6]

Indeed, Molière's own position was not unambiguous: of humble origins, he arrived in Paris in 1658 after hard-won experience with his troupe roving in the provinces. He had the patronage of 'Monsieur' (the King's brother) and in 1665, after the suspension of *Dom Juan*, his company became the 'troupe du roi'. Molière was thus heavily dependent, financially and otherwise, on the court theatre and on private performances in the establishments of the nobility. However, though Molière wrote in his embittered preface to the banned *Tartuffe*: 'Si l'emploi de la comédie est de corriger les vices des hommes, je ne vois pas par quelle raison il y en aura de privilégiés', he was circumspect enough never to ridicule the royal personage himself and would appeal to Louis whenever his vitriolic 'peinture' got him into hot water. There is some justification for inferring from Molière's career a condoning of the evils of absolute monarchy (just as, for that matter, the position of Brecht in East Berlin after 1949 was determined by his equivocal relationship with the governmental apparatus which supplied his theatre with copious subsidies). But whereas Molière, even had he wanted to, could not make his portrait of a young nobleman in *Dom Juan* so explicitly condemnatory that it would have implied a censure of the whole system of feudal aristocracy right up to and including the King,[7] Brecht built his adaptation squarely on the historical rejection of this system with its concomitant ills. Brecht's collaborator, Benno Besson, outlined the situation that might have motivated the Don Juan that Molière had converted into a French nobleman:

Geschichtlich für den Don Juan interessant ist auch das Zustandekommen einer einheitlichen Nation, die Zerschlagung des Adels in Frankreich, der Absolutismus Ludwig XIV., der sich auf ein Recht von Gottes Gnaden stützt, ökonomisch auf die bürgerliche Klasse gegen den Adel, die Verknechtung des Adels in Versailles, der mit Ehren und Geld zwar überschüttet wird, aber doch geknechtet. Die Position von Don Juan, der französischer Adliger ist, ist die, daß er nicht mehr zum Zuge kommt, was die normalen Appetite eines Adligen anbetrifft: Eroberung.[8]

From this point Brecht could go on to transfer Don Juan's instinct for conquest to the sexual sphere and emphasize his desire to emulate the deeds of Alexander. The axis of Brecht's adaptation of Molière is thus constituted by this outright condemnation of the feudally stratified society that was to be overthrown by the French Revolution after a century of convulsions. In keeping with the confessedly Marxist viewpoint he brings to bear on the text Brecht introduces — in Sganarelle, the fisherman, oarsmen and servants — a coherent ethos of the have-nots that gives a consistent view of the aristocratic world from below, where Molière contented himself with only implying it.

Indicative of Brecht's intent to attack every aspect of the nobility is his rendering of the expressions for them and the gentry that occur in *Dom Juan*. Not only are *gentilhomme, homme de qualité* and *monsieur* absorbed entirely into the aristocratic ambience but even that ubiquitous ideal of seventeenth-century France, the *honnête homme*, is unambiguously expressed in terms that bring into prominence class opposition. To Molière's age the *honnête homme* suggested a person of good breeding, politeness and elegant manners, of a wide culture worn lightly and urbanely, and with a refined and easy way of handling the world.[9] Though the *honnête homme* was not confined to any one class the tacit assumption was that only a member of the nobility or upper middle class had the wealth, leisure, heredity and power to develop such qualities. This is the factor that Brecht reveals and brings to the fore. In the very first scene of the adaptation Sganarelle talks of 'les honnêtes gens' as 'die Großen dieser Welt' (though also calling 'un honnête homme' 'ein Mann von Welt'), and later Don Carlos, Elvira's brother who is so passionately attached to honour, refers in the same breath to 'gentilhommes' as 'Edelleute' and 'un honnête homme' as 'ein Edelmann' (III, 5), unconsciously voicing the unvarnished social reality. Don Juan too draws class distinctions when he catches sight of Don Carlos being attacked: 'Un homme attaqué par trois autres?' (Molière, III, 2) becomes 'Ein Edelmann von drei Rüpeln angefallen!'. At the other end of the scale Pierrot (Pieter) the fisherman describes Don Juan, 'quelque gros, gros Monsieur' whom he has saved in a shipwreck, as 'ein ganz großes Tier' (II, 1) while his fiancée Charlotte talks of 'les Monsieux' as 'die großen Herrn'. In these slight variations of phrase the class antagonism that smoulders through the play is already lit.

As in the case of other adaptations Brecht seeks in *Dom Juan* a play standing in a disturbing and provocative critical relationship to its time or containing themes that can be developed and magnified in this direction. In *Dom Juan* he found, in addition, an abundance of implicit condemnations of Molière's social environment that could easily germinate into full-blown life in an age when the restraints imposed by Molière's own situation were no longer operative. However, when Brecht rhetorically asks 'Wie soll man Molière spielen?' and asserts that a Marxist approach will allow the full power of a work to be felt without warping or distorting the original author's intention, we must be on our guard. There is no guarantee of the nature of Molière's attitude to his time apart from the play itself, and any alteration — whether in text or production — is bound to result in a *different* play that may or may not be congruent with Molière's opinions. What is certain is that Molière obviously could not have at his disposal all the apparatus of a Marxist interpretation of history and even less a view of his own time filtered through three centuries. So it is not surprising that, despite his protestations, Brecht does in fact craftily put his own interpretation on the text he claims to study 'as accurately as possible' and superimposes on it a pattern (and a new rhythm) derived from modern political thought. This he does while ostensibly un-covering the subtle range of beauty and reality in his source:

Die alten Werke haben ihre eigenen Werte, ihre eigene Differenziertheit, ihre eigene Skala von Schönheiten und Wahrheiten. Sie gilt es zu entdecken. Das bedeutet nicht, daß man Molière so spielen soll, wie er 170x gespielt wurde; es bedeutet nur, daß man ihn nicht so spielen sollte, wie er 1850 gespielt wurde (und 1950). Gerade die Vielfalt der Erkenntnisse und Schönheiten seiner Werke erlaubt es, Wirkungen aus ihnen zu holen, die unserer Zeit gemäß sind.[10]

Brecht goes on to cite one of the effects of Besson's production that emerged from a discussion with students at Leipzig University who found 'die Satire auf die feudale Auffassung der Liebe als einer Jagd noch so aktuell, daß sie mit vielem Gelächter über die heutigen Herzensbrecher berichteten.' He is convinced that they would have been far less interested by 'dämonische Seelentöter'.

The various hints suggesting that the points of view of Molière and Brecht do not tally are brought together and formulated in the note *Zur Figur des Don Juan*:

Wir befinden uns nicht auf der Seite Molières. Dieser votiert für Don Juan: der Epikuräer (und Gassendischüler) für den Epikuräer. Das Gericht des Himmels verspottet Molière, es würde zum Himmel passen, dieser dubiosen Einrichtung zur Abtötung der Lebensfreude. Gegen Don Juan läßt er nur gehörnte Ehemänner und so weiter sein. — Wir sind gegen parasitäre Lebensfreude. Leider haben wir als Lebenskünstler nur den Tiger vorzuweisen![11]

This opens a wide gulf between the two dramatists and is a serious charge against Molière's outlook and way of life. But the accusation derives from a misunderstanding of the epicurean thought of the seventeenth century. Molière was indeed a follower of Gassendi whose anti-abstractionist rejection of systems of philosophy and religion led him to rehabilitate the teachings of Epicurus. This Greek philosopher had taught that happiness was the *summum bonum*, but a happiness emanating from peace of mind resulting from the assiduous cultivation of all the virtues, not just the satisfaction of sensual enjoyment. The all-important stress is on the repose of mind — and consequent absence of pain — that virtue entails. In seventeenth-century France this form of epicureanism gained a strong foothold among the *libertins*, the free-thinkers who adopted an empirical approach to religious matters and many of whom sought a heightening of life — moral and spiritual — in the moderate, balanced pursuit of civilized and refining activities. It is thus necessary to be very tentative as to the nature of Molière's epicureanism: if he was a disciple of Gassendi it would be manifested in a serious endeavour to equate pleasure and virtuous conduct, if he 'voted for Don Juan' sensuous delights and good living would be ends in themselves. Brecht clearly comes down against Molière who is even accused of mocking the divine judgement as if he considered heaven a rather suspicious invention designed to kill all joy in life. The charge is difficult to substantiate from evidence in the text, which actually shows signs of the struggle Molière had to weld into his realistic treatment of the theme the traditional elements (statue's appearance, descent into the abyss) that were expected by the public.

Brecht appears to ignore this aspect of the genesis of the play and, with a residual rancour against Molière for his assumed connivance at 'parasitical enjoyment of life', proceeds to turn Don Juan into an exquisite fop given over entirely to licentious self-gratification. He becomes the predatory tiger in the social sphere, disrupting the human community to snatch his booty where he will. To drive this view home Brecht sprinkles the text with stage directions and remarks by the characters that maintain the tone of self-indulgence generating all of Don Juan's actions. For example, a tailpiece is added to Sganarelle's instructions concerning the boat trip ('Und vergiß den Wein nicht' (I, 4); and later on Don Juan orders: 'Was ich sagen wollte, es muß eine Chaise bereit stehen, wenn wir mit dem Boot zurückkommen' (I, 7). The wine serves its purpose after the shipwreck when Don Juan escapes from the pair of fisher-girls he has been courting (end II, 5): Sganarelle is ordered to crack a bottle with them while his master pursues his machinations. Even under pressure Don Juan's epicurean tastes do not falter, for he has the sangfroid to call after the defeated tailor Dimanche as he leaves the house empty-handed: 'Schicken Sie mir zwei Röcke von der üblichen Art! Ich verlobe mich' (IV, 6). The very way in which Brecht several times weaves this trait of fastidiousness into the structure of a scene is sufficient indication of its intrinsic importance. Throughout Don Juan's first encounter with his father (brought forward from IV, 4 in Molière to I, 6) while the old man's tirade

flows over him, he coolly arranges the details of the boat outing with Sganarelle. The same technique recurs in IV, 9 when a second visit by his irate father
is unexpectedly announced while Don Juan is having his make-up put on:
'DON JUAN *zu La Violette*: Geh, halte ihn eine Weile auf. *Zu Sganarelle.*
Lege mir etwas Weiß auf. *Sganarelle schminkt ihn.*' He follows this up with a
laconic 'Ein Fleck unter die Augen' in answer to Sganarelle's shocked astonish-
ment that Elvira's words of warning have had no effect on his master. The next
scene (when Don Luis does manage to burst in with his vehement denuncia-
tions) is also punctuated by the servants coming and going with letters and
flasks of wine. The most significant revelation of Don Juan's concern for and
reliance on impressive externals is added in III, 5, when he catches sight of
his fleeing quarry Angelika and orders Sganarelle to dress him carefully, if
hurriedly, in his own clothes while the wounded Don Carlos lies by untended:

DON JUAN: Schnell, Schurke, schnell! Die Kleider her! Sie füttert auf der Lichtung
Rehe!
SGANARELLE *Don Juan, umkleidend, entschuldigt sich bei dem stöhnenden Don
Carlos*: Geduld, junger Herr, Wenn der Rock geknöpft ist, sollen Sie Wein haben.
DON JUAN: Knöpf ordentlich, er kommt von alleine zu sich. *Der Rock ist geknöpft.
Sganarelle will zu Don Carlos.* Schärpe! *Sganarelle bindet Don Juan die Schärpe um.*
Bandelier! *Sganarelle arbeitet weiter an ihm.*
SGANARELLE *zu Don Carlos, der schwankend aufsteht*: Nichts Ernstes, junger Herr,
ein Ruderschlag. Mich traf es am Knie.
DON JUAN: Perücke!
DON CARLOS *zu Don Juan, dem Sganarelle die Perücke richtet*: Mein Herr! —
DON JUAN *der noch nicht vollends hergerichtet ist, bedeutet ihm durch eine Hand-
bewegung zu warten.*

Don Juan is thus reduced to a cowardly dandy flaunting the finery of
his appearance and a lavish setting to achieve his seductions. To reinforce
this image Brecht inserts the completely new motif (introduced in IV, 8) of
Don Juan's detailed preparations for an intimate tête-à-tête supper party
during which he plans to take the fortress that is Angelika:

DON JUAN: ... Hast du alles für das Souper angeordnet, wie ich es haben will?
Laß sofort die Musiker kommen und dazu die vielgepriesene Sängerin Belisa;
sie soll das Mahl mit einer Serenade verschönen. Und schick nach den entzückenden
Fischermädchen. Sie sollen um Mitternacht ihre Austern und Krebse bringen. Den
Wein überprüfe ich.

This is a clever conversion of the awkward scenes in Molière (IV, 7 and 8)
where the Statue makes its first appearance on stage, moving and speaking
with a total lack of verisimilitude; beyond this, it enables Brecht to exploit
Don Juan's para-military tactics in the epicurean sphere and preludes IV, 11
where we are escorted on to the actual field of amorous battle: *Während dieser
Szene wird der Tisch vollends gedeckt, und Diener bringen die ankommenden
Musiker mit ihren Instrumenten im Blattwerk der Bäume unter.* Don Juan
intends to use this scene as a rehearsal of his manoeuvres for capturing
Angelika. At this point Don Juan acts out — with interspersed comments by

his servants — how he will receive Angelika, and then Sganarelle goes to answer a knock. That the knock on the door heralds the entrance of the Statue and not Angelika, his daughter, does not hinder Brecht from pursuing the epicurean thread to the very end. In the following scene Don Juan is engulfed in the abyss, *seinen Hut vergeblich festhaltend*, and the final laments of the bystanders peering down into the gaping hole confirm the hold that unproductive pleasure has in this society:

DIMANCHE: ... Die zwei Röcke, gnädiger ... Ah! Mein bester Kunde! ...
SERAFINE: Ah! Wer ißt nun meine Enten in Orangen? ...
DIE FISCHERMÄDCHEN: Ah! Wer nimmt unsere Austern?

To be sure, the specific comic dimension nevertheless takes over as the final stage direction unmistakably establishes the absurdity of this superficial epicureanism: *Aus der Höhe nieder flattert langsam Don Juans Hut.*

The deployment of epicurean elements in *Don Juan* illustrates one aspect of the reinterpreted personality of the hero that Brecht is anxious to delineate; for him the demonic seeker and irresistible lover give way to the ruthless campaigner exploiting every advantage of position and power:

Der große Verführer läßt sich nicht zu besonderen erotischen Kunstgriffen herab. Er verführt durch sein Kostüm (und diese Art, es zu tragen), seine Stellung (und die Unverschämtheit, sie zu mißbrauchen), seinen Reichtum (oder seinen Kredit) und seinen Ruf (oder die Sicherheit, die ihm seine Berühmtheit bei sich selbst gewährt). Er tritt auf als sexuelle Großmacht.[12]

This is the language of *Realpolitik* transferred to the field of love, the amoral premises of power politics intervening in and poisoning the personal relationship of individual to individual. The target of criticism is Don Juan and through him the behaviour of the class he stands for: his costume he parades before the fisher-girls and Angelika; his rank is brought to bear on Pieter (who is sent on an errand while Don Juan courts his fiancée); his wealth procures food, wine, finery and hired assassins; while his reputation gives him the hollow pretensions and dangerous activities of a misplaced Alexander the Great. The contextual relevance of the Macedonian general (who is mentioned only fleetingly in Molière's play) is seized on and expanded by Brecht to bolster his revision of Don Juan's personality — similar procedure to that adopted in *Der rote Hahn* where the peripheral Navy Day of Hauptmann's play is amplified into thematic significance. In Molière's second scene Don Juan confesses to Sganarelle the thrill he experiences in gradually overcoming the resistance of his prey and concludes his amorous philosophy with: 'Il n'est rien qui puisse arrêter l'impétuosité de mes désirs: je me sens porté à aimer toute la terre; et comme Alexandre, je souhaiterais qu'il y eût d'autres mondes, pour y pouvoir étendre mes conquêtes amoureuses.' One critic thinks that in this speech 'the imagery of military strategy, and particularly the final sentences leading up to the reference to Alexander, suggest that Dom Juan derives intellectual rather than sensual satisfaction from his conquests'.[13]

Another adduces the same outburst as evidence that Dom Juan is not simply a sensualist but 'un artiste de la séduction'.[14] Brecht emphatically does not share this indulgent view of military tactics in the sphere of love: for him Don Juan is not satisfying intellectual and artistic (i.e. aesthetic) urges in imitating Alexander; on the contrary, he is unscrupulously applying all the power he can muster as an aristocrat to achieve certain selfish ends. His is not the private activity deriving from purely mental or aesthetic delight, it is the brutal and destructive assault of a 'sexuelle Großmacht' on the rights of others.

With the aim of castigating Don Juan's tactics as *socially* reprehensible Brecht in his adaptation increases the references to Alexander. In I, 7 Don Juan confesses to Sganarelle in cold statistics his need for urgency: 'Geduld? Das ist gerade, was ich nicht habe. Schurke, ich bin 31 Jahre alt. Alexander starb mit 33. Er hatte 618 Städte erobert. Es ist klar, ich muß mich beeilen. Los jetzt! Das Boot!'; and on the heels of the rebuff given to his opportunist advances by his rejected wife in IV, 8 he turns his attention to Angelika: 'Sganarelle, was wird aus unserem Ruf? Er ist in der Liebe wie im Krieg mehr wert als alles andere. Die Festung ergibt sich dem, dem sich schon Festungen ergeben haben. Sie nimmt es als ein Naturgesetz hin. Der Ruf Alexanders hat ihm mehr Städte unterworfen als seine Waffenmacht. Dem Feldherrn ohne Ruf bleibt nur übrig, wie ein Berserker zu kämpfen. Auf eine Niederlage [i.e. Elvira's refusal to stay] muß sofort ein Sieg folgen.' The frenetic quality of this Don Juan is unmistakable, as is the incongruity of his actions and their aim; like an automaton he wields his destructive power, but there is neither pleasure nor profit in it. The robot-like exercise of his powers is underlined in IV, 11 when he rhetorically rehearses Angelika's arrival with Sganarelle as audience. In an earlier version the intentionally hollow pathos of his effusions (not untinged by an obvious irony) was crowned by a superficial comment (later suppressed) on feminine psychology:

Das weibliche Geschlecht nämlich, mein lieber Sganarelle, wünscht nichts, als von allen Skrupeln befreit zu werden, die es hindern, uns zu lieben. Um von uns sich umarmen zu lassen, genügt ihnen jedoch der absurdeste Grund. Es macht ihnen das größte Vergnügen, sich einzureden, sie täten, was sie auf jeden Fall tun wollen, ausschließlich um Reiche zu retten oder zu zerstören oder aus noch dümmeren Motiven.

The cumulative effect of these pseudo-military attitudes of Don Juan is to point their essential meaninglessness. Brecht and his collaborators discussed Don Juan's absurdity in this respect:

BRECHT: Molière wollte den Hof kritisieren; die Eroberung dieses bürgerlichen Finanzmannes [presumably Colbert] war eine solide Angelegenheit. Er schuf Handelsbeziehungen, die sich mehr oder weniger lohnten. Es gab auch Kriege auf dem Gebiet, die Sinn hatten, Handelsverträge, dann kriegerische Abenteuer, die zur Ausbreitung der Macht beitrugen. Das übertragen auf das Gebiet der Erotik, so vertritt Don Juan einen Eroberer, bei dem nichts herauskommt.

BESSON: Die Komik des Don Juan scheint mir einer der Hauptpunkte: mit

Legionen zieht er ins Feld für merkwürdige Ziele. Einen Traum verfolgt er, den Traum des Alexander, der durch das Mittelalter geht.[15]

The image of Alexander is thus no longer an arbitrary comparison to express the purposive drive of Don Juan nor can it now be interpreted positively as showing his aesthetic pleasure in ever more successful solutions to the game of seduction. By divorcing the means from the ends in the actions of Don Juan, Brecht achieves the true comedy of this figure, for now he is shown in his real isolation in a society where his function and therefore his power are rapidly becoming redundant. Brecht reduces to social terms a fact intuitively perceived by Molière in whose play the irresistible lover, in contrast to tradition, does not make even one conquest.

If Brecht appropriates the terms of Alexander the Great's exploits to mark his more overt condemnation of Don Juan, he also retains a further much-debated aspect of the hero, namely his atheism and seventeenth-century *libertinage*, but in a somewhat different focus from Molière. This element was of vital topical importance for the French playwright in his tussle with the forces of established religion and morality that had succeeded in suppressing his masterpiece *Tartuffe* in the previous year. Molière's immediate antagonists in this affair were the *faux dévots*, many of them in the Compagnie du Saint-Sacrement, the sanctimonious hypocrites who exerted secret pressures and on whom he tried to take some measure of revenge on his own ground in *Dom Juan*. Thus, Dom Juan's notorious 'Je crois que deux et deux sont quatre' in III, 1 and his mocking trifling with the faith of the Poor Man in the following scene are not to be taken as a profession of atheistic sentiments on Molière's part, as a foretaste of the free-thinking Enlightenment, but rather as a bitter — if oblique — attack on the *dévots*. Certainly Dom Juan has little in common with the earnest *libertins* of Molière's time, but, in view of the fact that Molière retains the traditional fate of the hero, the play has actually been seen as a criticism of *libertinage*. Brecht of course was not concerned with the personal beliefs of Don Juan as an individual; he directed his attention primarily to the wider field into which these views fitted and so treated him as the representative of his class in a distinct historical and social context. In common with other commentators Brecht detected the essential root of *libertinage* — which, revealingly, was especially widespread among the younger nobility in Paris — in the overweening power of the aristocracy and its gradual divorce from any meaningful function it might once have had in society, culminating now in a disregard of those very factors it had assiduously promoted to establish its power.[16] Brecht could thus in his notes draw attention to the negative nature of Don Juan's atheism:

Don Juan ist kein Atheist im fortschrittlichen Sinn. Sein Unglaube ist nicht kämpferisch, indem er menschliche Aktionen fordert. Er ist ein Mangel an Glauben. Da ist nicht eine andere Überzeugung, sondern keine Überzeugung. — Don Juan glaubt vielleicht sogar an Gott, er will nur nichts von ihm hören, da dies sein Genußleben stören würde. — Er benutzt jedes Argument — ohne eines davon zu glauben —, das die Dame legt, wie jedes, das ihn von der Dame befreit.[17]

And Besson's production reasserted the serious comedy inherent in Don Juan's specious atheism:

Er [Besson] stellt die Komik der Don-Juan-Figur wieder her, ... indem er die sozialkritische Aussage des Stückes wiederherstellte. In der berühmten Bettlerszene, die bisher dazu benutzt wurde, Don Juan als Freigeist und damit fortschrittlichen Typ hinzustellen, zeigte Besson lediglich einen Libertin, zu arrogant, irgendwelche Verpflichtungen anzuerkennen, so daß sichtbar wurde, wie die herrschende Clique sich auch über den staatlich konzessionierten und befohlenen Glauben hinwegsetzte.[18]

Though retaining the Poor Man scene Brecht negated the validity of the religious exchanges by having him erroneously address Sganarelle (disguised at this point as Don Juan) as the gentleman and by interpolating impatient expletives such as 'in Teufels Namen!' and 'Ihr Dummköpfe!' in Don Juan's utterances.

In the adaptation Don Juan's apparent atheism is thus stripped of any pretensions to an intellectual basis and is exploited as one symptom of the decay of feudal aristocracy; indeed, in discussing Don Juan's disastrous end Brecht ascribes to Molière his own arguments for condemning Don Juan's anti-social misuse of atheism:

Der Atheismus des großen Parasiten täuscht viele; sie fallen darauf herein, bewundern ihn, rühmen ihn als fortschrittlich. Aber Molière war weit entfernt davon, seinen Don Juan wegen seines Atheismus als einen vorurteilsfreien Mann zu empfehlen; er verurteilt ihn dafür — entzieht er sich, wie der ganze Hofadel der Zeit, durch seinen zynischen Unglauben lediglich den elementaren sittlichen Anforderungen! Molière läßt ihn am Ende vom Himmel bestrafen, aber nur in komisch-theatralischer Weise, damit überhaupt den Verbrechen endlich ein Ende gesetzt wird. In einer Gesellschaftsordnung wie dieser gibt es keine Instanz, die dem Parasiten Einhalt gebieten könnte, als — allenfalls — der Himmel, das heißt die Theatermaschinerie. Wenn der Bühnenboden sich nicht öffnen würde, das glänzende Scheusal zu verschlingen, ginge es ungehindert und unhinderbar weiter über die Erde.[19]

In unpublished programme notes to the Berlin production Brecht slyly indicated how he turned to account the totally artificial and improbable crushing of the parasitical Don Juan by a *deus ex machina* rather than a *deus ex coelo*:

Die steinerne Statue des Komturs holt ihn [Don Juan] in die Hölle. Lachend zeigt Molière, daß nur das sehr unwahrscheinliche Eingreifen des Himmels im Frankreich Ludwigs XIV. die frechen Übergriffe und Ausschweifungen der Adligen hätte verhindern können.[20]

The quasi-magical conclusion to the play that Molière kept in deference to a strong tradition allowed Brecht to turn it surreptitiously into a dialectical *pointe*: only a blatantly fairy-tale ending of this nature would be sufficient to check the arrogant dominance of the nobility, yet the very unlikelihood of this really happening highlights the ineffectualness of established religion, which anyway stands itself in a symbiotic relationship to what it should condemn.[21]

From whatever point this play is approached it becomes evident that Brecht wanted to exclude deliberately and systematically every aspect of Don Juan that was purely individual and unique to this particular figure and that could not be shaped in such a way that the sociological motivation emerged sharply. The whole *raison d'être* of the adaptation is expressed cryptically in the notes: 'Wir haben von der (Molière näheren) Satire mehr als von der halbtragischen Charakterstudie. Der Glanz des Parasiten interessiert uns weniger als das Parasitäre seines Glanzes.'[22] The social dimension is indispensable to satire and Brecht categorically rejects the opportunity of treating Don Juan as a 'tragic hero' — the reactions of an Œdipus, a Hamlet, a Phèdre betray little of the social fabric in which they live. Hence Brecht's interest not so much in the fine feathers of Don Juan but in the behaviour they facilitate and the consequences for others; Brecht's aim is not to paint an uncommitted portrait of the parasite but to bring out the parasitical — and therefore undesirable — essence of the figure. The comedy becomes in every essential a hostile revelation of the presumption of the feudal aristocracy in France, as manifested in the particular exploits of Don Juan. Brecht re-structures situations and dialogues to create a critical distance between audience and Don Juan, to obviate empathetic immersion in the details of his personality and to focus attention on to the *group* he is typical of in all he does. Since the target of Brecht's satire is the dominant aristocracy it is to be expected that the most decisive alterations carried out should be found largely in the presentation of the nobleman Don Juan as well as in the interplay of Sganarelle with him, servant and master, and their conscious and unconscious behaviour as determined by their respective social standing in mutual reference groups.

Molière had not made it his concern to show the aristocracy to be bad *per se* (even had he wished to, he would scarcely have survived the repercussions) but limited himself to showing Dom Juan as a nobleman who also happened to be bad. To put the audience in the picture in the expository first scene Sganarelle describes to Gusman some of his master's more relevant characteristics and uses the celebrated phrase 'Mais un grand seigneur méchant homme est une terrible chose', a comment that has been worried by critics ever since but is seldom taken to apply to anyone beyond the particular nobleman Dom Juan. Paradoxically, though not unexpectedly, the lines that include this one disappear from the adaptation. Dom Louis's tirade in IV, 4, so clearly based on a worthy belief in firm principles that make a man into a nobleman and that Dom Juan is regrettably not living up to, is re-fashioned by Brecht to show Dom Louis's fear for the good *image* of the *class* they belong to, not for the qualities this class should display; so the emotional

Ne rougissez-vous point de mériter si peu votre naissance? Êtes-vous en droit, dites-moi, d'en tirer quelque vanité? Et qu'avez-vous fait dans le monde pour être gentilhomme?... Apprenez enfin qu'un gentilhomme qui vit mal est un monstre dans la nature, que la vertu est le premier titre de noblesse, que je regards bien moins au nom qu'on signe qu'aux actions qu'on fait, et que je ferais plus d'état du fils d'un crocheteur qui serait honnête homme, que du fils d'un monarque qui vivrait comme vous.

turns into the calculating, rational

Mit welchem Recht genießest du unsere Privilegien? Was hast du getan in der Welt, ein Edelmann zu heißen? Glaubst du, es sei noch rühmlich, aus edlem Blut abzustammen, wenn man ein Schandleben führt? Kannst du nicht mehr erröten? Soll es heißen, ein Edelmann ist ein Ungeheuer in der Natur? Soll es heißen, die Söhne der Lastträger stellen die unseren in den Schatten, was die Tugend betrifft, sind sie besser?[23]

Brecht is thus bent on making Don Juan representative of his class (which, being parasitical, can have only negative characteristics) and he lets no opportunity slip by of emphasizing the hero's lying, ruthless, egoistic and irresponsible behaviour. The deepening of the Alexander theme is an example of this blackening of the nobility, drawing attention to their overbearing exercise of power. But Brecht goes much further in putting the qualities Dom Louis refers to in an equivocal light, so that in the dramatic context of the play they negate themselves. When Don Juan outrageously pretends to Elvira in I, 3 that he has left her through fear of the divine wrath for his 'adultery' in snatching her from the convent, the sole addition is his 'Gnädige Frau, um dem Himmel und aller Kreatur gerecht zu werden, müssen wir oft schmerzliche Opfer bringen —'. And in I, 6 (absorbing most of Molière's IV, 4) Brecht again has Don Juan hypocritically plead to his father the obligations demanded of a nobleman's honour — in order to rid himself of his troublesome wife (by allowing her to return to the convent whence he had abducted her) and loosen the parental purse-strings.

Further, Brecht deprives Don Juan of the attribute of courage. Molière did not discredit his Dom Juan for taking sensible measures to elude the twelve horsemen searching for him. Brecht, on the other hand, makes the most of Don Juan's fear at the thought of the three fishermen pursuing him after he himself had taught them to wield their oars as weapons:

DON JUAN: In der Tat, das Spiel scheint zu ungleich. Mit roher Gewalt will ich nichts zu tun haben. Das Schicksal trennt uns. Adieu, meine schönen Kinder, ich kann Ihnen nichts abschlagen. Sganarelle, ich sehe mich in der Lage, dir einen Herzenswunsch zu erfüllen, Sganarelle, du kannst meinen Rock anziehen, gib mir deine Lumpen.
SGANARELLE: Gnädiger Herr, Sie belieben zu spaßen. Soll ich in Ihren Kleidern sterben?
DON JUAN: Nicht, wenn es nicht nötig ist. Bereite alles für die Heimreise vor![24]

When a little later Don Juan is about to give chase to a new beauty, Angelika, whom he has just glimpsed in the park, Sganarelle has to restrain him as he has forgotten he is wearing his servant's clothes. Don Juan hurriedly urges him to give him back his finery, but while Sganarelle is reluctantly unbuttoning his coat their attention is diverted by the oarsmen's attack on a nobleman. Whereas Molière's Dom Juan goes himself to the aid of the belaboured gentleman, Brecht strikes a markedly different note:

DON JUAN: Was ist das? Ein Edelmann, von drei Rüpeln angefallen!
SGANARELLE: Die Ruderer!
DON JUAN: Der Kampf ist zu ungleich; eine solche Feigheit kann ich nicht mit ansehn. Komm dem Mann sofort zu Hilfe! Ich selbst schlage mich nicht mit Leuten, die mit Balken zuhauen. In den Kampf, Schurke! *Er gibt Sganarelle einen Fußtritt, der diesen auf den Kampfplatz befördert, und geht abseits.*[25]

The motif of an exchange of clothes between Don Juan and Sganarelle (although used by Cicognini, Dorimon and Villiers) is dropped at the rudimentary stage at the end of Molière II, 5 ('DOM JUAN: Je veux que Sganarelle se revête de mes habits') and Sganarelle turns up in the next scene in the guise of a doctor. Brecht falls back on the original idea of an exchange of clothes, not in order to achieve the comic misunderstandings that this transparent device traditionally causes but to focus attention on the relationship between clothes and wearer and call in question the worth of a Don Juan masquerading under his finery and, indeed, the intrinsic value of the finery itself that evokes such predictable reactions in others. Mention has been made of the scene where Don Juan ignores the battered Don Carlos while hurriedly changing back to rush off after Angelika — a case of dog eat dog. When the preparations are completed Don Carlos pours out profuse thanks, only to be brusquely cut short by Don Juan whose thoughts are elsewhere:

DON JUAN *sich ungeduldig umblickend*: Ich habe nur getan, mein Herr, was Sie an meiner Stelle auch getan hätten.
SGANARELLE *beiseite*: Nämlich nichts.
DON CARLOS: Tatsächlich genügte Ihr Auftauchen. Ihre gebieterische Erscheinung, Ihre Stimme, gewohnt des Befehlens . . . [he then describes his encounter with the oarsmen] Mich nicht kennend, belästigten sie mich mit der Geschichte eines Edelmannes, von dem sie behaupteten, er schulde ihnen Geld, und den sie gräßlich verleumdeten. Als ich ihnen Vorhaltungen machte über die schändliche Beschimpfung unseres Standes, ließen sie sich zu solchen Injurien hinreißen, daß ich sie, ungeachtet ihrer Überzahl, bestrafen wollte.[26]

The audience knows, and Sganarelle voices, the irony of what Don Juan says: the audience also knows that the imperious presence and the commanding voice belong to the servant who, though unwillingly booted into battle, did in fact rescue Don Carlos. Aristocratic apparel is thus shown to be an external camouflage, the noble beneath exposed as the miserable wretch he is. The physical visual impact of this dissociation between the man and his clothes is of course heightened by the dramatic irony of Don Carlos in a sense defending the very man he wishes to kill; it becomes questionable what 'die schändliche Beschimpfung unseres Standes' really means. Molière, of course, has no ambiguities in the equivalent scene (III, 3) where Dom Juan says: 'Je n'ai rien fait, Monsieur, que vous n'eussiez fait en ma place' and asserts that it would have been as cowardly as the robbers not to have gone to Don Carlos's aid. The latter had himself not got into the fight because of an insult to his class: '. . . j'ai fait rencontre de ces voleurs, qui d'abord ont tué mon cheval, et qui, sans votre valeur, en auraient fait autant de moi.'

What Brecht is aiming at altogether in the sequence of scenes spanned by the exchange of clothes (III, 1–5) is an alienation of 'noble appearances'. This is the point of the scene with Don Carlos and is even more wittily structured in III, 1 where we see Don Juan and Sganarelle in a neglected park, the servant having donned his master's clothes:

SGANARELLE: . . . Erlauben Sie, gnädiger Herr, daß ich mich eine Weile setze. Die Aufregungen, die Last Ihrer Kleider und nicht zuletzt dieses Korbes haben mich stark ermüdet.

DON JUAN: Dummkopf, wozu mußt du auch diesen Korb mitschleppen? Habe ich dir befohlen, ihn mitzunehmen? Don Juan schleppt keine Körbe.

SGANARELLE: Ihre Kleider haben mich nicht so verändert, daß ich die Pflicht, mich um Don Juans Magen zu kümmern, außer acht lasse. Laßt uns speisen, gnädiger Herr.

DON JUAN: Schurke! Es gehört sich nicht für einen Edelmann, am Wegrand wie ein Hund in ein Stück Pastete zu beißen. Tu meinen Kleidern mehr Ehre an. Benimm dich so wie ich. Ich werde mich zwingen, deine Manieren nachzuahmen. Schurke, du rührst keinen Happen an! *Don Juan ißt und trinkt.*

SGANARELLE *während Don Juan ißt*: Ich denke immer noch an den guten Doktor. Vielleicht hätte ich mich doch in seine Behandlung geben sollen. Mir ist sehr schwach, und mein Bauch fängt wieder an, so merkwürdig zu kullern: von links nach rechts. Meine Gesundheit ist weiß Gott nicht die beste, gnädiger Herr. *Don Juan wirft ihm einen strengen Blick zu.*

While on the one hand it is evident that though Sganarelle is now wearing the finery he will not be let off any of his chores as servant, he must on the other attempt to impersonate in both clothes and manners.[27] For this reason he can still be exploited by his master while at the same time providing him with a camouflage in case of danger. Even Sganarelle's veiled references to the state of his health do not bring him any food, and while they discuss doctors and religion he serves Don Juan wine to his meal. Only at the end of the scene, when Don Juan wishes to ask for directions to the town and they call to a passing Poor Man, is Sganarelle able to pounce on the food, for it would indeed have seemed odd if the servant ate while his master went hungry. Even now Don Juan manages to put a brake on Sganarelle's voracity: 'Iß wenigstens anständig. Du bist ich, vergiß das nicht. *Sganarelle macht sich ans Essen, er ißt verschwenderisch wie Don Juan.*' Throughout the next scene, notorious in Molière for Dom Juan's efforts to get the pious Poor Man to blaspheme for the sake of a *Louis d'or*, the latter naturally addressed Sganarelle as if he were master. All these scenes, then, are pressed into service by Brecht to demonstrate how noble appearances may cover nothing but meanness, how clothes and not qualities make the aristocrat.

While outer appearances are analysed to show up very vividly the 'Glanz des Parasiten' and 'das Parasitäre seines Glanzes', the same end is achieved no less effectively in the inherent dialectical tension between master and servant which runs through the play and generates the consequences of the disguise motif. This relationship (with a long tradition in the theatre and especially in comedy) is actual and visual as well as being dramatically urgent throughout the action. Though Molière makes good use of the *confidant* Sganarelle it is left to the adaptation to make the lower classes — valet, servants, fishermen — really an organic yet contradictory element of the play, functionally integrated in the image of society presented. Sganarelle is naturally the focus of his class (he is after all present in all but two scenes of the adaptation; Don Juan is absent from six) but not the only one to establish a reaction to his master. In this respect Brecht adds a dimension to Molière's play. The remarks and actions of Pierrot, Ragotin and the fisher-girls mark out an area of society that has its own ideas, shows critical insight and is not afraid to voice its sometimes inimical opinion. Brecht typically constructs in this way a reflective aspect to the 'comedy', the historical perspective of the audience is fostered by those moments that are themselves comments on Don Juan's behaviour and thereby alienate it.

In II, 3 Molière portrays a servile fear in Pierrot who catches Dom Juan kissing the hand of his fiancée Charlotte; when Dom Juan buffets him he cringes away and takes refuge behind the girl. In II, 4 of the adaptation Pierrot stands up to the aristocrat's arrogance and presumption, thus establishing a critical position. A little later, after Mathurine and Charlotte have successfully entreated Don Juan to flee from the coming oarsmen, II, 7 closes with the stage direction : *Die Fischermädchen schauen sich an, fangen an zu lachen und geraten so in Gelächter, daß sie sich auf den Boden setzen müssen*, lines that evoke — if more modestly — the type of 'historical moment' described for the end of Scene 6 in *Mutter Courage* in the notes to that play. This is the alienation that isolates the characters from their situation and enables them — and with them the audience — to view what they are doing coolly and dispassionately: the laughter of the fisher-girls is the dialectical synthesis of their historical situation within the play and the knowledge that such a situation (nobleman seducing poor women) was to be superseded in time. Similarly in IV, 1 Don Juan's riding-master Ragotin answers Sganarelle's query as to whether Angelika is coming or not in flat, unemotional words and tones that pinpoint his condemnation of what he is doing, without for all that preventing him from carrying out his orders:

Sie kommt oder kommt nicht. Was weiß ich? Warum soll sie nicht kommen? Man könnte sagen: sie ist noch im Trauerjahr um den Komtur. Aber geht's mich an? Ich hab genug zu tun: einen Parkwächter umlegen, einen Hund vergiften, eine Gouvernante bestechen. Briefe hin und Briefe her. Zwei Pferde sind dabei zuschanden geritten, im Stall sind nur noch drei. Sind es meine? Also. Kommt sie, kommt sie nicht? Ich frag nicht, ich weiß nichts, ich reite.

This reply prompts Sganarelle, who is implicated up to the neck in his master's affairs, to one of the few demonstrations of fear that Brecht allows him:

Glücklicher Mensch! Ich weiß zu viel. Ich fühle, wie sich über diesem Haus ein fürchterliches Unwetter zusammenzieht, und ich fürchte sehr, der Blitz könnte mit dem Herrn auch den Diener treffen.

In the ensuing scene — totally new in the adaptation — Sganarelle gets the cook Serafine to read his hand, half-scared and half-blustering — a reminiscence of the soldiers' reactions to Mutter Courage's black crosses:

SGANARELLE *zögert*: Ich will die volle Wahrheit.
SERAFINE *nimmt seine Hand*: Ich sage immer die volle Wahrheit.
SGANARELLE *zieht die Hand zurück*: Aber du kannst dich irren . . . Hier hast du meine Hand. Ist also mein Schicksal an das eines großen Herrn gekettet? Sei vorsichtig! *Nach einer Pause*: Nicht gekettet, wie? *Klimpert mit Geldstücken in der Tasche*. Schau scharf hin.

Apart from his — justifiable — fear of an approaching catastrophe, and some signs of panic (in IV, 8 Sganarelle sees flashes of lightning *mit Schrecken* and trembles, while he admonishes Don Juan 'Der Himmel möge Ihnen verzeihen'; in IV, 12 he swoons as the statue is about to lead Don Juan off), the cowardliness of the servant is played down by Brecht. Many asides in Molière's text that serve to show how Sganarelle is coerced into doing his master's bidding disappear from the adaptation ('Ah! quel abominable maître me vois-je obligé de servir!' (I, 3); 'O complaisance maudite! à quoi me réduis-tu?' (IV, 5)). So, of course, do the incidents in Molière III, 3–4 where Sganarelle watches from behind a tree while Dom Juan goes to the aid of Dom Carlos and where he runs off to hide when Dom Alonso lights on his master and wants to attack him.

As a matter of fact it is of little moment whether Sganarelle shows fear or not; this will not make him a hero or otherwise, nor will it throw light on the intent and quality of the adaptation. Indeed, in keeping with his partiality for copious and explicit stage directions in all his plays, Brecht inserts many exact indications in the text that in the convention of Molière's time were left to actor and producer; the impression is thus given that Don Juan relies first and foremost on the most primitive communication between master and servant — physical force, especially towards Sganarelle: *droht ihm mit dem Stock, bedroht ihn, nimmt ihn am Ohr, winkt Pieter zu sich* are typical stage directions. Molière's valet is a plaintive, whining, would-be moralist who lives in fear of his master and, where possible, comments on his unjust power in asides for the benefit of the audience. In this respect he is an interpretative intermediary between hero and audience, but the more he fulfils his role the less is he capable of really being rooted in the action of the play. In the last analysis master and servant move through the play along parallel tracks that nowhere cross, despite apparent clashes of mind in the pseudo-arguments on religion, philandering and fidelity; on the other hand Sganarelle *is* the ubiquitous foil to Don Juan and his censure of the latter inevitably imparts to the audience some criticism of the irresponsible noblemen of seventeenth-century France. Further, this does not mean that Sganarelle is colourless and amorphous: the contradictory forces of moral sense and terrified (yet lucrative) submission produce a tension in his character that is entirely his own. Brecht makes him more than 'un mélange d'esclave romain et de larbin moderne'[28] by articulating the element of class consciousness more flexibly; where Molière had allowed Sganarelle to voice criticisms of Dom Juan that anyone could have made, that is, criticisms founded on a 'universal' morality, Brecht derives them more strictly from Sganarelle's particular and unique position as paid servant. This adds a serious facet to his personality that was lacking in Molière for, instead of mouthing received moral principles, he now anchors his comments in the realities of his own experience of his master — in matters of money, brutality, opportunism. That Sganarelle does not turn his element of class consciousness to use, that he fails to arrive at positive action, can be accounted a failure on his part. Brecht endows him with a later historical insight into the class structure of his time but Sganarelle nevertheless remains caught in a comfortable acquiescence in the status quo; he lacks the energy for revolution.

The very first speech of the play in its altered form brings together these two factors that will dominate Sganarelle throughout: participation in Don Juan's exploitation of his fellow-men and simultaneous condemnation of it in socio-political terms. Brecht indicates the setting: *Eingang eines vornehmen Stadthauses. Davor Gepäckstücke*; then Sganarelle appears and *fischt aus Don Juans Gepäck eine Schnupftabakdose und betrachtet sie.* Already, before uttering a word, Sganarelle has climbed on the band-wagon of those who have and hold: within the limits of his subordinate position he is going to exploit every chance and — where possible — batten on Don Juan; his master's snuff will be a minor perquisite. The confused and aimless tirade against the enemies of snuff[29] (dragging in Aristotle and philosophy) is adroitly channelled by Brecht into a penetrating criticism of the rich entrenched behind their comforts: 'c'est la passion des honnêtes gens' becomes 'er [der Tabak] ist die Leidenschaft der Großen dieser Welt', and Sganarelle adds in the adaptation:

Ah, sie wählen ihre Leidenschaften mit Bedacht! ... Nur der Tabak ist es, der die Großen dieser Welt instand setzt, die Leiden zu vergessen, besonders die der anderen. Ein paar Bauernhöfe gehen einem in die Binsen? Nehmen wir eine Prise Tabak, und alles sieht nicht halb so schlimm aus. Ein Bittsteller wird unangenehm, ein Gläubiger zudringlich? Nehmen Sie eine Prise Tabak, mein Guter, seien Sie Philosoph!

In the light of these remarks the remainder of his speech (which modifies the original slightly) invites a fresh reaction: snuff appears as a means of stifling opposition, while the dubious reliability of Sganarelle is made plain as he offers Gusman his master's snuff-box.

In Molière too Sganarelle had kept his eye to the main chance but in the adaptation this trait is deliberately fostered to underline his acquiescence in exploitation; there are several instances where Sganarelle shows harshness and unscrupulousness in dealing with others, especially those below him. He is ordered by Don Juan in a new scene (I, 5) to hire some oarsmen and teach them to use their oars as weapons:

DON JUAN: Erteile den Kerlen den nötigen Unterricht.
SGANARELLE: Geld wäre da der beste Lehrer, gnädiger Herr.
DON JUAN *wirft ihm eine Börse zu*: Das muß genügen.
SGANARELLE *prüft die Börse*: Mit 20 Dukaten wird es gehen. *Er steckt die Börse ein*:
Hierher, Leute! Wir bezahlen eure Dienste mit zwei Dukaten pro Mann.
Die Ruderer sind überglücklich.
. . .
SGANARELLE *hart*: Fechten könnt ihr also nicht. Ich werde euch Unterricht geben
müssen.
ANGELOT: Unterricht im Totschlagen? Die scheinen keine Religion zu haben.
SGANARELLE: Wir bezahlen nicht zwei Dukaten für's Rudern.
BERTHELOT: Es wird nicht gehen, Herr. Ich kenne ihn. *Zeigt auf Angelot.*
ANGELOT *zu den zwei anderen*: Wollt ihr für zwei Dukaten Mitmenschen totschlagen?
BERTHELOT: Mein Herr, er hat recht, dafür sind in der Tat zwei Dukaten zu wenig.
COLIN *zu Angelot*: Du würdest es nicht einmal für drei machen, wie, Angelot?
ANGELOT *schüttelt den Kopf.*
BERTHELOT *zu Angelot*: Für vier?
SGANARELLE: Drei Dukaten kommen überhaupt nicht in Frage.
ANGELOT: Vier Dukaten sind eine Menge Geld. *Er schüttelt aber doch noch den Kopf.*
COLIN: Er hat einfach ein zu weiches Gemüt.
SGANARELLE: Drei Dukaten von uns erpressen zu wollen, das nennt ihr ein zu
weiches Gemüt.
BERTHELOT: Unter fünf Dukaten nichts zu machen.
DON JUAN *ruft Sganarelle zu*: Wird's bald?
SGANARELLE *knirschend*: Gut, ich werde euch den horrenden Preis von vier
Dukaten . . .
ANGELOT: Fünf!
SGANARELLE: Gut. Aber Achtung kann ich vor euch nicht mehr haben; Freunde
sind wir nicht mehr . . .
ANGELOT: Nein und abermals nein. Mein Gewissen erlaubt es nicht. *Er läuft weg.*
SGANARELLE: Geh zum Teufel!
COLIN: Aber zu zweit schaffen wir es nicht.
DON JUAN *zu Sganarelle*: Erhöhe den Sold.
COLIN *ruft Angelot nach*: Sechs Dukaten! Komm sofort zurück!
ANGELOT *kommt langsam zurück*: Jetzt sind es schon sechs geworden. Das tut mir
leid.

In the hard, pitiless bargaining that goes on in this scene Sganarelle, who
wishes to keep back all the money he can for himself, meets his match; the
simple oarsmen know the rules of *this* game and get the better of him. Sganarelle cannot swallow the thought of this 'wasted' money and in II, 3, after the
shipwreck, when he and Don Juan stand bedraggled on the beach, he is all
for making off before 'these damned boatmen' can find them and demand
payment. As he says reproachfully to his master: 'Und Sie haben ihnen, als
das Gewitter aufzog, um sie zum weiteren Warten zu bewegen, dreimal den
Lohn verdoppelt! Unsere Kasse aber hat die Flut verschlungen.' Later, in
II, 7, the new character Doctor Marphurius (who himself covertly desires to
make money from duels: 'Ich spreche nicht vom Geld, ich spreche von der
Heilkunst') says he has met some angry oarsmen:

MARPHURIUS: Sie schreien frech in der Gegend herum, ein edler Herr schulde ihnen 54 Dukaten! . . .
SGANARELLE: Schufte! 54 Dukaten!

Likewise, when Pieter stands up to the nobleman importuning his fiancée, Sganarelle takes the side of might and threatens him in intimidating tones: 'Hör zu, mein Junge, schrei nicht, verschwinde.' Pieter, however, will not allow himself to be browbeaten: 'Ich will aber schreien.'

These activities of Sganarelle as an exploiter of others makes him a ruthless illustration of survival through asocial behaviour in an asocial society, like the beatnik self-centred poet Baal in Brecht's very first play. Sganarelle lives according to the philosophy sung about in the second finale of *Die Dreigroschenoper* ('Erst kommt das Fressen, dann kommt die Moral'). This is the practical means of survival in a disordered society also expressed in the lines Jenny sings in Scene 16 of *Aufstieg und Fall der Stadt Mahagonny* ('Und wenn einer tritt, dann bin ich es / Und wird einer getreten, dann bist's du'); a pragmatism that operates right down the line and leaves no room for ideals or mercy. It is not only Sganarelle who acts by this code; the oarsmen, too, are prepared to sell their services dearly for a nefarious purpose and to insult and fight the nobility when looking for their money. Even Molière's peasant-girls Charlotte and Mathurine, to whom (in II, 4) Dom Juan makes simultaneous promises and who then keep their dispute on a fairly genteel verbal level, are turned by Brecht (II, 5) into two boisterous fisher-girls who engage in a vituperative clog-fight echoing the 'Eifersuchtsduett' of Polly and Lucy fighting over Macheath in *Die Dreigroschenoper*:

CHARLOTTE: Oh, doch. *Sie zieht eine Holzpantine aus.*
MATHURINE: Du hinterlistige Person! . . .
DON JUAN *zu Mathurine*: Lassen Sie doch; sie ist vom Teufel besessen!
MATHURINE: Das werde ich ihr schon austreiben. *Nimmt ebenfalls eine Holzpantine in die Hand.*
CHARLOTTE: Du tücksches Aas! . . .
MATHURINE: Was ich mir denke? Von dir? *Sie schlägt zu; Charlotte schlägt zurück* . . .
CHARLOTTE: Schietkram! . . .
MATHURINE: Scheusal! . . .
CHARLOTTE: Selber Scheusal! . . .
MATHURINE: Daß ich nicht lache! . . .

Both struggles, here and in *Die Dreigroschenoper*, are tooth and nail for a prize, with no quarter given. But it is eventually Sganarelle, poised between the privileges of the few and the powerlessness of the underdogs, who gives the cue for amoral opportunism to those of his class. In this respect he has the quality of hardness born of necessity that is not evident in the more light-hearted treatment by Molière. J. Arnavon ascribes Sganarelle's irresponsible advice to the Poor Man ('Va, va, jure un peu, il n'y a pas de mal' (III, 2)) to 'la mollesse de sa conscience, qui n'a rien du héros ni du martyr' and to his 'facilité et bongarçonnisme'.[30] There is not the same easygoing Sganarelle in the adaptation: here he is in earnest whether in grabbing what he can or in condemning the state of things that drives him to it.

This then is the polarity of Sganarelle evidenced in the nexus of his specific socio-historical situation: if he were not forced by circumstances perhaps he would not be brutal, but we do not know for sure. Many of his actions are unscrupulous because the urge to survive forces him to exploit his fellows. His is a betrayal of his class parallel to the examples in Scene 4 of *Die heilige Johanna der Schlachthöfe*, where a lad is prepared to take on the clothing and job of the worker Luckerniddle who has disappeared into the boiling-vat, Luckerniddle's wife is ready to forget him in exchange for twenty free canteen meals, and Gloomb leaps at the chance of replacing the foreman in the hated job that has caused the loss of his own fingers; but Johanna saw in this free-for-all only proof of 'der Armen Armut'. This is one side to Sganarelle: the fear for his position that emerges as a swashbuckling bravado in his submission to his master's morality. In his very first appearance we witness how some of Don Juan's overbearing attitudes have rubbed off on him but are conditioned too by his feeling of powerlessness to alter things. Sganarelle says to Guzman:

Eines muß man ihm immerhin lassen: er zieht die Weiber an wie süßer Essig Fliegen. Keine, die diesem Magneten widerstehen kann. Sein armer alter Vater weiß nicht, wie er die immer neue Schande überstehen soll! Und die Schulden! Aber was kann man tun? Nichts kann man tun.

The approach of Don Juan cuts short this speech, and the scene ends with Sganarelle callously shrugging his shoulders at Guzman's predicament as to what he should say to his mistress.[31] Nonetheless, though fear and expediency qualify Sganarelle's behaviour to a great extent, the adaptation does bring a far more ironical tone into this figure and, while Molière had relied on the aside to complete Sganarelle's dual outlook, Brecht uses more the direct comment to establish the valet's sceptical aversion from Don Juan's morals. A step in this direction is represented by Sganarelle's tongue-in-cheek rejoinders (e.g. 'Sie können nichts dafür. Bei Ihrer Anziehungskraft, bei Ihrem Feuer!' (I, 2)) that preserve the ambiguity of his identification with and censure of Don Juan's mode of action, as in I, 4:

SGANARELLE: Und unsere Briefe? Und unsere Geschenke?
DON JUAN: Alles zurückgeschickt.
SGANARELLE: Was? Die Dame verabscheut Sie!
DON JUAN: Sie bildet sich das nur ein. Sie will diesen Burschen tatsächlich morgen heiraten. Ich werde hier zum Äußersten greifen. Sie wird entführt.
SGANARELLE: Oh! Nein! . . .
DON JUAN *droht ihm.*
SGANARELLE: Ach, gnädiger Herr! — Das wird wieder eine Ihrer . . .
DON JUAN: Meiner —
SGANARELLE: . . . großen Aventüren!

But the switch to a completely new characteristic in the figure of Sganarelle is essentially to be found in those additions to — and omissions from — the source play that convey his view of Don Juan as a *type*, a paradigm of the ethos of the governing aristocracy. In so far as Don Juan is a portrait of the French nobleman of his time it can be said that Molière's Sganarelle also has this dimension, at least embryonically. But where Molière puts the individuality of his personages first Brecht shifts the centre of gravity to their socially conditioned and representative behaviour. The factor introduced by Brecht (which Molière obviously could not have at his disposal) is the historical awareness incorporated in Sganarelle; this allows him to stand aside and comment on situations with an assessment of his times that in actuality belongs to a much later period. Brecht thus employed the same device as in other adaptations but kept it within the logical bounds of his material. Sganarelle could not be turned into a *politically* conscious left-wing activist like Rauert in the adaptation of *Der rote Hahn* — this would have been too crudely anachronistic; his political awareness has to be limited and remains *in spe*, more like that in *Der Hofmeister*. What Sganarelle sheds by distancing himself decisively from his master (even if only at a few points) is the aura of ludicrous buffoonery surrounding the traditional valet to Don Juan; what he acquires is a serious dignity that sharpens the dialectic of his acquiescence and independence.

Within the limitations imposed by historical time and the accepted lines of the play Sganarelle is comparable to that other Brechtian servant in *Herr Puntila und sein Knecht Matti* who dissociates himself sharply from the actions of his master while at the same time humouring him. In this latter play there is no hindrance — and therefore no ambiguity — to the chauffeur's attitude. Brecht could deploy at will the class consciousness of Matti, and indeed gave directions to this effect in the notes: the material subjection but intellectual superiority of Matti to his master were to be crucial in establishing the antagonism between their respective classes. The intellectual superiority is bound to be with Matti as he is the analytic commentator on Puntila's trickery and hypocrisy and in scene after scene soberly and dispassionately strips off the veil of specious plausibility from the lies and presumptions of Puntila and his cronies. This is the quality that Brecht adds in his Sganarelle; with cool scepticism he deflates certain of Don Juan's antics, orientates his behaviour and gives it more than individual significance within a historical context.[32] In keeping with this dignity he accords the valet Brecht wisely eradicated the whole sequence in Molière IV, 3 where Sganarelle, who also owes Dimanche money, prevaricates with a flurry of fine phrases and promises directly imitated from his master's handling of the merchant. This was a scene that raised a laugh at the valet's expense, but his pretentious aping aroused a stereotyped ridicule that came nowhere near the mordant satire of Dom Juan's encounter with Dimanche. For the same reason Brecht omitted most of Molière IV, 7 in which, after being invited by Dom Juan to join him at table, Sganarelle is involved in a comic ballet with the flunkeys deftly removing his dishes one after the other before he can touch them. This makes Sganarelle look foolish in front of the *lower* servants and would fit ill with the independence that Brecht wants to attribute to him. The same is true of the following scene which is left out in its entirety; this was the unexpected first appearance of the Statue, and Dom Juan had ordered the abjectly frightened Sganarelle to sit down with them despite his protestations that hunger and thirst have left him.

These excisions remove Sganarelle from the sphere of the comic valet of the *commedia dell'arte*, traditionally the focus of derision and buffoonery, and stand him on his own feet as a sensible observer not afraid to make trenchant comments on his master, either in word or deed. Thus, instead of aquiescing as Don Juan taunts the Poor Man in III, 2, Sganarelle (who in disguise is now taken for the master) tries to moderate the baiting and Don Juan has to jolt him out of his passivity before he will tell the Poor Man to blaspheme. His reluctance to join in his master's sport is patent. Right at the opening of the adaptation Sganarelle's remarks on the use of snuff, mentioned above, are sufficient indication of where he stands in the clash between the top dogs and the underdogs. These are backed up by quips and asides throughout the play, and in II, 6 he evinces class solidarity with the fisher-girls as he advises them to be on their guard against Don Juan, whose success he ascribes solely to the power of his position:

SGANARELLE: Ihr armen Dinger! Fallt mir nicht auf den rein. Der! Kunststück, euch den Kopf zu verdrehen!
Don Juan tritt näher.
SGANARELLE: Gebt mir seinen Rock, seine Bänder und seine Federn, und ich verführ' euch spielend; aber dann habt ihr was davon! Ich rate euch zum Guten: Nehmt euch vor dem in acht! *Bemerkt Don Juan*: Nehmt euch in acht vor dem, der schlecht von meinem Herrn spricht...
DON JUAN: Sganarelle... *Nimmt ihn am Ohr.*
SGANARELLE: Ihr kennt meinen Herrn nicht!

Molière's Sganarelle had also warned the girls in II, 4 against his master's philandering (which he treats as a personal characteristic, not the consequence of social power) but without the brutally realistic tone of the adaptation. The movement of the scene is unchanged by Brecht but while Molière's Sganarelle, on sighting his master, had exclaimed 'Monsieur est homme d'honneur', Brecht, by switching to the ironical ambiguity of 'Ihr kennt meinen Herrn nicht!', shows how Sganarelle tries to convey caution to the threatened girls.

Another significant illustration of this shift in him from sighing resignation to militant opposition occurs in IV, 11 (a merging of Molière V, 2 and V, 4). Brecht takes over the gist of Dom Juan's speech in which he cynically claims that 'la profession d'hypocrite' will provide a perfect cover for his pursuits; the adaptation transforms 'Enfin c'est là le vrai moyen de faire impunément tout ce que je voudrai' into the more vivid 'Wenn es einem ehrlichen Mann verboten ist, sich die Nase zu schneuzen, so ist es einem Heuchler erlaubt, eine ganze Stadt zu stehlen. Laß sie uns denn stehlen!' This is then followed by Don Juan's surprise announcement that the Komtur's daughter Angelika is coming to supper and by his rehearsal of her reception, at the end of which

Sganarelle's accumulated hate for his master's privileged impunity bursts out uncontrollably:

Und ehrlich währt am kürzesten, und Lügen haben lange Beine, und wer zuerst lacht, lacht am besten, und wer zuletzt kommt, mahlt zuerst, und faule Fische, gute Fische, und vergib uns unsere Unschuld, und das Kamel geht durch das Nadelöhr! Ah, zu denken, daß eine Persönlichkeit wie die Ihre alles tun kann, ohne daß irgendeine Macht einschreiten könnte! Gibt es wirklich niemanden, den der Himmel schicken könnte? Findet er keinen?

Deftly Brecht telescopes into this inversion of proverbial phrases all the incoherent, illogical arguments that Sganarelle stutters out in Molière: on tobacco (I, 1), on God and religious faith (III, 1), and at this point on damnation (V, 2):

Sachez, Monsieur, que tant va la cruche à l'eau, qu'enfin elle se brise; et comme dit fort bien cet auteur que je ne connais pas, l'homme est en ce monde ainsi que l'oiseau sur la branche; la branche est attachée à l'arbre; qui s'attache à l'arbre, suit de bons préceptes; etc. etc.

By reversing the apparently reliable logic of gnomic sayings Brecht cunningly achieves two goals through Sganarelle's words: he describes the reality of Don Juan's behaviour and indicates the intrinsic disjointedness of a social order in which Don Juan can freely act out his deceits, and at the same time he presents Sganarelle as a coolly thinking observer resisting the status quo with factual succinctness, like the unemployed Rauert in *Der rote Hahn*.

The social and historical comment projected through the new configuration of Sgnanarelle's character is crowned in the final added scene (IV, 13) which shows how all the figures in the play are in one way or another conformists to and promoters of the society they live in despite their temporary protests and rebelliousness in the course of the action.[33] As Don Juan descends into the pit they crowd round the edge and give vent to their material reactions at the dandy's disappearance — and not one mentions his soul:

LA VIOLETTE: Welch ein Unglück! Er ist weg!

ANGELIKA: Ich habe mich ein wenig verspätet. *Sieht das Loch*: Ah! Entsetzlich!

DIMANCHE *zwei Röcke bringend*: Eine Erpressung! Die zwei Röcke, gnädiger ... Ah! Mein bester Kunde!

ELVIRAS BRÜDER: Wo ist der Schurke? — Ah! Die Ehre unserer Familie ewig befleckt!

SERAFINE: Ah! Wer ißt nun meine Enten in Orangen?

MARPHURIUS: Ah! Das Duell!

DON LUIS: Ah! Mein Sohn! Mein Erbe!

DIE RUDERER: Ah! Wo ist er? — Vierundfünfzig Dukaten futsch!

DIE FISCHERMÄDCHEN: Ah! Wer nimmt unsere Austern? — Der schöne gnädige Herr!

    Alle stehen erschüttert vor dem Loch. Aus der Höhe nieder flattert langsam Don Juans Hut.

SGANARELLE: Mein Lohn! Mein Lohn!

This twist in the tail of the play grew out of the embryonic 'Mes gages! Mes gages!', Sganarelle's despairing cry at the loss of his master that Molière found in Cicognini and that Brecht kept as the closing line.

An analysis of the manifold changes that a committed playwright such as Brecht makes in adapting another man's work (changes in conception of character and role, in plot and action, in content and ideological purpose) cannot ignore their structural consequences. This must not be reduced to a routine of counting scenes; nor is it at all significant that Brecht points out how the producer Besson had made the superficial modification of removing the traditional 5-Act division of *Dom Juan* (Brecht had done that himself so often that with him it was now almost a convention in reverse). The internal logic and rhythm of the play is the important aspect of structure. In the case of *Don Juan* the question arises as to how far and how successfully Brecht related alterations in content to consonant changes in form; indeed, whether his adaptation is more or less 'dramatic' than his source. The critic Reinhold Grimm devotes some attention to a formal comparison of the two plays, and though he first pays tribute to Brecht's sense of theatre ('Diese Neufassung quillt über von glänzenden Einfällen und szenischen Erfindungen') he questions whether Brecht actually succeeded in making this adaptation fit the paradigm of epic theatre and even suggests it is less epic than Molière.[34] After quoting a French editor's assertion that Molière's aim 'fut, évidemment, non de nouer une intrigue dans une crise brève comme la foudre, mais de dérouler autour de la forte personnalité du héros, pour mieux l'éclairer, une diversité d'aventures humaines',[35] Grimm continues:

Diese Definition, bis auf die positive Bewertung des Helden und die Überbetonung der Persönlichkeit, hätte Brecht ohne weiteres übernehmen können, sollte man meinen . . . Verblüffenderweise ist beinah das Gegenteil der Fall. Gewiß, das von Molière vorgegebene Schema einer episierenden Reihe von Begebenheiten behält Brecht bei. Innerhalb dieses Schemas aber hebt er schon bestehende Zusammenhänge hervor und fügt neue ein, so daß der Kausalnexus dichter wird. Dazu kommt, daß die oft sehr langen Repliken des Franzosen in kleinere, dramatisch bewegtere Dialogstücke aufgelöst werden; außerdem steigert die ständige Berufung auf den von Anfang an prophezeiten Zorn des Himmels das Präzipitieren der Handlung und erhöht die Spannung.

In support of his argument Grimm enumerates the main alterations made by Brecht. Yet the examples given can more cogently be seen to strengthen the epic structure: the oarsmen hired by Don Juan — equivalent to Molière's peasants — are identical with the robbers who attack Don Carlos and incorporate the lower class element that both obeys and strikes against authority; the incident of Sganarelle dining with Don Juan which is removed to the roadside, now does more than just illustrate the servant-master relationship and is dovetailed with the exchange of clothes (this adumbrated in Molière) so that both elements establish the alienation of noble appearances and create that dual perspective of the social *données* of the time that complies

with Brecht's definition in *Kleines Organon für das Theater*: 'Eine verfrem-
dende Abbildung ist eine solche, die den Gegenstand zwar erkennen, ihn
aber doch zugleich fremd erscheinen läßt.'

The omission of the first apparition of the statue of the Komtur provides
Grimm with what he takes to be indisputable proof that Brecht was making
an 'Aristotelian' drama of *Dom Juan*; he sees in the one and only appearance
of the Statue, 'wirkungsvoll aufgespart' until the end, a revocation of Brecht's
stubborn principle that his theatre could only exist in and through a con-
cordance of ideological content matched with epic form. Grimm claims
that Brecht's own description of *Die Gewehre der Frau Carrar* as 'aristotelische
(Einfühlungs)Dramatik' could apply even more aptly to *Don Juan*. But
other reasons can be found for the exclusion of the Statue's first arrival. It
must be remembered that Molière too was manipulating a traditional plot
and material and had to use great ingenuity in his effort to blend the supernatural elements with his socio-psychological study of contemporary *mœurs*.
Most critics have undoubtedly felt that the French playwright failed to marry
the warring disparates, with a consequent arbitrariness in both motivation and
final solution. Arnavon constantly harps on the weakness of the motifs that
Molière had to incorporate in deference to tradition (the Statue, the 'souper',
the spectre) and categorically states that in production 'plus le merveilleux,
seule partie réellement faible de la comédie, sera diminué, plus l'œuvre gran-
dira en force, en portée, en durée'.[36] It is thus premature to judge the mere
fact that Brecht reduces the Statue's appearances to one; this can only be done
after investigating the functional value of the change.

In this respect Grimm equates the two arrests of Macheath in *Die Dreigroschenoper* — the reasons for which Brecht explained in detail in his notes
— with the two appearances of the Statue, though in terms of function the
two cases bear no resemblance to each other. *Die Dreigroschenoper* deals with
bourgeois notions as its central theme and endeavours to work out a congruent form. Since Brecht wishes the exemplary life of Macheath the high-
wayman to dispel the erroneous belief that 'ein Räuber sei kein Bürger'
(itself begotten of another false idea that 'ein Bürger sei kein Räuber') he
depicts his 'hero' with all the habits of a Bürger. It is in fact the obstinate
adherence to an ordered routine that makes Macheath as predictable as any
Bürger; the regular patronage of prostitutes — even when on the run — is
the habit specifically selected by Brecht (not least because it is ostensibly
frowned on by society) in the form of *two* arrests in a whorehouse to convey
the affinity between a 'Räuber' and 'Bürger' in Macheath. The question of
this repetition touches on the essence of Brecht's conception of drama and he
was very alive to it; hence the explanation in the notes entitled *Warum zwei
Verhaftungen des Macheath und nicht eine?*:

Diese erste Gefängnisszene ist, aus dem Gesichtswinkel der deutschen Pseudoklassik
betrachtet, ein *Umweg*, nach unserer Ansicht ein Beispiel primitiver epischer Form.
Sie ist nämlich ein Umweg, wenn man wie diese rein dynamische Dramatik, der Idee
das Primat zuerteilend, den Zuschauer ein immer bestimmteres Ziel wünschen

macht — was hier der *Tod* des Helden wäre —, sozusagen . . . eine Zwangsläufigkeit in gerader Linie braucht.[37]

Seen in this light the apparent holding up of the action by the dual arrest actually depicts the most significant fact about Macheath's character and serves the integral *dramatic* purpose of bringing about his downfall. There is thus no real point of comparison between the number of Macheath's arrests and the Statue's appearances in *Don Juan*. Molière had introduced the Statue three times (one in each final scene of Acts III, IV, V); the first time, in the mausoleum, it had nodded; on the second occasion it had entered, sat down at Dom Juan's table and invited him to dine the following night; on the third, it had led the libertine off to his doom. Brecht telescoped the first two incidents into the mausoleum scene (III, 8), dropping the entirely irrelevant and somewhat farcical visit to Don Juan's house but retaining the essential invitation, though with the important difference that it is now Don Juan who insolently invites the Statue to dine *à trois* (the spice for him will be the Statue's daughter whom he is seducing). The essential dramatic fact of the invitation that points towards the end of the play is thus present in both original and adaptation; and if Molière's play is first and foremost a portrait of the unprincipled nobleman of his time and Brecht's a critical depiction of the extent and misuse of this power, neither relies intrinsically on the Statue nor even on the hero's catastrophic end.

Many dramatic elements that are to be found among the traditional features of the Don Juan legend were re-introduced by Brecht to add incisiveness to his thesis: Angelika, the Komtur's daughter (Donna Anna in *Don Giovanni*), described as 'eine minderjährige Tochter' (I, 2) and promised as 'angenehme Gesellschaft' in the invitation to her father, adds piquancy to Don Juan's pretence of reform (IV, 10); the exchange of clothes between servant and master — used in Dorimon's version — gave way in Molière to a doctor's garb and what was at that time a topical polemic on medicine; the oarsmen in Brecht participate more meaningfully in the action than do Molière's peasants. Brecht also achieved a subsidiary concentration of the action largely by omitting many of the rhetorical *longueurs* in Molière's text; the sermonizing diatribes by Don Juan's father and the wordy involutions around their honour by Elvira's brothers are two of them. Parallel with this is the reduction of formal aspects of Molière's language: except for the purpose of parody the poetic, near-verse flight of classical French prose (the rhythm of Molière's prose in *Dom Juan* is demonstrably rich in alexandrines) would have been an erratic block protruding incongruously from the bed of social comment in the adaptation.[38]

However dramatic Brecht may appear to have made his adaptation, a careful examination of the text shows that the ideological content and the epic form are not independent of one another as Grimm argues, and that the critical comment on social realities impinges on the audience through both the interaction of characters and the formal means by which this is presented. In all essentials Brecht has epicized the action. He presents a cowardly Don

Juan who relies on the power of his position; the discrepancy between his words and actions therefore relativizes both (e.g. in II, 7; III, 1–5). Sganarelle, too, is ambivalent in his actions, attitudes, asides — as are the oarsmen in their willingness and yet unreliability as trained thugs. The several instances of 'interleaved' scenes — preparations for abducting a fresh quarry (I, 4), Don Juan dressing while Don Carlos lies wounded (III, 5), Don Juan at his toilet while his irate father waits, and his cold-blooded reawakening of feeling for Elvira (IV, 9), etc., are examples of the epic technique that alienates by mutually distancing both incongruent substances in the scene. Similarly, the alienating effect of mime and run-through is pressed into service — Sganarelle telling Don Juan what violent abuse he would hurl at a hypothetical master (I, 2), Sganarelle instructing the boatmen in the use of their oars as weapons (I, 5), the dumb show of the fight between oarsmen and noblemen (III, 4), Don Juan rehearsing the seduction of Angelika, thus exposing his unfeeling egoism (IV, 11). The tendency to mime was already present in Molière (lurking as it does close below the surface of all comedy) but Brecht handles it deliberately as a powerful constituent of epic technique, in that it allows the actor to put a *model* — a stylized abstraction — before the audience; the actor can detach himself from the personality he is portraying and this diminishes the 'Aristotelian' empathy and constantly jerks the audience back into critical distance.

There can be no doubt that in the adaptation Don Juan is more negatively and Sganarelle more positively presented, but it is false to infer that, like a see-saw movement — the people are therefore on the way to being idealized. Brecht's play is a trenchant and all-pervading criticism of the assumptions of the *whole* of that society, at every level; if Don Juan struts on to the stage as a 'sexuelle Großmacht', his behaviour is nevertheless half-expected and also half-accepted by those who suffered the ravages of his actions. All the 'lower' characters are shown as conformists and time-servers and the ludicrousness of their compliance culminates in the actual spatial arrangement of the final scene as Don Juan's feathered hat floats down among them. A strong leaning to social comment flavours Molière's play too, though the censure here is concentrated on the representative of one narrow — though dominant — class.

The exigencies of the traditional Don Juan plot, made even more restrictive through the popularity of the theme in the preceding years, hampered Molière's freedom in his treatment of it and forced him to retain the cumbersome supernatural paraphernalia connected with Don Juan's punishment. The linking of Don Juan and the divine judgement opened the door to those metaphysical and philosophical interpretations that take off from strict reality and measure Don Juan with the inflated rules of the absolute and the general. For this reason the critic is tempted to remove Molière's hero to the safely determined symbolic sphere of the myth: 'Au fond, Don Juan doit être considéré comme appartenant au domaine de la fable plutôt qu'à une classe sociale déterminée'.[39] In making such a comment the critic is corroborating the evidence found in numerous artistic formulations of the Don Juan theme. Mozart's *Don Giovanni* is probably the most renowned treatment based on an interpretation within the religious framework. Here Don Juan operates on such a gigantic scale that he is no longer judged an ordinary man — he is elevated instead to the sphere of legend and direct confrontation with the deity. His profligacy is of such dimensions that divine wrath and retribution automatically assert themselves in the emissary from the beyond — the statue of the Commander which is a baroque invention of the Spanish religious plays that first forged the Don Juan theme. Quite clearly such a positive rounded view of Don Juan and his fate rests on an unshakable belief in an eternal order that allows the demonic to appear on earth — whether in the guise of a profligate or a natural catastrophe — in order to prove its own divine power and permanence. This is the essential myth of Don Juan that must necessarily exclude such disturbing possibilities as a psychological interpretation (in which Don Juan can be seen to express the fulfilment of driving fantasies in individual men) or the social considerations that preoccupy Brecht.

In this respect, perhaps, Brecht really diverges from Molière, so that the adaptation finally reveals itself as working both with and against Molière just as *Der Hofmeister* was with and against Lenz. Brecht takes over those components that have a direct social bearing — such as the episodes involving the fishermen or Dimanche — but stops short of anything that might allow Don Juan the slightest hope of escape into the realm of mythology. Hence the subduing of the spectre, Statue and religious allusions; all the divine machinery calculated to instil awe-struck silence and respect in the audience is reduced to a minimum and remains in Brecht too only a concession to the inherited plot. Instead Brecht builds into his adaptation the factor of the historical perspective. In this way the adaptation is partly a re-interpretation of Don Juan the French nobleman (from a twentieth-century documentary point of view) and partly a comment on Molière's own attitudes as expressed in the detail of *Dom Juan*. In his conception of the hero Brecht puts on the stage a *model* of the overbearing attitudes of a ruling social class, a *representative* of uncurbed impunity rather than just a particular individual; and he so organizes the adaptation that Don Juan acquires weight and value as a model through the articulation of social awareness in Sganarelle. The servant becomes the dynamic fulcrum of the adaptation as so frequently in Brecht's work where the audience is made to look at the great from below, through the eyes and life of the anonymous underling.

The question remains: is *Don Juan* a comedy, and of what nature? Molière called his work a *comédie* despite the disaster that overtakes the hero; it is less the substance than the manner that makes Molière's play unquestionably comedy. This is borne out by his own pronouncements on 'la comédie' in the *Préface à Tartuffe*: 'On connaîtra sans doute que, n'étant autre chose qu'un poème ingénieux, qui, par des leçons agréables, reprend les défauts des hommes, on ne saurait la censurer sans injustice.' And after the banning of *Tartuffe* he was moved to defend his play in the *Premier Placet* addressed to the King: 'Le devoir de la comédie étant de corriger les hommes en les divertissant, j'ai cru que, dans l'emploi où je me trouve [i.e. as 'chef de la troupe du roi'], je n'avais rien de mieux à faire que d'attaquer par des peintures ridicules les vices de mon siècle.' The important fact for Molière was the aesthetic 'par des leçons agréables' and 'en les divertissant'; the didactic message ought to reach the audience entirely in terms of its presentation, or the playwright should desist from attempting to convey it.

Given Brecht's views on the function of drama, it is not surprising that he shows a bias towards comedies as models for his adaptations. This tallies with his own proclaimed distaste for tragedy that is prone to cloak social realities in favour of the 'universal' in human nature. Most dramatists and theorists, from Lessing to Sternheim, see tragedy as concerned with the individual and comedy with the social nexus. If there is any justification for this differentiation of tragedy and comedy, then Brecht's characters are firmly anchored in comedy: they are not just exemplars of human 'vices' (the miser, the bully, the hypocrite, etc.) but they are constructed in such a manner as to illustrate how such characteristics are more often than not a concomitant of a particular social group in a historically specific context. Brecht demonstrates how human behaviour is largely the outcome of conditioning through social, political and economic influences, how the individual characteristics become a variable in the formula composed of factors derived from social impulses. In *Don Juan* the audience is invited to examine closely the 'Parasitäre seines Glanzes' (the type), not the 'Glanz des Parasiten' (the individual).

The characters in a play are a matter of content, but the question of illusion is the concern of form. Lessing indicated how the tragedian must promote and sustain the illusion of the audience while the comic dramatist may fracture it with impunity:

Der tragische Dichter sollte alles vermeiden, was die Zuschauer an ihre Illusion erinnern kann; denn sobald sie daran erinnert sind, so ist sie weg . . . Dem komischen Dichter ist es eher erlaubt, auf diese Weise seiner Vorstellung Vorstellungen entgegenzusetzen; denn unser Lachen zu erregen, braucht es des Grades der Täuschung nicht, den unser Mitleiden erfordert.[40]

The shattering of the theatrical illusion has, of course, become a commonplace of Brecht's drama. The technique of alienation is his method of achieving this and it provides a deliberate means of countering the willing absorption of the audience into the 'suspension of disbelief'. Brecht recognized that alienation was an essential element in comedy ('Allgemein angewendet wird der V-Effekt in der Komödie, besonders der niedrigen'),[41] and he fostered its dynamic intervention by every means at his command — in the structure of individual scenes and their interaction, in language and the parody generated by discrepant levels, in techniques of acting. In *Don Juan* Brecht intensifies the devices that had already served Molière to destroy the illusion and hinder indiscriminate empathy; from the start the attention of the spectator is demanded on two separate but simultaneous levels, that of the assimilation of real happenings before his eyes and that of a distancing critical assessment of their bearing in a socio-historical context. This is the essence of Brecht's comedy (and his drama in general): the event and its evaluation, the history and the historian are inextricably welded together in the one complex, so that each tempers the other in a continuous dialectical discourse. For this reason, all Brecht's drama is comedy, and all his comedy serious, built as it is on the twin pillars of the aesthetic and the ethical, enthralment and detachment, 'lachen' and 'verlachen'.[42] Though Brecht manipulates the Don Juan theme more consciously than Molière in order to depict a certain society through its representatives, he recognizes the aesthetic need for this didactic pre-occupation to be totally absorbed into the autonomy of the drama, and the value of contradictions and inconsistencies in human beings.[43] Whether in his own plays or in adaptations Brecht seldom allowed sociological behaviourism to overwhelm his sense of theatre. In Molière too he acknowledged a sharp critical insight akin to his own that expressed itself in the satire of *Don Juan* at a distance of three centuries.

NOTES

1 L. Weinstein, *The Metamorphoses of Don Juan* (Stanford, 1959), surveys in detail the vast literary heritage of the Don Juan theme with its many idiosyncratic and spectacular accretions, without mentioning Brecht's reworking of Molière. Brecht probably used E. Neresheimer's translation of *Dom Juan* as the basis for his adaptation.
2 Jules Lemaître, *Impressions de Théâtre*, 2 vols (Paris, 1890), I, 67, indicates the later nineteenth-century brand of the Romantic in the 'dilettante' conception. In the Romantic epoch, however, Stendhal stands out with his characteristically realistic slant; compare *De l'Amour*, II, in *Œuvres complètes*, edited by P. Arbelet and E. Champion (Paris, 1926), p. 127.
3 *GW*, 17/1259.
4 BBA 1579/06.
5 Compare P. Bénichou, *Morales du Grand Siècle* (Paris, 1948), pp. 172 f., who draws attention to the absence of a positive *bourgeoisie* in Molière's works; its representatives are almost always ineffectual and no more likely to throw up the ideal of the *honnête homme* than is the nobility.
6 BBA 1579/05.
7 Bénichou, op. cit., pp. 214 f., detects, however, a perhaps unconscious attack on the monarchy in Molière.
8 BBA 1579/05.
9 See Chevalier de Méré: 'Si quelqu'un me demandait en quoi consiste l'honnêteté, je dirais que ce n'est autre chose que d'exceller en tout ce qui regarde les agréments et les bienséances de la vie.' Quoted in Blaise Pascal, *Pensées et opuscules*, edited by L. Brunschvicg (Paris, 1913), p. 116.
10 This and the following quotation, *GW*, 17/1260.
11 *GW*, 17/1258.
12 *GW*, 17/1257 f.
13 W. D. Howarth, edition of *Dom Juan* (Oxford, 1958), p. 78 n.
14 J. Cairncross, *Molière — Bourgeois et Libertin* (Paris, 1963), p. 28.
15 BBA 1579/08.
16 See Bénichou, op. cit., pp. 171 f., who ascribes the phenomenon of *libertinage* to the post-Renaissance decline of the aristocracy.
17 *GW*, 17/1258.

18   *GW*, 17/1260 f.
19   *GW*, 17/1261 f.
20   BBA 1092/101.
21   See Brecht's comments in BBA 1579/08: 'Da ist etwas Widersprüchliches: Ein Mann glaubt nicht, daß der Himmel eingreifen kann. Er ist als fortschrittlich gedacht, Molière glaubt auch nicht. Dann greift der Himmel aber doch ein. Dann hat er sich sehr geirrt.' Thus the improbable intervention of heaven is turned neatly to account; Don Juan's apparent progressiveness in religious thinking is refuted. At the same time a modern audience is still not likely to think the *deus ex machina* probable in real terms.
22   *GW*, 17/1260.
23   *GW*, 6/2607 f.
24   *GW*, 6/2580 f.
25   *GW*, 6/2587.
26   *GW*, 6/2589.
27   Brecht has a fondness for such scenes that involve disguise, as they inevitably lay bare the essentials of socially-conditioned reality — it is easier to change one's clothing than one's habits and nature. Compare *Der kaukasische Kreidekreis*, in which Grusche pretends to be a lady but is found out because she knows how to make a bed, and where Azdak has to teach the disguised and fleeing Großfürst how to eat like a hungry man if he wishes to escape detection.
28   J. Arnavon, *Le Don Juan de Molière* (Copenhagen, 1947), p. 117.
29   It is generally considered that this is part of Molière's polemic with the Compagnie du Saint-Sacrement, which consistently campaigned against snuff takers; see F. Baumal, *Tartuffe et ses Avatars* (Paris, 1925), pp. 224 f.
30   *Le Don Juan*, p. 310.
31   Molière has a more abject ending; Sganarelle says: 'je t'ai fait cette confidence avec franchise, et cela m'est sorti un peu bien vite de la bouche; mais s'il fallait qu'il en vînt quelque chose à ses oreilles, je dirais hautement que tu aurais menti.'
32   Compare Bénichou, *Morales*, pp. 167 f., who analyses Sganarelle's claim that he hates Dom Juan and is only ruled by fear.
33   If Dom Juan was Dimanche's best client, for example, the effort it must have cost the tailor to extract payment from other noblemen can only be left to the imagination.
34   All the following quotations are taken from R. Grimm, *Bertolt Brecht und die Weltliteratur* (Nürnberg, 1961), pp. 41–7.
35   R. Jouanny, *Molière. Théâtre complet* (Paris, n.d.), I, 710.
36   Arnavon, *Le Don Juan*, p. 174. Howarth, too, draws attention to the tenuous and arbitrary role of the Statue, op. cit., p. xxxi.
37   *GW*, 17/997 f.
38   See in this connexion Friedrich Dürrenmatt's pertinent reflections on the near-impossibility of translating Molière into German, in 'Zum Tode Ernst Ginsbergs', *Theaterschriften und Reden* (Zürich, 1966), pp. 202 f.: 'Die beiden Sprachen sind zu verschieden, das Französische besitzt eine angeborene Rhetorik, im Deutschen wirkt das Rhetorische fast immer zu wuchtig, und was gar den Alexandriner betrifft, will man ihn überhaupt nachahmen, so wirkt er bei Molière ebenso selbstverständlich wie im Deutschen unnatürlich. Molière ist vielleicht prinzipiell unübersetzbar ... Molières Bedeutung auf der deutschsprachigen Bühne liegt allein in seinen Gestalten. Seine Form und seine Stoffe entstammen einer Komödientradition, die weit in die Antike zurückreicht, doch die Weise, wie er die ewigen Typen des Geizigen, des betrogenen Ehemannes oder des Menschenfeindes sah, stoßen sie aus dem Typischen in den Charakter und ins Dämonische. Seine Menschen sind stärker als seine Sprache, der Unübersetzliche wird auf deutsch spielbar.' Ginsberg, together with Kurt Horwitz, succeeded in his Molière productions by 'translating' Molière's 'Realistik' and 'bittere Menschenkenntnis'.
39   Cairncross, *Molière*, p. 54 n. Bénichou, *Morales*, p. 167, compares *Dom Juan* and *Amphitryon* in similar terms: 'Toutes deux pièces reposent pourtant sur la conception d'un héros souverain, dont les désirs se prétendent au-dessus du blâme et de la contrainte; et dans toutes deux des relations réelles apparaissent à travers une action légendaire.' Bénichou further derives from the 'prolongement fabuleux de l'action' a fairy-tale magnification of Dom Juan that releases him from the ballast of reality, pp. 168 f.
40   *Hamburgische Dramaturgie*, 42. Stück.
41   *GW*, 15/366.
42   Compare Lessing's remarks on 'lachen' and 'verlachen' in *Hamb. Dram.*, 28–9. St.

43 See BBA 1579/11 for Brecht's observations on Molière and his fellow-playwrights: 'Schön ist, daß diese Komödienschreiber wirklich die vollen Widersprüche behalten und nicht eine Formel liefern, die sofort zu fassen ist. Das ist lebendig. Er [Molière] wendet sich nach allen Seiten mit Gelächter, verlacht Atheisten und Theisten, wenn sie komisch sind. Wo etwas komisch ist, wird gelacht, ohne Verantwortungsgefühl. Deshalb wollen wir diese Gegensätze nicht zu sehr auf eine Formel bringen. Die Widersprüche sind in einer Art großartig, andererseits oberflächlich.'

CHAPTER V

PAUKEN UND TROMPETEN

Pauken und Trompeten, made and first performed in 1955, was the last adaptation Brecht was to undertake (*Coriolan*, though unfinished, occupied him in 1952/3). It is also the one in which he handled his source most freely, as a scene-by-scene comparison with George Farquhar's *The Recruiting Officer* immediately makes apparent. Yet, paradoxically, despite the replacement of several motifs and long stretches of dialogue, the *effect* of *Pauken und Trompeten* is very close to the original text and we do not feel that the latter has been treated in cavalier fashion. This is because Brecht found in Farquhar's play a kindred intelligence at work, realistic and rebelliously-minded, and so he was able to build on what he found without first having to carry out extensive demolition. As Reinhold Grimm put it: 'Obwohl Brechts Eingriffe in Handlungsführung und Personengestaltung hier, ähnlich wie im *Don Juan*, viel weiter reichen als im *Coriolan*, spüren wir keinerlei Bruch: das witzig-freche, turbulente Stück wirkt in der neuen Fassung wie ein Original. Der Grund dafür ist, daß Brecht diesmal nicht *gegen* den Geist seiner Vorlage dichtet, sondern *aus* ihm *heraus*. Er brauchte, um das Stück zu ideologisieren, nur die vorhandenen Ansätze aufzugreifen und weiterzuführen: Kritik an gesellschaftlichen Mißständen, nämlich an den Methoden der Soldatenwerbung, war bei Farquhar, wenn auch versteckt, zweifellos vorhanden.'[1] Thus, though the changes in *Pauken und Trompeten* are at first sight surprising, the *direction* of the two plays is essentially the same, and qualitative differences are a result of Brecht's travelling further along the path tentatively indicated by Farquhar.

Brecht's apparently radical external alterations turn out to be a tightening and intensification of embryonic or implied attitudes already present in Farquhar:

Da Brecht außerdem die Geschehnisse vom Anfang des 18. Jahrhunderts auf die Zeit des amerikanischen Unabhängigkeitskrieges verlegte, konnte er die Themen der kolonialen Ausbeutung und der Revolution einbeziehen und schuf sich damit zusätzliche Möglichkeiten der Ideologisierung. Sie äußert sich vor allem in der Verschärfung der Werbemethoden, in der Darstellung der Hinterbliebenen gefallener Soldaten sowie in der Einführung des mit den aufständischen Kolonisten sympathisierenden Paares Lucy (die bei Farquhar nur das typische Kammerkätzchen des Lustspiels ist) und Mike ... Durch seine rigorosen Streichungen, Umstellungen, Änderungen und Einfügungen baut er die auch bei Farquhar komödiantisch bewegte Handlung noch wirkungsvoller auf; durch die Einführung einiger neuer Gestalten, vor allem der sittenstrengen Lady Prude und des Butlers Simpkins, schafft er ein bunteres Bild. Daß durch diese Eingriffe die eine oder andere hübsche Szene aufgegeben werden muß, nimmt Brecht, wie bei allen seinen Bearbeitungen, in Kauf.[2]

The final result would not merit particular attention, however, if it were nothing more than a reiteration of Farquhar's late-Restoration comedy; as always, Brecht's adaptation becomes a qualitatively different organism, indeed it is doubtful whether it can ultimately be called a comedy at all.

What does Brecht do to the framework of the play? He first of all goes through the familiar process of getting rid of act divisions and accommodating Farquhar's seventeen scenes[3] in only a dozen numbered scenes of his own. The counting of scenes, however, is largely otiose since *Pauken und Trompeten* has at least as many shifts of situation and characters as *The Recruiting Officer*; Brecht's plays are frequently busier than the already busy comedies of Farquhar's time. In actual length (of script, not performing time) the two plays are roughly equal; the surprising statistics concern the alterations, for Brecht omits about two-thirds of Farquhar's text, providing wholly new dialogue in its stead. That is, two-thirds of *Pauken und Trompeten* does not figure in the source, a remarkable and revealing fact for what is termed an adaptation. A re-structuring is also evident in the overall pattern. *The Recruiting Officer* has an even, though fast-moving and complicated flow of intrigue with no marked peripeteia at any point, since the author's chief concern is to juggle dexterously with three main threads of plot — recruiting, Silvia's efforts to ensnare Plume,[4] Melinda's fencing with Worthy — until he can bring them safely to a serene resolution in the haven of the final scene. Farquhar is so enamoured of his subsidiary plots that his play shows unmistakable traits of epic theatre — who can say that the contemporary mores of courting and matrimony are secondary to malpractice in methods of recruiting?

Brecht seems to have imposed a different design on *Pauken und Trompeten*: the eighth and the twelfth are nodal scenes in the adaptation, and not by chance the longest, each of them absorbing four scenes from Farquhar partly or wholly and between them accounting for over a third of the total play. In the first of these scenes there is some sort of turning-point in the action with the openly vocal declaration of opposition to the ruling system and its methods on the part of several characters. The subsequent scenes until the harshness of the sardonic end are darkened with the brutality of the authorities as they enforce their will in a successful bid to retain power and further self-interest. In keeping with this intensification of mood there is a noticeable injection of fresh dialogue in the second half of *Pauken und Trompeten*; this contrasts materially with the first six scenes where Farquhar is more closely adhered to. Appropriately, Brecht marked the break by inserting a first *Zwischenspiel vor dem Vorhang* between Scenes 6 and 7; a sombre second *Zwischenspiel* forms a prelude to the all-important climactic final scene.

In another respect Brecht reversed a structural procedure recurrent in his dramatic work: he not only did not provide a commentary in the shape of a prologue and epilogue for *Pauken und Trompeten* but even omitted those appended by Farquhar to his play. A closer look at them explains why. The Prologue to *The Recruiting Officer* is a tame affair in bad verse alluding to the classical enlisting of Achilles by Ulysses in the struggle against the Trojans, an episode Homer described as the 'listing of kings' for the sake of one Helen; Farquhar concludes with a pretty (and pretty artificial) compliment to the galaxy of Helens in the audience every night, who should inspire the Britons to write 'beyond compare'. One does not have to ponder why Brecht cut out this 'graziösen kleinen Prolog'.[5] The Epilogue is just as irrelevant, announcing as it does with laboured wit that there will be music (including the Grenadier March) to accompany the play; an epilogue in Farquhar's day was anyway likely to be a trivial matter, being habitually dropped after the third performance and frequently composed by a friend of the playwright. Brecht contented himself with transferring Sergeant Kite's opening speech to a Prologue before the curtain is raised (as he had done in *Der Hofmeister* where the private tutor introduced himself to the audience), though now he retains several lines from the original. The few he adds at once set up a different resonance from Farquhar's jokingly inoffensive opening:

Ich bin der Sergeant Barras Kite und werbe ein Heer
Für unsern guten König George, denn über dem Meer
In seiner Majestät Kolonie Amerika
Gibt's Umwälzung und Ungehorsam, das war noch nicht da.
Hätte also irgendwer Lust, sich zum Heeresdienst zu melden
Einige ehemalige Kriegsteilnehmer oder enttäuschte Helden
Freunde des Aufenthalts im Freien, unruhige Geister . . .
Als welchen ehrlichen Mann Sie hiermit oberflächlich kennengelernt haben.
Meine Herren, wer verteidigt gegen einen bunten Rock und reichliches Futter
Das gute alte England (ausgenommen seine Schwester, seinen Bruder,
     seinen Vater und seine Mutter)?[6]

The Prologue to *Pauken und Trompeten* is a warning of how rash it would be to base an assessment of the adaptation on a purely quantitative comparison: the mechanical counting of lines and speeches retained or jettisoned is a misleading guide — a programmatic suggestion such as is contained in Brecht's Prologue (or a divergent final scene) can by itself swing the adaptation completely away from the conceptual path of the original. Two factors are of overriding importance in estimating the relationship of *Pauken und Trompeten* to *The Recruiting Officer*, namely the intellectual impetus and the dramatic procedure providing in their fusion the dynamic and individuality of a play. The extent of their agreement in these two aspects determines how far the thought and manner of Farquhar and Brecht are consonant.

In his essay *A Discourse upon Comedy*, published several years before *The Recruiting Officer* in 1701, Farquhar furnished valuable insights into his own mode of creation while formulating his views as to the nature of comedy, the way in which the dramatist should set about handling his matter and to what end. His constant irritation at the stultifying strait-jacket of Aristotelian rules, in which 'the Criticks' try to imprison the playwright, does not diminish the value of the Discourse as a complement to the fragmentary observations on comedy in Aristotle's *Poetics*. Farquhar declares his empirical approach openly, saying that he intends to 'inquire into the first Invention of Comedy; what were the true Designs and honest Intentions of that Art; and from a Knowledge of the *End*, seek out the *Means*, without one Quotation of *Aristotle*, or Authority of *Euripides*'.[7] He proceeds to develop a formula for comedy, claiming 'that old Aesop must wear the Bays as the first and original Author':

Comedy is no more at present than a *well-fram'd Tale handsomely told, as an agreeable Vehicle for Counsel or Reproof*. This is all we can say for the Credit of its Institution, and is the Stress of its Charter for Liberty and Toleration. Then where shou'd we seek for a Foundation, but in *Aesop's* symbolical Way of moralizing upon Tales and Fables . . .

It will be noted that Farquhar's emphasis lies on comedy as a lively theatrical experience, and is close in spirit to Molière's 'corriger les vices des hommes en les divertissant' and even to Gottsched's more pedantic dictum later in *Versuch einer Critischen Dichtkunst*: 'Die Comödie ist nichts anders, als eine Nachahmung einer lasterhaften Handlung, die durch ihr lächerliches Wesen den Zuschauer belustigen, aber auch zugleich erbauen kann.' Yet the notorious dryness of Gottsched is worlds apart from the vivacity of Farquhar who ascribes the motto *utile dulci* to Aesop and sees in it the twin impulses that can generate a fit comedy in terms of his own age:

Then without all Dispute, whatever Means are most proper and expedient for compassing this End and Intention, they must be the *just Rules of Comedy*, and the *true Art of the Stage*.

Now, Sir, if our *Utile*, which is the End, be different from the Ancients, pray let our *Dulce*, which is the Means, be so too . . .

The burden of Farquhar's essay is that comedy must be judged by its ability to please, more particularly to please the audience as it sits before the stage:

To make the Moral instructive, you must make the Story diverting: The Splenatick Wit, the Beau Courtier, the heavy Citizen, the fine Lady, and her fine Footman, come all to be instructed, and therefore must all be diverted; and he that can do this best, and with most Applause, writes the best Comedy, let him do it by what Rules he pleases, so they be not offensive to Religion and good Manners.

But *hic labor, hoc opus*; how must this Secret of pleasing so many different Tastes be discover'd? Not by tumbling over Volumes of the Antients, but by studying the Humour of the Moderns: the Rules of *English* Comedy don't lie in the Compass of *Aristotle*, or his Followers, but in the Pit, Box, and Galleries.

This denotes a marked aesthetic attitude as well as a pragmatic concern to set up a productive relationship with the living spectator, and in its essentials it coincides with Brecht's awareness of the audience as a functional element in the dramatic process. It is no accident that the *Programmheft* accompanying the Berliner Ensemble production of *Pauken und Trompeten* quoted Farquhar's pronouncement that the rules of comedy lay 'in the pit, box and galleries'. It amplified this further by pointing out that in Restoration Comedy the characters do not only talk amongst themselves but also address the audience to explain their feelings, thoughts and decisions through word and gesture:

Das 'zahlende Publikum' hat Anspruch darauf, daß man es ins Vertrauen zieht und genauestens in die Geschichte einweiht. Es übernimmt die vergnügliche Rolle des Mitwissers, darf sich auch als Schiedsrichter fühlen in den Händeln, die auf der Bühne ausgetragen werden.

Other comments indicate that Brecht wished to hold the interest of the spectator by every resource of text and staging:

So sind die Verwandlungen schnell und elegant zu bewerkstelligen. Das braucht das Stück, es ist auf Spannung gebaut, und der Betrachter — ungeduldig, die Abenteuer der Liebenden und Werbenden weiter zu verfolgen — darf nicht durch zeitraubende und plumpe Umbauten auf die Folter der Langeweile gespannt werden.

There is thus enough evidence pointing to a sufficiently shared view of the *modus operandi* of comedy to explain why Brecht could accept the basic structure of *The Recruiting Officer*.

Real differences between the two playwrights occur in the content and purpose of their plays, in the *utile*. This may be a question of degree of seriousness, or temperament, or personality, or intensity of feeling, or ideological commitment. One does not have to look far for proof of divergent attitudes to their subject-matter. Few observers would apply to Brecht what was said of Farquhar: 'He lash'd the Vices of the Age, tho' with a merciful Hand; for his Muse was good-natur'd, not abounding overmuch with Gall, tho' he has been blam'd for it by the Criticks.'[8] Both Farquhar and Brecht were capable of biting satire, but Farquhar tempered his with a certain relaxed amiability. The circumstances that contributed to the making of *The Recruiting Officer* are well known: Farquhar was commissioned a Lieutenant of Grenadiers in 1704 and sent on recruiting duty to Lichfield and then to Shrewsbury in 1705.[9] *The Recruiting Officer* contains the precipitate of his experiences in the techniques of recruiting, but the essence of Farquhar's mood in writing the play is not to be found in any prologue or epilogue but in *The Epistle Dedicatory* that prefaced its first publication and was addressed 'To All Friends round the Wrekin'. The few paragraphs of this *Epistle* clearly state that the comedy was to be in the nature of a thank-offering for, as Farquhar said, 'the entertainment I found in Shropshire commands me to be grateful, and that's all I intend'. He describes his urbane treatment at the hands of the citizens of Shrewsbury in eulogistic terms that clash discordantly with what we find in *Pauken und Trompeten*:

'Twas my good fortune to be ordered some time ago into the place which is made the scene of this comedy ... The kingdom cannot show better bodies of men, better inclinations for the service, more generosity, more good understanding, nor more politeness than is to be found at the foot of the Wrekin.

The discrepancy in the spirit of the two plays is further emphasized by Farquhar's placatory remarks on his harmless and sympathetic depiction of characters who might be mistaken for local personages:

I have drawn the justice and the clown in their *puris naturalibus*: the one an apprehensive, sturdy, brave blockhead; and the other a worthy, honest, generous gentleman, hearty in his country's cause, and of as good an understanding as I could give him, which I must confess is far short of his own.[10]

This is a far cry from the polemical belligerence that permeates *Pauken und Trompeten* and is expressed in diametrically opposed terms in the *Programmheft* (which, as a 'declaration of intent', is in a sense the counterpart of *The Epistle Dedicatory*). Here the explanation is given for placing the action seventy years later; namely, to depict the pressing of men for a brutal colonial war (American War of Independence) rather than a political struggle of the absolutist era (War of the Spanish Succession):

Die Bearbeitung zeigt auch die Interessenten des Kriegs klarer, den ehrenwerten Richter Balance vor allem, aber auch die Smuggler, Prude, Worthy: Die Bourgeois führen das Vaterland im Mund und ihren Reichtum in der Tasche und benutzen, Arm in Arm mit der feudalen Klasse, das Heer für ihre selbstischen Interessen.

So wurden die kritischen Einblicke Farquhars in die Mechanik des Militarismus verschärft, sie treffen nicht allein die britische Rekrutierungsmühle Anno 1705, sondern alle Versuche, Söldner in Raub- und Kolonialarmeen zu pressen . . .

In einem Prolog, der der Komödie vorangestellt wurde, erläutert der Werber Kite, was hier gespielt wird.

Farquhar deals with the reality (of recruiting) which Brecht abstracts to an idea around which he builds his adaptation; that is, the theme of recruiting is no longer of contemporary relevance and becomes instead a springboard for the deployment of ideas about war familiar to us from *Mutter Courage*. Farquhar's Captain Plume, like Farquhar himself, shows evidence of being attached to the glory of war (what idealists claim is worth dying for) and attracted by gaudy appearances (a red coat and uniform). In modern terms the meretricious glamour of a military career is integral to any recruiting poster (good pay and prospects, see the world, every girl loves a uniform, it's a good life in the Army), and so, though the *method* of recruiting in Farquhar's day is no longer topical, the spirit behind it is still prevalent, and this allows Brecht plenty of scope for exposing such cant and malpractices. In shifting the action to the American War of Independence he also made a careful adjustment to strengthen his attack on recruitment. Brecht did not believe any abstract glory worth dying for, only that one's own freedom as a human being justifies fighting; from this derives the significance of the War of Independence (which was a 'good' war of liberation), while the War of the Spanish Succession was in one sense a struggle of capitalists with capitalists. This change allowed Brecht to attack a war of aggrandizement and debunk its methods of attracting men to the soldiery.

Farquhar, unlike Brecht, certainly had no desire to lash the vices of his age in *The Recruiting Officer*, and it is in this ideological perspective that the two authors differ most. As far as the sugar on the pill was concerned, Brecht was determined to sacrifice nothing of Farquhar's lightness of touch: 'Freilich wurde sorgfältig darauf geachtet, weder die leichte Schreibweise Farquhars, noch die abenteuerliche Lustigkeit der Liebesintrigen darüber zu verlieren' (*Programmheft*). So in his adaptation he set out to marry bitter censure to suave, well-proportioned elegance, and the tension of *Pauken und Trompeten* emerges most sharply in visual presentation on the stage, in the clash between brutal motives and civilized exterior.

In embarking on the adaptation of *The Recruiting Officer* with such a clearcut critical aim in view, Brecht's handling of it had of necessity to effect two operations simultaneously: he had to reduce his source material drastically in order to make way for additions that would bring about a new figuration of the play around the hub of fresh notions he was building into it. The two procedures were, of course, inevitably reciprocal; what Brecht left out of his adaptation is only the complementary aspect of what he added. Several themes that accord with the tone of the accommodating *Epistle Dedicatory* are radically curtailed or modulated. Short work is made of the soldiers' optimism in their recruiting (which they hold despite Plume's constant lament about 'the fatigue of recruiting') and the relative ease with which they enlist the men they want (a success that does not tally logically at all with the forcible pressing of men by the magistrate in the last act). Brecht extracts the friendliness from Sergeant Kite's gentle persuasion, his 'purse of gold' and 'tub of humming ale' (I, 1), and does not allow him the pleasure of tricking the doltish smith and butcher into enlisting (IV, 3). Farquhar's Captain Plume had made his first entry to buoyant drum-beating ('By the Grenadier March that should be my drum and by that shout it should beat with success') and his confidence received confirmation from Kite's report on his activities:

PLUME: . . . But how stands the country affected? Were the people pleased with the news of my coming to town?
KITE: Sir, the mob are so pleased with your honor and the justices and better sort of people are so delighted with me that we shall soon do our business. (I, 1)

The temper of this becomes sombre in the adaptation:

PLUME *geht herum*: Shrewsbury! *Seufzt.* Wie steht es mit der Werbung? Wie empfing Shrewsbury dieses Jahr seine militärischen Freier? *Kite macht eine wegwerfende Handbewegung.*
PLUME: Keine Erfolge?
KITE: Spärlich, Captain. Ich habe diese Leute pflichtgemäß gefragt, ob ihnen nicht das Blut kocht, wenn diese amerikanischen Dreckfarmer und Pelzjäger dem guten

König George nicht mehr die Steuern zahlen wollen.
PLUME: Und?
KITE: Die Antworten waren sehr häßlich.[11]

The change from Kite's cheerful 'I have been here but a week and I have recruited five' to 'Ich bin jetzt eine Woche hier und rekrutiert habe ich ganze fünf Stück' is indicative of the uphill struggle the recruiters are faced with in *Pauken und Trompeten*. In the same vein Brecht whittled down the more gentlemanly, humane characteristics of both Plume and Justice Balance. He omitted Plume's defence of the stratagem of recruiting that got at the men by kissing their girls: 'Some people may call this artifice, but I term it stratagem, since it is so main a part of the service. Besides, the fatigue of recruiting is so intolerable that unless we could make ourselves some pleasure amidst the pain, no mortal would be able to bear it' (IV, 1). He also ignored Plume's defence of his own probity to the disguised Silvia: 'No, faith, I am not that rake that the world imagines. I have got an air of freedom which people mistake for lewdness in me as they mistake formality in others for religion. The world is all a cheat, only I take mine which is undesigned to be more excusable than theirs, which is hypocritical. I hurt nobody but myself, but they abuse all mankind' (IV, 1). Further, all his improbably idealistic opinions of women, and Silvia in particular, are rejected as incompatible with his purposeful ambitiousness: 'If your town has a dishonourable thought of Silvia, it deserves to be burned to the ground. I love Silvia, I admire her frank, generous disposition. There's something in that girl more than woman. Her sex is but a foil to her . . . Show me another woman that would lose an inch of her prerogative that way, without tears, fits, and reproaches . . .' (I, 1); '. . . and I haven't the vanity to believe I shall even gain a lady worth twelve hundred' (III, 1); 'No, she's above my hopes, but for her sake, I'll recant my opinion of her sex' (IV, 2). Similarly, there is no trace in *Pauken und Trompeten* of Plume's original solicitude for Balance: 'Ill news! Heavens avert it; nothing could touch me nearer than to see that generous, worthy gentleman afflicted. I'll leave you to comfort him, and be assured that if my life and fortune can be any way serviceable to the father of my Silvia, she shall freely command both' (II, 1).

Balance, too, had cherished at least amicable, if not paternal, feelings for Plume — 'I love him so well it would break the heart of me to think him a rascal' (II, 2) — although he wished to save his daughter from seduction, and he looked with tolerant eye on the sexual incursions of the military; 'Look'e, Mr. Scale, for my own part I shall be very tender in what regards the officers of the army. They expose their lives to so many dangers for us abroad that we may give them some grains of allowance at home . . . Consider, Mr. Scale, that were it not for the bravery of these officers we should have French dragoons among us that would leave us neither liberty, property, wife, nor daughter. Come, Mr. Scale, the gentlemen are vigorous and warm, and may they continue so. The same heat that stirs them up to love spurs them on to battle. You never knew a great general in your life that did not

love a whore' (v, 2). It is a different state of affairs in *Pauken und Trompeten*:
now Balance matches Plume's opportunism with a distrustful wariness alive
to all the dangers of the recruiters. He no longer asks his daughter to leave
town for his sake, but simply orders her away after subjecting her to a harsh
interrogation in order to extort a confession of her relationship with Plume.
When she remonstrates that he had had nothing but praise for the Captain,
he retorts: 'Aber als Werbeoffizier. Als Werber von Soldaten und nicht
meiner Tochter.'[12]

Parallel with major modifications in the function of Plume, Balance,
and the recruiting theme, Brecht also pared down the subsidiary plot revolving
around Melinda and her triangular relationship with Worthy and Captain
Brazen. There is a consequent simplification in the intricacies of a superficial
intrigue: the tacking operations engineered by Melinda (her divulging letter
to Balance, the counterfeit letter and signature to Brazen, the visit to the
fortune-teller — Kite in disguise — by Melinda and Lucy also disguised, the
subsequent appearance of Lucy pretending to be her mistress that almost
precipitates a duel between Worthy and Brazen), all these contrivances go by
the board. So does most of the dialogue in which Plume and Worthy periodic-
ally commiserate with each other on the unsatisfactory course of their love-
affairs. The most significant result of the reduction in Melinda's participation
in the play is that Lucy, her maid, is released from the role of *confidante* that
had enabled Farquhar to keep the spectator abreast of events as they occurred.
Brecht sacrificed much indisputably witty dialogue between mistress and maid
in order to make each of them a more accurate representative of her station in
life. The tone of their relationship in *The Recruiting Officer* was dissociated
from reality to the extent that they met on a common neutral ground of
dialogue whose only purpose was to favour the hatching of plans; Lucy was
'the typical kittenish lady's maid', used as an object by Melinda: 'Women
must discharge their vapours somewhere, and before we get husbands, our
servants must expect to bear with 'em' (IV, 1). By not involving her so heavily
in the love intrigue and especially by making her the fiancée of the unsub-
missive barman Mike, Brecht turned Lucy into a spirited antithesis to Melinda,
a foil whose off-hand compliance in the latter's antics is at the same time
ironical mockery of them.[13]

In trimming away so much material from *The Recruiting Officer* it was
inevitable that Brecht would have to surrender some sparkling repartee
along with more long-winded stretches of dialogue. In fact, frothy wit gratui-
tously generated (usually between flirting or skirmishing couples) is often
taken to be a determining characteristic of Restoration Comedy until it gave
way to eighteenth-century sentimental drama, and it can be argued that
Brecht's transposition of Farquhar's play into German miscarries because he
dispensed with this formal feature. On the other hand, he retained a sufficient
amount of the vivacious dialogue (quite apart from what he added new) to
ensure that Farquhar's deftness was not lost. In other ways, too, he consciously tried to preserve the particular spirit of this comedy; the message of

advice addressed by Brecht eleven days before his death to the members of the Berliner Ensemble, boldly about to take their production of *Pauken und Trompeten* to London, demonstrates his full awareness of the aesthetic need to perform the play at a brisk, elegant pace:

[Es] besteht in England eine alte Befürchtung, die deutsche Kunst (Literatur, Malerei, Musik) sei schrecklich gewichtig, langsam, umständlich und 'fußgängerisch'.

Wir müssen also schnell, leicht und kräftig spielen. Es handelt sich nicht um hetzen, sondern um eilen, nicht nur um schnell spielen, sondern mehr um schnell denken. Wir müssen das Tempo der Durchsprechproben haben, aber dazu leise Kraft, eigenen Spaß fügen. Die Repliken sollten nicht zögernd angeboten werden, wie man jemandem die eigenen letzten Schuhe anbietet, sondern sie müssen wie Bälle zugeworfen werden.[14]

Nevertheless, it is undeniably evident that Brecht's main effort was directed — as always — to penetrating and crystallizing the essentials of the society that motivated the workings of the characters in the play. Actions interested him, and conversations only as an expression of them. For this reason, Brecht kept firmly in mind the dominant social characteristics in Restoration drama that were inherited by Farquhar, in particular the hard, ruthless disregard for other individuals when it was a matter of self-interest; he clung firmly to the convention of having the characters jockeying for the most favourable position *vis-à-vis* lover, prospective wife or husband. This convention itself derived from the normal practice (among the ruling classes) of basing marriage on money; a man would most often seek a woman with an income, so that he would be left his freedom — after ensuring his security.[15] Brecht exploited the theme of the callousness and indifference of this society to the full by exposing with less charity than Farquhar the lawless jungle warfare going on beneath the civilized surface. It is all the more surprising, therefore, that he omitted some elements in *The Recruiting Officer* that tallied perfectly with his own less lenient attitudes. Brecht leaves out, for instance, the revealing first encounter between Plume and Silvia when the girl counters the Captain's fiery protestations of love with the cold douche of materialism — which he, however, is ready for:

SILVIA: Well, well, you shall die at my feet, or where you will, but first let me desire you to make your will; perhaps you'll leave me something.
PLUME: My will, madam, is made already, and there it is. (II, 1)

There are also several comments of ironical value on matters concerning the military that Brecht might well have turned to account. One is Balance's jingoistic blood-and-thunder patriotism:

Look'e, Captain, give us but blood for our money and you shan't want men. I remember that for some years of the last war we had no blood nor wounds but in the officers' mouths, nothing for our millions but newspapers not worth a reading. Our armies did nothing but play at prison bars, and hide and seek with the enemy, but now ye have brought us colors and standards and prisoners. Odmylife, Captain, get us but another Marshal of France and I'll go myself for a soldier. (II, 1) or his later remark on Plume's methods of pressing men: 'We must get this mad captain his complement of men and send him a-packing, else he'll over-run the country' (III, 1). Again, Brecht ignores Melinda's opinion on a different kind of pressing: 'The devil take all officers, I say; they do the nation more harm by debauching us at home than they do good by defending us abroad' (III, 2). Considering also the intensified part played by the military in *Pauken und Trompeten* it is surprising that Brecht let slip the disguised Silvia's enlightening outburst on the sons of the well-to-do: 'Me for a soldier! Send your own lazy, lubberly sons at home, fellows that hazard their necks every day in pursuit of a fox, yet dare not peep abroad to look an enemy in the face' (V, 5). Her caustic sketch of an officer that precedes this also disappears:

SILVIA: I'm called Captain, sir, by all the coffeemen, drawers, whores, and groom porters in London, for I wear a red coat, a sword *bien troussée*, a martial twist in my cravat, a fierce knot in my periwig, a cane upon my button, piquet in my head, and dice in my pocket.

SCALE: Your name, pray, sir.

SILVIA: Captain Pinch. I cock my hat with a pinch; I take snuff with a pinch, pay my whores with a pinch. In short, I can do anything at a pinch but fight and fill my belly.

BALANCE: And pray, sir, what brought you into Shropshire?

SILVIA: A pinch, sir. I knew that you country gentlemen want wit, and you know that we town gentlemen want money, and so —. (V, 2)

It would thus be mistaken to conclude that the great reductions effected by Brecht in his source material implied that Farquhar's play consisted of little other than the clockwork motions of vapid characters as they performed their minuet-like intricacies of flirtation. In fact, in developing his pragmatic interpretation of *The Recruiting Officer*, Brecht builds on the firm foundations of Farquhar's accurate social observation. The young Irish dramatist in Shrewsbury not only had a sharp ear for differences of accent and expression[16] but also incorporated in his comedy all the tacit assumptions that were vital determining factors in that society. It is extremely unlikely that a nostalgic whiff of the drawing-room was what persuaded a group of convicts to act *The Recruiting Officer* at Sydney in 1789 — the first play ever seen in Australia. *The Mutiny and Impressment Acts* of Queen Anne's reign and their topicality in Farquhar's play are only one dramatically striking element of the many that lie latent under the deceptively humorous and amiable dialogue. The arranging of a marriage as a sober transaction in commodities underlies the frivolous encounters between Silvia and Melinda and the men they are out to net. Trading (and property) was in fact the motive force operative in all the ramifications of society: 'The country gentlemen ruled Eighteenth Century England, but they ruled it largely in the interest of commerce and empire.'[17] The majority of Acts passed in Queen Anne's time reveal quite clearly the dominant concern with maintaining and expanding economic prosperity by imposing tariffs to protect English commerce — especially the cloth trade. Entry into the exhausting War of the Spanish Succession and the acquisition of the American Colonies were also primarily business enterprises undertaken for profit.[18] The booming expansion of trade signalled by these ventures required powerful military support, and the evil practices concomitant with the raising of large armies from a recalcitrant population were brought to the surface in *The Recruiting Officer*, although Farquhar no doubt subdued his satire in order to get his play staged at all (he had to submit it to his commanding officers for approval).

If all these social, economic and political premisses can be postulated for *The Recruiting Officer*, then the major encroachment immediately evident in the adaptation — the shift forward seventy years to the War of American Independence — does no intrinsic damage to Farquhar's play, and serves instead as a clear-cut focal point around which Brecht undertakes a re-alignment. He showed no hesitation in exercising his discretion as adaptor to intensify the tendentious hints and sharpen the social contrasts in Farquhar's comedy. The American Revolution was a happy choice for a change of era as it remained sufficiently close to Farquhar's time not to impair the validity of the basic assumptions on which *The Recruiting Officer* rested, yet at the same time it introduced into the fabric of the play a cluster of events that heralded the sweeping transformations in political thought and reality that were to be set in motion or accelerated a few years later with the French Revolution. In this way Brecht was able at one stroke to preserve in *Pauken und Trompeten* the explicit social structure of *The Recruiting Officer* (England ruled by a stable squirearchy, the mores of the middle-class, the waging of war overseas as aggrandizement and not in self-defence) and to call these *données* in question from the secure vantage-point afforded by hindsight.

It is possible from one point of view to condemn Brecht's relentless re-structuring of source plays in the light of a historical perspective that comes later and indeed to fault the logic and accuracy of this procedure. The Communist Manifesto could not have been written in 1748, and in 1948 it would have appeared as a whimsical throwback; analogously, when Brecht introduces into a play the dimension of ideological scrutiny appropriate to modern political analysis, he is committing an anachronistic intrusion, more so in the case of *The Recruiting Officer* than, say, in *Der Biberpelz*. Yet he never inserted his ideas into the original surreptitiously, never tried to hide the fact that his versions were simultaneously artistic constructs *and* historical assessments, and always handled the adaptations openly as revisions in the light of intervening events. *Pauken und Trompeten* gives *The Recruiting Officer* a fresh significance, while the latter adds depth to Brecht's play.

This is the justification, if one were needed, for the shift of time to the American Revolution. The year 1776 was a seminal date for modern developments and a bridge to later ideologies — the year of Jeremy Bentham's *Fragment on Government*, Adam Smith's *Wealth of Nations*, Gibbon's *History*, and of course the Declaration of Independence. It was thus a date that allowed

Brecht to implant the modern premisses of his thought smoothly and pain-lessly in his 'revision' of *The Recruiting Officer*. It has to be remembered that the idealistic conception of the American War of Independence throughout *Pauken und Trompeten* is a deliberate reduction of the complex issues in the Colonies. Numerous historians of different convictions and at different times have seen the events of 1760–76 from widely divergent viewpoints. Of greatest currency is the opinion that the revolt pivoted on the twin questions of home rule and who should rule at home. Brecht's simplification takes the form of ignoring that the structure of the Colonies closely followed the pattern of eighteenth-century England, and that the Colonists themselves were composed of very diverse elements — wealthy merchants in the seaports, modest and often struggling farmers and planters, labouring groups (a nascent prole-tariat) in the centres of population. These all shared a common belief in the interlocking values of property and liberty, for property had grown to be, in their circumstances, the guarantee of security and therefore of liberty. It emerges that Brecht chooses to crystallize the intricate facts around the resounding abstractions of the Declaration of Independence; in so doing, he projects a modern chiliastic interpretation on to the situation in 1776, coloured to a great extent by the sanguine mass immigrations from Europe through the nineteenth century that were themselves initiated and assimilated by capitalism and acquiesced in the prime liberty of capitalism — that of self-assertion and self-betterment, regardless of others.

Brecht transferred the operations of Captain Plume and his sergeant from the relative nebulousness of Queen Anne's reign to a direct confronta-tion with burgeoning democratic attitudes under George III (he seems to have one or two details wrong: for instance, this king could scarcely have been in the words of the recruits' song 'gebeugt und alt' in 1776 when he was only thirty-eight years of age. Probably 'das große Schiff der Königin' in the song in Scene 8 is also imprecise, while the Boston Tea-Party which appears to have just come to the notice of Balance in Scene 12 happened in 1773, three years before the events of *Pauken und Trompeten*). To highlight the official purpose of this recruiting, Brecht exploits the pyrrhic victory of the British at Bunker Hill in 1775, the Declaration of Independence by the insurgent colonists and their siege and capture of Boston in 1776. Against the rising tide of independence the glory of being a soldier is dulled into dangerous and profitless reality; no longer does an inveigling Plume hold out hopes of booty to woo the yokels: 'What think you now of a purse full of French gold out of a monsieur's pocket, after you have dashed out his brains with your firelock, eh?' (II, 3). This glitter is replaced by prospects of promotion ('Schaut mich an: eine kleine Weile trug ich die Muskete, und heute führe ich eine Kom-panie!') that are ferociously quashed by Kite as soon as the men have risen to the bait:

KITE: . . . Wer will meinen Sergeantenspieß haben?
BEIDE REKRUTEN: Ich.
KITE: Hier. — In die Gedärme! — Marsch! Ihr Hurensöhne! *Jagt sie ins Quartier*.[19]

From the moment Kite steps in front of the curtain to add some cynical lines in the *Prologue* and his initial report to Plume on the hostility of the population, the play is skilfully deflected from the deft path of comedy that Farquhar had trodden, and a heavy oppressiveness hangs over the nefarious activities of 'Ihro Majestät Menschenfänger'. Brecht could alter the overall tone of the play far more effectively and rapidly by adding scenes and snatches of dialogue than by omissions. The apathy of the body of townsfolk and their virtual ostracism of the recruiters serves to illustrate the exclusion of the latter from the spoils of empire. In Scene 5 Plume and Kite sit listlessly in the market-place recruiting-booth as an unemployed man passing by curtly rejects their advances. They are roused from their despondence by the arrival of Rose and her brother Bullock, and while Kite entices the peasant into enlistment with the help of pornographic pictures, Plume makes off with the sister in an effort to lure her six village swains through her. On their next appearance in the recruiting-booth (Scene 7) the situation has not changed, and Kite explains why: rumours of the heavy English losses at Bunker Hill have filtered through even to Shrewsbury.

They not only lack recruits but money as well; Plume has doubts about organizing a Sunday concert ('Mit nichts in der Kasse!') and even has to refuse Brazen the loan of a few shillings, while Kite reports: 'Wir haben keine Kompanie. Da sind noch die 10 Pfund des Fähnrichs für den Sonntag, aber wir haben keine Idee.'[20] It is small wonder, then, that when on the banks of the Severn the barman Mike exposes Kite in his disguise as a parson, the sergeant gives vent to his mortification in a snarling assertion of discipline over the enlisted Appletree, the only person present who must obey him: 'Fahnenflüchtige werden standrechtlich erschossen';[21] or that he follows this up with a shattering of the Sunday afternoon idyll as he savagely rounds up his recruits:

Kite treibt alle Soldaten aus dem Wäldchen. Die Mädchen wollen ihre Freunde zurückhalten und rufen sie flehentlich bei ihren Namen.
KITE: Inspektion aus London! Alles, was den Rock des Königs trägt, in die Stadt zurück! Marsch, ihr Hundesöhne! *Zu den Mädchen*: Zivil kann zurückbleiben. *Zu Sally, die sich schluchzend an Appletree klammert*: Laß das Flennen![22]

The critical point is reached in Scene 9 when Plume admits to Balance and Worthy that his recruiting efforts have been brought to a standstill: 'Der Herr Armeeinspekteur aus London hat in meinem Quartier ganze elf Rekruten vorgefunden.'[23] Gloom hangs over the conversation until, in view of the latest news that Boston is in the hands of the rebels, the Justice of the Peace decides to break the stalemate by reviving the coercive recruitment laws of Anne's reign (laws necessitated by the War of the Spanish Succession and designed 'to raise and levy such able-bodied men as have not any lawful calling or employment, or visible means for their maintenance and livelihood, to serve as soldiers'.) With high-sounding phrases and iron intransigence Balance brushes aside all objections:

BALANCE: ... Ich hielt es bis heute nicht für notwendig, die Zwangsrekrutierungs-gesetze anzuwenden. Es ist notwendig, ich sehe es ein. *Er holt das Gesetzbuch aus dem Bücherschrank.* Rekrutierungsgesetz 1704.
WORTHY: Aber jetzt haben wir 1776. Die Anwendung dieser Gesetze hat in Welsh-pool einen Skandal hervorgerufen.
BALANCE: Aber sie hat auch zwei Kompanien kampffähiger Männer aus den Gefängnissen hervorgerufen. Sollen in unseren Gefängnissen schlechte Elemente fett werden oder das Straßenbild verschandeln? Ins Feld mit ihnen! Man könnte sogar sagen, es ist in einer Weise unmenschlich, diese Leute in Gefängnissen oder arbeits-los auf der Straße vegetieren zu lassen, wenn sie in der Neuen Welt als Helden für Englands Freiheit sterben können. Unsere vaterländische Pflicht ist es in jeder Hinsicht, auch ihnen ihre Chance zu geben. Captain Plume, begleiten Sie mich ins Gefängnis.[24]

This is the turning-point at which passive guile is transformed into active duress as the civilian Balance resolutely takes over the recruiting campagin: 'Worthy, wir sind seit Jahren in Shrewsbury zu milde gewesen. Das Gefängnis ist leer. Ein Kinderschänder, das ist alles; ein Tropfen auf den heißen Stein.' The scene ends with Balance's assurance to Lady Prude that he will clean up the dissoluteness in the town:

PRUDE: ... Diese Stadt wimmelt ja von Elementen jeden Alters, die ungestraft sündigen, Trunkenbolden, Taschendieben und Arbeitslosen. Werden die Behörden denn niemals ...
BALANCE *der aufmerksam geworden ist, hebt die Hand*: Mylady! Die Behörden *werden*, Sie haben recht, vollkommen recht. Wir werden dem Gesindel zeigen, wie man sich patriotisch aufführt. Wir werden der Moral freien Lauf lassen, und wenn das Gefängnis von Shrewsbury platzt!
PRUDE: Sie denken an eine Säuberung ...?
BALANCE: Im größten Stil, Lady Prude.[25]

The invention of a fresh character in Lady Prude enabled Brecht to transfer to her the concern for 'justice' and morality that should properly have been the charge of Balance. In *Pauken und Trompeten* it is she (not the magistrate) who takes up Bullock's complaint that Plume has 'pressed' his sister Rose. In this fashion Balance is stripped of the humane behaviour that Farquhar had attributed to him and sacrifices the country girl Rose to the sexual appetite of the soldiers in the tooth-and-nail fight to protect his own interests:

PRUDE: Mr Balance, Sie sind der Friedensrichter dieser Stadt, aber was ist geworden aus dem Frieden dieser Stadt?
BALANCE: Sprechen Sie etwa von dem Offizier, den in seinen Mauern zu beherbergen Shrewsbury die Ehre hat?
PRUDE: Zum Teufel mit ihm!
BALANCE *groß*: Lady Prude, Sie können die Töchter dieses Landes nicht hindern, seinen Soldaten den schuldigen Respekt zu erweisen!
PRUDE *trocken*: Ich wollte, Sie dächten, wenn Sie so etwas äußern, an die eigene Tochter, Mr Balance.
BALANCE *ebenso*: Lady Prude, ich habe an sie gedacht.[26]

Deprived of all scruples, the magistrate becomes a very different character from his prototype in *The Recruiting Officer*. He is given a toughness and dramatic impact that emerges in the contradictory twists of his actions noted down by Brecht: 'Balance weigerte sich zunächst, Militär moralisch zu machen. Jetzt macht er aus Unmoralischen Militär.' On this basis Balance can stoutly defend the 'morals' of the soldiers to the outraged Lady Prude immediately before he comforts her with the deceptive promise to fill the prisons.

The vicious quality introduced by Balance with his determination to implement the Impressment Acts floods through the remaining three scenes; these are permeated by febrile and widespread arrests (in *Pauken und Trompeten* Plume, Wilful and the merchant Smuggler[27] are all hustled off to prison) followed by the more discriminating condemnation to military service of the poorer people. The constable Bridewell wields his power and lines his pocket:

Durch die Gittertür sieht man, wie hinten Verhaftete vorbeigetrieben werden.
BRIDEWELL *draußen*: Elf Shilling, und du kannst laufen!
TASCHENDIEB *draußen*: Elf Shilling? Das ist Halsabschneiderei.
BRIDEWELL *draußen*: Rin!
BERGMANN *draußen*: Ich habe mindestens 15 Shilling zu Hause; schickt zu meiner Frau.
BRIDEWELL *draußen*: Rin! . . .
ARBEITSLOSER *draußen*: Ihr könnt mich doch nicht ins Gefängnis stecken, nur, weil ich keine Arbeit finde.
ANDERER GEFANGENER *draußen*: Die Mühlen sind geschlossen!
BRIDEWELL *draußen*: Aber die Kasernen sind offen. Rin!
ARBEITSLOSER *draußen*: Das ist eine Schande!
BRIDEWELL *draußen*: Halt! Wer hat das gesagt? Du hast die Polizei beleidigt, du kommst zu den Dragonern.[28]

But even Bridewell succumbs to the wholesale impressment conducted by Balance from the magistrate's bench in the final scene. Farquhar had adumbrated the reason for the flow of prisoners drying up (because Bridewell had let those go who could pay him eleven shillings) and Brecht seizes on this to drive his point ruthlessly home:

BALANCE *zu Bridewell*: Du bist entlassen, unwürdiger Mensch. Nein, du bist nicht entlassen, vielmehr du wirst Mr Kite überhändigt. Abmessen.
BRIDEWELL *greift in die Tasche*: Einen Augenblick, Mr Balance. Dann beabsichtige ich, mich loszukaufen. Ich würde es mich 2 Pfund kosten lassen.
BALANCE: 2 Pfund? Alles.
BRIDEWELL: Alles?
BALANCE: Alles auf den Tisch — Alles! Auch was du von dem Fähnrich bekommen hast. *Bridewell zahlt.* Fertig. Abmessen.
BRIDEWELL: Aber ich *hab* doch bezahlt!
Pearmain holt ihn unter die Meßlatte.[29]

Throughout this last scene Balance maintains a grinding momentum that crushes the crafty with the innocent in an atmosphere of betrayal recalling the anarchic struggle for survival in an asocial world that dominated Brecht's plays in the 1920s. Both the miner and the unemployed man are pressed (as they had been in *The Recruiting Officer* (v, 5)) and Brecht toyed with a fragmentary incident in which the same happens to a group of five men who have no ready cash about them.[30] Though this was not used in the final version, Brecht did insert a characteristic episode in which the pimp, the pickpocket and the whore prove there is no honour among thieves. After the pimp has given evidence against the pickpocket (who is led off to war for his theft) he in turn is convicted and punished in like manner when the girl he lives on gives him away. The paroxysm of hysteria that grips Balance in this scene is reflected structurally in his frenzied shuttling back and forth between library and courtroom; even the youthful Mike is pressed on impulse (at least temporarily) as he brings in the beer called for by the magistrate:

BALANCE: Sage mal, Mike, wieso bist du nicht bei der Armee?
MIKE: Ich kann nicht, Euer Gnaden, ich bin noch nicht achtzehn.
BALANCE: Hast weder Vater noch Mutter gekannt, bist in der Waisenanstalt groß geworden, und du willst dein Alter wissen? Dein Alter bestimme ich, Lümmel, so lauten die Gesetze. Achtzehneinhalb, abmessen.
Mike wird gemessen und abgeführt.
BALANCE: Waisen sind mir anvertraut. Bridewell, der nächste![31]

The treatment of the axial theme of recruiting undergoes a distinct qualitative change in *Pauken und Trompeten*. Whereas Farquhar (no doubt as a result of his own toilsome experiences in Lichfield and Shrewsbury) only perfunctorily allows the questionable recruiting methods of his day to come through to the surface and his indulgence verges on acquiescence (he could not jolt his elegant London audiences too rudely), Brecht exploits his material to the point of caricature (black or white characters) in his denunciation of the methods and ends of that form of society. The Justice of the Peace in *Pauken und Trompeten* is a far cry from the somewhat traditional paternal figure in *The Recruiting Officer* who will see to it that all comes right in the end — 'a worthy, honest, generous gentleman, hearty in his country's cause'. The new Balance is a wily campaigner, certainly hearty in his country's cause — as long as the national interest coincides with his own: 'Patriotismus und Egoismus decken sich in der herrschenden Klasse',[32] and under pressure patriotic sentiments are the first to yield. All benevolence is drained out of Balance, and from his very first appearance in Scene 2, where he callously subordinates his daughter's feelings to his own intentions, he evinces a two-faced cunning that makes him a match for anyone and the prime protagonist of 'die Interessenten des Krieges'. Immediately after crushing Victoria's romantic hopes, he advances to welcome Plume 'mit ausgebreiteten Armen'; the equivalent scene in *The Recruiting Officer* (ii, 1) with Balance's sentimental patriotism and Plume's tidy description of the defeat of the French at Hochstadt as 'a very pretty battle as one should desire to see' is replaced by Plume's evasions regarding the military 'Situation drüben', Balance's violent indignation at the Declaration of Independence manifesto, and his promise of support on behalf of the town.

Balance is the king-pin in Brecht's adaptation and sufficiently justifies the discarding of the original title. All the dramatic strands of the play emanate from or touch him at some point or return to him as the final instance of their resolution. His handling of Captain Brazen (who has given up his uniform for the sake of the rich Melinda and is only an embarrassment to her intention of marrying Worthy) exemplifies the tenacious control he has of his own class:

MELINDA: Sie *müssen* ihn nach Amerika schicken, Onkel.
BALANCE: Keine Sorge . . . Lucy, geh und such Captain Brazen auf. Sag ihm, du kämst im Auftrag deiner Herrin, die zu Hause in Tränen ersticke. Ihr ganzes Vermögen sei in einer Ladung Tee investiert gewesen, und die Rebellen hätten sie freventlich in den Hafen von Boston geschüttet . . .
BALANCE: Dieses Unglück mache es Miss Moorhill völlig unmöglich, von ihm zu verlangen, daß er ihretwegen seine glorreiche militärische Laufbahn aufgäbe. Sollte er daraufhin irgendwelche Zeichen von Edelmut, Opfersinn und echter Hingabe zeigen, was ich nicht annehme, dann bittest du ihn sofort noch um zwei Pfund für euren Haushalt, das müßte ihn zur Besinnung bringen.[33]

To his consternation, Brazen does arrive and Balance, thinking at first that he has lost his firm grip on the workings of his own kind, apologizes to Melinda: 'Meine Liebe, ich bin untröstlich, ich habe mich geirrt.' But his acumen was sound, only the facts were misleading: Lucy had not managed to intercept the impatient lover, and as Brazen releases Melinda from her promise on hearing the news, Balance can complacently say 'Ich verstehe die Welt wieder' — an ironical parody of Meister Anton's final line in *Maria Magdalene*. Hard on the heels of Melinda's dilemma Balance is brought face to face with his own daughter in the shape of Wilful. In keeping with his uncompromisingly realistic conception of the magistrate, Brecht drops entirely the pretence that Balance does not recognize his own daughter. The piquancy of Farquhar's dialogue gives way to straight-forward unpleasant interrogation by the father who asks his daughter if she is out of her mind to adopt such a ridiculous disguise. Victoria lies to him that she is pregnant so Balance acts quickly: he calls in Plume, sends for Brazen, and in between bouts of administering 'justice' in the courtroom, carries on a running argument with the former over the financial terms of marriage with Victoria, for Plume is out to drive as advantageous a bargain as he can:

BALANCE: . . . Es muß sofort geheiratet werden, sofort! . . . Sie quittieren sofort den Dienst, Plume.
PLUME: Das ist lächerlich.
BALANCE: Was ist lächerlich?
PLUME: Sir, mein Beruf!
BALANCE: Ihr Beruf! Und mein Ruf?
PLUME: Und meine Pflicht gegenüber England?

BALANCE: Und Ihre Pflicht gegenüber meiner Tochter?... Sie haben gesetzwidrig eine Frauensperson in die Armee gepreßt mit dem Vorsatz, sie nach Amerika zu verschleppen. Ich gebe Ihnen fünf Minuten Bedenkzeit. Entweder meine väterliche Fürsorge: meine Tochter und 1200 Pfund im Jahr — oder sagen wir 1000 Pfund — oder mein richterlicher Zorn: bei Wasser und Brot in einem Kerkerloch, Sir. *Zu Victoria*: Zieh den bunten Fetzen aus![34]

Balance insists on a quick decision, while Plume plays for time which he knows to be on his side and unsuccessfully tries to wring a much larger annual allowance from his prospective father-in-law. Finally, after a last attempt, Plume settles for Balance's offer, exchanges his uniform for Brazen's civilian clothes and also presents the latter with his recruits (which vindicates Balance's perspicacity in summoning Brazen). Plume marks his satisfaction with the terms of the bargain by a speech of high-sounding hypocritical phrases that is punctuated by Brazen's background voice reading out the Articles of War in the Court-room:

PLUME *in der Bibliothek*: Sir, wenn eine Sadt belagert wird von einem Regiment, mag sie sich verteidigen... Einem ganzen Heer übergibt sie die Schlüssel... Vor Wunden auf dem Schlachtfeld sicher, sehe ich gefaßt der Gicht entgegen... Ihrer Liebe, Victoria, opfere ich meinen Ehrgeiz... Ruhmreicher, von Ihren Reizen besiegt zu werden, als ganz Amerika zu unterwerfen.[35]

The ironical capitulation to Victoria is only the logical final stroke in keeping with the new configuration of Plume's character in *Pauken und Trompeten*. Gone is the gay, easy, zestful officer of Farquhar's comedy who is assured of a pleasant welcome in Shrewsbury. Brecht turns him into a watchful, calculating figure, bored by the town, with no illusions about the hostility he and his men arouse and which he must counter with native cunning and resourcefulness. He sketched the rough outline of character he had in mind for Plume in a note:

Kein Grund, dem Werbeoffizier der englischen Restaurationskomödie mehr gesellschaftlichen Status zu verleihen, als etwa der Weinreisende im Preußen des angehenden zwanzigsten Jahrhunderts genoß. Das war nicht etwa der Beruf des Adels. Dessen Söhne besaßen Regimenter mit acht Jahren. Plume ist ein Bauernjunge, der sich durch Mutterwitz und vielleicht durch Tapferkeit hochgedient hat und keinerlei Tischmanieren benötigt. Die Fabel des Stücks verlangt, daß er halbwegs gut gewachsen ist, und niemand im Publikum braucht Victorias Gefühle für ihn zu teilen. Andrerseits braucht ihm nicht sein Stand zuschlechte gehalten werden. Der Subalterne ist hier auch der Plebejische. — Etwas über das 'Äußerliche': Stramme und elegante Haltung ist zu vermeiden. Plume kann in seiner hübschen Uniform stecken, wie er will, er imitiert nicht einen Edelmann und bewegt sich nicht wie ein Flamingo.[36]

The dynamic of Plume's character is generated by the contradictions he embodies. In *Pauken und Trompeten* Brecht aggravates them to such a point that the relative positions of all the personages are modified — Plume is both indispensable to the ruling class and a danger to it, yet even more ominous for the lower classes from which he possibly sprang. A note on the contradictions indicates his tensions and their questionable resolution:

Beruf und Berufung des Offiziers.

Der Offizier schützt das Vaterland, wo immer er kämpft, und lebt von dem Land, in dem [er] stationiert ist, also eventuell auch vom Vaterland, möglichst gut.

Er versorgt sich mit den Töchtern des Lands in gleicher Weise im eignen wie im fremden Land.

Der Eroberer läßt sich erobern.[37]

Throughout *Pauken und Trompeten* Plume displays an eminently pragmatic sense that enables him to economize in the efforts he must be ready to make in opposite directions in order to maximize the return on them — either a company of recruits or a profitable civilian marriage. As a consequence the adaptation loses most of the conventional scenes of mutual commiseration between Plume and Worthy on the disheartening progress of their respective courting affairs; instead, in Scene 8, Plume spells out a hard-hitting plan of campaign for Worthy:

PLUME: Man will Ihre Eifersucht erregen. Und da werfen Sie Ihre Flinte ins Korn? Worthy, wenn Sie jetzt nachgeben — ja, dann ist alles verloren. Sie müssen Melindas Verzweiflungsmanöver sich im Sande verlaufen lassen. Sie trifft Brazen nur Ihretwegen. Ich gebe zu, es mag unangenehm für Sie sein, die beiden im Wäldchen verschwinden zu sehen . . .
WORTHY: Unangenehm! Es ist unerträglich!
PLUME: Ach was! Unerträglich! Man opfert eine Stadt, um ein Land zu gewinnen. Man duldet eine Schlappe, um den Endsieg zu sichern. Worthy, Sie sind in Gefahr, durch Kleinzügigkeit die Chance Ihres Lebens zu verpassen.
WORTHY: Was? Ich soll zuschauen, wenn die Frau, die ich liebe, mit einem solchen Kerl . . .
PLUME: Unbedingt. Mit größter Kaltblütigkeit. Geben Sie ihr doch Gelegenheit, den Unwert Ihres Rivalen festzustellen.[38]

Plume's own connexion with Victoria runs along quite different lines too. In *The Recruiting Officer* the sentimental link is strong from the start, Plume had already wooed Silvia during his previous stay in the town and he maintains throughout this idealized image of her womanly perfection. There is no place for these elements in *Pauken und Trompeten*: now Plume can hardly recall the girl at the window of the boarding-school ('Ach, die Sechzehn-jährige' (Scene 1)), and he parries with a cold rebuff when she (as Wilful) hands him a romantic letter in the billiard-room of The Raven. Soon after, however, Plume hints that he would not be averse to a passing affair with Victoria, which characterizes the astute, unfeeling quality of his attitude to the girl — she is a commodity, like Rose: 'Kite, was hältst du von dieser briefeschreibenden kleinen Balance? Du meinst, so was legt sich hin auf dem Papier, aber ehe es zu einem Kuß auf die Stirn kommt, verlangt sie Glocken, Myrte und Stempel. Nichts für uns, was?'[39] Just as men were a commodity handled quantitatively in the commerce of war, so women here become merchandise to be traded for profit. From this point on showing none of the cordiality that Farquhar had endowed him with, Plume pulls his rank on Wilful and snaps orders at him to procure him Victoria in exchange for Rose without delay. When Wilful turns up in the next scene having failed to carry out the order, Plume hectors him further and demands the return of Rose.[40]

This antagonism of self-interest and behaviour determines the course of the affair until the compromise on a purely business footing is reached with Balance. Plume reprimands Wilful for dissoluteness while Boston falls, then steps out of his role momentarily to address the audience when Rose's words enlighten him as to Wilful's identity: 'Ich falle aus den Wolken. Sie selbst erscheint nicht, aber jede andere hält sie von mir weg! Ich werde ihr heimleuchten.'[41] The sparring intensifies: Plume promises Rose that he will make up to her Wilful's deficiencies as a lover. Wilful swiftly retaliates by having the Captain arrested for not being able to honour his IOU to her, and then when Wilful refuses obdurately to strip and wash in prison, Plume is prepared to waive the order if Wilful will tear up the IOU. Throughout the added scene in prison (Scene 11) Plume bullies Wilful mercilessly and rounds it off by sobering her passion for him by revealing that he knows she is Victoria. The shock of this cold douche provokes her outburst: 'Gehen Sie zum Teufel, Sie Scheusal.'[42] It is essential to grasp Plume's total indifference to Victoria as a person in order to realize the divergent functions of their union in original and adaptation. In *The Recruiting Officer* the two had been united after all the vicissitudes of the plot to provide a conventional anodyne ending, while their coming together in *Pauken und Trompeten* is a cold-blooded transaction virtually decided at the conference-table between the opportunist adventurer and the commercially-minded magistrate.

By their behaviour Captain Plume and Justice Balance show that they can see through each other and that their identity of interests can also be made to coincide neatly with patriotism. It is Plume who suggests to Balance early on the desirability of drawing recruits from the prisons, and he invites Worthy to a glass of wine to demonstrate that his interest in enlisting men is not alone on behalf of King and country:

PLUME: ... Dort können wir das Geschäftliche besprechen.
WORTHY: Richtig, deshalb kam ich. Wo werden Sie Stiefel für Ihre Grenadiere hernehmen? Hoffentlich von Worthy & Co.
PLUME: Zuerst muß ich wissen, wo ich Grenadiere für Ihre Stiefel hernehme, Worthy. Ich werde dem Richter Balance unverzüglich meine Aufwartung machen.[43]

Worthy, in fact, far from being any longer a 'Shropshire gentleman', is transformed into a 'Schuhfabrikant' which adds pungency to his role in *Pauken und Trompeten*; the cares of his infatuation for Melinda are augmented by worries about the military market for his boot production. Here Brecht seizes the opportunity of demonstrating the interdependence of commercial and military interests (capitalism and war) in a model case, and so Worthy is to be found numbered among those with a vested interest in war glumly concerned at the slow pace of recruiting: 'Ich fürchte, das, was da an Rekruten auf dem Marktplatz steht, wird meine Schuhlager nicht leeren.

Es genügt nicht, Schuhe für die Mannschaft zu haben, man muß auch Mannschaft für die Schuhe haben.'[44] Apart from drawing Worthy firmly into the circle of those who profited from war, Brecht enlarged it to include Lady Prude and Smuggler, at the same time dropping a brace of Justices of the Peace, Scale and Scruple, who had somewhat tempered Balance's viciousness in *The Recruiting Officer*. But, as in many other plays as well as adaptations, Brecht did not content himself with giving the measure of those on top by depicting only *their* actions: he incorporated into *Pauken und Trompeten* a dozen extra characters — all of the lower class — who decisively swing the play away from *The Recruiting Officer* into a different conceptual orientation.

Though these added characters are all from the same stratum of society, there is a marked differentiation of outlook, occupation and function amongst them that gives the utmost significance to their introduction into the adaptation. Certainly, Farquhar is rightly singled out among the dramatists of his time for having dared to put the provinces on the stage and for his depiction of rustics such as Rose and Bullock, the fairly easily recruited Appletree and Pearmain, the gullible butcher and smith, the defenceless miner and unemployed man. Brecht consciously built on this foundation from the perspective of later political theory. The people he was dealing with were not working-class in the modern industrial sense, their political consciousness inevitably lacked the sharp focus and directional thrust given to it later by the cumulative development of factories, trade unions, Marxism and revolution.[45] It would be incongruous to expect a clear and coherent anticipation of the Marxist class-struggle in the working-man of the early or mid-eighteenth century.

In this respect the degree of awareness given to some of the new characters (in particular Simpkins, Mike and Der Breitschultrige) is really an anachronistic intrusion, serving once again to build into the structure of the play the most telling factor that alone is enough to alter its whole tone and quality, and that frankly acknowledges the time-gap between original and adaptation with its unavoidable effects. The representatives of the lower classes are by no means all angels; even more than in his younger work, Brecht was here conscious of the contradictions in individuals as well as in society. (Although in 1954 he described the behaviour of his first major character, Baal, as 'asozial, aber in einer asozialen Gesellschaft', it is by no means certain that Brecht believed unconditionally that a 'good' society would improve men; his concept of man and society as (variable) functions of each other implies a realization that this process, if at all possible, would be slow and painful. However, this need not mean a rejection of optimism.) The pickpocket, pimp and whore who shop each other without compunction are undesirable specimens to be found at all levels of society; by inserting them into the final scene, Brecht guards against lumping all the have-nots together into an undifferentiated mass whose automatic virtue it is to be down-trodden. These three batten on the social order that perhaps produced them; just because they are small fry amongst the bigger sharks, their failure need cause no tears.

The subtle gradation of personalities and functions embraces all the new characters introduced in conflict with or as commentary on the social system. In a number of scenes Simpkins, the butler in Balance's house, interjects terse comments that, *by virtue of their context*, take on a double meaning. His very job makes him ambiguous: does he accept the ethos of his employer and side with him (in the image of the 'faithful retainer'), or is he using his position within a powerful household to undermine it wherever occasion offers — the classic infiltration tactic in the theory of revolution? The exclamations with which he punctuates Balance's virulent attack on the Declaration of Independence in Scene 2 appear to share his master's anger, but at the same time, through their imprecision, they ironically convey a sympathy with the Colonists. The central importance of an apparently peripheral character like the butler is brought home even more strikingly in Scene 4 where he is again serving whisky to the dignitaries of the town as military music blares below their platform:

BALANCE: Das Blech gießt ein wenig Heroismus in die blutarmen Herzen der Bürger. Ah! Ich bestehe auf einer Schilderung der Schlacht von Bunker Hill, Plume.
PLUME: Sie bringen mich in Verlegenheit, Mr Balance. Eine Schlacht ist wie die andere.
SIMPKINS: Oh!
BALANCE: Sagten Sie etwas, Simpkins?
SIMPKINS: Pardon, Sir. Man weiß in Shrewsbury alles über Bunker Hill, Sir, Captain.
BALANCE: Was weiß man?
SIMPKINS: Der Fluß heißt Hudson, Mr Balance. Weiter oben befindet sich ein Wehr und ein Stausee, Sir, weiter unten Gerstenfelder. Die Rebellen hatten den Hudson bereits überschritten, aber im Schutze der Nacht manövrierte Captain Plume, Sie entschuldigen, Sir, 80 Grenadiere und eine Kanone durch ihre Linien. Mit einem wohlgezielten Schuß, bin ich recht berichtet, Captain, wurde das Wehr hinweggefegt, und das Wasser beginnt, die Gerstenfelder zu überfluten. Ein vernichtendes Feuer dezimiert zwar unsere tapfere Kompanie, aber dann geschieht das von Captain Plume Vorgesehene. Die Rebellen sind nicht Soldaten, es sind gemeine Kuhbauern, die sich in Waffenröcke gezwängt haben, und angesichts einer Überschwemmung von einigem Ausmaß verwandelt sich so was sehr schnell wieder in gemeine Kuhbauern, hehehe. Ein ganzes Korps von Kuhbauern läuft in dieser Nacht auseinander, den Damm flicken und das treibende Vieh aus den versinkenden Farmen zu retten. Früh um acht greifen wir an. Das Ergebnis ist bekannt. Pardon, Sir. Pardon, Captain.[46]

The telling force of Simpkins's account springs from what he does *not* say, namely his own condemnation of the tactics of Bunker Hill, obliquely put in his sardonic formulations: 'Ein vernichtendes Feuer dezimiert zwar unsere tapfere Kompanie', 'gemeine Kuhbauern, hehehe.' The irony and the attitude are not conveyed in *what* but in *how* he describes, and a mental effort is demanded of the spectator to go beyond the text in its interpretation ('Das

Ergebnis ist bekannt' laconically sums up the loss of a third of the British troops). In Scene 9 the arrival and spread of ill-tidings (Boston has fallen to the rebels) gives Simpkins yet another opportunity for concealing real joy and emotion beneath an apparently shattered exterior:

BALANCE: Captain Plume . . . Boston ist in den Händen der Rebellen.
SIMPKINS: Unmöglich!
BALANCE: Bitte? *Schickt Simpkins mit Geste hinaus* . . .
SIMPKINS *herein*: Tee, Mr Worthy.
WORTHY *brüllt*: Whisky!
SIMPKINS: Sir, ich bitte Sie, heute kleinere Versehen entschuldigen zu wollen. *Mit brechender Stimme*: Boston ist in der Hand der Rebellen.
Simpkins ab. Balance und Plume kommen in düsterer Stimmung herein. Sie setzen sich stumm.
BALANCE *ruft*: Simpkins!
SIMPKINS *herein*: Mr Balance!
BALANCE *brüllt*: Whisky!
SIMPKINS: Ich darf heute um Nachsicht bitten. *Ab.*
BALANCE: Was hat er denn?
WORTHY *über die Schulter*: Boston.[47]

To the very end Simpkins is at hand tossing out provocative remarks that in their tone or timing are a revocation of themselves.

As is only to be expected in this play, the head-on collision between the rulers and the ruled occurs in the sphere of recruiting. Brecht took over where Farquhar left off, for the latter had not taken denunciation of the methods of raising men to any great lengths.[48] Brecht starts from differentiated premises about war: a war of principle — a spontaneous struggle for freedom — is vastly different from a war of oppression that depends on the impressment of a powerless section of the population to fight for the ends of the ruling class. He attributes a massive resistance to his lower classes that makes the task facing Plume and Kite well-nigh impossible and as a consequence provokes Balance's iniquitous conscription measures. Though Brecht follows *The Recruiting Officer* in allowing both Appletree and Pearmain to be recruited, he drops almost the whole scene (IV, 3) where Kite, disguised as a fortune-teller, tricks the credulous smith and butcher into parting with their money and their freedom. The vestiges of these two gullible characters are found in the smith William who in Scene 8 of *Pauken und Trompeten* proves recalcitrant to the persuasions of Kite (this time in the garb of a flower-girl with attendant connotations of superstition and fortune-telling). But Kite is persistent — and desperate; he reappears later in the scene in the guise of a parson and inveighs against such obdurate churls as William who refuse to fight for king and country. The young barman Mike demolishes his rhetoric (which is nothing less than a caricature of the established church backing the established system) and finally unmasks him:

KITE: Ihr Lieben, es ist der Kirche zu Ohren gekommen, daß der oder jener davor zurückschreckt, die englische Freiheit in Amerika zu verteidigen, aus Schwäche und

Furcht des Fleisches. Das ist Unsinn. Fleisch ist Staub und wird wieder zu Staub werden, aber England ist England und wird immer England sein. Auch in diesem gottvergessenen Amerika, ihr Leuchten von Micklesbury.
MIKE: Aber ist es nicht so, Reverend, daß die Leute drüben auch Leute sind?
KITE *donnernd*: Und was ist mit der Geographologie, du Rotzer? Und was ist mit dem neunten Gebot Mose, ihr Misteimer? Heißt es 'Du sollst nicht begehren deines Nachbarn Weib noch Haus!' oder nicht? Und gehört Amerika etwa nicht dem guten König George von England, seit Gott es geschaffen hat? Und jetzt begehren es diese Amerikaner, der Teufel soll sie persönlich holen, die Ladies entschuldigen schon.
MIKE: Aber ist es nicht so, Reverend, daß es in Amerika keine Lords und keinen König gibt? ... Ist es nicht so, Reverend, daß Sie überhaupt kein Reverend sind, sondern Mr Kite, Sohn der Zigeunerin Cleopatra, Zuchthausvogel, lebenslänglicher Sergeant?[49]

Both appearances by Kite enlist the opium of the people — 'fate' and Bible texts — to neutralize the tangible needs and concerns of ordinary people. By juxtaposing grand (but inaccurate) generalizations and practical questions Brecht uncomfortably exposes old *clichés* which, by a sleight-of-hand, he has distorted for the purpose of caricature.

The greatest single factor that significantly alters the whole tone of the adaptation is the introduction or development of the 'historical' awareness of these lesser characters. The snatches of conversation or comment from the wives of the men being dealt with by Balance in the closing scene are exactly parallel to the caustic, sceptical interjections by the onlookers in Act 5 of the *Biberpelz — Roter Hahn* adaptation when von Wehrhahn attempts to implicate the socialist Rauert in a charge of arson. Both are inequitable court scenes, and clearly seen to be so as the objections from the public are ignored from the bench with overbearing arrogance on the part of Balance. The ex-soldier described as Der Breitschultrige is the focus of resistance in the public gallery; he knows the law and the rights of the individual but has no illusions about the sanctity of those rights. Though he advises the miner's wife 'Ihr Mann verdient sichtlich seinen Lebensunterhalt, dann kann er nicht ins Heer gepreßt werden. So lautet das Gesetz', he is not surprised when the miner is nevertheless sent to join the ranks. A similar unsuccessful attempt by Der Breitschultrige to save the unemployed John Workless and his wife ends on the same note of disillusion:

BALANCE: Saal räumen! *Bridewell und der Gerichtsdiener räumen den Saal.*
FRAU COBB: Aber irgendwo muß man sich doch beschweren können.
BREITSCHULTRIGER: Ja, beim Friedensrichter.
JENNY: Aber der preßt sie doch hinein.
BREITSCHULTRIGER: Eben.[50]

Altogether, Der Breitschultrige is very much alive to the realities of the situation in *Pauken und Trompeten* and incorporates more than any other character the hindview of later times on the historical events that form the background to the play. His organized awareness is supported in minor ways, for example by the instructive song in the *Zwischenspiel* between the last two scenes, that is, between Worthy's rescue of the banker Smuggler from prison and the appearance of the remaining less influential prisoners (including the miner who sings the song) before Justice Balance:

> Alle doch, mehr oder wenig
> Zahlten sie dem guten König
> Alle zahlten sie die teuern
> Ungeheuern Heeressteuern
> Ausgenommen I. N. Smith.
>
> Doch es war dem guten König
> Immer noch ein wenig wenig.
> Alle nahm man am Schlafittchen
> Alles rin in das Kittchen
> Ausgenommen I. N. Smith.

Put at this point, the verses provide a prelude to what is about to happen — the pressing of the men — and also a point of view about it: that justice is being flouted. Like the figure of Der Breitschultrige the song thus eminently performs that dual function intended by Brecht of being dramatically integrated with the action (here it underlines the low morale of the prisoners and the preparations for bringing them before the Justice) and at the same time expressing an informative comment on that action.

Der Breitschultrige immediately notices that the arrival in court of a disguised Victoria has caused some sort of embarrassment as Plume is curtly summoned into the library ('Der Captain hat, scheint's, auch Dreck am Stecken.') and senses the possibility of exploiting this when voices are raised off-stage ('Was ist da drinnen los?'). The audience is already aware of the significance of this ex-soldier from his first appearance in Scene 4. Like Rauert in *Der rote Hahn* he is intelligent and factual (perhaps made so by the loss of a leg at Bunker Hill), and though he unflaggingly drinks the ale paid for by Kite, he keeps a clear head that saves him from the grinding system, but marks him as dangerous and seditious:

KITE: ... Darf man fragen, Sir, wie Ihnen das Ale des Königs gemundet hat?
BREITSCHULTRIGER: Vorzüglich, Sir.
KITE: Der Dienst des Königs würde Ihnen noch besser munden, Sir.
BREITSCHULTRIGER *trinkt seinen Krug aus*: Können vor Lachen, sagte der Stieglitz, Sir. Und damit besten Dank für die Bewirtung. Ich sitze jetzt hier schon den ganzen Tag auf Ihre Kosten. *Er steht auf.*
KITE: Auf ein Wort, Sir. Sie kennen den Severn, aber kennen Sie den Mississippi? *Der Mann stapft weg. Man sieht, er hat ein Holzbein.*
KITE: Was ist das? *Hinterherrufend*: Wo hast du denn dein Bein?
BREITSCHULTRIGER: Bunker Hill.
APPLETREE: Sein Bein ist weg!
KITE: Aber für den König. Hut ab. Gut, er hat sein Bein verloren, aber so ein verdammter Rebell da drüben verliert es genau so.
BREITSCHULTRIGER: Aber für sich! *Ab.*

PEARMAIN: Aber für sich. *Lacht.*
KITE *starrt dem Breitschultrigen nach*: Das ist ein Fall für die Polizei![51]

Kite's attempt to recruit by bribery — an echo of contemporary electioneering practices — demonstrates on a small scale the principle determining the whole structure and morality of that society. The action of Der Breitschultrige in *not* repaying Kite for the beer, his separation of 'Fressen' and 'Moral', is like Lucy's when she reserves the right to despise her 'benefactors'. Both these characters deliberately break out of the accepted transaction pattern on which society works and thus represent meaningfully realistic condemnation of it.

Pauken und Trompeten is given a new feature of the utmost importance with the introduction of Der Breitschultrige, and the effect is reinforced by the addition of the young barman Mike and his dreams of emigrating with Lucy to the promise of a more expansive life in the American Colonies. While Der Breitschultrige embodies the cerebral, analytical assessment of this particular epoch in the evolutionary process of British history, Mike represents the experiential, non-articulated aspect of the same situation. His vision of a new freedom stands in sharp contrast to the reality of the time — until they gained independence the Colonies were easily and systematically exploited sources of raw materials, crops and taxes for British trade —, but it does prefigure the irresistible weight of a whole century and a half of urgent longings among distressed millions scattered throughout Europe, longings that created a mythology still active in such books as Kafka's *Amerika* and Thomas Mann's *Felix Krull*. Whereas Mike's ambition of opening a hotel in North America is not as arbitrary as the entry into the hotel trade of the heroes of these two novels (he is, after all, now employed at The Raven) it does subsume all that was restless, footloose and dynamically independent in the future United States. Lucy is to be Mike's partner in this venture. In *Pauken und Trompeten* she ceases to be the traditional chambermaid whose individuality (if she is allowed any) is confined within the limits of her interest in her mistress's affairs; instead she is outspokenly conscious of distinctions of class and active in promoting the interests of those like her (when Balance pretends that Melinda has lost her fortune so that Brazen will cease his importunings, Lucy's first thought, like Sganarelle's, was 'Mein Lohn!', which she immediately justifies with a curt 'in Geldangelegenheiten sehe ich gern klar'). A generous tip given her by Worthy for delivering a message from Melinda has value in bringing their hopes one step nearer realization; she despises the message and the giver. The Sunday afternoon walk by the Severn provides the idyllic setting for their dreamings:

LUCY: ... Noch zehn solche Botschaften, und wir haben unsre Überfahrt beisammen. Und 'Auf nach Amerika!'
MIKE: Aber nicht wie die uns drüben haben wollen, mich als Grenadier und dich als du weißt schon was, sondern im Hotelgewerbe.
Der Schwan schwimmt heran und wird gefüttert.
LUCY: Ich schreibe Tante Emmy noch heut abend nach New York.
MIKE: Wozu? Wir gehen nach Boston. Nicht in dieses Kaff.

LUCY: Kaff! New York ist zwar eine von den kleineren Städten, aber es hat Aussichten.
MIKE: Zu klein für ein Hotel mehr.[52]

A little later in the same scene Mike produces a copy of the Declaration of Independence that had aroused such ire in Balance. Though he cannot read he has memorized its contents, and the way it sparks off the enacting of a touching and humorous incident in the future hotel of the young people is sufficient proof of the intensity of their dreams:

LUCY: Was ist das?
MIKE: Aus der Neuen Welt. Ich hab's von einem Kutscher, der hat's von einem Matrosen aus Liverpool. Paß auf! Geh, Felix! Weg mit dem König, weg mit dem Erzbischof, weg mit den Lords! Wir brauchen in der Neuen Welt keinen König und keine Lords, die von unserem Schweiß fett werden. Wir in den Staaten von Amerika wollen keine Kolonie Englands mehr sein. Gezeichnet: Franklin.
LUCY: Mike! Seit wann kannst du lesen? *Nimmt das Blatt.*
MIKE: Ach, Fred hat mir gestern gezeigt, wie man das macht.
LUCY: Da steht was ganz anderes drauf.
MIKE: So? — Was?
LUCY: 'Unabhängigkeitserklärung'.
MIKE: Auch gut. Lies.
LUCY: 'Daß alle Menschen gleich geschaffen sind, und von ihrem . . .', das Wort kann ich nicht lesen, '. . . mit gewissen . . . Rechten ausgestattet sind: Leben, Freiheit, und dem Streben nach Glück . . .'.
MIKE: Lucy, da gehen wir hin!
LUCY *sagt eine kleine Szene an*: Mr and Mrs Mike W. Laughtons Hotel 'Zum Schwan'. *Spielt*: Nimm nicht immer neue Gäste an, Mike W. Laughton, wenn ich nur noch zwei Ochsenrücken am Spieß habe.
MIKE: Gut, dann werde ich den Lord-Mayor von Philadelphia vor die Tür setzen, Mrs Mike W. Laughton. Aber zuerst noch ein kleines Tänzchen in der Küche; schließlich bezahlen wir die Musiker.
Sie tanzen.
LUCY: Verrammle die Türen des Hotels, Mike W. Laughton, die Rotjacken kommen.
MIKE: Lad mir die Flinte, Frau! Diese gottverdammten Engländer! Bumm — Bumm! Die Flinten sind schlecht geölt, Mrs Mike W. Laughton!
LUCY: Mein bestes Salatöl!
MIKE: Bumm. Getroffen![53]

The scene of idyllic reverie and miming by Mike and Lucy, coming after the burden of the Declaration of Independence has been established, has the effect of clarifying visually the anomaly of the unprivileged fighting for King George in a war to destroy the kind of society they themselves crave. This paradox is brought to a climax when Mike so wholly enters the role of an American that he shoots the English, while at the same time he is patently English himself. The result is a brilliant plastic formulation of the Marxist view of a capitalists' war, where the ordinary man kills his fellow (his 'brother', himself) and strengthens the very society which crushes

10

him. This scene is a less conscious presentation from the point of view of the participants than the one in which the one-legged Breitschultriger is involved, for the latter distinguishes between a leg lost for a remote principle (the interests of King George) or for the vital essence of one's own existence (American freedom, 'für sich'). However, although the historical situation is not articulated consciously by Mike and Lucy, the *scene* is articulate in every aspect, structured into powerful meaning by Brecht's purposeful condensation and the alienating effects achieved. The whole scene can be taken as an exact objective correlative to the situation it presents: the ordinary man intuitively grasps the relevance of the Declaration of Independence for himself without actually comprehending the printed words.

Yet Mike and Lucy are not just castle-builders who take refuge from present irritations in the security of reverie. The barman is not afraid to stand up to his 'superiors' when Victoria tears a rent in the billiard-cloth; he demands immediate payment for the damage and reminds Plume of other outstanding debts. He is sufficiently on the *qui vive* to realize the significance of Kite's words when the sergeant lets drop to Victoria that the British had lost 11,000 men in gaining the victory of Bunker Hill. Mike is quick-witted enough to evade Kite's threats for having overheard this 'official secret', and he is matched by Lucy's presence of mind in threatening to expose Victoria's disguise to the public if Balance refuses to release her Mike who is under military age:

LUCY *die inzwischen durch den Gerichtssaal in die Bibliothek gestürzt ist*: Mr Balance! *Sie zieht Balance in den Gerichtssaal*: Sie nehmen meinen Mike fort.
BALANCE: England braucht ihn.
LUCY: Und ich?
BALANCE: Was du?
LUCY: Ich brauche ihn ebenfalls.
BALANCE: Schlag dir den Jungen aus dem Kopf, er wird Grenadier.
LUCY: Mike W. Laughton hat andere Absichten, Sir, und wenn Sie ihn nicht freilassen . . .
BALANCE: Was dann?
LUCY: Dann wird die Welt erfahren, wer alles hierzulande Fähnrich wird.
BALANCE: Lucy!
LUCY: Mr Balance . . .
BALANCE: Gerichtsdiener, den Schankburschen vom Raben zurückholen.[54]

Lucy gains her point, Balance bows to blackmail, and Mike and Lucy are reunited with the buoyant prospect of emigration before them, proudly anticipated by Lucy in the Americanized form she gives to Mike W. Laughton's name!

With the insertion into *Pauken und Trompeten* of more than passive representatives of the lower class (the most important being Simpkins, Mike and Der Breitschultrige) the focus of the play is switched to their sociopolitical situation, and the frivolous society game of *The Recruiting Officer* remains only as a contrast to and in conflict with them. Brecht was always alive to the protective seduction of excluding hard facts from one's mind, the inertia that bathes the past — however evil — in a cosy, analgesic glow. In *Pauken und Trompeten* he countered any tendency to mental sloth in the audience by intensifying the contradictions in action and structure to such a degree that there is no simple resolution at the end — only a disturbing uneasiness.

Farquhar fittingly has his recruiting officer round off the action neatly in rhyming couplets that reflect the smooth unproblematic end to the play:

> With some regret I quit the active field,
> Where glory full reward for life does yield;
> But the recruiting trade with all its train,
> Of lasting plague, fatigue, and endless pain,
> I gladly quit, with my fair spouse to stay,
> And raise recruits the matrimonial way.

The ethical — if not aesthetic — complacency in these obedient lines finds no place in Brecht's version; the dialectic of contradiction in content and in form that he has assiduously built up in the course of the play is maintained until the final curtain and continues beyond. The tableau that dominates the end brings together all the chief protagonists, not in the spirit of reconciliation usually associated with such scenes (one thinks here, for example, of *Nathan der Weise*) but in the full discordance of an open breach:

Alles hat sich in der Halle versammelt. Simpkins hat Champagner und Gläser gebracht. Man hört ein Soldatenlied von der Straße her, von den ausmarschierenden Rekruten gesungen.

REKRUTEN: Komm, mein Junge, kleid dich ein
In Virginia hörst du kein
Kindergeschrei und Weibergefleh
Dort über den Hügeln und über der See.

BALANCE *hebt sein Glas*: Auf das gute alte England!
MIKE *heimlich zu Lucy*: Auf ein neues, gutes!
SMUGGLER: Lang lebe die englische Freiheit, daheim und übersee!
LUCY *leise zu Mike*: Auf uns!
PRUDE: Auf unsere Kolonien, daß sie uns gedeihen!
MIKE *leise zu Lucy*: Daß sie sich befreien!
SIMPKINS: Das walte Gott!

Ein Propfen knallt.

REKRUTEN König George, gebeugt und alt
Hat auf der Stirn eine Kummerfalt
Daß ihm sein Reich in die Binsen geh
Dort über den Hügeln und über der See.

BRAZEN *von der Straße herauf*: Mr Lakonisch, Ihr Diener und so weiter — Tag, Mr Smuggler! *Zu Plume*: Glückwunsch zu dem fetten Braten, Plume!
PLUME *am Fenster*: Kite!
KITE *auf der Straße, kalt*: Einen angenehmen Abend, *Mister* Plume.

REKRUTEN: Mädchen, kehr ich nicht zurück
                      Ist es aus mit unserm Glück.
                      Doch König George sitzt fester denn je
                      Dort über den Hügeln und über der See.
                      Das Lied entfernt sich.
SIMPKINS *schluchzt*: England, England über alles!
BALANCE: Und jetzt: auf zur Fasanenjagd!
ALLE: Ah!
BALANCE: Simpkins! Kutsche vorfahren! Vierspännig![55]

This vignette no longer mirrors the untying of a dramatic knot, the levelling of differences, the apportionment of shares with all in equanimity. It barely conceals Balance's bitter struggle to retain and impose his power by violence, his frenetic running back and forth between court-room and library (a dozen times in all) in the effort to protect the opposing interests of his family and his country. The successful outcome is toasted in champagne: those in the room experience a serene and irresponsible catharsis, but the recruits marching past outside cast a sombre shadow across the scene and beyond the play. The peaceful ending of *The Recruiting Officer*, devoid of critical comment, yields to the confrontation at the close of Brecht's version which is all the more caustic for not being spelled out. Contradictions glossed over by Farquhar in a witty line ('And raise recruits the matrimonial way') are differentiated sufficiently by Brecht to produce the dialectic implications of the recruits' song. While Plume has seen fit to settle for the perquisites of domesticity no such choice is allowed the soldiers. What the soldiers may really want is concealed by their song which implies that they are joyfully evading the negative aspects of family life ('In Virginia hörst du kein | Kindergeschrei und Weibergefleh'). Society can thus salve its guilty conscience in the pretence that these actually are the singers' sentiments.

    The play is about domesticity and life on the one hand, war and death on the other; Brecht demonstrates how those who control society make capital out of each as opportunism demands. This closing scene also points the contrast of age and exhaustion with youth and vigour: King George ('gebeugt und alt') and a weary colonialism clash with the young couple Lucy and Mike and the stirring dynamic of emergent America. England's rebuke to the fractious colonies — the paternalistic whipping of a naughty child — will fail through its feebleness. With this clenched climax Brecht imposes a historical perspective on the play that is not only evident throughout in the content itself but is also achieved by an accumulation of formal characteristics operating dialectically that are congruent with it. The staple motif in Restoration Comedy of a woman disguising herself as a man is used by Farquhar to rouse fairly predictable laughter through misunderstandings on the stage and superior knowledge in the audience.[56] There is, it is true, a modicum of dialectic in the course Silvia takes, as she herself explains in the concluding scene: 'But, I hope, you'll excuse a change that has proceeded from constancy. I altered my outside because I was the same within, and only laid by the woman to make sure of my man. That's my history.' Brecht sharpens the dialectic: 'Um unter die Haube zu kommen,| Zog sie Männerkleidung an| Und gespornte Stiefel.' He invests Victoria's disguise with social significance and allows her a whole *Zwischenspiel* in which to present herself to the public as a guinea-pig to be observed coolly and with detachment:

VICTORIA *unter dem Arm die Uniform*: Meine Damen und Herren, Sie sehen Ihre Victoria vor einem schweren Entschluß. Sie ist ins Heer eingetreten, um dem geliebten Mann nahe zu bleiben! Kann es ihre Absicht sein, tatsächlich nach Übersee zu fahren? Wie dem auch sei: diese letzten Tage in England nicht an seiner Seite zu verbringen, kann ich mich nicht entschließen, so sehr es vielleicht der Vernunft widerspricht. Wie heißt es im Lied? *Sie singt*:

> Es gibt im Leben Augenblicke
> Wo vor dir herrisch eine Frage steht:
> Folgst du der Leidenschaft und dem Geschicke
> Folgst du nicht lieber dem, was die Vernunft dir rät?
> > Doch die Brust, sie schwillt von Gefühlen
> > Bedrängend den armen Sinn
> > Es runden die Winde die Segel
> > Und das Schiff fragt nicht lange: Wohin?
>
> Schwester, aus was für einem Holze
> Bist du gemacht, daß du dir was vergibst?
> Was ist mit deiner Scham und was mit deinem Stolze?
> Ach, danach fragst du nicht mehr, wenn du einmal liebst!
> > Es folgt dem Hirsche die Hirschkuh
> > Und dem Löwen die Löwin ins Feld
> > Und es folgt dem Geliebten das liebende Weib
> > Wohl bis ans Ende der Welt.[57]

Both the situation and the song emphasize that something is amiss in a society that demands such subterfuge; even the song crudely equates the love of man and woman with an animal experience.

Time and again in *Pauken und Trompeten* Brecht unfolds the dialectic of speech and action. The nature of language in drama is essentially dialectic, for the drama is a happening between people who can express their actions dramaturgically only in words, theatrically in gesture and demeanour. Brecht seeks out the contradictions of speech and action in their minutest ramifications. For example, the same words used by Balance to Plume (in *The Recruiting Officer*) and to Victoria (in *Pauken und Trompeten*) tell us totally different things about his true attitude; and Simpkins's report of the battle of Bunker Hill is couched in such a form that it is evident he is mocking his hearers. Similarly, the pathos of Balance's patriotic speeches stands in direct and stark contrast to the reality that emerges in his actions. The pathos is shown up to be hollow and ludicrous, but this discrepancy also renders the reality suspect, for if the personage does not use speech congruent with his actions the spectator will be alerted to the danger of concealed actions.

As has been indicated above, the final tableau contains the greatest concentration of this dialectic fracture in individual words. Balance raises his glass to 'das gute alte England' at the very moment when the victims of the callous system he is lauding pass by the window; the simple words 'gut' and 'alt' contain contradictions and a negation of Balance's toast, as Mike's immediate reaction ('Auf ein neues, gutes!') murmured to Lucy emphasizes. What is more, the phrase 'good old England' is merely a platitude in English.[58] When Balance then invites everybody (but not the servants!) to a pheasant-shoot Brecht closes the play on a dialectical note of the utmost economy. The 'Ah!' which greets his announcement is not only a spontaneous gasp of anticipatory pleasure but also an expression of dramatic relief at adventures endured and overcome. More profoundly than either of these, however, it is a self-condemnatory statement about the participants themselves — their ranking on the ladder of society, their frivolity at this hour when the country is engaged in a struggle, and their shifting of the responsibility of defence on to those who have nothing at all to gain from either victory or defeat. The coquetting with life of the rulers stands damned out of their own mouths. In its re-assertion through a visual tableau of the saddlefast privileged class this scene is identical in quality with the idyll stage-managed by the Major von Berg at the close of Scene 16 in Brecht's version of *Der Hofmeister*, where the servants are gathered together for a toast and the Majorin imposes a uniform and suspect *bonhomie* with a sugary song that glosses over the harsh events in the preceding action.

In settling on Farquhar's comedy for adaptation Brecht was unquestionably advocating a thesis, namely that the evil methods of pressing soldiers in eighteenth-century England were symptomatic of more widespread malpractices and characteristic of a rotten — or undesirable — social and political system. By adding certain elements to the play (such as the articulate individuals of the lower classes, the ambiguous actions of Judge and Captain) he sought to present dramatically through contradictions the inherent dialectic of the theme. This is one aspect of the adaptation. Its complement rests in the simultaneous need to engross the attention of the audience in the dramatic spectacle without obscuring the historical perspective indispensable to an evaluation of the image of society presented. Brecht's way of maintaining in balance these two requirements (thesis and enjoyment, or criticism and empathy) was to cultivate the verve and dash of Farquhar's dialogue while at the same time bringing into relief the historical context through evocation of the period in elegant scenery (as he had also done with *Don Juan*) and consciously 'stiff' clothing. The *Programmheft* contains details of this procedure:

Die Szenerie hat den Charakter des Stahlstichs, jener eleganten und pedantisch exakten grafischen Technik, die vor der Erfindung moderner Bilddruckverfahren im 18. und frühen 19. Jahrhundert zu bildlichen Darstellungen aller Art diente ... Diese Soldaten und Dämchen, diese Bauerndirnen und Landedelleute, die unser Papier-Shrewsbury bevölkern, sind wie aus der Spielzeugschachtel gestiegen, in der sie sorglich in Holzwolle eingepackt lagen.

The dual function and aim of the adaptation in promoting critical judgements and providing aesthetic pleasure is a dialectic pattern embracing the internal dialectic tension of content and structure; it is thus hardly surprising that irony is a necessary element in the reactions of Brecht or his audience. For this reason the short sketch in the *Programmheft* outlining the action of *Pauken und Trompeten* is entirely ambiguous in the information it conveys and the language used. It is to be a comedy telling the story of Victoria, the judge's daughter:

Wie sie in heftiger Liebe zu einem Kapitän Seiner Britischen Majestät Grenadiere entbrannte, wie sie den Zorn des Vaters und manch andere Fährnis auf sich nahm, wie sie in Mannskleidern sich dem Geliebten näherte, auch in allerlei Abenteuern ihren Mann stand, und wie sie zum guten Ende den Kapitän ihres Herzens in den Hafen der Ehe einbrachte. Auch erfährt man einiges über die Kriegswirren im fernen Amerika und sieht, wie ein junger Offizier vor ihnen bewahrt wurde, indem er den Stimmen des Herzens und der Vernunft gehorchte.

With a sardonic twist Brecht here gives pride of place to the successful outcome of the love-affair; in the play itself he may have sugared the pill for reasons of entertainment, but it is the bitter taste that lingers at the end.

NOTES

1 Op. cit., p. 49.
2 Ibid., pp. 49 f.
3 I have followed the scene divisions adopted by Leigh Hunt and William Archer who start IV, 2 after Plume's 'I had forgot; pray be kind to her' and thus have three scenes in this Act.
4 Brecht added point to Silvia by altering her name to Victoria with its military overtones, hinting especially — for the modern audience — at the classical age of British capitalism and colonial imperialism. The reverse process applies to the young barman, Mike Laughton, who was called George in draft versions of *Pauken und Trompeten*. This would have been an inappropriate name for a person aspiring to achieve freedom by emigrating to the rebel colonies; instead, the Irish ring of Mike Laughton evokes the brutal redcoat suppression of that people.
5 Grimm, op. cit., p. 50.
6 *GW*, 6/2619. Brecht had written even more aggressive lines that were discarded; compare the fragment BBA 984/114:

Ich bin der Sergeant Barras Kite
Im Dienst seit William the Conquerors Zeit
Seit Arundel und Tenchebrai
Trieb ich zu Land und über See
Für einen schmal und kargen Lohn
So mancher Mutter letzten Sohn
Den Nil hinauf, den Ganges lang
Hinter einer Fahnenstang
Für König, Erzbischof und Lord.

7 *The Works of the late Ingenious Mr George Farquhar*, eighth edition (London, 1742), I, 95. Subsequent quotations from this essay are taken from this edition. Quotations from the text of the play follow George Farquhar, *The Recruiting Officer*, edited by Michael Shugrue (London, 1966).
8 *Some Memoirs of Mr George Farquhar, prefacing The Works*, op. cit., p. 7. These memoirs were probably written by W. R. Chetwood, according to W. Connely, *Young George Farquhar* (London, 1949), p. 314.
9 For a detailed description of Farquhar's induction into the military, see Connely, op. cit., Chapters XIV and XV.

10 Compare Archer's comment bearing upon this matter in his introduction to Farquhar's plays in the Mermaid Series (New York, 1959), p. 21: 'in all his plays, from *The Constant Couple* onwards, and especially in the last three, Farquhar gives a general preponderance to kindness over cruelty and good over evil . . .'; and in a footnote: 'It may be said that *The Recruiting Officer* treats heartlessly of the cruelties perpetrated under the Enlistment Acts. But denunciation of these abuses was scarcely to be expected from an officer actually employed in the work of recruitment; and, on the other hand, though the comedy is gay and irresponsible in tone, it is no eulogy, but rather a satire, on the methods employed.'

11 *GW*, 6/2621. The darker aspects of recruiting were, of course, by no means ignored in the eighteenth century; in Isaac Bickerstaff's ballad-opera *The Recruiting Sergeant* a mother inveighs against the sergeant in a cataract of abuse.

12 *GW*, 6/2628.

13 Compare an earlier version of the scene where Lucy re-enacts to Mike (at that time still called George) with disparaging tone her participation in the Melinda/Worthy intrigue, BBA 983/95 f.: 'Die gnädige Frau muß ihre Launen irgendwie los werden, und vor sie einen Mann hat, müssen die Dienstboten herhalten. (Sie macht Melinda nach). "Es ist das größte Mißgeschick für eine Frau, wenn sie Jemand braucht, dem sie ihr Herz ausschütten kann!" — Ein Geheimnis quält die gnädige Frau tatsächlich schlimmer als eine Kolik. (Melinda nachmachend) "Lucy, hilf mir!" Ihr ist von ihrem Geheimnis so übel, daß sie jede Minute ohnmächtig werden könnte! — Was fehlt Ihnen, Miss Moor-hill? — (Melinda nachmachend) "Du bist ein Dienstbote, ein Geheimnis macht euch unverschämt." — In dem Fall, Madam, würd'ich Ihnen raten, Sie nehmen mich aus dem Dienstbotenstand heraus und stellen mich darüber. 500 Pfund [versprochen, wenn Lucy ihr zur Heirat mit Worthy helfen würde] würden aus mir eine Dame machen, würdig, die Vertraute der vornehmsten Frauen im Lande zu sein. Es würde mich außer-dem in dem großen Vorhaben unterstützen, mit dem George und ich uns nun einmal befassen. (Sie küßt George. — Melinda nachmachend) "O Lucy! Ich kann es nicht länger bei mir behalten! Lucy, geh sofort zu Mr Worthy", das ist ihr Schuhfabrikant, "und sage ihm du wirst ihm mein Geheimnis verraten, wenn er dir ein Trinkgeld gibt." — Und ihr Geheimnis, Madam? — "Das geht dich nichts an, du Erpresserin!" — Aber wenn ich das Geheimnis nicht weiß, wie soll ich es ihm verraten? — "Du sagst einfach, Miss Moorhill hat ein Rendez-vous am Severn mit einem Captain. Etwas Schreckliches wird geschehen, wenn nicht etwas dazwischenkommt." . . . George: Und du bist gegangen zu dem Schuhfritzen? Lucy: Ja. Er machte Augen wie ein Kalb und gab mir zwei Schilling. Hier. Ich habe ein Taschenmesser für dich gekauft.'

14 *GW*, 17/1296.

15 This theme, though a dominant one in drama from 1600–1720, is by no means a literary invention, as any social historian can show; see G. M. Trevelyan, *English Social History* (London, 1942), p. 313.

16 See Archer, op. cit., p. 24, on the novelty of Farquhar's country types: 'He introduced the picaresque element into English comedy, along with a note of sincere and original observation. To have made the good folk of Shrewsbury and Lichfield express them-selves with the modish, stereotyped wit of the London chocolate-house and boudoir would have been the height of absurdity.'

17 Trevelyan, op. cit., p. 310.

18 Ibid., p. 323.

19 *GW*, 6/2644.

20 *GW*, 6/2660.

21 *GW*, 6/2673.

22 *GW*, 6/2675.

23 *GW*, 6/2676.

24 *GW*, 6/2677.

25 *GW*, 6/2682. In BBA 981/42 there is an extended version of this scene that betrays the intimate collaboration of military and civilian power boding ominously for a defenceless section of the community:
BALANCE: Heute nacht wird zugepackt und morgen werden wir im Gericht diese demoralisierten Elemente zu braven englischen Soldaten verknallen.
PLUME: Auf meinen Sergeanten Kite können Sie sich für eine bravoureuse Leitung der Razzia verlassen, Mr Balance!

BALANCE: Und um das Zusammenwirken des Militärs und der Zivilbehörden vollkommen zu machen, erwarte ich Sie, Captain Plume, morgen vormittag elf Uhr. Ich
bitte Sie als Beisitzer neben mir auf der Richterbank Platz zu nehmen.
PLUME: Sehr wohl. Um elf Uhr im Gericht. Um die Stunde, in der das ganze übrige
Königreich Tee trinkt.

26 *GW*, 6/2649.
27 One of several new characters in *Pauken und Trompeten* (in *The Constant Couple* (1699)
Farquhar had a merchant of the same name) with a small but typically Brechtian part:
when Kite brings him to prison from a brothel — he is wearing 'ein Damenmorgenrock
über feiner Unterwäsche' — he offers cigars to Plume and complains of the treatment he
has been given, at which point the indignant Worthy rushes in to release him: 'Meine
Herren, Boston fällt, und damit fallen die Aktien. Begreiflich, daß wir strenge Maßnah-
men benötigen, die gelichteten Reihen unserer Regimenter wieder aufzufüllen — aber
doch nicht mit Bankiers! Wenn man anfängt, uns einzuziehen, ist es möglich, daß wir
auf die Neue Welt verzichteten. Junger Mann, was wird dann aus Ihrer Profession?'
(*GW*, 6/2690).
28 *GW*, 6/2688 and 2690.
29 *GW*, 6/2705.
30 It might be thought that for the destitute and unemployed in this epoch there was little
to choose between death by slow starvation and death by violence as soldiers — if they
enlisted they might at least be fed after a fashion. However, the famous though inaccurate estimates of Gregory King made in 1696 classed 'common soldiers' together
with 'labouring people and outservants' and 'cottagers and paupers' at the bottom of
the income scale, all these groups being 'persons decreasing the wealth of the country',
that is, spending more than they earned in order to survive. A century later (1801)
Colquhoun still placed the common soldier at the low level of the labouring people and
paupers. Figures given in M. D. George, *England in Transition*, second edition (London,
1953), Appendix.
31 *GW*, 6/2704.
32 *GW*, 17/1263.
33 *GW*, 6/2694.
34 *GW*, 6/2701 f.
35 *GW*, 6/2707. The contrasting essentials of the sentences are taken from Farquhar, but
not the cynical situation that alters their tone; compare *The Recruiting Officer*, v, 7:
'Why then, I have saved my legs and arms and lost my liberty; secure from wounds
I'm prepared for the gout. Farewell subsistence and welcome taxes. Sir, my liberty and
hopes of being a general are much dearer to me than your twelve hundred pound a
year, but to your love, madam, I resign my freedom, and to your beauty, my ambition,
greater in obeying at your feet than commanding at the head of any army.'
36 *GW*, 17/1264.
37 *GW*, 17/1263.
38 *GW*, 6/2663 f.
39 *GW*, 6/2660.
40 That Brecht was determined to eradicate any pleasantness from Plume's character is
evidenced in an earlier draft of this scene (BBA 981/04) in which Plume is dictating to
Wilful a letter addressed to Victoria. The missive voices romantic sentiments and feelings
out of keeping with the new conception of Plume and the whole incident therefore
disappears from the final version.
41 *GW*, 6/2685.
42 *GW*, 6/2692.
43 *GW*, 6/2625.
44 *GW*, 6/2676. In an unused draft passage (BBA 983/60) Worthy gives vent to his gloom
in elegiac, nostalgic terms reminiscent of Puntila's lyrical effusion on the beauties of
Tavastland: 'Wenn ich so in meinem Laden sitze, werde ich trübsinnig beim Ansehen
meiner Stiefel. Da waren Zeiten, wo Marlborough kampflustige Soldaten mit sich nach
Frankreich führte. Auf schlechten Wegen, im Kot und Schnee sehnten sich unzählige
Soldaten nach gutem englischem Schuhwerk. Jetzt schreien in ganz England die
Stiefel nach Soldaten. Plume, Sie sind kein Handwerker, Sie verstehen die Sprache der
Dinge nicht.' Krupp a craftsman! Worthy's sentiments illustrate — in an early stage of
industrialization — the Marxist tenet that in a capitalist society the worker (producer of
the goods) has become 'entfremdet' from his product and that the spurious materialist

principles by which this social structure is organized lend a fetishistic mystique to objects and possessions that dehumanizes the individual. Men become secondary to things.

45 It is essential in evaluating Brecht's adaptation to keep clearly in mind that he freely operates with terminology and concepts that are familiar to us now but did not exist or were at best nebulous at the time the original play was written, though the circumstances defined by these concepts were often the reality; compare in this respect E. J. Hobsbawm, *The Age of Revolution 1789–1848* (London, 1963), p. 1: 'Let us consider a few English words which were invented, or gained their modern meanings, substantially in the period of sixty years with which this volume deals. They are such words as "industry", "industrialist", "factory", "middle class", "working class", "capitalism" and "socialism". They include "aristocracy" as well as "railway", "liberal" and "conservative" as political terms, "nationality", "scientist", and "engineer", "proletariat" and (economic) "crisis". "Utilitarian" and "statistics", "sociology", and several other names of modern sciences, "journalism" and "ideology", are all coinages or adaptations of this period. So are "strike" and "pauperism".'

46 *GW*, 6/2636. That Brecht attached some importance to this description of the battle can be gauged from the fact that it survived through various drafts. In BBA 991/53 it is George (i.e. Mike) who tells it to Victoria and adds his opinion: 'Wenn Sie mich fragen, ich halte nicht viel von einem solchen Sieg.' In BBA 651/124 f. Kite recounts the battle to Smuggler languishing in prison, and the latter draws a parallel between these tactics and 'Robert O'Shires Coup auf dem schottischen Wollmarkt 1761', somewhat clumsily forging a bond between the military and merchant spheres: 'Meiner Meinung nach bestehen keine grundsätzlichen Unterschiede zwischen unseren militärischen und kommerziellen Unternehmungen. Was für ein General wäre Robert O'Shire gewesen, und Sie, Plume, würde die Geschäftswelt von London mit offenen Armen empfangen! Was hilft es, wenn Leute für England sterben, wenn es nicht Leute gibt, die von England leben!' In the published play these two versions disappear and the report of the battle is left to Simpkins. In fact, his narration of the episode of Bunker Hill is topographically crudely inaccurate. What actually happened was that the rebels entrenched themselves in a hastily improvised redoubt on Breed's Hill (adjacent to and little more than half the height of Bunker Hill on a promontory just north of Boston). They were repeatedly attacked frontally by redcoats under Major-General William Howe, and finally dislodged and dispersed after inflicting heavy losses on the British troops. The Hudson river flows well over a hundred miles to the west down to New York, and a weir and flooded fields could scarcely figure on the tiny area where the battle took place. Brecht actually distorted the real events in order to invent an anecdote that illustrates the 'blackness' of the British by emphasizing the peaceable 'whiteness' of the farming Colonists.

47 *GW*, 6/2677 and 2681.

48 See Connely, op. cit., p. 247: 'He had shown how Queen Anne raised her armies for Marlborough's wars; if there was corruption in the methods, Farquhar exposed them rather than condoned them; if some recruits were kidnapped, others joined up willingly; if Army life had its demoralizing side, it was in other ways regenerative. Not alone the civilian public, but the Services as well, should benefit from the exhibition of this play.' Compare also M. S. Anderson, *Europe in the Eighteenth Century* (London, 1961), p. 136 f.: '[The] assumption that the productive and educated parts of society were too valuable to be squandered in battle, that their function was to pay for wars not to fight them, was almost universally accepted . . . Under these circumstances almost every eighteenth-century army was likely to contain an element of ne'er-do-wells, social misfits and even criminals . . . In the War of American Independence three British regiments were composed entirely of reprieved criminals, while vagrants and other undesirables were often forced into the army in wartime.'

49 *GW*, 6/2672 f.

50 *GW*, 6/2703 f.

51 *GW*, 6/2640.

52 *GW*, 6/2665.

53 *GW*, 6/2671 f.

54 *GW*, 6/2707 f.

55 *GW*, 6/2709 f.

56 Altogether, Farquhar seems in his plays to have relied quite heavily on disguises: in *Love and a Bottle* Roebuck is pursued by Leanthe dressed as a man; Oriana (*The Inconstant*) in the guise of a nun, later a boy, attempts to win young Mirabel from the

courtesan Lamorce; and there is an exchange of clothes between Beau Clincher and Tim Errand in *The Constant Couple*. Programme notes to the National Theatre production of *The Recruiting Officer* in London describe how these 'breeches parts' extended outside the theatre.

57 *GW*, 6/2657.
58 The effect of throwing the meaningless use of a word into relief is to alienate it: in a flash the 'gut' and 'alt' are scrutinized by the same process that probes the verbs in the poem *Fragen eines lesenden Arbeiters* to question whether the famous generals of history really built the cities and conquered realms themselves.

CHAPTER VI

CORIOLAN

Of all the adaptations tackled by Brecht in Berlin his version of Shakespeare's *Coriolanus* provoked the most complex responses, raising as many questions as it answered. Although he proposed a new handling of Shakespeare's play as early as April 1951, he had not completed the text on his death over five years later. In the published adaptation the battle scenes (Shakespeare, I, 4–10) are represented by the classic Tieck translation which Brecht had intended to replace by a single scene to be written while the rehearsals were actually in progress. This lacuna is not in itself a serious impairment, but it does draw attention to the absence of a factor that was of particular importance to Brecht as playwright and producer, namely the transposition of the potential of a text into actual and unique performance on the stage. In the *Programmheft* accompanying the first Berliner Ensemble production eight years after Brecht's death (first night 25 September 1964) the audience is told quite straightforwardly that Brecht's *Coriolan* lacked 'jene wesentliche letzte Phase des Arbeitsprozesses, in dem die Dramaturgie einer praktischen Kontrolle unterzogen, Fabel- und Figurenführung vom Regisseur gemeinsam mit dem an der Aufführung arbeitenden Kollektiv — von Darstellern, vom Bühnenbildner, Komponisten und den anderen künstlerischen Mitarbeitern — erprobt, durch Vorschläge bereichert und weiterentwickelt wird'. The adaptor becomes the adapted one; a reviewer, with Brecht's text open in his lap, was startled by the contrast with the earlier Frankfurt production that had used the published version: 'Was da zu lesen stand, konnte nur mit Mühe und durch dauerndes Vor- und Zurückblättern zu dem, was ich sah und hörte, in Verbindung gebracht werden; . . . die Abweichungen Brechts vom Shake-speare-Text sind nicht zahlreicher als die (oft wieder näher an Shakespeare heranführenden) Abweichungen der Brecht-Bearbeiter vom Brecht-Text. Es ist ein ganz neues Stück entstanden, das mit dem, das 1962 in Frankfurt aufgeführt worden ist, kaum mehr etwas zu tun hat.'[1]

In this same year of the Ensemble production Günter Grass called in question the whole basis of Brecht's ideological position with regard to the adaptation in a talk entitled *Vor- und Nachgeschichte der Tragödie des Corio-lanus von Livius und Plutarch über Shakespeare bis zu Brecht und mir*.[2] This iconoclastic demolition of Brecht's supposed ideals is a lively reassessment of the theme and an idiosyncratic — yet partly justified — unmasking of the aesthete Brecht intent on creating a reflection of life on the stage while the living are trampled down outside the walls of his theatre: 'In die Zeit der

Bearbeitung fällt das fatale Datum: Der siebzehnte Juni. Während sich Brecht, von Livius gestützt, den Kopf zerbrach, wie er Shakespeares nur mit Knüppeln bestückte Plebejer zu Beginn des Aufstandes schlagkräftiger bewaffnen könnte, erhoben sich, ungeprobt und unbewaffnet, die Bauarbeiter der Stalinallee, um gegen die erhöhten Normen zu protestieren, wie dazumal die Plebejer gegen den unerschwinglichen Kornpreis.' The provocative outcome of Grass's speculations was his play *Die Plebejer proben den Aufstand*; in it he establishes an unresolved tension between Brecht's declared bias in adapting *Coriolanus* and the notorious ambiguity of his reaction in June 1953 when the East Berlin workers' uprising took place on his doorstep. (Needless to say, he was not rehearsing *Coriolan* at the time, but Erwin Strittmatter's *Katzgraben*.)

However, though Brecht's *Coriolan* remains open-ended into the future, Shakespeare's play too is not really a conclusive source, but heavily dependent on the account of the Graeco-Roman chronicler Plutarch, who in his turn was indebted to the succinct Livy and a wordier Dionysius of Halicarnassus. Indeed, these historians themselves handed on unauthenticated material of a semi-legendary nature: the figure and exploits of Coriolanus were shrouded in the uncertain events connecting the expulsion of the Tarquin rulers from Rome and the establishment of the young republic (*c.* 500 B.C.). Such imprecision naturally allows great latitude to the dramatist (who is thus not exposed to the pedantic charge of falsifying history) both in the marshalling and arranging of facts to serve his purpose and in the interpretation of motive and event. In this respect Brecht is to be accused of despotic manipulation of Shakespeare's play only to the extent that the latter can be reprehended for having plundered Plutarch in his search for dramatic material. The shafts of insight of historians and dramatists that have illuminated Coriolanus from several angles make him into an enigmatic figure. This chapter will centre on the interplay of dramatic imagination between Shakespeare and Brecht which at some points may be elucidated by the perspective of the ancient chroniclers or that of the Berliner Ensemble.

A comparison of *Coriolanus* and Plutarch's *Life of Martius Coriolanus* (in the translation by North that Shakespeare knew) quickly reveals how the Elizabethan kept close to the guide-lines of his source for the major sweep of the action as it moves through successive phases: opening unrest in Rome followed by the campaign against the Volscians and the capture of Corioli; the victorious Coriolanus standing for Consul, but needing the votes of the multitude he scorns; his opposition to the tribunes and to the distribution of cheap corn, arousing the anger and hostility of the people; his swift trial and banishment; the sudden and unexpected *volte-face* that allies him with the Volscian leader Tullus Aufidius; his march to the gates of Rome and the embassy of women sent to plead with him; his surrender to his mother's entreaties and withdrawal from Rome; his death at the hands of the Volscians. Shakespeare, writing drama not history, elaborated the story-line with extra scenes and features that emphasized the personal and individual situation in a 'historical' context, and gave intuitive aesthetic coherence to his ready-made theme. Such elements are Coriolanus's wife receiving the visit of Valeria and the episode with his bellicose young son; the intensification of the personal rivalry with Aufidius and the latter's disclosure of his motives to his soldiers; the meeting of the Volscian and the Roman informer; the implication that the tribunes manipulated the trial and the voting out of spite and animosity; Coriolanus's reluctance to stand for Consul and his even greater aversion to complying with the traditional forms; the early introduction of Volumnia to urge him to placate the people; Coriolanus's subsequent anger against *all* the Romans including the 'dastard nobles'; his death incurred through the 'ungovernable violence' of his speech to the Volscians (while in Plutarch Aufidius has him cut down before he can defend himself with eloquence).

These deviations from the source all add greatly to the individualization of the drama, shifting the centre of force from the historical record to the interplay of human personalities. To make the grand simplicity of his tragic sweep even more effective Shakespeare omitted the plebeians' secession to the Mons Sacer and the social grievances leading up to it, together with the consequent granting of tribunes to represent the people; he simply has Martius announce in the opening scene that two of them will be Brutus and Sicinius — an inaccurate use of the sources, but at once identifying a pair of the main protagonists for us. Nor does Shakespeare mention the enforced colonization of the recently plague-ridden town of Vellitrae and the resulting hatred of the people when Martius woos their votes. These are exclusions that greatly strengthen the structure of the tragedy by concentrating the energy of motivation into few but powerful moments.

Notes to an early version of his adaptation show that Brecht initially intended to keep close to the accounts of the legend in order to be more credible in the interpreting of it; this meant starting the plot at an earlier point than Shakespeare had done, namely with the secession.[3] The original conception, with the curve of the play progressing from event to event, would in its chronicle flow have been congenial to Brecht's interest in the *process* of action, the 'Spannung auf den Gang'. Although the early division of his version into three acts comprising thirteen scenes gave way finally to Shakespeare's five-act shape, and the secession theme was also dropped, Brecht stuck firmly to his interpretation of the play in political terms, as his summary shows:

Erster Akt. Dieser Akt umfaßt den Spielverlauf vom Ausbruch der Revolution bis zu ihrem Sieg. *Zweiter Akt.* Der zweite Akt fußt auf den Erfolgen der Plebs am Heiligen Berge. Er umfaßt den Plan der Konterrevolution, den systematischen Aufbau des Prestiges von Coriolanus, die Wahl Coriolanus durch Trick zum Konsul und das Mißlingen der Gegenrevolution. Dieser allgemeine Verlauf der Handlung ist durch die Sage festgelegt und kann nicht verändert werden. *Dritter Akt.* Dieser Akt hat zum Inhalt den Landesverrat von Coriolan, die Entstehung des Imperialismus, der nach zwei Seiten hin siegt: einerseits über den revolutionären Flügel unter

Brutus und andrerseits über den reaktionären Flügel unter Coriolan. So weit er diese Dinge darstellt, ist er die absolut notwendige und logische und auch die historisch tatsächliche Schlußfolgerung aus Revolution und Gegenrevolution.[4]

In keeping with such a reading he asserted that any private action could only be admitted if it fitted into the overall political frame. This meant that Brecht had to re-think the function and motivation of many characters, especially Volumnia.

The stress laid by many commentators on Shakespeare's preoccupation with 'dramatic art' and 'human nature' *per se* seems to point to a vast gap between Shakespeare and Brecht. Dover Wilson claims that the central theme is 'not politics or fighting, but Nature, or if you will human-kindness, a leit-motif of all his last plays . . . In *Coriolanus*, as in his other plays, Shakespeare is interested in dramatic art and nothing else . . . If, therefore, in reshaping his source material, he seems to tilt the balance here in favour of the patricians or there in favour of the plebs, he does so for no other purpose than to keep his tragedy moving upon an even keel or to give a character an opportunity for an interesting speech'.[5] Yet Hazlitt, in his *Characters of Shakespeare's Plays*, had been quite vehement about the political 'message' of *Coriolanus*: 'Any one who studies it may save himself the trouble of reading Burke's Reflections or Paine's Rights of Man or the Debates in both Houses of Parliament since the French Revolution or our own. The arguments for and against aristocracy or democracy, on the privileges of the few and the claims of the many, on liberty and slavery, power and the abuse of it, peace and war, are here very ably handled, with the spirit of a poet and the acuteness of a philosopher.'[6] More recently D. J. Enright has maintained that *Coriolanus* embodies 'certain qualities of an intellectual debate' and is political in so far as the Rome here portrayed is peopled by factions.[7] MacCallum may be right in stating that 'despite the general appreciation which Shakespeare shows for the attitude of the Roman *Civitas*, he has no perception of the real issues between the plebeians and the patricians, or of the course which the controversy took'.[8] But a more accurate analysis of what Shakespeare was doing in *Coriolanus* is given by a critic concerned with the political aspect:

Shakespeare being Shakespeare, his political characters interest us also as private persons and have an interior life of their own, but they are essentially political characters . . .

Coriolanus presents the aristocrat in a vain effort to come to terms with the common man . . .

Shakespeare presented in 1609, without malice or favour, a Roman aristocrat who despised the electorate. Shakespeare was not primarily interested in the merits of aristocracy or democracy as a form of government. He was interested in Coriolanus as an individual who happened to be confronted with a political situation which arises in every period and remains with us today.[9]

For Shakespeare the individual destiny may be borne along and decided in political terms because the constellation of determining factors happens to take that form; for Brecht, reared on the historicity of Hegel and Marx, nothing is arbitrary, no man can be abstracted as an autonomous being from the social network of the *polis*. Thus the re-working of *Coriolanus* amounted to an investigation of the events of the hero's life in the context of the community, an undertaking justified for Brecht by the shifting perspective of each historical epoch that inevitably alters the attitude to and understanding of the past:

Ich glaube nicht, daß die neue Fragestellung Shakespeare davon abgehalten hätte, einen 'Coriolan' zu schreiben.
Ich glaube, er hätte ungefähr in der Weise, wie wir es taten, dem Geist der Zeit Rechnung getragen, vermutlich mit weniger Überzeugung, aber mit mehr Talent.[10]

There are two impulses simultaneously at work in Brecht's concern for adaptation. One is the immediate practical need for a repertoire providing aesthetic theatrical enjoyment which might, however, run the risk of being a mindless distortion if no account were taken of the enormous changes in society and sensibility that have come about between the time of the original and our own. This entails the second impulse that is inherent in Brecht's concept of epic theatre, namely that the theatre has an exegetic task to perform closely bound up with the evolution in the audience — Brecht dreamt of a proletarian one — of a reflective historical sense as a function of the aesthetic apprehension. A close collaborator on *Coriolan* has described this essentially didactic procedure:

Brecht betrachtete seinen Versuch, das Stück für heute spielbar zu machen, durchaus als vorläufig. Er schrieb: 'Bei stärkerer Entwicklung des Gefühls für Geschichte — und wenn das Selbstbewußtsein der Massen größer wird — kann man alles so ziemlich belassen wie es ist.' (Notiz vom 27.12.1952). Für heute jedoch hielt er die Aufdeckung der historischen Zusammenhänge für notwendig.[11]

In setting about the task of laying bare the causal historical mechanism in *Coriolanus* Brecht appears on the face of it to have adhered fairly respectfully to the structure of action provided by Shakespeare. A scrutiny of the two texts reveals, however, that Brecht's version is only about sixty per cent of the original in length (Act I, Scenes 4-10 are not included in the calculation as Brecht did not supply a battle scene). Moreover, of this about seventeen per cent is wholly new material concentrated in a few scenes, so that Brecht actually used only half of Shakespeare's text — a radical adaptation by any standard. But the *positive* changes remain few for Brecht relies to a great extent on omission rather than alteration; almost every scene shows a drastic curtailment of speeches and metaphorical language that turns this already austere tragedy into an even more astringent analysis of an uncompromisingly harsh theme. Bullough concluded that the manner in which Shakespeare used Plutarch made *Coriolanus* 'the most economical and closely designed of all Shakespeare's plays, the history-play with least "surplusage", the most intense from start to finish, structurally one of his finest achievements'.[12] It was the soundness of this structure that allowed Brecht to dismantle so much of it without impairing its stability.

The principles of adaptation subsequently formulated in the essay *Einschüchterung durch die Klassizität* had to be applied to a complicated situation in *Coriolanus*. Brecht claimed that to bring out the original conceptual content of a work the adaptor had to subject both its historical context and the individual attitude of the author to intensive study. Out of these exponential factors should emerge, as he never tired of reiterating, the socio-critical statement of the play. *Coriolanus*, in contrast to the plays by Lenz, Hauptmann, Molière and Farquhar, is the only work (apart from the *Antigone* in Hölderlin's translation) handled by Brecht in which the playwright and his theme are not synchronous. A significant element actively incorporated into Brecht's other adaptations is his assessment of the author's own attitudes to his time, conditioned as these are by the relevant epoch. This becomes more complex in *Coriolanus*, for the core of Brecht's interest lies in ancient Rome and he substitutes a historical analysis for Elizabethan notions. The perspective of the seventeenth century swings through an angle to become that of the twentieth. This does not diminish the impact of late Tudor and Jacobean conditions on Shakespeare's play and Brecht was well aware of this. The Reformation had generated widespread social unrest, especially as a result of the rapacity of the new landlords who had taken over the monastery lands, the eviction of peasants to make way for sheep-rearing that supplied the expanding wool trade, and the increasing acquisitive enclosure of common land. Kett's Norfolk rebellion in 1548/9 was economically motivated; in 1604 the people of Northamptonshire protested to Parliament against 'the depopulation and daily excessive conversion of tillage into pasture', and not long after, in 1607/8, scarce food and high prices brought about the Midland Revolt, when rebellion spread from Northamptonshire to Warwickshire and Leicestershire. All these troubles provided parallels with Plutarch's 'sedition at Rome, by reason of famine' and the prolonged struggles over the agrarian laws.

Of more significance for *Coriolanus* than *events* in England is the manner in which the underlying postulates of the drama reflect and incorporate in action the contemporary political notions to which Shakespeare was necessarily exposed. Paramount in the conception of the structure of the state at this time was the ideal of a stable organic entity wholly dependent on the peaceful interrelation of its separate constituents and that must be protected at all costs against disintegration stemming from internal strife or the injurious malfunctioning of any single part. Many critics have interpreted this view as the rational inference from the political equilibrium brought about by the consolidation of Tudor power and absolutism, and point to 'the very real horror with which Renaissance writers regarded the presocial state of disorder and bestiality'.[13] Phillips describes how Tudor thought 'presented the state as a structure established by God or by natural reason, designed for the common good of all its members, governed by a sovereign authority, and composed of functionally determined ranks and degrees each of which, performing its appointed task, contributed to the welfare of the whole.'[14] Foremost in importance was the concept that every man had his allotted place and purpose in the state (ordained from on high in a Hegelian sense, for whom whatever structure existed was right and God-given by the very fact that it *was* that structure), and 'the very and true Commonweal' could only survive if this were accepted on all sides. Harmony and order would immediately be jeopardized by any challenge to these assumptions, so writers 'constantly warned against the social disruption which would follow failure to maintain the established order of degree and vocation'.[15]

This critic musters three grand metaphors from three opening acts by Shakespeare to exemplify the insistence on natural and ordered processes in political organization: in *Henry V* Canterbury points to the pattern of the beehive for the production of honey; Ulysses in *Troilus and Cressida* paints a dreadful picture of the catastrophic discord that would ensue if the heavenly bodies left their predestined courses; and Menenius placates the hungry citizens in *Coriolanus* with Plutarch's fable of the belly. These are, of course, representative of a vast abundance of Shakespearian imagery, especially in the Histories and Roman Plays, where factious elements and their disruptive effects play such a vital role, but no less in dramas where the micro-unit of personal relationship (father to child, husband to wife) is the centre of interest. It is not only in the state of Denmark that something is rotten, for disease and infection lurk everywhere, ready to emerge and canker and corrupt the smooth functioning of the healthiest organism. Wilson Knight locates the malady of Rome in *Coriolanus* in the internecine struggle between plebs and patricians, and sees Coriolanus as 'a poisonous agent in the political organism'.[16] But this is not to imply that Coriolanus alone is pernicious to the city, his rampant aggression can only materialize in collision with the insurgent vehemence of the plebs, and it is probably true that 'this is not the tragedy of a ruler alone or of a people alone, but a picture of the threatened disintegration of an institution including and yet superior to them both — the state'.[17]

The maintenance of an ordered state, its welfare dependent on each individual respecting and adhering to his appointed function in it — this then is a preoccupation of the Elizabethan mind. But such thinking also ensures the maintenance of a status quo on grounds that are anathema to modern social attitudes and especially to a committed person like Brecht. This is demonstrated specifically in the specious reasoning and spurious analogy of the classic fable of the belly, embroidered from Plutarch's laconic mention into a grand rhetorical figure by Menenius. In Plutarch's narrative Menenius had been among 'the pleasantest old men and the most acceptable to the people' sent by the Senate to persuade the plebeians to end their secession. Livy described him as 'an eloquent man, and one who was a favourite with the people, because he derived his origin from them', while Dionysius stressed his diplomacy and how he was 'looked upon as a person of superior wisdom and was particularly commended for his political principles, since he pursued a middle course, being inclined neither to increase the arrogance of the aristocratic party nor to permit the people to have their own way in everything'. However, in all the chronicles Menenius had died soon after the campaign in which Martius (later Coriolanus) captured Corioli, whereas Shakespeare retains him as the 'portrait of an average member of the privileged class in any community, the speaking likeness of an English squire removed to a Roman setting'.[18] He is a smooth-tongued propagandist for the patrician party, able to render the somewhat ignorant people amenable with his unctuous suavity. Jan Kott calls him 'a tactician and philosopher of opportunism',[19] and Brecht too, according to the *Programmheft*, 'hat die Figur des Menenius Agrippa vom üblich gespielten Witzemacher zum Realpolitiker aufgewertet'. The metaphor of the belly obviously has a principal part to play in the sophistry that easily sways the fickle mob in Shakespeare's play, but it is remarkable that Brecht kept it almost in its entirety simply for its celebrity, although he knew it ill fitted his own conceptions. The most he does is to hint more strongly than Shakespeare that Menenius is an empty talker by having the Erster Bürger announce him to be 'Senator und Schönredner' and alter the grudging 'yet you must not think | To fob off our disgrace with a tale' into an ironical willingness to be instructed in honeyed speech: 'Aber ich für mein Teil möchte schon lang gern schön reden lernen, und das kann man von dir, Agrippa. Schieß los!'[20]

The inherent fallacy in the fable of the belly reduces to very simple terms: in the organic whole of the human body the belly (the patricians) may appear to gorge itself but is patently performing a primary function in the economy of the natural process, the failure of which would be detrimental to the continued existence of the remaining parts. Indeed, 'the great toe' (First Citizen) is the part that could be cut off with no loss to the welfare of the body. But the image loses all force, and even masks the truth, when applied to the estates that make up the city: in economic terms, the patricians accumulate wealth and corn through power, and at the end of Menenius's oratory the plebs are no less hungry nor is the price of corn any lower. There is no natural bond between those who take and those who lose. Uncharacteristically, Brecht made no alteration or interpolation to expose this subterfuge with which Menenius vindicates a false 'natural law' in the order of society.

From elsewhere in Shakespeare, however, Brecht did borrow the gist of yet another extended metaphor extolling the supreme merit of the harmony achieved in a proper and moderate integration of the different parts of the state. Typically, natural growth in the garden (controlled by the civilizing and thoughtful care of man) provides the imagery. The scene occurs in *Richard II* (III, 4) at the point where the downcast Queen and her ladies overhear a gardener and his men discussing their work amongst the plants with unconcealed allusion to the news that Richard is about to be toppled through not exercising enough foresight and authority. While Shakespeare's protracted metaphor relies entirely on the maintenance of order, Brecht adjusts the focus and introduces the notion of equality of rights to supplant the idea of a pre-determined hierarchy. When Coriolanus is canvassing the voices of the people he finds out the trades they follow:

FÜNFTER BÜRGER: Ich bin ein Gärtner, Herr.
CORIOLAN: Und was lehrt Euch Euer Gewerbe, was den Staat angeht, denn hier sollt Ihr etwas für den Staat entscheiden.
FÜNFTER BÜRGER: Herr, mein Garten lehrt mich —
Dies kleine Reich der Beete und Rabatten —
Daß selbst die edle Rose von Milet
Von allzu üppigem Wuchs beschnitten sein muß
Soll sie gedeihn. Auch muß sie sich drein finden
Daß Kohl und Lauch und allerlei Gemüse
Von niedrer Abstammung, doch ziemlich nützlich
An ihrer Seit ihr Wasser abbekommen.
CORIOLAN: Was soll das heißen, Stimme?
FÜNFTER BÜRGER: Der Garten müßt verwildern, dächte man
Der königlichen Rose nur.[21]

The gardener's words are symptomatic of the 'New Order' that Brecht embeds in *Coriolan*; fresh factors are distinguished in the structure of the state, and value will depend on an open assessment of usefulness, not on preformed categories. Brecht jettisons the deployment of the metaphor that best conveys the Tudor ideal of the state, but keeps the political problem firmly at the core of his adaptation: it is still a question of who rules, and, perhaps, who ought to rule.

This theme of government and power in *Coriolanus* provokes conflicting views that are never likely to be resolved: is it an argument about politics or a drama of human emotions and character, is it debate or event? Dover Wilson adamantly refuses to interpret the play as a political gloss:

Inasmuch as its main theme or rather its political shell or envelope bears an accidental resemblance to the political controversies that dominate the modern world, the play is often read, and sometimes produced, as if it were a political pamphlet. The fact that some interpret in fascist and others in communist terms should be enough to prove the fallacy of such anachronism.[22]

On the other hand, in his *Causerien über Theater*, Fontane commented on a performance he attended at Sadler's Wells in 1857: '. . . wenn ich auch nirgends dem antiken Gegensatz zwischen Patriziat und Plebejertum begegnete, so hatte ich wenigstens überall den Gegensatz zwischen englischer Aristokratie und englischem mob. Diese Kerle mit ihren Knitteln waren wie von der Straße genommen.' Heine, too, detected the play's topicality for English politics in the nineteenth century and its links with a social reality outside the auditorium: 'Man sollte manchmal glauben, Shakespeare sei ein heutiger Dichter, der im heutigen London lebe und unter römischen Masken die jetzigen Tories und Radikalen schildern wolle.' And in *Shakespeare und kein Ende* Goethe voiced the common attitude that sees in Coriolanus the struggle of innate excellence to retain its rightful control over the state: 'So geht durch den ganzen *Coriolan* der Ärger durch, daß die Volksmasse den Vorzug der Bessern nicht anerkennen will.' But, though arguments about forms of government may be a strong motive force in *Coriolanus*, Shakespeare creates individuals who are far more than mouthpieces. Thus Hazlitt's assertion that the stuff of this drama consists of arguments for and against democracy can fairly be rebutted:

There are no such arguments. There are only aristocrats and democrats. He refers to power and the abuse of it. There is no discussion of this problem. There is only a proud man who assumes the right to despise persons of a lesser breed ... 'Coriolanus' is not the dramatisation of a political thesis. It is not a play in which the supreme conflict is one of political principle.[23]

Balancing the public theme are a number of aspects concerning the men and women of the drama in their private relationships and reactions. There is the personal envy and spite of the tribunes towards Coriolanus, and his pride and ambition and suicidal urge to be true to his own nature in the teeth of all practical argument. There is the motif of Coriolanus's aesthetic perception of experience: he loves bravery and the 'aristocracy of courage' for their own sakes, and his bond with Aufidius is stronger than patriotism; he seeks personal glory, and power only as an enhancement of that glory; his hatred of the populace is more aesthetic than political, and their stinking breath rather than any threat to his freedom excites his gall. There is the tense homosexual trait in Coriolanus that explains why the seasoned Menenius was set a-trembling when he received a letter from the youthful warrior (II, 1), and why he 'godded' him; it also intensifies the relationship with Aufidius, for Coriolanus loves war more than a woman, prefers his opponent in battle to a wife, thinks of his mother as a Hercules, and is welcomed like a beloved by Aufidius ('our general himself makes a mistress of him', 'Let me twine | Mine arms about that body' (IV, 5, 109 f. and 200 f.)). But in the end the 'natural' woman triumphs, Coriolanus's betrayal to Volumnia is an infidelity, Aufidius is left as the discarded lover and takes furious revenge. Such elements add immeasurably to *Coriolanus*, making it humanly exciting, injecting passion into politics within the bounds of a unique set of situations. Brecht whittles them down, either intentionally — as with the personal motives for the tribunes' loathing of Coriolanus — or as a penalty to be paid for omitting such lengthy tracts of Shakespeare's text.

As a result the play is drained of a great deal of the dramatic energy that was engendered by Shakespeare's subtle equilibrium of conscious and unconscious promptings, public and private psychology. In this respect Günter Grass sees Brecht's adaptation as a lifeless substitute for the intuitive power of the original, alleging that this version 'hat der Tragödie das naive Gefälle genommen und an dessen Stelle einen fleißigen Mechanismus gesetzt, der zwar sein Soll erfüllt und die gewollte Tendenz geschmackvoll ästhetisiert', but claiming that this spoliation does not warrant the 'Griff nach dem fremden Stoff'.[24]

Thus Brecht converts the attraction and repulsion of Coriolanus's vibrant personal rivalry with Aufidius almost entirely into the clear-cut terms of suspicion and opportunism. It is true that Shakespeare had not minimized the vein of conspiracy colouring Aufidius's behaviour towards Coriolanus: the conflict of mercy and honour when Coriolanus yields to his mother is welcomed ('Out of that I'll work | Myself a former fortune' (v, 3, 201 f.)) and exploited ('therefore shall he die, | And I'll renew me in his fall' (v, 6, 48 f.)). But the 'dark' speech ('All places yield to him . . .' (IV, 3)) with which Aufidius concludes his discussion of the situation with his Lieutenant, a meditation on the philosophy of power spawning half-articulated hopes and lurking desires, is subjected by Brecht to radical change in both content and tone that narrows the general's musings down to objective facts and attendant possibilities:

> . . . hat er Rom, dann hab ich ihn.
> Denn was er dann auch macht, ist falsch, weil er's macht.
> Faßt er den Adel unzart an, ist's aus —
> Dann lamentiert der volskische Adel, und
> Faßt er den Adel zart an, ist's auch aus —
> Dann lamentiert der volskische Adel auch.
> Der Mann hing ab vom Glück und konnte Glück
> Nicht nutzen.[25]

Brecht then keeps the skeleton of Aufidius's ponderings on services and rewards, virtue and power: the general reflection ('So our virtues | Lie in th' interpretation of the time' (IV, 7, 49 f.)) is anchored in the practical reality ('Und unser Wert hängt ab von dem Gebrauch | Den unsre Zeit macht von uns').[26] Altogether, Brecht makes the motif of suspicion in the tussle for power dominant in the relationship of the competing generals, thereby blurring less manifest factors suggested in Shakespeare's text; in the adaptation Aufidius presses his rival urgently and with less tact to action that will destroy him:

> AUFIDIUS: Wie lang willst du noch warten?
> CORIOLAN: Wir lagern morgen vor den Mauern Roms.
> AUFIDIUS: Warum nicht heut?
> CORIOLAN: Partner in diesem Feldzug
> Ihr müßt den Herrn in Antium bestätigen
> Wie rückhaltlos ich die Aktion betrieb.
> AUFIDIUS: Nicht allzu hurtig. Rückhaltlos? Gewiß . . .
> Doch auch von diesem alten Mann [i.e. Menenius], der dich
> Vergöttert, nichts von Unterwerfung, nur
> Beschwörung und die Bitte 'Geh und häng dich!'[27]

The more central theme of Coriolanus's relationship to his mother demonstrates even better how Brecht curtails imagination in favour of the aridity of political argument and decision. In Shakespeare's text there are several facets to this relationship that cohere in the intensity of emotion induced by Volumnia's kneeling before her son to plead for Rome. She is the symbol of his mother-city, but also a dominant woman who has moulded him to her ideals from childhood. His 'own nature' is as much a product of upbringing as of innate qualities; and her kneeling before him is a violation of the moral and social order that is tantamount to an infraction of natural law. Many arguments of a logical, psychological, emotional character converge in the near-blackmail of her entreaties, but the motive force that pulses through this encounter is the clash of wills between two individuals, not the question of Rome's survival:

This is not, in essentials, a conflict of class prejudice with civic patriotism, though Volumnia is free enough with references to her country. It is a conflict of personal pride with a sense of what is due from Marcius to 'great Nature'.[28]

This scene is crucial in the assessment of Brecht's version, for he and his collaborators were fully aware of its appeal to passion and intended instead to elucidate the self-interest concealed by the fire. Concerning the legend and its interpretations we read in the *Programmheft*:

Fast ausnahmslos spricht man vom Hohenlied der Sohnesliebe, die mit dem Tod bezahlt wurde ... [Brecht noticed] daß William Shakespeare die Rede merkwürdig schwunglos, mit schwachen Argumenten seitens der Mutter ausgestattet hat ... Brecht, der die Kunst Shakespeares zu hoch schätzte, um Zufälligkeiten zu unterstellen, stellte die Frage: Was, wenn Shakespeare die Rede absichtlich mit schwachen Argumenten ausgestattet hat? Vielleicht wollte Shakespeare andeuten, da seien noch andere Gründe für die Umkehr des Coriolan im Spiel; daß die Rede der Mutter zwar Anlaß zur Umkehr, keinesfalls aber alleinige Ursache ist. Und wenn dem so ist, was sind das wohl für andere Ursachen?

Perhaps Brecht had good reason to look behind the scenes of Shakespeare's dramatic construct, for we find that none of the ancient chroniclers mentions that Coriolanus was consumed by totally intransigent rage; he was instead prepared to spare Rome on 'honest and just conditions of peace' which he gave the Roman emissaries — before Volumnia's appearance — thirty days to think over. As Plutarch says: 'he willed them to restore unto the Volsces all their lands and cities they had taken from them in former wars; and, moreover, that they should give them the like honour and freedom of Rome, as they had before given to the Latins'. Shakespeare, naturally intent on shaping his material to achieve the maximum impact as drama, suppresses this 'fact', makes much of Coriolanus's unbending spurning of Cominius and Menenius in turn, and so throws into greater relief Volumnia's appeal to her son to serve both duty and honour by reconciling the two peoples. Brecht, on the other hand, severely limits Volumnia's intuitive eloquence that is designed to move Coriolanus through his better instincts. Of her two major impassioned speeches ('Should we be silent and not speak ...' and 'Nay, go not from us thus ...' (v, 3, 94–125 and 131–82)) Brecht replaces lines 94–107, retains the remainder of that speech, and effectively substitutes an entirely new text for the whole of the second:

VOLUMNIA: Könnt ich schweigen, schwiege ich.
Dann hätt ich nichts gesagt, was dich bewegte

Und tötete, und auch nicht, was umsonst.
Denn ich ging nicht wie andre Mütter weg
Das Kind zu retten, sondern zu verderben
Und zwar, wenn ich's noch menschlich find, ansonsten
Fällt's mich an . . .
        . . . Vergiß
Das kleine Ungemach, daß es mir schwerfällt
Weil mich dein Vater nicht daran gewöhnte
Jetzt mein Gesicht ins Tuch zu hüllen, wenn ich
Aus dem Haus geh, laß die kindische Rührung, wisse
Daß du auf ein sehr andres Rom marschierst
Als du verließest. Unersetzlich
Bist du nicht mehr, nur noch die tödliche
Gefahr für alle. Wart nicht auf den Rauch
Der Unterwerfung! Wenn du Rauch sehn wirst
Dann aus den Schmieden steigend, die jetzt Schwerter
Wider dich schmieden, der dem eignen Volk den
Fuß auf den Nacken setzen will und dafür
Sich seinem Feinde unterwirft. Wir aber
Der Glanz und Adel Roms
Muß nun die Rettung vor den Volskern
Dem Pöbel danken oder deinen Volskern
Die Rettung vor dem Pöbel![29]

Gone is the tearful supplication of mother to son, in its place we hear the rational persuasion of an argument that is measurable in public terms. Volumnia is made to evince a clarity of political insight and a realism in evaluating her conclusions that is not unprepared for in Shakespeare (she had earlier been successful in urging Coriolanus to curb his disdain of the populace for reasons of expediency); but the ground of this important scene is shifted from emotion to reason and its dimensions are scaled down, with a resultant change in quality. Coriolanus yields to Volumnia in petty fashion, like a politician forced out of office for an error of judgement. He is no longer the man of heroic mould invested with grandeur and expressing himself in magniloquent gesture. The fall of a tragic hero acquires an ironical connotation for Brecht who refuses to see the hero and his greatness as forming an indivisible entity; for him, personal worth is a variable of service to the community. Thus, since the hero does not necessarily carry his greatness to the grave, there is no contradiction in Brecht's reducing the stature of Coriolanus when his behaviour is socially reprehensible. Brusque notes outline the reasoning that sees the individual as not indispensable from the public point of view, for he might well hold society to ransom if he were thought irreplaceable:

Sieg Roms — Untergang Coriolans und Sieg des Plebs über den römischen Adel, dagegen [ist Volumnia] als Mutter und Patriotin. Frieden: würde Herrschaft des Plebs — demokratisches Gemeinwesen bedeuten.
    Volumnia bittet den Sohn nicht um Umkehr, sie kniet nicht nieder, sie zeigt ihm nur die Ausweglosigkeit der Lage. Rom ist nicht auf seine Umkehr angewiesen, der

Plebs wird die Stadt verteidigen — die Demokratie setzt sich aber in jedem Falle durch. Mit der Alleinherrschaft des Adels ist es vorbei. Coriolan verschuldet den Untergang seiner Klasse.

Coriolan kehrt nicht um, weil er der Sohnesliebe nachgibt, sondern weil er erkennt, daß er sich selbst überschätzt hat.

Seine neue Tragik: Coriolan wird nicht, wie er hoffte, von Rom zurückgerufen, sondern die Stadt hat sich gegen ihn bewaffnet. Der Nimbus seiner Unentbehrlichkeit ist dahin. Es stellt sich heraus, daß jedermann, auch er, entbehrlich ist. Er war als Held nützlich, aber sein Preis — die Unterwerfung Roms — ist zu hoch für die Gesellschaft. Die Tragik Coriolans ist damit aus dem Privaten — Konflikt Mutter/ Sohn — ins Gesellschaftliche gehoben: Nützlichkeit des Individuums für die Gesellschaft.[30]

Brecht's undisguised intention is thus to make public issues the fulcrum of his version, whereas Shakespeare's problem was how to create the drama of an individual out of the material of political ideas and parties. Evidence of this ambivalence in *Coriolanus* is the significant intrusion of the concept of loyalty — abstract and yet a very emotional concern — to Rome, to the Volscians, to his class, to his mother, to himself. It can be said that Shakespeare solved this problem intuitively by carrying through the *action* of the drama on the individual plane through the impingement of one life on another, while the *tone* set by the language and background reflects the collective affairs that are at stake. Wilson Knight talks of 'the sheeted iron of this play',[31] and draws attention to the essentially 'civic' setting in the imagery packed with the materials of buildings and war, hard stone and metal. Perhaps because Shakespeare used the language of the play as a vehicle to convey the harsh, uncompromising clash of party interests, few people find any poetry in it. There is no softness of language because there is no love, but as a correlate of the implacable struggle for power fought out in the city the fabric of this language is of immense expressive potency. This is possibly why Jan Kott can say that to the classicists 'it seemed incoherent, vulgar, brutal' and for the romanticists 'it was too bitter, flat and dry'; he tacitly accounts for these reactions by describing how the human interest in *Coriolanus* shrinks in the face of such bulk of public matter: 'There is only a historical chronicle, dry as a bone, though violently dramatized. There is also a monumentalized hero, who can rouse all sorts of emotions, but never sympathy.'[32] This grey, cold, inimical world in which the play unfolds is more congenial to Brecht's rigorous playing down of passions, his practice of flooding the stage in neutral white light to expose motives visually, his predilection for greys and browns and muted tones, worn articles of everyday life that channel attention to the matter under elucidation.

The core of the contrast between Shakespeare and Brecht is to be found ultimately in the attitude of the playwright to the relationship of history and drama, subject-matter and its treatment. Lessing believed that the 'inner probability' of events is what makes them credible and authentic in drama, and he advocated a handling of history that adequately describes Shakespeare's approach: 'Auf dem Theater sollen wir nicht lernen, was dieser oder jener einzelne Mensch getan hat, sondern was ein jeder Mensch von einem gewissen Charakter unter gewissen gegebenen Umständen tun werde. Die Absicht der Tragödie ist weit philosophischer, als die Absicht der Geschichte.'[33] Lessing was here combating the ingrained demand for factual verisimilitude in historical events which Shakespeare had long since jettisoned for the sake of psychological and aesthetic truth. But Brecht — like Schiller with whom he had so much in common — is an analytical interpreter of history through the medium of drama, and his plays are animations of historical textbooks rather than events relived as immediate experience. Jan Kott dismisses the superficial use of history as a mere background for personal dramas and contrasts with this the deeper historical drama of Brecht and Schiller on the one hand, and Shakespeare on the other:

They know history, have learnt it by heart, and do not often go wrong. Schiller was a classic author of this kind of historical drama. Marx used to call his characters speaking trumpets of modern ideas. They interpret history because they know the solutions it offers. They can sometimes express real trends and conflicts of social forces. But even this does not mean that the dramatization of history has been effected. It is only a historical textbook that has been dramatized. The textbook can be idealistic, as in Schiller and Romain Rolland, or materialistic, as in some dramas of Büchner and Brecht; but it does not cease to be a textbook.

Shakespeare's concept of history is of a different kind . . . History unfolds on the stage, but is never merely enacted. It is not a background or a setting. It is itself the protagonist of tragedy.[34]

The difference between the unique happening and the analysis of that happening is the difference between Shakespeare and Brecht; the latter's primary concern *is* how a particular individual acted in a precise historical context and with specific implications for the future. Thus the unending arguments about Shakespeare's *personal* opinions on the populace, the merits and faults of democracy and aristocracy, or contemporary social and political structures, are essentially peripheral to the central dramatic interest. This does not exclude the fact that Shakespeare's consciousness of his own time has relevance where circumstances are similar, but it is quite unlike the total framework of historical perspective brought to bear by Brecht, of which contemporary parallels are only a chronological culmination.

It is thus almost inevitable that a detailed and exhaustive study of the formative stages of Rome after the expulsion of the Tarquins and their dynasty should be a prerequisite for Brecht's interpretation of *Coriolanus*. The *Programmheft* presents the analysis of 'Sage und Geschichte', describing how the newly-established Roman republic had a predominantly peasant population still dominated by the aristocracy, and how the latter's attempts to crush the small (middle class) property owner and keep the peasants in subjection led to a long-drawn-out class struggle:

In diesem Klassenkampf war die Verweigerung des Kriegsdienstes die wirkungs-
vollste Waffe der Plebejer, deren Anwendung u.a. zur Wahl eigener Interessenvertreter, der Volkstribunen, führte und damit zu weiteren Erfolgen der um ihre
ökonomischen und politischen Rechte kämpfenden Klasse . . . Shakespeare benutzte
die Aufzeichnungen des Plutarch als Stoff, um in seiner 'Tragödie des Coriolanus'
— einem Stück mit Parabelcharakter — auf Ereignisse im England seiner Zeit zu
reflektieren: auf die mit dem Ende der Tudorherrschaft ausbrechenden Kämpfe
zwischen Adel und dem erstarkten, politische Anerkennung fordernden Bürgertum.

Brecht's collaborator Käthe Rülicke, after summarizing the background of
Shakespeare's time — especially the contradictions arising from the collision
between the feudal Stuarts and the rising Puritan bourgeoisie — defines the
contrasting approaches of the two dramatists, Shakespeare going for the
individual hero and his fate, Brecht taking into account the historical repercussions of his actions:

Shakespeare gestaltete die Krise der untergehenden Aristokratie. Brecht gestaltete
das Heraufkommen der neuen Klasse. Shakespeare zeigt seinen Coriolan als einen
glänzenden Helden, der an seinen Leidenschaften zugrunde geht, den sein Stolz zum
Feind des Vaterlandes gemacht hat, und er zeigt das Volk als einen rohen und unge-
bildeten Haufen, der für den großen Mann kein Verständnis aufbringt. Brecht zeigt
Coriolan, durchaus im Stück ablesbar, als reaktionärsten Interessenvertreter des
Adels. Nicht sein Charakter führt zu seinem Unglück, sondern sein Unverständnis
gegenüber der historischen Entwicklung. Indem er den gesellschaftlich überholten
Zustand der Monarchie wiederherstellen will, gerät er in Gegensatz zu Rom — nicht
nur zu den Plebejern, sondern auch zu seiner eigenen Klasse. Seine historisch rück-
läufigen Anstrengungen führen zu seinem Untergang.[35]

It is inaccurate to argue that Shakespeare was vindicating in *Coriolanus* the
aristocratic form of government, and that Brecht reversed this by promoting
the plebs; instead he introduced bias where it was absent in Shakespeare by
exploiting the latter's powerful realism. Tendentiousness is not a yardstick for
measuring Shakespeare's play, though it is for the adaptation. In clouding this
differentiation Käthe Rülicke distorts Shakespeare:

Nur eine handfest gebaute, auf echten Klassenwidersprüchen basierende Fabel
konnte diese Umkehrung der Tendenz vertragen. Das Stück Shakespeares bleibt
auch bei Einnahme des entgegengesetzten Klassenstandpunktes intakt, lebendig und
erweist sich als in hervorragendem Maße realistisch.[36]

Another East German critic, Friedrich Dieckmann, suggesting with cautious
respect for Shakespeare that it is 'der Widerstand einer großen und gültigen
Form, der ihn [Brecht] zu veränderndem Eingriff reizt',[37] discriminates more
perceptively between the realism — and consequently the aims and methods
— of the two playwrights. He acknowledges that there must be some sort of
affinity of viewpoint between them which is crystallized in 'der realistische
Bezug . . ., in den Shakespeare hier einen politischen Stoff zu seinen sozialen
Bedingungen gestellt hat', and goes on to argue that Brecht's task was to make
the adaptation hinge on the socio-political reality immanent in the situation,

not on the moral make-up of the hero. It was necessary to show the reaction of the hero to the demands of his position in that society rather than the reactions of other people to him.

In keeping with his 'textbook' conception of history Brecht makes no pretence of being truly objective; unashamedly he sides with the plebeians and effectively transposes the ideological action to a modern context. If we accept that Shakespeare imposed the political and social thinking of his own era on the Roman situation, then Brecht is only adopting the same procedure in grafting on to Shakespeare's play the categories of the twentieth century. The discrepancy between them is a measure of the gap separating their periods: the idea of a harmonious hierarchical commonwealth is very far removed from the representation of society as a stratification into classes locked in bitter struggle, the outcome of which is as historically and impersonally inevitable as the order of the 'commonweal' was in accordance with natural and divine law. Whether these political philosophies are absolute or relative is itself a philosophical question; it suffices that Brecht subscribes to and *operates* with the criteria of post-Marxian consciousness — his ideological framework is cast entirely in terms of the class structure. The realistic resilience of Shakespeare's drama is proved by the fact that many critics of *Coriolanus* talk almost unawares in terms of class division.[38] But Brecht goes beyond Shakespeare and is qualitatively different in that he has *consciously* superimposed the modern perspective, even to the point of applying anachronistic terminology in designating Menenius a 'Realpolitiker' and discussing whether Sicinius (in an early version) possesses 'die meisten Fehler eines sozialdemokratischen Kompromißlertums'.[39] Dieckmann recognizes the intensity of Brecht's reaction to events he had lived through, and construes this as the reason for the almost rabid projection of his virulence towards Hitler on to Coriolanus, after shattering the dictator's contemporary image in Arturo Ui. This reading of Coriolanus is 'ein unhistorisches Unterfangen, das eine Über-Entlarvung zeitigt, aber geboren aus dem Trieb, den gehaßten Zeitgenossen bis in den letzten Schlupfwinkel zu verfolgen und ihm nach der Gegenwart auch die Vergangenheit zu rauben'.[40]

As has been said, Brecht scrutinizes the Roman context analytically, where Shakespeare, bent on a quite different dramaturgical intention, could ignore the historical factor and create a realistic setting for his individuals. What Shakespeare does suggest is that there existed already in this rudimentary stage of what was to become a mighty empire the ethos of city republic, family organization, great patriotic deeds and greater reputations, that was to leave its mark and its myths imprinted on the consciousness and imagination of Western civilization. MacCallum describes how this sense of grandeur emerges from Volumnia's actions to create in the spectator a feeling of the 'majesty and omnipotence of the Eternal City'.[41] In contrast to this stands Brecht's dry formulation of the Roman situation in modern terminology:

Nur in Rom ist ein politisches Problem kaum ein religiöses, und nur in Rom findet sich diese Simplifizierung und dabei diese strenge Klassenschichtung, die für das Stück notwendig ist . . .
Zweitens bietet Rom eine besonders starre und eindeutige Klassenscheidung. Drittens ist ein Klassenkampfmittel wie die Auswanderung absolut einmalig und nur im antiken Rom durchführbar und vorgekommen. Viertens dadurch, daß man als Schauplatz Rom wählt, gewinnt die ganze Handlung weltpolitische Bedeutung . . .
Dann ist es auch eine Tatsache, daß Rom seine inneren Klassengegensätze vermittels einer antiken Form von Imperialismus ausglich.[42]

Such cool probing of the mechanism of the Roman state cannot accommodate the emotional fascination of the Idea of Rome, and begins to dispel the aura of untouchable majesty that instills uncritical awe. An outline of the action of the drama in the *Programmheft* — again in modern terms — is a further characteristic step in the deflation of the myth of Coriolanus's greatness. However, the appraisal of a situation in up-to-date terms is not of itself truly historical; to be so it requires an awareness of the consequences of events, the resultant of counterbalanced forces in time, projected into the future. This is illustrated especially in the added final scene where Brecht attempts to integrate the historical impulse into the dramatic fabric of his adaptation by opening the play into the future. We see a placid Senate dealing with its everyday business *after* the death of Coriolanus, which for Shakespeare had been the end of the drama and with it the play:

Brecht deutet mit nur einer kleinen Schlußszene die tatsächliche historische Weiterentwicklung an. Es wird deutlich, wie die Parteinahme für die Plebejer eine Fabelführung ermöglicht und erzwingt, die den objektiven gesellschaftlichen Gesetzmäßigkeiten entspricht.[43]

It is worth noting that Brecht did not adhere, any more than Shakespeare, to the 'historical' facts: he kept to the assassination of Coriolanus (though Livy hints at discrepant accounts of how he met his death, and that he may even have lived on in exile), but had no authority for depicting the peaceful business in the Senate nor for implying that control was in the hands of the tribunes and therefore of the plebs. Brecht was not, however, presenting a re-enactment of events, he was postulating here historical potentiality, as in the brief scene he substitutes for the victorious return of the ladies, and their welcome, in v, 5:

> BOTE: Die Neuigkeit!
> Die Volsker ziehen ab und Marcius mit!
> BRUTUS: Der Stein hat sich bewegt. Das Volk erhebt
> Die Waffen, und die alte Erde bebt.[44]

The messenger's news comes from the preceding scene ('The Volscians are dislodged, and Marcius gone' (v, 4, 42)), but Brutus's couplet — ironically Shakespearian in its closing position — skilfully reverts to the image Menenius had used (v, 4, 1–8) to illustrate the immovability of Coriolanus's stubbornness:

MENENIUS: See you yond coign o' th' Capitol, yond cornerstone?
SICINIUS: Why, what of that?
MENENIUS: If it be possible for you to displace it with your little finger, there is some hope the ladies of Rome, especially his mother, may prevail with him. But I say there is no hope in't: our throats are sentenced, and stay upon execution.

In the adaptation it is not left at this: Brutus replies, in the knowledge that Volumnia had more persuasive matter than tears to take to her son: 'Er mag unbeweglich sein durch ihre Rede — obgleich das nicht so sicher ist, sie hat ihm manches zu berichten, was ihm neu sein wird — der Stein dort ist unbeweglich. Ein Erdbeben, und ich bewege ihn vielleicht danach doch.'[45] By cleverly repeating the motif, Brecht creates a sudden tension that leaps between the two moments and matches the *real* convulsion that has taken place in the state; it is the signal that the revolution, which is indeed an earthquake, has toppled the patrician power embodied in Coriolanus.

It becomes very apparent from any consideration of the handling of the political and historical content of *Coriolanus* that neither Shakespeare nor Brecht is objective, and neither would claim to be so. The latter is evidently the more outspokenly committed — it is certainly easier to identify radical commitment which tends to change rather than support for the status quo — but many critics accuse Shakespeare of sustaining the nobility because of his unflattering portrait of the mob. Phillips argues that this is inevitable, given the political ideas current in Shakespeare's time: 'In the turbulent history of Rome in this period Tudor theorists who argued in defense of monarchy and the hierarchy of degrees found a convincing demonstration of the dangers of democratic government.' He describes how Shakespeare's 'expressions of contempt for the plebeians are qualified by a sympathetic presentation of the grievances of the people' and thinks this impartiality suggests that Shakespeare's main political interest was 'not in the privileges of a special class, but in the welfare of the whole state.' Coriolanus demonstrated 'the disastrous consequences of violating those principles by which a healthy political society is maintained'.[46]

In the light of this argument it is reasonable to deduce that the idea of 'specialty of rule' was for Shakespeare and his contemporaries a tacit assumption underlying their political attitudes, conducive therefore to a maintenance of existing structures and a hindrance to change. Brecht leaves no one in the dark about his intentions: he sets the class struggle between plebs and patricians squarely at the heart of his adaptation, unblushingly asserting his right — just as the bourgeois had done — to 'kräftig interpretieren, d.h. parteiisch vorgehen, umso mehr als man damit die Partei des Volks nehmen kann'.[47] His blunt aim is to demonstrate the political maturity and reliability of the lower classes:

Grundlinie: Sh[akespeare] behandelt den Plebs als 'unreife Klasse'. Das sind die Argumente der heutigen Bourgeoisie: das Proletariat ist nicht reif für die Führung.

Bei uns muß der Plebs in der Lage sein, die Macht zu übernehmen. Das ist zu zeigen.[48]

Brecht thus introduces a single, goal-directed criterion, defines its values uncomprisingly and creates schematically in accordance with it.

The treatment that Brecht metes out to Shakespeare's play is thus not based intrinsically on dramatic grounds but reflects a far more fundamental problem, that of comparing the value of two inherently diverse organisms or political philosophies. The question we are driven to ask is whether the 'democratic' rule of the plebs advocated by Brecht is in any way an advance on the 'specialty of rule' conditioning Shakespeare's play. In a philosophical sense it is difficult to maintain that historical change is progress any more than are changes in art or other areas of human activity. The concept of progress necessitates self-generating axioms through which history can be categorized and evaluated; a phenomenistic apprehension of consecutive events in time could not accept as objective the Marxist analysis of history as an inevitable sequence of necessary stages within the conceptual framework of an evolutionary view. For Marx, as for Brecht, a later stage in development is *necessarily* better, but such discrimination is impossible in an existential conception of experience. The modernity of *Coriolanus* lies in this problem which overshadows the arguments engrossing Marxists and historians, and disturbs because the answer to it can only be relativist and pessimistic. Critics sense the irresolvable contradictions that make *Coriolanus* enigmatic, dramatic and at the same time a subject of speculation about the moral value of history. Jan Kott is well aware of the doubtful accuracy of objectivity:

Eagles do not lower themselves to the level of rats and crows. Coriolanus wants the world to recognize his greatness. But the world is divided into plebeians and patricians. Coriolanus's hierarchy of nature does not agree with the real world. Rats have no wish to consider themselves worse than eagles.[49]

Wilson Knight, too, resorts to the animal world to define the relativity of perspective:

Coriolanus is shown as infinitely superior to the tribunes in all noble qualities, in all exquisite strength. He is proud as a lion might be proud among jackals. But that is no reason why jackals should tolerate a lion in their midst.[50]

Eagles and rats, lions and jackals: superiority in the phenomenal world is a matter of greater strength or staying power. The reasoning faculty of human beings superimposes a moral scheme of value on the chaos of occurrences and especially on the affairs of men. Part of the richness of Shakespeare is that this drama does not allow the phenomenal world to be reduced to nothing more than a well of illustrations for mental constructs.

A major contradiction arises from the personality and position of Shakespeare's Coriolanus. A great general, he has the virtues of a leader; turned against those he leads, these same virtues become grave demerits as he takes on the appearance of a tyrant. A double moral emerges: 'An ambitious general aiming at dictatorial power is extremely dangerous for the republic . . . The moral drawn from the second chapter is very bitter indeed. The city that exiles its leader becomes defenceless. The people can only hate and bite, but are unable to defend their city.'[51] Coriolanus complicates the deceptively simple-looking class struggle; he 'accepts two of the classic opposites of the plebeian theory: the rich — the poor, the rulers — the governed. But to these two, he adds two more: the noble — the base, the wise — the fools'.[52] That is, to a clear factual situation concerning the actual distribution of wealth and power, Coriolanus links a philosophy, a value judgement regarding the worth of individuals. That is perhaps the point in which the adaptation deviates in essentials from its source; Brecht insists on gearing value judgements to the factual class struggle — the worth of a man is a function of his use to society.

This conception leads once again straight to the core of the adaptation, namely the preoccupation with the individual's irreplaceability, in particular the position of that servant of the state, Coriolanus. For Shakespeare, the irreplaceability of Coriolanus resides in his uniqueness as an individual. Unambiguously, Brecht adopts a different standpoint from either Plutarch or Shakespeare, for he categorically denies that Coriolanus was necessary to Rome, and hinges the drama on the hero's mistaken *belief* in his indispensability:

Die Geschichtsschreibung Plutarchs und das Stück Shakespeares haben etwa die gleiche Tendenz.

Der römische Plebs erpreßt den Senat, als die benachbarten Volsker auf Rom marschieren. Da der Plebs zum Kriegführen gebraucht wird, erhält er als Gegenleistung Volkstribunen zugestanden. Die Haltung beider Schreiber richtet sich gegen den Plebs; die Tribunen sind Intriganten.

Bei Plutarch wie bei Shakespeare ist CORIOLAN die Tragödie eines großen und unentbehrlichen Mannes. Auch wenn Coriolan in seinen Ansprüchen zu weit geht, ist das nur die Überstiegenheit einer an sich großartigen Haltung, an der er ja dann auch tragisch zugrunde geht.

In der Bearbeitung verschiebt sich die TRAGÖDIE DES INDIVIDUUMS zu der TRAGÖDIE DES GLAUBENS AN DIE UNENTBEHRLICHKEIT. Es stellt sich heraus, daß der Glaube an die Unentbehrlichkeit zwar das Individuum vernichtet, nicht aber ohne weiteres das Volk. Es kann zwar eine große Anzahl von Personen in eine tragische Situation kommen, — sie müssen sich dann von dem Individuum, das sich gegen sie erhebt, befreien.[53]

This represents a significant alteration in attitude to the tragic theme, for on this new conceptual basis the dramatic function of the plebs undergoes a qualitative dialectical change. The people are no longer a foil to Coriolanus, a stone that makes him stumble or on which he sharpens his blade, they are instead equal to him in importance and potential value. Whereas Shakespeare handled the plebs as an unavoidable element in his massive concentration on the lone hero, Brecht reorganized the dramatic pattern so that in place of the single axis of the hero's path, around which everything moves, the adaptation is shaped as a system of co-ordinates mutually interacting to produce an independent resultant — namely, a view of social structure. Hence Brecht can make observations on audience interest in the hero, revealing his view that events are explicable in terms of conscious mental attitudes and judgements, and not to be left to the arbitrary vagaries of individual characteristics of personality. Pride may be a feature of Coriolanus but is not to be taken as the dominant motive to vindicate his actions; the collective fate also demands recognition and must be presented so that the audience experiences it as the price paid for Coriolanus's rise to power, leading ultimately to defiance of this hero:

Und was den Helden betrifft, ist die Gesellschaft an einem andern Aspekt interessiert, der sie unmittelbar angeht, nämlich dem Glauben des Helden an seine Unersetzlichkeit. Diesem Glauben kann sie sich nicht beugen, ohne den Untergang zu riskieren. Das setzt sie in unabdingbaren Gegensatz zu diesem Helden, und die Art des Spiels muß ihr das gestatten, ja muß das erzwingen.[54]

One of Brecht's most direct and abruptly effective methods for scaling down the sheer size of the traditional hero to dimensions that will minimize his apparent indispensability and the undiscriminating, purely emotional involvement of the audience in his life, is the device of underplaying the magnitude of the single deed or situation. Brecht's resistance to individual greatness is motivated in part by the conviction that the community is only viable as a true collective of mutually enhancing efforts and in part by the knowledge that the accompaniment of celebrity is the expendable small person, the object of injustice and exploitation, an outrage to the dignity of man. Brecht found his technique for deflating the great man in what can be termed the Icarus syndrome, from the brief notes he made (about 1939) analysing the 'narrative' elements figuring in a number of paintings by Pieter Bruegel, especially the *Landscape with the Fall of Icarus*. This painting closely follows the account in Ovid's *Metamorphoses*, but Bruegel offsets and firmly neutralizes the mythical occurrence by various means such as the minute space to one corner of the canvas actually taken up by the plunge into the sea (only the legs appear above the surface), and the sailors on the merchant vessel, the ploughman, shepherd and fisherman in the foreground going about their tranquil daily tasks, looking away from and totally unaware of the tragedy:

Winzigkeit dieses legendären Vorkommnisses (man muß den Gestürzten suchen). Die Figuren wenden sich von dem Ereignis ab. Schöne Darstellung der Aufmerksamkeit, welche das Pflügen beansprucht. Der fischende Mann rechts vorn, der zum Wasser in besonderer Beziehung steht. Daß die Sonne schon untergeht, was viele erstaunt hat, bedeutet wohl, daß der Sturz lang währte. Wie anders darstellen, daß Ikarus zu hoch flog? Daidalos ist längst nicht mehr sichtbar. Flämische Zeitgenossen in antiker, südlicher Landschaft. Besondere Schönheit und Heiterkeit der Landschaft während des grauenhaften Ereignisses.[55]

It must be made clear that the dispersal of attention involved in this 'narrative' process does not disparage the colossal deed, but sets it in a total configuration of simultaneous events each of which can be assimilated rationally as well as affectively by the observer. This is the distance induced by concurrent focuses. Brecht inserts a fine example of the Icarus syndrome into *Coriolanus* by subordinating to his own ends Shakespeare's IV, 3, in which a Roman informer betrays the valuable knowledge of Coriolanus's banishment to a Volscian spy. Bullough censures Shakespeare for this 'not entirely necessary scene, intended to bridge the few days during which in Plutarch Marcius was in a turmoil of indecision and choler'.[56] The small incident does in fact prefigure the greater betrayal by Coriolanus — Shakespeare knew his business better than Bullough. But whether or not Brecht also thought that Shakespeare had nodded with this scene, he replaced it by a completely new text:

RÖMER: Warum kehrt Ihr um? Ich komme aus Rom, aber ich bin kein Räuber!

VOLSKER: Wenn das nicht der Gerber Lätus aus der Gasse der Sandalenmacher ist!

RÖMER: Piger! Sieht man sich endlich wieder?
   Sie umarmen sich.

RÖMER: Wie geht es der Frau? Bäckt sie noch die kleinen Hirseflanden?

VOLSKER: Immer noch; sie kann die Rosinen bekommen, aber mir fehlt in der Seilerei der Hanf. Deshalb gehe ich nach Rom, Alter.

RÖMER: Und ich gehe nach Antium, zu sehen, ob sie dort meine Lederhocker brauchen können.

VOLSKER: Bist du durch Corioli gekommen, das ihr uns gestohlen habt? Wie ist es dort?

RÖMER: Du wirst es sehen. Es hat sich kaum geändert. Man ißt, schläft und zahlt Steuern. Wie ist es in Antium?

VOLSKER: Man schläft, ißt und zahlt Steuern. Und in Rom?

RÖMER: Man ißt auch, schläft auch und zahlt auch Steuern. Aber wir haben einen Aufstand gehabt und den Coriolan vertrieben.

VOLSKER: Wirklich, seid ihr ihn los? Ich kann dir sagen: ich werde Rom leichteren Herzens betreten.

RÖMER: Ich verließ es mit geringerer Furcht.

VOLSKER: Mensch, daß endlich wieder Friede ist!

RÖMER: Gute Reise, Piger, und glückliche Geschäfte in Rom!

VOLSKER: Gute Geschäfte in Antium, Lätus![57]

Here are all the elements Brecht detected in the alienating epic painting of Bruegel: the unknown small artisans, the trivial details of daily life with its repetitions and sameness in different places, the strong sense of unassuming idyll, and above all the attenuation of what should be the central, all-absorbing fact — the banishment of Coriolanus — that has been shrunk to the effect of a minor ripple on a placid pool. This is the view from below of massive, world-shaking events that are relativized in the perspective of the common man. It may appear that this scene is identical in function with the well-known Shakespearian technique of inserting brief episodes in his tragedies that give humble people a chance to comment on the doings of their masters — as in the conversation (omitted by Brecht) among Aufidius's serving-men after their master has made Coriolanus welcome as an ally. The significant difference is that the Shakespearian remarks from the common people still have their focus entirely in the lives of their superiors, while Brecht, aiming at an all-embracing 'historical' assemblage of situations, ascribes at least the same weight to the private circumstances of the two artisans as to the calamity that has befallen Coriolanus and will find a place in the history books. As Brecht noted in the *Fall of Icarus*, the catastrophe and the idyll are dialectically reciprocal and throw each other into relief.

From being a minor scene in *Coriolanus* this meeting on the highway between Volscian and Roman becomes a king-pin in the dramatic conception of Brecht. It is backed up by the vital closing scene in the Senate added in the adaptation to provide the final blotting-out of the aggressive hero who has dominated so much of the action:

> KONSUL: Der Antrag der Tribunen, Ländereien
> Nach der Erobrung eingezogen, den Bewohnern
> Coriolis zurückzugeben, ist Gesetz.
> SENATOR: Antrag, betreffend eine Wasserleitung
> Vom dritten Hügel zu den östlichen Gärten.
> *Ein Bote bringt eine Nachricht.*
> KONSUL: Hier eine Meldung, daß in Antium
> Am gestrigen Vormittage Cajus Marcius
> Erschlagen wurd.
> *Stille.*
> MENENIUS: Antrag: Sein Name, nunmehr, da er tot
> Der ihn einmal so groß trug und einmal
> So wenig glücklich, sei am Kapitol
> Als eines Römers und als eines . . .
> BRUTUS: Antrag:
> Daß der Senat fortfahre mit der Sichtung
> Der täglichen Geschäfte.
> KONSUL: Eine Frage:
> Die Marcier bitten, daß, nach der Verordnung
> Numa Pompilius' für die Hinterbliebenen
> Von Vätern, Söhnen, Brüdern, doch den Frauen
> Erlaubt werd öffentliches Tragen
> Von Trauer für zehn Monde.
> BRUTUS: Abgeschlagen.
> *Der Senat setzt seine Beratungen fort.*[58]

Parallel with the everyday tasks and cares of the tanner and sandal-maker is the day-to-day, somewhat dull business of the Senate; again the news of Coriolanus's death scarcely stirs the surface.[59] It is possible that Brecht went beyond the bounds of the psychologically probable in not allowing even a hint of relief to enter at the disappearance of this dangerous man. The naked directness of juxtaposition practised by Brecht in this scene poses with brutal frankness the question of fame and greatness — not the less powerful for being only implied — although the complete obliteration of Coriolanus in the public memory was avoided in the Ensemble production by omitting the Konsul's request and therefore Brutus's curt 'Abgeschlagen'.[60]

The alienating effect of these two scenes stands in startling contrast to their relative insignificance among the properly *dramatic* nodes of the play. They represent nothing less than the regrouping of the historical molecules to give a new pattern and quality to our understanding of past events, and a revaluation of accepted norms of fame, prestige, value. For this reason the figure of Coriolanus is subjected to a rigorous investigation, his possible motives are scrutinized within Brecht's fresh conceptions of the causal concatenation of events rather than the erratic outbursts of personality. Wilson Knight entitles his essay on *Coriolanus* 'The Royal Occupation', this being indeed a traditional idea of the kingly qualities: pride, bravery, skill in war, indifference to pain and injury, delight in battle and success in slaughter. Coriolanus is 'a slaying-machine of mechanic excellence',[61] and his son, too, is being reared to fit into this mould of military prowess.[62] Brecht, and later in production the Ensemble, was concerned with the *application* and target of Coriolanus's abilities. War-making is the only value for the warrior, but it is a value, especially in the context of the emergent Roman republic fighting for survival. Hence the need to recognize the important function of the battle-scenes in establishing the general's initial worth to Rome, justifying the acclamation of the masses and determining his rough-shod methods in a civilian situation.

The heart of the matter, for Shakespeare as well as Brecht, lies in the relationship of the individual to society: 'People of the Renaissance were fascinated by the problem of absolute power; the mechanism by means of which a good prince is transformed into a tyrant. To them it was an everyday affair. It was one of the great Shakespearian themes.'[63] Such a theme can be extrapolated from Shakespeare's drama and is obviously a strong subconscious undercurrent pressing right through it from the opening lines. Brecht brings it to the surface as an issue for open debate, and while in the early stages of considering how to adapt Shakespeare's play he had thought of turning the war of defence into one of aggression, he soon discarded this in favour of Coriolanus's 'Streben nach der Monarchie'[64] that explains his attitudes and bid for power more cogently:

Beiseitegelassen werden muß das Motiv Angriff oder Verteidigung. Angriffs- oder Verteidigungskriege waren in dieser hist[orischen] Situation immer fortschrittlich, da sie zur Errichtung des röm[ischen] Imperiums führten.

Coriolan jedoch will die Monarchie wieder aufrichten, d.h. zu einer überlebten Gesellschaftsordnung zurückgehen, war also *persönlich reaktionär*. Dieses Motiv macht ihn zum Gegner sowohl Roms als auch Antiums. Er muß aus Rom fliehen, und in Antium versagen.[65]

By this means Brecht implants a coherent dialectic in Coriolanus that operates outside the purely personal attributes of pride and expertise in war. The individual may be useful but is not essential to society, and the energy built up by the confluence of achievement and ambition reaches the critical explosive point where the virtues of Coriolanus (his military successes on behalf of

Rome) become evils (his attempt to attain despotic power by usurpation). The vast quantity of violence massed in the service of the state undergoes the qualitative change to danger that basically alters and nullifies the social value of Coriolanus.

Brecht's adaptation pivots largely on this question of *appropriate* and *false* ends; he emphatically refuses to see the hero's tragedy in terms of a personal choice between pride and patriotism, duty to himself and to his mother. Coriolanus's sword is valuable if devoted to an acceptable purpose; if abused, it becomes reprehensible. The *Programmheft* explains how important it is to show that Coriolanus's greatness is measurable and that the acclamation of the people is in recognition of his usefulness:

Von hier erhalten auch die Darsteller der Tribunen gestisches Material: sie müssen nicht aus abstrakter Aversion den Coriolan unaufhörlich verurteilen, sondern sie werden gezwungen, den Feldherrn in jeder Situation neu zu beurteilen. Sie können Fehler begehen in der Beurteilung des Nutzens und des Schadens. Aber auch Nutzen und Schaden stehen nicht dualistisch gegenüber. Der Nutzen des Feldherren *wird* zu einem Schaden, wenn er seine Fähigkeiten im Kampf ausdehnt auf seine Mitbürger.

Pursuing its ramifications in the actions of the parties involved, Brecht elaborates this theme in all its consequences. In a note dated 20 May 1951 he stated the basis of Coriolanus's position:

Die Tragödie des einzelnen Mannes interessiert uns natürlich weit weniger als die des Gemeinwesens, veranlaßt durch den einzelnen Mann. Wir müssen aber zugleich nahe beim Shakespeare bleiben, wenn wir nicht seine Vorzüge gegen uns mobilisieren wollen. So scheint es uns am besten, aus dem verletzten Stolz des Coriolan eine nicht allzu shakespeareferne andere bedeutende Haltung zu machen, nämlich den Glauben des Coriolan an seine Unersetzlichkeit. Sie ist es, die ihn zugrunde richtet und das Gemeinwesen eines wertvollen Mannes beraubt.

This change in 'Tendenz' was reaffirmed in July 1952: 'Das Individuum erpreßt die Gesellschaft mit seiner Unentbehrlichkeit ... Die Lösung muß positiv für die Gesellschaft sein, das heißt, sie hat es nicht notwendig, sich von einem Individuum erpressen zu lassen.' Consistent with his denunciation of the 'personality cult' Brecht arranges a crucial encounter in II, 3 (absorbing elements from Shakespeare II, 3 and III, 1) between the victorious general attempting to bludgeon his way to the Consulship with a hail of vituperation and accusations of blackmail, and the populace who stand up to him with irony and counter-charges. Coriolanus brushes aside the restraining pleas of Menenius and Cominius:

CORIOLAN: ... Denn mit jedem Wunsch
Den ihr der schmutzigen Brut erfüllt, erzeugt ihr
Die neuen Wünsche.
FÜNFTER BÜRGER: Oho!
MENENIUS: Laßt es gut sein ...
BRUTUS: Allwo
Das Volk nicht nur auf dem Papier befragt wird!

CORIOLAN: In Griechenland! Warum geht ihr nicht
Nach Griechenland? Die Stadt heißt Rom.
COMINIUS: Genug.
SICINIUS: Genug im Übermaß.
CORIOLAN: Nein, nehmt noch einiges
Für die Klienten mit! 's ist gratis. Mir ist
Bekannt, daß, als der Krieg die Stadt bedrohte
Mit jähem Untergang, sich das Geschmeiß
Der stinkenden Bezirk' am untern Tiber
Korn ausbedungen für den Waffendienst.
Gewisse Leute sahn die Zeit gekommen
Für einen kleinen Fischzug durch Erpressung
Des Staats.
COMINIUS: Nicht weiter, Herr, ich bitt Euch.
VIERTER BÜRGER: Gewisse andere erpressen nicht, sie stehlen.
Wo bleibt die Beute von Corioli? . . .
CORIOLAN: Jetzt
Wo Rom nicht mehr den äußern Feind am Hals hat
Und das durch mich, kann Rom von seinem Aussatz
Sich lachend waschen.⁶⁶

In the first act, too, Coriolanus had challenged the rabble to leave the city
if they were not satisfied: 'Als ich dann einschritt | Schrien sie im Gehn "Wir
wandern aus!" Ich rief | Ihnen ein "Gute Reise" nach.'⁶⁷ By omitting whole
stretches of Shakespeare's text Brecht succeeds in reducing the effects of
Coriolanus's courage, patriotism and nobility; the speech on dust-laden
custom (Shakespeare, II, 3, 111–23) becomes squalidly contemptuous
doggerel:

CORIOLAN: . . . Aber wenn ihr auf Unterhaltung dringt, kann ich euch
ein Lied singen von der Dankbarkeit der Wölfin.
*Zum Spiel eines Sackpfeifers, der angefangen hat, für kleine Münzen,
etwas aufzuspielen:*
Hier seht ihr Cajus Marcius Coriolan
Bei dem Versuch, sich Hinz und Kunz zu nahn.
Er hat römische Adler zu verkaufen
(Bitte die lieben Kleinen, sich nicht um die Federn zu raufen!)
Ich bitte die Herrn, von Amtes wegen
Die Finger in meine Wunden zu legen.
Gegen ein kleines Almosen bin ich bereit
Zu jedwedem Dienst. Tretet heran! Letzte Gelegenheit!⁶⁸

The violence done to Shakespeare's text is for Brecht a necessary step towards
diminishing the glamour of Coriolanus in readiness for the demonstration
that he is not indispensable, and the climax of this endeavour is reached when
the people of Rome, after an initial moment of panic, take up arms against
the threat of the mighty general.

Certainly, Brecht bends the legendary story in order to devise an action
that is congruent with his modern view of historical situations and his intention

of relativizing the importance of the individual *vis-à-vis* the communal achievement. The Icarus syndrome in Brecht's thought is reinforced by his championship of the anonymous hero, the unnamed individual whose mark can usually be detected only in collective effort.[69] Needless to say, in advocating the democratic principle — the city equals the citizens, a man's worth is a function of his value to society — Brecht is really positing a new absolute in place of one felt to be antiquated, unjust, and unsuited to the conditions of his own contemporary world. The chief goal of the adaptation — to demonstrate that society must not allow itself to be blackmailed by an apparent dependence on the qualities of a single man — cannot be attained simply by censuring the peremptoriness of Coriolanus. He must be negated and surpassed in a real collision with a force that can prove itself capable of providing an alternative ethos for the common weal.

The counterpoising of forces necessitates a two-pronged approach to Shakespeare: the deflation of the hero, and the upgrading of the populace. One decisive point in this clash between the single and the collective hero is reached when Coriolanus demands the capitulation of Rome: by taking up arms in answer, the people show not only that there exists a positive force in Rome despite Coriolanus's absence, but also that they would have been ready to defend themselves against the Volscians in the earlier war even without their general. There is no doubt of Brecht's partisanship for the people. He insisted in the germinal stage of his version that the plebs should be depicted as the positive, progressive faction in Rome from the very first scene — the subject of a long analysis and discussion in 1953:

Hier spielt das Volk die Hauptrolle. Hier muß dem Volk der andere gewünschte Charakter gegeben werden. Erhalten bleiben muß die Rede 'Was macht die Patrizier zu Patriziern?' denn aus ihr folgert sich der Entschluß zur Auswanderung. Ob die 'sogenannten' 'humoristischen Lichter' erhalten bleiben sollen, ist fraglich. Irgendwelchen Wert besitzen sie nicht. Es fehlt mir an Urteil, wie sie hier wirken. Falls sie die Rüpelhaftigkeit des Volkes unterstreichen, sind sie wegzulassen und zu ersetzen.[70]

In handling the function of the plebs Brecht had to carry out a dual operation: in order to invest them with dignity and acumen he first had to strip them of the image encrusted since Shakespeare's day that the lower orders were pithy, coarsely witty, somewhat dull in mind, and a source above all of comic relief.[71] Much comment has been made on Shakespeare's virulent descriptions of the noxious, stinking, vacillating, stupid populace in *Coriolanus*, yet it is usually ignored that the contemptuous epithets issue from the disdainful lips of the patricians. MacCallum talks of 'Shakespeare's inability to conceive a popular rising in other terms than the outbreak of a mob', yet claims that Plutarch attributed to all classes of citizens in the young republic an 'intuitive political capacity'.[72] Brecht indeed makes no bones about endowing his plebs with a political sagacity that is anachronistic (since it derives from a maturity acquired over a century of working-class struggle) and idealistic. He was quite aware of this incongruity:

Es ist selbstverständlich ein Fehler, wenn das Volk, bei der Rolle, die es im Coriolan spielt, irgendwie etwa an Shakespearesche Rüpelszenen erinnert. Auf der anderen Seite kann aus historischen Gründen die römische Plebs nicht ohne weiteres als ein fortgeschrittenes, klassenmäßig stark bewußtes Proletariat geschildert werden. Wenn auch die Klassengegensätze im alten Rom durch ihre gesetzliche Verankerung schärfer sind als im modernen Kapitalismus, wo sie nur halb gesetzlich, halb ökonomisch und halb gewohnheitsrechtlich fixiert sind, so kann man doch von einer antiken Masse in Italien im 5. vorchristlichen Jahrhundert zwar Würde, aber nicht politische Klarheit verlangen.[73]

Brecht suggests that with some caution the dignity of the people and its revolutionary will could be emphasized. Nowhere in Brecht's work is a stupid peasant or worker to be found, or one incapable of learning. The extent of Brecht's bias leads him to replace the alleged idealization of the aristocracy in *Coriolanus* with the idealization of the plebs, despite his stated desire to avoid doing so. In this Roman play several of the plebs display exactly the same political acumen as Rauert, Der Breitschultrige, Sganarelle in other adaptations. The self-possessed meeting of the Roman and the Volscian artisans, the political awareness of the gardener and others, the tactics of the tribunes, the final scene in the Senate, all rightfully belong to a modern context. Indeed, Dieckmann criticizes the artificial flatness of Brecht's last scene precisely because it is an idealization coming after the one which closed Shakespeare's play. The Ensemble created a violent finale out of Coriolanus's death, and, coming after it, Brecht's scenic coda

hat die Harmlosigkeit des Hinterbliebenen-Sextetts, mit dem, nach dem feurigen Verschwinden des Helden, der *Don Giovanni* schließt, und kommt aus demselben, nur eben säkularisierten, Geiste, der alle individuelle Dramatik in einen höheren Zusammenhang, eine unverrückbare Ordnung einbettet, die den Sieg des Guten von vornherein garantiert und vor der das Einzelschicksal episodal wird.[74]

The classical Christian 'Lobet Gott den Herrn' becomes 'Am Ende siegt doch das Volk', and Dieckmann concludes that though the practicability of Brecht's Utopian dream is questionable, the impulse towards it deserves respect.

Within the framework of his ideologizing tendency Brecht imparts clarity, irony, dignity and resistance to his citizens. Although functioning in the dramatic happening on stage as a collective, these men are differentiated and endowed with 'die sorgfältig durchgeformten, individuell aufgewiesenen Verhaltensweisen des einfachen Mannes, in denen sich Coriolan nach anfänglichem Triumph verstrickt'.[75] The simplest method of improving the image of the populace was, of course, to divest it of such menial traits as the cowardice and scrabbling greed of the soldiers.[76] More effective dramatically than such face-lifting are the distinctions made between the citizens. As the curtain rises Brecht puts among the mutinously-minded crowd a man holding a child and carrying a large bundle, thus contrasting the First Citizen — who incites to action — with the inertia and frightened evasion of other plebeians:

ERSTER BÜRGER: Ihr seid bereit, nicht eher umzukehren als bis der Senat zugestanden hat, daß den Brotpreis wir Bürger bestimmen?... Und den Preis für die Oliven?... Cajus Marcius wird uns mit Waffengewalt entgegentreten. Werdet ihr davonlaufen oder werdet ihr kämpfen?... Ich frage, weil ich nicht mitmache, wenn in der Sache nicht zu Ende gegangen wird. Wozu bringst du den Sack mit und das Kind?

DER MANN MIT DEM KIND: Ich will sehen, was ihr erreicht. Wenn ihr nichts erreicht, werde ich mit denen vom dritten Bezirk auswandern.

ERSTER BÜRGER: Obwohl die Ebene, wo sie sich niederlassen wollen, unfruchtbar ist wie eine Steinplatte?

DER MANN MIT DEM KIND: Trotzdem. Wir werden Wasser dort haben, Luft und ein Grab, und mehr gibt es für uns Plebejer hier in Rom auch nicht. Dort werden wir zumindest keine Kriege für die Reichen führen müssen. *Zum Kind*: Wirst du brav sein, Terzius, wenn du keine Ziegenmilch bekommst?

Kind nickt.

ERSTER BÜRGER: Seht ihr, solche Leute haben wir unter uns. Der fürchtet den Cajus Marcius mehr als die wilde Natur in den Allegibergen. Bist du nicht ein römischer Bürger?...

DER MANN MIT DEM KIND *Zum Kind*: Terzius, sag, daß du in einer solchen Stadt nicht Bürger sein willst.

Kind schüttelt den Kopf.

ERSTER BÜRGER: Dann hau ab, und schnell, du feiger Hund, aber das Kind laß da; wir werden für Terzius ein besseres Rom erkämpfen.[77]

The submissive acceptance of the status quo by such citizens — despite an ironical insight into its workings — is accentuated later when Coriolanus roughly requests his vote and the man points out the general's toga to his child:

Das ist die schlichte Toga, mit der sie sich auf dem Markt bewerben müssen, Terzius. Sie hat keine Taschen, damit er keine Stimmen kaufen kann, hahaha. Sonst möchte er sie vielleicht kaufen, wie? Hahaha. Aber er bekommt meine Stimme, weil er Rom eine Stadt dazu erobert hat, er bekommt sie. *Ab.*[78]

From this easy conquest Coriolanus turns to notch up a further success with a cobbler in a bantering exchange plagiarized from the opening scene of *Julius Caesar*. The Fourth Citizen assures Coriolanus that he can rely on the cobbler's vote 'weil der Krieg den Schuhpreis hinauftreibt und Ihr eine wahre Personifikation des Krieges seid, Herr'.[79] The sting in the tail here condemns such commoners as the cobbler who cannot see beyond their private, immediate gain to the contradiction inherent in it: the war which is making him rich will debilitate the city, lay it open to possible conquest and ultimately deprive him of his profit. On the heels of the cobbler's acquiescence comes the intelligent metaphor of the rose and the cabbage; the gardener is careful not to commit his vote, as is the Sixth Citizen, whereas the Third and Fourth Citizens are intent only on appeasing Coriolanus. In this way divergent or conflicting views among the plebeians are synoptically and economically adumbrated: fear of Coriolanus, awe before his deeds, and the profit motive on the one hand — scepticism, hard common sense, trenchant questions about his policies and the booty of Corioli on the other.

Since the plebeians are now the mainspring of action in Brecht's reading of their historical situation, the motives for any modifications of their attitudes and conduct have to be carefully sifted and functionally determined within the limits of the drama. The wavering irresolution and fickleness of Shakespeare's citizens serves largely to confirm — and so enhance — the packed determination and hard courage of Coriolanus; they are extensions of the bulking consciousness of his own self, and as a foil to him are used as material for the construction in dramatic terms of his figure. Brecht seeks to make the play epic by dispersing this concentration of dramatic movements in the one individual. In his version the plebeians are invested with a dramatic function at least equal to that of Coriolanus; in this way an over-saturation of energy does not occur at any single point since contradictions exist throughout and neutralize each other continuously. However, in unreservedly admitting his partisanship for the plebs, Brecht ran the risk of swinging the axis of the drama into a different but as extreme a position as he implied that Shakespeare had done. In other words, he tended to substitute the idealization of the people undiscriminatingly for the idealization of the nobility. When it came to staging the adaptation, the Ensemble foresaw the pitfalls and shortcomings of this intention of Brecht's. The rehearsal notes in the *Programmheft* indicate the importance of showing a qualitative change in the attitude of the plebeians from hero worship to defiance of Coriolanus:

Coriolan ist eine Gefahr für die Republik, nicht nur durch seine eigene Kraft, sondern vor allem durch die Bewunderung, die man seiner Kraft zollt. Denn zum Heldenkult gehört nicht nur ein Held, sondern auch eine Gesellschaft, die den Kult macht, weil sie ihn anscheinend braucht. Nicht nur der Held kostet Spesen, sondern vor allem auch die Heldenverehrung. Ohne den Jubel für den Helden ist der Held nicht gefährlich. Ohne die Blindheit des im nationalen Taumel befindlichen Volks von Rom ist der später gewonnene Blick, der Coriolan als Schaden erkennt, kein Fortschritt; ja, ist die Kandidatur Coriolans unentschuldbar, da von den Tribunen im Keime zu ersticken. Es ist die alte Sache: bevor einer seinen Herren um besseren Lohn angeht, muß er den Rücken gerade richten.

The problem was one of differentiation: if the plebs were to be adequate to their function in the reorganized dramatic economy of the play, their reactions had to be resolved into stages that displayed a change — and a progress — in the quality of their actions, resulting from insights gained in dealing with Coriolanus and the patricians. On these grounds the Ensemble graded the role of the plebeians into three phases: unreflecting initial acclamation of the general (who has served Rome well); a growing apprehension of the danger of tyranny inherent in his very qualities; the final progression from blindness to insight and preventive action. This structure entailed particularly the discarding of Brecht's 'idealistic' justification of the disorganized arming of the citizens in the opening scene, in order to throw into relief the subsequent changes in quality. The problem then was to show how the plebeians had progressed in political consciousness by deliberately taking up arms later:

Die Lösung dieses Problems für die Fassung des Berliner Ensembles 1963 fanden wir — angeregt durch entsprechende Darstellungen des Livius und Plutarch — im Streik, in der Kriegsdienstverweigerung der Plebejer, einer historisch revolutionären Haltung, welche Senat und Patriziat zwingt, Volkstribunen zu ernennen ... Unsere Änderung: Das Stück zeigt am Anfang in einer großen Weise die Kriegspläne der Oberen, und es endet mit den Friedensplänen der Unteren.

The principal keystone of the adaptation — and this is retained by the Ensemble — lies squarely in the decision of the plebeians to defend their city against the menace of Coriolanus (by inverting the order of v, 3 and v, 4 Brecht significantly makes this vital scene (v, 3) *precede* the confrontation of Coriolanus and Volumnia, by which it is thus uninfluenced). Collaborators' notes describe how the plebeians act while the nobles talk:

Cominius, der von Coriolan abgewiesen wurde, geht zu den Tribunen über und verteilt die Waffen an das Volk Roms. Diese Art 'nationale Front' ist angelegt bei Plutarch — tatsächlich konnte das Volk nicht allein kämpfen —. Auch die Senatoren wollen Römer bleiben und nicht in Abhängigkeit von den Volskern geraten. Das patriotische Interesse von Adel und Volk stimmt eine Zeitlang überein.

In der Verteidigung Roms liegt der Kern der Bearbeitung, der Anlaß für die Umwandlung des tragischen Punktes: Rom wird nicht gerettet, weil Coriolan umkehrt, sondern Coriolan kehrt um, weil Rom entschlossen ist, sich selbst zu retten. Die Plebejer bewaffnen das Volk vor der Unterredung Mutter-Sohn: Der Ausgang des Krieges hängt nicht von dem Ausgang des Gespräches ab. Sie lassen Volumnia nur gehen, um Zeit zu gewinnen. Coriolan wartet zu lang. Als der Krieg nicht ohne Volk ging (Anfang), machte man ihm Konzessionen. Coriolan irrt sich aber, als er glaubt, daß der Krieg nicht ohne großen Mann geht.[80]

The gap between Brecht's conception and Shakespeare's depiction yawns wide: the latter's panic-stricken citizens had at once repented the banishing of Coriolanus and turned on their leaders to vent their guilt and fear. The disconcerted Sicinius is warned by a messenger (v, 4, 35-9):

> Sir, if you'ld save your life, fly to your house:
> The plebeians have got your fellow-tribune,
> And hale him up and down; all swearing if
> The Roman ladies bring not comfort home
> They'll give him death by inches.

Alarm and recrimination evaporate from among Brecht's plebeians, dismay is reserved only for the patricians:

Im 4. Akt 4. Szene [an early numeration for v, 3] dürfen nicht — wie bei Shakespeare — die Bürger ihre Meinung ändern und die Verbannung Coriolans bereuen, sondern der Adel muß deutlich seine Angst (um das eigene Leben, nicht um Rom) zeigen. Dies kann zum Ausdruck gebracht werden.

1. Müssen die Bürger feststellen, daß es besser ist, daß ein Geier wie Coriolan *gegen* sie ist, als in den eigenen Reihen kämpfen.

2. Der Adel muß in Panik ausbrechen, wie kopflose Hennen, denen der Hahn auf den Nachbarhof geflogen ist. Sie zittern vor ihrem Standesgenossen, daß ihnen die Waffen aus den Händen fallen, die sie aufsammeln.[81]

The active plebeian rebound to meet the challenge of Coriolanus is master-minded and steered by the tribunes. These two men are the leaders of the popular resistance, and in the adaptation they are subjected to a thorough overhaul that totally transforms their image. Shakespeare's portrayal of them is not flattering, for it becomes clear that much of their enmity towards Coriolanus stems from personal envy and spite. Dr Johnson spoke of their 'plebeian malignity and tribunitian insolence', and many commentators see them delineated as 'utter scoundrels' in agreement with R. W. Chambers that Shakespeare 'hated and despised the tribunes in *Coriolanus* with a bitterness which he rarely felt towards any of his creatures'.[82] Enright says that 'the conversations of the tribunes reveal a plain jealousy of Coriolanus as a man which has nothing to do with their jealous concern for the people's rights. At least, we feel, he is more of a man than they are',[83] and Brents Stirling maintains they are 'the real villains of the Shakespearean story'.[84] A careful comparison with Plutarch's descriptions of Brutus and Sicinius led Mac-Callum to the conclusion that Shakespeare blackened their characters,[85] and they do indeed figure as abject jackals snarling at the hero's heels. They do incite the mob, they are afraid of losing office, they do blench at the thought of Coriolanus menacing Rome, they are cowardly when the mob howls for revenge on them. Yet there is in them too a nugget of devotion to the public weal, the possibility of self-sacrifice for the advancement of their class, as Jan Kott colourfully suggests:

It is these two indolent half-wits, proud, violent and petulant, who represent the people in *Coriolanus*. They are 'the herdsmen of the beastly plebeians' and stink just as the populace does. They suffer from scabies and have to scratch themselves all over their bodies. They are like mongrels. But these mongrels know how to defend their herd. These two ridiculous tribunes, Brutus and Sicinius, short and misshapen, envious and suspicious though they are, possess a class instinct.[86]

More clearly than some critics Palmer understands that Shakespeare's tribunes are not simply base and vile, that they do represent the outlook on the world of an ill-used class and they do fight for a cause. Faint shadowings of modern worker movements are perceptible in Shakespeare's pair of probing trouble-makers: 'For better or worse, these tribunes are Shakespeare's counterfeit presentment of two labour leaders. They are the natural products of a class war in the commonwealth. They use their wits to defend the interests of the popular party and to remove from power a declared enemy of the people.'[87] And when Brutus suspects ulterior motives in Coriolanus's promptness to serve under Cominius, 'the tribunes are right and they are giving proof of precisely that "realism" and precisely that suspicion of their political rulers which are characteristic of popular leaders in all times and places.'[88]

The glimmer of political stresses and configurations that properly belong to a later century is painstakingly uncovered by Brecht and fanned into a glow that colours every feature of his interpretation. And the central axiom of this interpretation is the transfiguration of the tribunes into alert and altruistic public officials, solely taken up with the welfare of the citizens. From the very first scene Brecht takes care to throw into relief the calmness and wisdom of the tribunes as they exercise a benevolent watchfulness over the interests of their charges. Brutus advises the plebeians to enlist with Coriolanus in a justified war of defence against the Volscians who are intending to attack Rome 'Auf die Nachricht großer| Teurung und Rebellion hier':

> BRUTUS: Geht, Freunde, folgt ihm! Schreibt euch in die Listen!
> Seid gute Krieger für ein gutes Rom!
> Und was den Kampf in seinen Mauern angeht
> Um Korn, Olive, Pacht- und Zinserlaß
> Wir schauen aus, dieweil ihr für es fechtet.[89]

It is Brutus who tempers Sicinius's blunter assessment of the hero with a hint that he might be used to protect the interests of the plebeians, at least in the face of foreign aggression:

> SICINIUS: Solch ein Mann ist
> Gefährlicher für Rom als für die Volsker.
> BRUTUS: Das glaub ich nicht. Solch eines Mannes Schwert
> Ist mehr, als seine Laster schaden, wert.[90]

It would, in fact, be a misrepresentation to identify these prudent and deliberate tribunes of Brecht's with Shakespeare's turbulent fomenters; paradoxically, they show 'die Arbeiterklasse als Verteidigerin der bürgerlichen Demokratie' and are not at all 'Anwälte des Umsturzes, sondern Wahrer der Rechtsordnung wider den Über-Anspruch der Besitzenden'.[91] In his antagonistic appraisal of Brecht's version, Günter Grass shows a tinge of scepticism towards the unashamed partisanship of his endeavour to instil class-consciousness into the plebeians:

Die erste Szene des zweiten Aufzuges bestätigt, beim Vergleich beider Fassungen, Brechts Vorhaben, das Original — und sei es unter Verzicht auf die blühendsten Dialogpassagen — zu einem Tendenzstück umzuformen, in welchem sich Coriolan mehr und mehr zum Kriegsspezialisten vergröbert, der weise Narr Menenius zum reaktionären Kasperle wird und beide Volkstribunen sich zu Klassenkämpfern wenn nicht erster, dann zweiter Güte mausern.[92]

In the scene mentioned Brecht omits or curtails Brutus's poetic description of the popular acclaim that greeted Coriolanus's victorious return, the enumeration of his wounds, and the tribunes' plan to stir the mob against him.

As a result of cuts and judicious additions, the tribunes emerge as clear-sighted politicians with the makings of statesmen, unswervingly analytical as they assess each new situation in turn:

SICINIUS: Die guten Priester beehren mich nicht mit mehr Vertrauen als dich, Brutus, aber ich weiß, es sind schlechte Nachrichten.

BRUTUS: Warum unter allen Umständen schlechte?
SICINIUS: Weil entweder die Volsker gesiegt haben, dann sind sie Herrn in Rom, oder Cajus Marcius, dann ist er Herr.
BRUTUS: Das ist richtig. Da kommt Menenius Agrippa.
Menenius tritt auf.
MENENIUS: Wie geht es, ihr Hirten des Plebejerviehs?
SICINIUS: Das Essen ist etwas knapp am Tiber, aber Ihr sollt neue Nachrichten haben?
MENENIUS: Ja, von Cajus Marcius, aber den liebt ihr nicht . . .
BRUTUS *im Abgehen zu Sicinius*: Jetzt wissen wir, wie die Nachrichten sind, die sie haben. Marcius hat gesiegt. Der Bursche wäre sonst nicht so frech.[93]

When Sicinius predicts a runaway election of Coriolanus to Consul, Brutus answers 'Das hieße Gute Nacht mit uns Tribunen' — but this remains the only allusion to a private interest in office on their part. They switch at once to a consideration — demanding some vision — of future eventualities and the psychology of the citizens' shallow insight:

> SICINIUS: Sein Auftrag war, die Volsker abzuschlagen
> Nicht mehr. Genausogut kannst du dem Wolf
> Befehlen, er soll dir vom Hühnerstall
> Den Fuchs verscheuchen, doch nicht mehr tun!
> Er nimmt Corioli.
> BRUTUS: Und hetzt uns so
> Die Volsker für Jahrzehnte auf den Hals.
> SICINIUS: Und horch, wie jetzt ein siegbesoffnes Rom
> Vom Ruhm des Unbotsamen widerhallt!
> Heut kündet jeder Sattler seinem Weib
> Er hab Corioli hinzubekommen
> Sie planen, wo sie zwei, drei Marmorvillen
> In ihrem Keller unterbringen wollen.
> Wir sind nur Spielverderber.[94]

Concluding from their estimation of the circumstances that the onus of action devolves upon them, Brecht's tribunes quickly display their tactical skill in varying the pace and pressure of their political struggle. In the forum, the most public place, they insist on clear words from Coriolanus on his policy and attitude if he is elected Consul:

> SICINIUS: Eins vielleicht
> Verbliebe noch zu tun: vor allem Volk
> Den Kandidaten nach Programm und all-
> Gemeiner Haltung zu befragen.
> MENENIUS: Halt!
> Dies steht nicht in der Charta.
> SICINIUS: Die Tribunen
> Stehn auch nicht in der Charta. Neues Recht
> Erfocht das Volk im Krieg und mag's nun nützen
> Im Sieg, Ihr Herrn . . . Coriolanus
> Soeben liefen in den Hafen unsre

Kornschiffe ein aus dem besiegten Antium.
Die Fracht ist Korn. Tribut und Beute aus
Dem blutigen Volskerkrieg. Was, edler Marcier
Würdst du als Konsul tun mit diesem Korn?[95]

Having soon after provoked Coriolanus's ire and compassed his banishment, Brutus and Sicinius stand firm and cool-headed when news is brought
of his destructive advance on the defenceless city. Shakespeare (IV, 6) shows
them gripped by panic and the agitated citizens repenting they have exiled
him, while the nobility find nothing reprehensible in Coriolanus's threats.
Brecht attributes panic only to the patricians, and a few extra lines establish
the bond of trust uniting the plebeians and their imperturbable leaders:

SICINIUS:　　　Seid nicht entmutigt. 's gibt
Ein Pack in Rom, das gern bestätigt sähe
Was es zu fürchten vorgibt. Leute, geht, und
Ich sag nicht lauft, in die Bezirkslokale
Und zeigt, daß ihr nicht Furcht habt.
ZWEITER BÜRGER:　　　　　　Lieber zeigt ich
Als Mut jetzt eine Waffe. War es klug
Ihn zu verbannen?
SICINIUS:　　　Ja.[96]

This solid class front proceeds from steadfastness to action; in place of
Menenius's refusal to attempt to intercede with Coriolanus on behalf of
Rome:

Go you that banish'd him;
A mile before his tent fall down, and knee
The way into his mercy.

(v, 1, 4-6)

Brutus castigates the patricians' alacrity to capitulate — Brecht ironically
gives him Menenius's lines for his scorn — and orders the arming of the
citizens. Words become hard facts:

BRUTUS:　　　　　　　Ihr hingegen
Wißt, wie Rom billig wird! Laßt doch den Rauch
Vom Kapitol aufsteigen, daß der Vetter
Erfährt, er ist willkommen. Fallt aufs Knie
Vor seinem Zelt, nein, eine Meile vorher
Und rutscht auf Eurem Knie in seine Gnade!
Heraus mit dem Beschluß: wer will den Rauch sehn?
　　　Pause.
Gut, keiner. Dann verteilt die Waffen, sonst
Wird, wer den kleinen Rauch nicht sehen will
Den großen sehen, in dem Rom aufgeht![97]

With the focus of attention narrowing to defence — defence against aggression, defence of a community worth fighting for — the definition of the values
which shape that community is outlined by Brecht in the key scene v, 3 when
all the Senators but Cominius leave:

BRUTUS: Sie gehen packen. Sie wollen lieber auf ihren Gütern sterben. *Zu den Bürgern*: Es ist, wie wir euch gesagt haben. Die Väter geben Rom preis. Wie steht es in euren Bezirken?

EIN BÜRGER: Die Mehrheit hat sich zum Kriegsdienst gemeldet. Wer noch wartete, ob Menenius etwas bei Coriolanus ausrichten würde, wird sich jetzt melden.

BRUTUS: Gut. Wenn diejenigen, die von Rom leben, es nicht verteidigen wollen, werden wir es verteidigen, von denen Rom bisher gelebt hat. Warum sollten nicht die Maurer die Mauern verteidigen?

COMINIUS: Rechnet einige von uns dazu. Ihr sollt die Waffen ausgehändigt bekommen, ich nehm's auf meine Kappe.

BÜRGER: Es lebe Cominius![98]

The faith of the citizens in their leaders' judgement is justified when Brutus, in disagreement with his more impetuous colleague, allows Volumnia to undertake her momentous appeal to Coriolanus. Brutus is not swayed by emotional considerations of filial piety, but by two real facts: the need to warn Coriolanus that the people are now in control of their city and ready to defend it, and the need to gain time for forging weapons. A citizen brings Volumnia's request to be allowed to parley with her son:

SICINIUS: Die Bitte ist abgeschlagen.

BRUTUS: Ist bewilligt.

SICINIUS: Willst du die Verräterbrut aus der Stadt lassen?

BRUTUS: Einige Familien, Patrizier, leben jetzt in Furcht, wegen ihrer Verbindungen mit ihm gesteinigt zu werden. Sie scheinen sich an die Marcier gewandt zu haben. Ich glaube nicht, daß die Alte uns fürchtet, aber ich denke nicht, daß sie dafür ist, daß in Zukunft der volskische Senat auf dem Kapitol sitzt. Sie ist in ihrer Art eine Patriotin, indem sie uns Plebejer lieber von Römern geschunden haben will als von Volskern ... Das Gespräch kann uns einen Aufschub verschaffen. Heute nacht und morgen den Tag über sind die Mauern schwach besetzt. *Zum Bürger*: Sie können gehen. Aber schick eine der Frauen des Gesindes mit, auf die du dich verlassen kannst, daß wir erfahren, was gesprochen wurde. Einverstanden?

SICINIUS: Einverstanden. Zwei schwere Tage vor uns.

BRUTUS: Mir scheint, und manchem, wie ich hör, dies Rom
Ein besserer Platz, seit dieser Mensch nicht mehr
In seinen Mauern geht, wert zu verteidigen
Vielleicht zum ersten Mal, seit es gegründet.[99]

Finally, after the success of this stratagem, the tribunes move forward to the concluding stage of their political battle — the fulfilment of peaceful power in the Senate meeting with which the adaptation closes, after the intervening stages of action and achievement.

There can be no doubt that Brecht set about reorganizing the matter of *Coriolanus* with the premeditated intention of achieving twin aims: to display the danger to society of an individual's abuse of power, and to demonstrate the healthy energies latent in the lower classes that can be harnessed to nullify such threats and create a desirable society. This is perhaps the tenor of a comment Brecht made on Shakespeare's achievement for his time, and the necessity on the modern stage of going beyond it — from the individual to society, from personal freedoms and passions to integration in a collective organism. Dieckmann analyses fundamental differences in the treatment of the hero between original and adaptation, describing how Shakespeare set out to show Coriolanus's value in war and dispensability in peace. The drama is not so much a 'tragedy of pride' as an excursus on 'die Grenzengerechtigkeit zwischen Politik und Heerführung, ein Plädoyer wider den Militärstaat, soziologisch konkretisiert durch die Aufdeckung des Klassenhintergrunds'.[100] In this conception of the warrior-hero Shakespeare had vividly in mind the ever-present threat in post-medieval times that the *condottieri* — mercenary leaders like Colleoni, Sickingen, Sforza — would prove tyrannously oppressive if they ever diverted their valuable services from military ends to the acquisition of power as peacetime heads of state. Dieckmann suggests, with Otto Ludwig, a comparison of Coriolanus and Wallenstein, since the tragedy of each is generated by an overreaching of himself and of the social structure, coupled with an inability to create a 'new order' out of his own nature. This tragic failure ensues because Coriolanus ('der Gewalt- und Willensmensch in seiner klassischen Gestalt, der leibhaftige Kriegsgott')[101] oversteps the bounds of his proper sphere of activity, and — in a sense — is untrue to himself. In the Ensemble production the 'natural', 'mythical' attributes of the hero are drained from him — there remains only a vicious, menacing, frenzied beast:

Nicht in schimmernder Wehr, mit wehendem Helmbusch steht Coriolan auf der Bühne, sondern als ein Gladiator und Schlagetot, ein wüster Draufgänger, unzähmbar und blutdampfend . . . er ist (in der Darstellung Ekkehard Schalls) im Ganzen zum Berserker, zum losgelassenen Rüpel herabgedrückt und dem Zuschauer wird kein ästhetisches Moment zur Ergötzung am Helden gelassen.[102]

This degraded image of Coriolanus that was handed on by Brecht is taken by Dieckmann to be the reflection of a modern *condottiere* figure, the sinister distortion of the charismatic idol in Nazi Germany. Brecht had already achieved an artistic formulation of this spurious hero in *Der aufhaltsame Aufstieg des Arturo Ui*. Dieckmann discusses two 'explosion' scenes: Ui's hysterical, declamatory, hollow eruption is part of his artificiality in contrast to the genuine, spontaneous outburst of unbridled self-assurance possessed by Shakespeare's hero. This critic implies that Ui is an impressively adequate satirical expression of the strident bastardized hero, and that Brecht, in pursuing his quarry — the debased counterfeit of the truly predatory beast — too vehemently, actually destroys the pristine image he wishes to restore. In other words, though Brecht's polemic is with the present, he joins issue with Shakespeare:

Coriolan ist bei Shakespeare das gleißende Raubtier — prächtig zu sehen, für sich genommen attraktiv, aber zerstörerisch von Natur, ein geborener Feind friedlicher Gemeinschaft. Aber eben: zerstörerisch *von Natur*, und die Shakespearesche Sprache, ihre Dynamik, ihr rhythmischer Schwung — selbst ein Stück natürlicher Schönheit —, spiegelt diese Seite seiner Erscheinung . . . Indem nun die Aufführung aus der Erfahrung einer Zeit, die zerstörerisch war aus Unnatur, . . . die klassische

Form aufzuheben trachtet, gibt sie sich den Anschein, das anzugreifen, was sie im Grunde verteidigen will: die von der faschistischen Verwechselung mit dem Zerstörerischen bedrohte Natur, die sich hier noch *in* diesem bekundet. Kunstmittel, die gegen den Verfall des Schönen geschaffen sind, werden hier gegen dieses selbst, das intakte Urbild, gerichtet.[103]

Dieckmann goes further and detects in Brecht's method of modernizing the language as well as the premisses of *Coriolanus* the danger of the anti-cliché and techniques of alienation hardening into just another dogmatic system.

Dieckmann's sensitively argued strictures on Brecht's adaptation are cogent and very pertinent if it is assumed that Brecht was trying to *oust* Shakespeare with his version; but it needs to be proved that such actually was his resolve. A more positive assessment of the relationship of original and adaptation can be reached through some remarks of another rebel playwright, namely Schiller. In his preface to *Die Räuber* Schiller enunciates certain principles of dramatic creation that underlie more than his own maiden play and are recognizably present in *Coriolanus*. He first acknowledges the advantages inherent in dramatic treatment generally 'die Seele gleichsam bei ihren geheimsten Operationen zu ertappen', and proclaims with specific reference to Franz Moor: 'Das Laster wird hier mit samt seinem ganzen innern Räderwerk entfaltet.' Shakespeare, like Schiller, lays bare the secret processes of the soul, and for him too the irrational, emotional, inexplicable motivations of men are an intrinsic part of the dramatic artifact. The characters in *Coriolanus* — the warrior, his mother, the tribunes, the rival general Aufidius, and others — are knit together by subterranean forces that draw their energy from deep pools of the personality on a level of response inaccessible to purely logical elucidation.

Schiller's second point — his main concern in this preface — relates to the portrayal of the 'wicked' character. He makes three assertions: no human being is an outright villain since all are made in the likeness of God; the playwright must give due prominence to the virtues that even the most depraved man possesses; finally — on a cautious note — there ought to be sufficient reasoning thought present for the playwright not to make vice so intellectually and aesthetically pleasing that the spectator is seduced or lulled into overlooking its ugly source: 'Wenn es mir darum zu thun ist, *ganze* Menschen hinzustellen, so muß ich auch ihre Vollkommenheiten mitnehmen, die auch dem bösesten nie ganz fehlen. Wenn ich vor dem Tyger gewarnt haben will, so darf ich seine schöne blendende Flekenhaut nicht übergehen, damit man nicht den Tyger beym Tyger vermisse.' Schiller is, of course, eager to justify his bandits to an eighteenth-century audience, and his notes are determined on the one hand by an idealistic view of the 'salvation' of the human being, on the other by a realistic insight into his diversity.

Shakespeare too, perhaps more resourcefully than any other dramatist, endows his characters with subtle gradations of faults and qualities that demand a matching complexity of response from the spectator. Coriolanus is a bundle of contradictions — pride and submission, loyalty and betrayal,

partnership and rivalry, ambition and disdain, love of Rome and contempt
for her citizens, private desires and public deeds — that in their delicate
equilibrium induce in the audience the final effect of 'a balanced judgement,
moral and intellectual rather than passionate, for the paradoxes of the hero's
character are seen to cohere in a credible personality which excites admiration
and dislike, disapproval and pity without engaging us as totally as do Hamlet,
Lear and Othello'.[104]

Crucial, too, to Schiller's conception of the hero is his extraordinary
stature. He speaks as heir to the wave of Shakespeare worship in the eighteenth
century; hence his insistence on the presentation of all aspects — good and
bad — of a hero, if the dramatist is to be 'der getreue Kopist der wirklichen
Welt' (*Unterdrückte Vorrede*); hence also the sheer magnitude of his characters, their huge potential either for good or for evil. Coriolanus, like Karl
Moor, has a dynamic capacity for action, but whereas Shakespeare leaves his
creations as monuments of themselves absorbed entirely in their own reality,
Schiller is drawn into the ethical undertow of contemporary aesthetics and his
final word subordinates realistic depiction to an overall moral: 'Der Verirrte
tritt wieder in das Geleise der Gesetze. Die Tugend geht siegend davon.'
The sketch of Karl Moor provided by Schiller in his *Avertissement zur ersten
Aufführung* is true in all essentials of Coriolanus:

Das Gemälde einer verirrten großen Seele — ausgerüstet mit allen Gaben zum
Fürtrefflichen, und mit allen Gaben verloren . . . Groß und majestätisch im Unglück,
und durch Unglück gebessert, rückgeführt zum Fürtrefflichen. Einen solchen Mann
wird man im Räuber Moor beweinen und hassen, verabscheuen und lieben.

This expresses the Aristotelian principle that is the bond between the Shakespearean and Schillerian hero; his orbit is determined by a philosophical
premise which qualifies the reactions of both character and audience. Whether
the outcome is tragic death or return to virtue, the hero acts according to rules
of belief that are consonant with aesthetic effects.

The Marxist Brecht rejects the isolated greatness of the individual as well
as secret promptings of the soul that have no source in external motivation.
Within the all-important social framework he does discover utter villains,
colossal and ominous through their total dedication to evil. One such is
Arturo Ui. Nowhere in Brecht's work is hugeness of stature a criterion of the
dramatic personage; his characters are never cast in the heroic mould, since
they are designed to be congruent to and answer the needs of our modern
sensibility. Characters who might possibly operate in vast dimensions, a
Galileo or a Puntila, are reduced by their own furtive pettiness or by the
opposition of a defiant antagonist, while Brecht's positive heroes are drawn
almost exclusively from the humble ranks of unassuming men and women
whom nothing marks as outstanding. Brecht converts the Schillerian tenets
into modern terms, confirming Dürrenmatt's answer to Brecht's own question
about the presentation of the world in drama: 'Mit einem kleinen Schieber,
mit einem Kanzlisten, mit einem Polizisten läßt sich die heutige Welt besser

13*

wiedergeben als mit einem Bundesrat, als mit einem Bundeskanzler.'[105] For this reason, if Brecht wished to adapt *Coriolanus*, he was bound to drag the hero down from the pinnacle of fame.

It is important to consider carefully in this connexion the implications of Brecht's definition of a realistic manner of writing: 'den gesellschaftlichen Kausalkomplex aufdeckend|die herrschenden Gesichtspunkte als die Gesichtspunkte der Herrschenden entlarvend| . . . |konkret und das Abstrahieren ermöglichend.' Brecht is not at all realistic in the manner that Shakespeare and the early Schiller were realistic, for he would refuse to be a faithful copyist of the 'real' world (this he would disparagingly term 'naturalist'). His realism is an abstraction, a schematic rendering of the reality that confronts him in an effort to convey an insight into that reality. This is an abstraction and a restriction because certain aspects are excluded from the vision so that it may gain in coherence, density and impact. Brecht abstains from depicting the 'dazzling' beauty of the tiger's 'Fleckenhaut', which is an aesthetic phenomenon divorced from the tiger's claws — a victim being mauled by the beast would have little appreciation for its 'fearful symmetry'. The dazzle *per se* is spurned by Brecht; as soon as externals are used to an end, however, as soon as they affect the lives of those around and therefore society, they become motivations and of gestic significance. Thus Brecht could say, speaking of Don Juan, that he was concerned not with the 'Glanz des Parasiten' but with 'das Parasitäre seines Glanzes'. In the same way, he does not allow Coriolanus a single atom of gratuitous greatness. The language of Shakespeare — and with it the deeds of the hero — is reduced to a level flow of hard argument and counter-argument; and the adaptation closes in a muted minor key with the almost total obliteration of the hero, his fame being equated with his worth to the community and so shrinking to nothing.

Dieckmann describes the versions of *Coriolanus* by Shakespeare and by Brecht as being like warring partners, 'deren jeder nur wirksam wird, indem er den andern retardiert: der Verfremdungsduktus den klassischen Jambus, der durchschneidende Impuls die Distanz der Analyse'.[106] The two dramas are certainly not to be weighed against each other, as they belong to such different epochs. Brecht has not aimed at producing a version to usurp Shakespeare's unique creation; what he has done is to re-structure the exploits of Coriolanus in such a fashion as to inject a twentieth-century consciousness of drama and of history into a legend so clearly pervaded by a political theme. That Brecht's adaptation does not shrivel into a dramatized political tract is due to the qualities that also inform his original work: a cold and fearless intelligence, sensitivity to the multiple and contradictory forms of human community, and, above all, compassion for the suffering and underprivileged.

NOTES

1 R. W. Leonhardt, 'Können wir den Shakespeare ändern?', *Die Zeit*, 2 October 1964.
2 Published in *Akzente*, 11 (1964), 194–221.
3 BBA 672/68.
4 BBA 672/69 f.
5 J. Dover Wilson, *Coriolanus* (Cambridge, 1960), pp. xix ff. No critical purpose is served by writing of Shakespeare in such blurred terms: dramatic art is not an entity that can be isolated, nor is there room in great plays for speeches that are only interesting.
6 W. Hazlitt, *The Complete Works*, edited by P. P. Howe (London, 1930–4), IV, 214.
7 D. J. Enright, *The Apothecary's Shop* (London, 1957), p. 47 f.
8 M. W. MacCallum, *Shakespeare's Roman Plays and their Background*, second edition (London, 1925), p. 521.
9 J. Palmer, *Political Characters of Shakespeare* (London, 1945), pp. vi ff.
10 *GW*, 17/1253.
11 Käthe Rülicke-Weiler, *Die Dramaturgie Brechts* (Berlin, 1966), p. 147. *Coriolanus* is, of course, perfectly actable in any age. The word 'spielbar' therefore requires some elucidation: for Brecht and his collaborators it connotes an interpretation meaningful, as they see it, in terms of a modern audience.
12 G. Bullough, *Narrative and Dramatic Sources of Shakespeare* (London, 1964), V, 494.
13 J. E. Phillips, *The State in Shakespeare's Greek and Roman Plays* (New York, 1940), p. 50. Phillips persuasively analyses Shakespeare's use of illustrations from natural law as analogical metaphor for the 'ordinances of eternal law' that affect the lives of men.
14 Ibid., p. 20.
15 Ibid., p. 90.
16 G. Wilson Knight, *The Imperial Theme* (London, 1931), p. 176 n. and 180.
17 Phillips, op. cit., p. 11.
18 Palmer, op. cit., p. 255.
19 J. Kott, *Shakespeare our Contemporary* (London, 1964), p. 154.
20 *GW*, 6/2400.
21 *GW*, 6/2440 f.
22 Op. cit., p. xxi.
23 Palmer, op. cit., pp. 309 ff.
24 Op. cit., p. 208.
25 *GW*, 6/2479 f.
26 *GW*, 6/2480.
27 *GW*, 6/2488 f.
28 Palmer, op. cit., p. 301.
29 *GW*, 6/2491 f.
30 BBA 650/24.
31 Op. cit., p. 193. Compare also p. 155: '. . . there is here a swift channelling, an eddying, twisting and forthward-flowing stream; ice-cold, intellectual, cold as a mountain torrent and holding something of its iron taste. We are in a world of hard weapons, battle's changing contacts, civic brawls about "grain" and "corn"; a town-life somewhat limited and provincial, varied with the sickening crashes of war. There is little brilliance, little colour.'
32 Op. cit., pp. 145 and 147.
33 *Hamburgische Dramaturgie*, 19. Stück.
34 Op. cit., p. 30.
35 *Die Dramaturgie*, p. 149.
36 Ibid., p. 153.
37 'Die Tragödie des Coriolan', *Sinn und Form*, 17 (1965), 466.
38 See Palmer, *Political Characters*, p. 250: 'Shakespeare in *Coriolanus* takes for his theme a recurrent political problem of all times and places . . . Politics are a predominating interest in scene after scene . . . in this particular tragedy the individual men and women are passionately concerned with their rights and wrongs as citizens in a community . . . the virtues and vices of the principal characters are all related to their place and function in the commonwealth; their actions and passions are almost wholly governed by their conceptions of what is due to them or expected of them as belonging to an estate of the nation.' Kott, with his Marxist background and his thesis that Shakespeare is our 'contemporary', goes even further, op. cit., pp. 151, 164, 167 ff.:

'But the history that breaks Coriolanus is not royal history any more. It is the history of a city divided into plebeians and patricians. It is the history of class struggle. History in the royal chronicles, and in *Macbeth*, was a Grand Mechanism, which had something demonic in it. History in *Coriolanus* has ceased to be demonic. It is only ironic and tragic. This is another reason why *Coriolanus* is a modern play . . . In this drama of class hatred Coriolanus is such as the plebeians see him, but the plebeians also conform to Coriolanus's view of them . . . At the Capitol and at the Forum, laws of revolution, attitudes and conflicts, are all exposed, sharply like formulas, condensed in bits of dialogue. Opposite each other stand: "top" and "bottom", Jacobins and Girondists, revolutionary democrats and liberals . . . History has proved the plebeians right: the enemy of the people has become the enemy of Rome. In the first three acts of *Coriolanus* a bare drama of class attitudes has been played out. One could call it also a drama of historical inevitability. There is in it no discrepancy between social situation and action, or psychology. Coriolanus could be nameless, just as the First, Second, and Third Citizens are nameless. He is just an ambitious general, who hates the people and has gone over to the enemy camp when unable to achieve dictatorial power.'

39 BBA 672/69.
40 'Die Tragödie des Coriolan', p. 471.
41 *Shakespeare's Roman Plays*, p. 547.
42 BBA 672/67.
43 Rülicke-Weiler, *Die Dramaturgie*, p. 153.
44 *GW*, 6/2493.
45 *GW*, 6/2487.
46 *The State*, pp. 146 ff.
47 BBA 93/25.
48 BBA 650/03.
49 *Shakespeare our Contemporary*, p. 163.
50 Op. cit., p. 184.
51 Kott, op. cit., pp. 148 ff.
52 Ibid., p. 154.
53 BBA 650/01.
54 *GW*, 17/1252 f.
55 *Verfremdungseffekt in den erzählenden Bildern des älteren Breughel, GW*, 18/281.
56 Op. cit., p.488.
57 *GW*, 6/2465 f.
58 *GW*, 6/2496 f.
59 Compare the tone of grand solemnity with which Shakespeare closes his play, and the temper of comments on 'a conclusion that proposes no enigma and inflicts no pang, but even more than in the case of *Macbeth* satisfies, and even more than in *Antony and Cleopatra* uplifts the heart, without troublesome questionings on the part of the reader' (MacCallum, *Shakespeare's Roman Plays*, p. 462). Wilson Knight, op. cit., p. 198, also enthuses over the tremendous spirit of the finale and wonders 'whether any speech gives a more exquisite thrill of delight than this final cry of triumph at the hour of his death. Like *Hamlet*, this play of death ends with a dead march. But long after that there rings yet Coriolanus's final cry, a note of triumph never struck in *Hamlet*, the cry of mighty value, vanquished indeed by a mightier, yet itself a thing of royal integrity and splendour.'
60 R. W. Leonhardt, op. cit., says of Brecht's ending and the alteration to it: 'Das ist ein schlechter Schluß, denn: da taucht unvermittelt eine unbekannte Verordnung eines bis dahin nie genannten Mannes auf; da entfernt man sich von Shakespeare (in dessen Stück die Frauen ja als Retter Roms geehrt werden) weiter, als nötig ist; da wird der Tribun Brutus als unerbittlicher Fürsprecher einer über den Tod hinausreichenden Sippenhaft unsympathisch — nachdem es doch ein Ziel der Bearbeitung gewesen war, die Volkstribunen als weise Männer guten Willens (was sie bei Shakespeare gewiß nicht sind) erscheinen zu lassen. Ich weiß nicht, ob Mut dazu gehörte, den vom Meister hinterlassenen Schluß zu streichen; auf jeden Fall verrät die Streichung tiefe künstlerische Einsicht.'
61 *The Imperial Theme*, p. 163.
62 Brecht's scepticism of the *need* for great rulers and their bloody deeds is summed up in the ironical close to his sonnet *Über Shakespeares Stück 'Hamlet'*, an attitude to Hamlet's decision to slaughter:

So daß man finster nickt, wenn man erfährt
Er hätte sich, wär er hinaufgelangt
Unfehlbar noch höchst königlich bewährt.

63 Kott, op. cit., p. 150.
64 BBA 1824/95. The phrase is by Rülicke-Weiler.
65 BBA 650/07 f.
66 *GW*, 6/2444 ff.
67 *GW*, 6/2403.
68 *GW*, 6/2441 f.
69 The poem *Fragen eines lesenden Arbeiters* is the simplest expression of this attitude and the inevitable enquiry it provokes, and its ideology is to be met at countless points in Brecht.
70 BBA 672/69.
71 See *Programmheft: Zur Inszenierung*, which opens with a bitter attack on the tradition of presenting a great individual against a background of knaves and petty scum so that the hero's glitter was enhanced: 'Der Zuschauer sollte seinen Shakespeare auf Anhieb haben, und er bekam ihn mit der blechernen Größe eines Gyges und dem traurigen Humor der Mundartstücke. Er rülpste, furzte, randalierte auf der einen Seite, damit auf der anderen Seite um so edler und einsamer herumstolziert werden konnte wie aufgeputzte Hähne.'
72 MacCallum, *Shakespeare's Roman Plays*, pp. 525 and 518.
73 BBA 672/67 f. Compare the more aggressive criticism of Grass, op. cit., p. 201 f.: 'Denn jene, bei Shakespeare von der ersten Szene an wankelmütigen Empörer schult Brecht, bevor sie überhaupt auftreten, also vorgefaßt und nicht im Verlauf der Handlung, zu handfesten Revolutionären um, die ihm mit seiner Schlußszene den Beweis erbringen sollen, daß die klassenbewußten Plebejer — wie Livius andeutet — bei ihm ganz gewiß siegen werden. Dem Schema dieser Tendenz folgend, benehmen sich seine Tribunen: zeigt Shakespeare zwei verwechselbare Nullen, intrigant und feige, gibt Brecht zwei listenreichen und fortschrittlichen Funktionären mehr und mehr die Macht.'
74 Dieckmann, 'Die Tragödie', p. 478.
75 Ibid., p. 475.
76 See notes on the unfinished scenes of Act I, BBA 650/07: '(zu 4.): bleibt. Stärker herauskommen muß das "ohne uns" der Soldaten, die Marcius zwar wegen seiner Tapferkeit loben, aber nicht für Rom kämpfen wollen.
(zu. 5.): Das Plündern hielten wir für uns ohne Bedeutung, es muß nicht gezeigt werden, d.h. nur soweit, als es Coriolan Anlaß zu Beschimpfungen gibt. Dann Übergang zu der Beschimpfung in [6].'
77 *GW*, 6/2397 f.
78 *GW*, 6/2439.
79 *GW*, 6/2440.
80 BBA 650/23.
81 BBA 1769/06.
82 R. W. Chambers, *Shakespeare's Hand in the Play of Sir Thomas More* (Cambridge, 1923), p. 168.
83 *The Apothecary's Shop*, p. 34 n.
84 Brents Stirling, *The Populace in Shakespeare* (New York, 1940), p. 42.
85 Op. cit., p. 501: 'They are described as "seditious tribunes" when they oppose the colonisation of Velitrae and the renewal of the war; but Plutarch shows they had good grounds for doing so. Even their action against Coriolanus for opposing the grant of corn and advocating the abolition of their office, was from their own point of view, and perhaps from any point of view, perfectly legitimate.'
86 *Shakespeare our Contemporary*, p. 166.
87 *Political Characters*, p. 259.
88 Ibid., p. 260.
89 *GW*, 6/2405 f.
90 *GW*, 6/2407. Compare Grass, op. cit., p. 204: 'Bei Brecht halten zwei selbstbewußte Funktionäre die Position.'
91 Dieckmann, 'Die Tragödie', p. 470.
92 Op. cit., p. 206.
93 *GW*, 6/2426 f. Compare BBA 650/09: 'Neu eingeführt am Anfang kurzes Gespräch zwischen den Tribunen. Es zeigt, daß das Volk immer am Kriege verliert.'

94 *GW*, 6/2430.
95 *GW*, 6/2442 f.
96 *GW*, 6/2478. Compare the helpless disarray into which tribunes and plebeians fall in *Coriolanus*, IV, 6, 139–61.
97 *GW*, 6/2481 f.
98 *GW*, 6/2486 f.
99 *GW*, 6/2487 f.
100 'Die Tragödie', p. 470.
101 Ibid., p. 467.
102 Ibid., p. 472.
103 Ibid., p. 486.
104 Bullough, op. cit., p. 495.
105 *Theaterprobleme* (Zürich, 1955), p. 44.
106 'Die Tragödie', p. 487. Compare M. Zéraffa, 'Shakespeare, Brecht et l'histoire', *Europe*, 35 (1957), 131: 'Brecht et Shakespeare s'opposent, mais s'appellent, et s'expliquent l'un par l'autre.'

CHAPTER VII

CONCLUSION

No critical assessment of an adaptation can afford to lose sight of the fact that two poles are constantly involved — the adaptor (a contemporary of ours) and the author (usually a 'classic'). A variety of sociological and cultural factors have helped to perpetuate the public image of the classics as sacrosanct monuments, never more strongly perhaps than in the nineteenth century, when the post-Romantic concept of the creative artist as inspired but bohemian became firmly embedded in the general consciousness. The business-like methods of a novelist like Dickens did nothing to shatter this picture, and it is said that when Trollope divulged the prosaic routine of his prose writing he drew on himself the censure of the critical élite who dictated taste. Hans Mayer can write of culture at the turn of this century: 'Die individuelle Besitzergreifung der "Bildungsgüter" geschah durch Klassikerbibliotheken. Wer Klassiker war, entzog sich ebenfalls der Erörterung.'[1] The term 'classic' in this sense has little meaning for creative artists themselves (of whom the adaptor may be one) who usually find they are involved to a greater or lesser degree in a struggle to come to terms with what has been achieved before them. 'Being influenced by' or working 'in a tradition' posits a critical and sympathetic dialogue with one's predecessors. 'These fragments I have shored against my ruins' describes the salvaged remnants of our literary past that T. S. Eliot erects as a protective bulwark against cultural disintegration. For various reasons Eliot stands poles apart from Brecht in his attitude to tradition, but they are both aware of one essential: that the writer can find his own identity and meaning only through an active relationship with the past. Like Brecht, Eliot uses the term 'historical sense' (though with different connotations) when he states that tradition 'involves, in the first place, the historical sense . . . and the historical sense involves a perception, not only of the pastness of the past, but of its presence . . . This historical sense, which is a sense of the timeless as well as of the temporal and of the timeless and of the temporal together, is what makes a writer traditional. And it is at the same time what makes a writer most acutely conscious of his place in time, of his contemporaneity.'[2]

In recent decades the reshaping of already complete and self-sufficient works appears to have become a feature of dramatic activity in particular, and many reasons can be adduced in explanation. In the first place a writer is now faced with new aesthetic tasks in having to modify material to suit the differing exigencies of a range of media — book, theatre, radio, cinema,

192

television. The need to satisfy the expanding demands of media and public calls for a proliferation of themes, plots and story-lines that is not feasible; individual experience does not extend its compass of variety and richness at the pace of material and technological development. Secondly, the modern artist's concern for the *process* of creating almost matches his commitment to the creation itself. Ever since Poe's essay *The Philosophy of Composition*, perhaps, the writer has become more and more engrossed in self-consciousness, and the reflective element in his activity has encroached on the 'naive' sureness of actual composition. This in turn has undermined the sense of absolute value, of uniqueness and perfection of the work of art; less than ever before is the artist convinced that his formulation is definitive, time and time again he makes a hesitant approach to 'perfection', 'completion' — and is happy to leave his statement tentative and provisional. Fragment, experiment, variation all indicate the quality of the present-day writer's consciousness of reality. It is not surprising that Brecht published his plays as 'Versuche', nor that Max Frisch subjects a meagre number of themes to permutation as diary entry, radio play, theatre play and novel. Finally, with the awareness that all creative work is a timebound articulation comes the view that the classics are now no longer inviolable. This could be another expression of the irony that marks the temper of our time and that, perhaps as a concomitant of the democratizing process, has eroded the prescriptive right of public figures to respect and reverence. One of the battles lost in recent years by authoritative censorship was fought in an attempt to preserve the immunity of public personages — the Royal family, the Prime Minister and so on. In the theatre a producer — or adaptor — is free now to seek out meaningful connexions with the present in a work and to modify it accordingly without compunction. Comments by Heinar Kipphardt in his 1968 adaptation of Lenz's *Die Soldaten* clearly state this (justifying his radical procedure to some extent with Lenz's own words from *Die Freunde machen den Philosophen*: 'Alle meine Stücke sind große Erzgruben, die ausgepocht, ausgeschmolzen und in Schauspiele erst verwandelt werden müssen.'):

Von den Schönheiten des Stückes angezogen und dessen Schwächen vor Augen, unternahm ich den Versuch, das Stück in einer verbesserten Fassung vorzulegen. Die Absicht ist, die Schönheiten des alten Stückes zur Geltung zu bringen, verdeckte Schönheiten sichtbar zu machen und gleichzeitig die Schwächen und Unschärfen der Vorlage zu beseitigen ... Das Prinzip der Bearbeitung war, den Lenz so weit wie möglich zu respektieren und soviel wie notwendig zu ändern ... Es ist das Ziel der Bearbeitung, den *Soldaten* des Lenz den Platz im Bestande der deutschen Schaubühne zu erwerben, der ihnen zukommt, und der ihnen seit nahezu 200 Jahren verweigert wird.[3]

Dürrenmatt has performed a similar operation on Shakespeare's *King John* and Strindberg's *Dance of Death* as Dramaturg for the Basler Stadttheater. The body of artistic creation inherited and added to by successive ages is a phenomenon that has exercised Dürrenmatt as much as Eliot, though with different results. The latter promoted the conservative attitude to tradition as a quasi-religious entity standing above the individual talent and having mandatory and formative properties. Without exactly negating these aspects of tradition Dürrenmatt launches a healthily pragmatic jeremiad in *Theaterprobleme* deploring the storehouse function of tradition and its detrimental consequences for the contemporary writer:

Es [the theatre] ist heute weitgehend ein Museum geworden, das kann nicht verschwiegen werden, in welchem die Kunstschätze alter Theaterepochen gezeigt werden ...

Das Theater, die Kultur lebt von den Zinsen des gut angelegten Geistes, dem nichts mehr passieren kann und dem man nicht einmal mehr Tantiemen zu zahlen braucht, und mit dem Bewußtsein, einen Goethe, einen Schiller, einen Sophokles auf seiner Seite zu haben, nimmt man die modernen Stücke entgegen. Am liebsten nur zur Uraufführung. Heroisch erfüllt man seine Pflicht, um beim nächsten Shakespeare wieder aufzuatmen.[4]

Since all museums are bursting at the seams with treasures and we have not even fully investigated the cultures of cave-dwellers, our own art will have to take its turn for the attention of future ages. Thus it is a matter of indifference whether new things are written.

Dürrenmatt's pessimistic conclusion underlines the relevance for both dramatist and audience of enquiring into the validity of tradition and why we continue to appreciate and concern ourselves with past drama. In the broadest possible terms, the motivation is human: modes of experience (sensory, social, psychological, emotional, aesthetic) are in their essentials common to humanity in all ages. Man is distinguished by his historical consciousness, simultaneously apprehending himself in a present context and his forbears in the past. Constantly renewed communion with the historical accumulation of art is probably the activity that most subtly satisfies the need men have for a past dimension in their imaginative experience of time. And the theatre may literally provide the best stage for the communal enactment and fulfilment of this need.

The importance of a past dimension in men's consciousness is beyond dispute; most of our activities take the past into account directly or indirectly and, indeed, the more 'purposeless' they are, the more they seem to be involved with the past (archaeology, history, collecting). Less certain in contemporary culture are the traditional modes of operation of the theatre and in what way its sociological function is still meaningful. Attempts to break away from institutionalized theatre, manifested in such phenomena as happenings, living theatre, Straßentheater, can all be understood as dynamic, if not always successful endeavours to inject into the theatre a consciousness that can more adequately cope with or at least reflect the modern world. No small part is played in this by the encroachment of document in the fictional field of literature, with a consequent sharpening of the historical sense.

In this context Brecht has been accused of employing the very forms of theatre — and theatrical experience — he was apparently claiming to expose.[5] But such criticism usually rests on an inadequate grasp of the interdependence of thought and form in Brecht's work, and even presupposes a fission between the processes that determined his intellectual structures (historicizing) and their aesthetic expression (alienation).[6] Brecht's didacticism is congruent with and generated by his conception of history as an understanding of human experience, not as the transmission of hard facts, which may well change their appearance if subjected to a different perspective. This didacticism is maieutic in putting the process of understanding at the centre of interest, and it achieves aesthetic pleasure in what Roland Barthes calls the 'connaissance naissante' of the audience. Such a view of 'history' naturally has close affinities with Marxist attitudes, especially in its effect of presenting different ideologies as relative in the effort to analyse the *process* of historical events. Like Marxism, too, its aim is to promote the reciprocal understanding of the past and the present, and to keep open an optimistic teleological approach to the future with the possibility of influencing it.[7]

Every element in Brecht's dramaturgy is directed to the active end of presenting history — which is a continual changing of circumstances — in such a manner that the presentation itself is an intervention in history, with the result 'daß das historische Stück durch das Stück für ein Publikum von Historikern abgelöst wird'.[8] The French critic Bernard Dort recently suggested that the three major dramatic trends since the Second World War (the theatre of the absurd, Brecht's epic-dialectical drama, neo-naturalism) have all reached the limits of their possibilities and there is only one way left open: 'Von nun an muß man die Begriffe der Schöpfung und des dramatischen Werkes revidieren. Der Schwerpunkt der theatralischen Tätigkeit hat sich verändert: er ist nicht mehr auf der Bühne oder im Stück zu finden, sondern gewissermaßen in einem Bereich zwischen Bühne und Zuschauerraum, oder genauer noch im Schnittpunkt von Theater und Welt.'[9] Dort too facilely dismisses the epic-dialectical theatre for it does seem that Brecht's dramatic mode, if kept free of the distortions of formalism, properly operates at the intersection of theatre and reality. His adaptations, no less than his original plays, make sense within the historical context as discharges of productive energy in the form of clarification and enlightenment. In the *Messingkauf* Shakespeare's *Julius Caesar* is taken to illustrate the active process of historicizing: the Philosopher suggests that the actor could handle the text 'wie einen authentischen, aber vieldeutigen Bericht',[10] but the immediate experience in real life of the events involved would not itself substantially enlarge one's knowledge of the world. The function of the theatre is to structure the actions in such a way that the audience would understand more from the representation of reality than an eye-witness of the original scene. Historicization is thus a procedure that adds import to a text.

The repertoire for the Berliner Ensemble that Brecht evolved over six years had the twin aims of offering entertainment to the audience while encouraging a reflective historical insight that itself would be of aesthetic quality. His adaptations of past plays are a significant contribution to the re-orientation of historical thinking away from an *a priori* transcendental 'truth' immanent in historical events towards an understanding of the ever-changing structure of reality with a view to influencing the future structure. The standpoint Brecht takes up is no more objective than the one he rejects except in so far as the process of history — and possibly progress — is its objective truth, and the meaning of history, not being determined, is not there to be apprehended, but must continually be established afresh. The analysis of historiography extends to drama, and Brecht demonstrates with his adaptations that a play, once created, need not be treated like a historical event — wholly self-sufficient, inviolable and in a sense unproductive — but can stand up to sympathetic re-interpretation in the time dimension of history. The sensitive adaptation in a new perspective enhances and enriches the original without in any way obliterating its factual reality. There ensues on this the obvious corollary that Brecht's adaptations cannot be seen as a purely personal matter peculiar to his manner of ordering reality through the medium of the theatre. The radical kind of adaptation may well prove to be more than a Brechtian idiosyncracy; indeed, there is no reason why these adaptations should not themselves be the subject of a re-working if a sufficiently coherent and articulate ideological and aesthetic apparatus should evolve to do this.

It is important to distinguish between the handling of traditional themes (e.g. St Joan, Amphitryon, Faust, Œdipus, Don Juan) where only the essential subject-matter is shared, and the true adaptation that compels the original into positive colloquy. In the drama the choice lies between alternative paths of adaptation. The playwright may draw on a common store for his theme, taking notice more or less at will of previous versions, or he may rework a specific creation, as Brecht does (or, in painting, Picasso with his famous variations on *Las Meninas* by Velasquez, and more recently on David's *Rape of the Sabine Women* and Manet's *Déjeuner sur l'herbe*). The second method is clearly more complex as it sets up a tension between one author, work and period and another. What is more, this tension will in all probability induce a qualitative change in our appreciation of the original, a fact Eliot was alive to in asserting that 'the difference between the present and the past is that the conscious present is an awareness of the past in a way and to an extent which the past's awareness of itself cannot show'.[11] Brecht's original plays could themselves well be subjected to intelligent adaptation, and this would guard against the ever-present danger that his abundant and explicit ideas on production might stultify the creatively dialectical staging of his own plays and turn them into museum pieces. An example of the rather purposeless adaptation was Günther Büch's 1967 production of *Die Dreigroschenoper* in Oberhausen which accommodated a topical attack on the shut-down of many Ruhr coalmines but went no deeper since it lacked a fresh ideological approach.

A play of any worth, whether it be by Brecht or an earlier writer, must always be at the service of the producer or adaptor who, in his turn, finds himself divided between some sort of loyalty to the original and the imperative task of making that play meaningful in the terms of his contemporary audience. The divergent attitudes that a passionate acceptance or rejection of the Brechtian mode can generate are well illustrated by two statements published in the same issue of *Les Lettres françaises* (9 June 1960). André Steiger, maintaining that realistic dramas like those of Calderon and Molière are perfectly amenable to Brechtian treatment, asserted of his 1958/9 production of *Les femmes savantes*: 'Et je n'aurais pas su le montrer [the social aspect] aussi clairement si je n'avais pas connu Brecht.' Jacques Mauclair, on the other hand, categorically rejected the application of Brecht's method to other plays than his own: 'Non, on ne peut pas monter *Dom Juan* ou *La Mouette* "à la Brecht" . . . C'est toujours une atteinte à la pièce. Les théories de Brecht ne peuvent se manier qu'avec prudence.' This sort of choice facing the producer is acknowledged in a programme note accompanying the presentation of *The Recruiting Officer* at the National Theatre, London, in December 1963; William Gaskill wrote:

No classic is timeless; at one period of history it may assume a particular relevance for its audience undreamt of by the author. For the 30's *Richard II* was another *Vortex*, when the audience saw its self-pitying hero as one of them, and for us today, Falstaff's questioning of honour in *Henry IV* is the same as Joan Littlewood's in *Oh, What a Lovely War*! The form and pressure of our time is essentially anti-heroic and we respond most to those writers like Middleton and Farquhar whose view of heroism is as sceptical as our own . . .

[In *The Recruiting Officer*] I think what we recognise from our experience is the systematic deception of the ignorant to a pointless end by the use of the heroic images of the past, a past no longer relevant. We may laugh at Pearmain and Appletree but we recognise our own plight.

Gaskill countered queries as to why he did not use Brecht's adaptation of Farquhar with the argument that *The Recruiting Officer* could be produced in a way to yield a sufficiently modern meaning without going all the way with Brecht:

It would be false to impose on Farquhar Brecht's statement of the social situation but we cannot ignore in Farquhar those elements which excited Brecht to make his version . . . In directing a play which observes social values without criticising them I have tried to make clear (without underlining) those points which will be more meaningful to a modern audience. To do more would be to destroy the framework in which Farquhar wrote, and would involve rewriting the play.

In spite of the reservations voiced by Gaskill, the National Theatre did, five years later, take into its repertoire a Brechtian rewriting of an English play — *Leben Eduards des Zweiten von England* — that Brecht had adapted with Lion Feuchtwanger in 1923/4, and was now translated back into the language of Marlowe's original. There is no question of the source play being usurped or invalidated; indeed, Brecht was at pains to point out how it could be enhanced by the contrast with an adaptation. One of his *Thesen zur Faustus-Diskussion* in defence of Hanns Eisler's opera *Dr. Faustus* (1953) may serve as an illustration:

Hat Eisler versucht, unser klassisches Faustbild völlig zu zerstören? Entseelt, verfälscht, vernichtet er eine wunderbare Gestalt des deutschen Erbes? Nimmt er den Faust zurück? Ich denke nicht. Eisler liest das alte Volksbuch wieder und findet in ihm eine andere Geschichte als Goethe und eine andere Gestalt, ihm bedeutsam erscheinend... So entsteht für mein Empfinden ein dunkler Zwilling des Faust, eine finstere, große Figur, die den helleren Bruder nicht ersetzen noch überschatten kann oder soll. Von dem dunklen Bruder hebt sich der helle vielmehr ab und wird sogar heller. So etwas zu machen, ist nicht Vandalentum.[12]

Brecht is here justifying vicariously in Eisler his own activity as adaptor. The following contributions to the Faust discussion are applicable in all essentials to Brecht's own re-interpretation:

Es sollte nicht abgelehnt werden, daß eine große Figur der Literatur neu und in einem anderen Geist behandelt wird. Ein solches Unternehmen bedeutet keineswegs den Versuch, die Figur zu zerstören. Die antike griechische Dramatik weist manche dichterische Unternehmungen solcher Art auf.

Ich lese den Inhalt so: Faust, eines Bauern Sohn, ist im Bauernkrieg zu den Herren übergelaufen. Fausts Versuch, seine Persönlichkeit zu entfalten, scheitert dadurch. Es ist ihm nicht möglich, den Verrat vollständig zu vollziehen. Sein schlechtes Gewissen zwingt ihn, seine ehrgeizigen Pläne im letzten Augenblick immer noch so rebellisch auszuführen, daß ihm der Erfolg bei den Herren versagt bleibt. Er hat die Wahrheit zu seinem Nachteil erkannt. Aus heilsamem Trunk wird sie ihm zu Gift. Als ihn die Bauernschinder endlich anerkennen, bricht er zusammen und kommt zur Einsicht, die er in seiner Confessio verkündet.[13]

The hero seen in a new perspective — from very close to the ground! — is one of the prime modifications Brecht makes in re-ordering the configuration of a character and work. But there are others. He explores and puts to use factors pertinent to the time of the play's action that subsequent historical assessment has revealed. He searches for what the author wanted to say, or what he said unconsciously or implicitly.[14] He injects a modern political consciousness into some representatives of the lower classes and thus secures a historical perspective of the play from below, at the same time fixing — often in one and the same 'Gestus' — the dispensable nature of the masters.

More characteristic than any other aspect is the dominance of reflection that stamps all Brecht's work and is responsible for a fundamental alteration of pattern in any adaptation by him. The dramatic movement of the original (for instance, in *Der Hofmeister* and *Coriolanus*) is submitted to the reasoning faculty of the audience. In this way the unique individual situation acquires explicit representative significance in the adaptation where in the original it remained implicit. By keeping a tight hold on the conceptual understanding of the dramatic action Brecht tries to ensure a close-knit dialectical unity of the text that is simultaneously an interpretation of itself. Put another way, he presents analysis (Vorstellung) of the original in place of portrayal (Illusion). This is the sense of Ihering's remarks in his review of the first night production in 1924 of *Eduard II* which Brecht called a 'history':

Historie bedeutet nicht 'historisches' Schauspiel, nicht Geschichte im zeitlichen Sinn, sondern Geschichte als Mitteilungsform. Historie wie Ballade, wie Moritat. Der Stoff ist kolportagehaft, jahrmarktsmäßig gesehen: 'Leben Eduards des Zweiten von England' — und doch gestaltete Form. Der Stoff ist weder durch Stil ausgetrieben (wie bei Hofmannsthal, wenn er alte Dramen bearbeitete), noch Rohmaterial (wie fast immer zuletzt, wenn ein Drama überhaupt einen Stoff hatte). Brecht hat Marlowe nicht 'bearbeitet'. Das alte englische Drama *Eduard II* ist wieder als Stoff, als Urmaterial erlebt und von neuem Gestalt geworden.[15]

This comment is equally relevant to Brecht's later adaptations for he always inserted into the process of adaptation the dynamic factor of a modern consciousness, with the effect of submitting the original to the double perspective proper to historiography — the event itself in its contemporary setting and that occurrence appraised from the present and in its relationship to the present. Thus in *Eduard II* 'the history is medieval English, but the impulse behind it comes from Germany in the immediate aftermath of the first world war', as Martin Esslin notes in the programme to the National Theatre production. In other adaptations Brecht engages in an extremely complex dialogue with the original that has far-reaching consequences in the structure, direction and impact of the play.

Needless to say, the incisive changes that Brecht made in adapting plays by other men necessitate a revision of traditionally accepted criteria of evaluation. First to go must be the ingrained idea that the original provides an inflexible norm against which the adaptation is to be measured and found wanting to a greater or lesser degree. The five adaptations analysed in this study are all *qualitatively* different from their originals and are as powerful alienations of them as Brecht's own plays are of the reality that they present. With the adaptations the audience moves into a Brechtian world and will search in vain for the individual stamp of the original masterpiece, for Brecht has eliminated the quirky eccentricity of *Der Hofmeister*, the powerful impact of Hauptmann's turgid emotion, the elegant frivolity of *Dom Juan*, the witty lightness of Restoration comedy in *The Recruiting Officer*, the towering hero in *Coriolanus*. The language too — that most important element in drama — shows that there is no question of half-measures with Brecht. He does not engage in dilettante pastiche; instead, the characters in his adaptations are not differentiated in speech by chronological factors but by social distinctions. The Roman Senator and the Wilhelminian worker both speak the language to be found in all Brecht's plays, and the adaptations are as likely to recall the latter as the originals which were their starting-point.

A simple but clear illustration of the operation of Brecht's technique of adaptation is his reworking for the stage of Anna Seghers's radio play *Der Prozeß der Jeanne d'Arc zu Rouen* in 1952. It is true that almost half of the total sixteen scenes are new, but nevertheless there is no substantial divergence from the radio play, and this for two reasons. First, Anna Seghers shaped her text very closely to the actual protocol preserved in the House of Deputies in Paris as well as to contemporary accounts; thus the narrative structure of

document is inherent in the subject-matter. Secondly, the harmony of ideological attitude between Anna Seghers and Brecht meant that the latter had
no need to alter the intent of the play but was left free to emphasize its
direction. This he did by concentrating on a historical handling of the material:
the 'Prozeß' is not only the trial but also the process that takes place gradually
in the course of the trial. Beneath the factual web of interrogation and answer,
judgement and execution, Brecht tries to reproduce the movement of history
by indicating how the views and decisions of different individuals and groups
condition each other in a dialectical relationship. Johanna is seen to waver,
weaken and give in suddenly as a result of what she believes to be the apathy
of the people, from whom her captivity cuts her off: 'Nicht die Todesdro-
hungen der Kirche, sondern die fälschlich vermutete Teilnahmslosigkeit des
Volks zerbrechen zeitweise Johannas Widerstand.'[16] The popular unrest in
Rouen shows this to be an error of judgement and a betrayal of the people:
'Nachdem sie von den Unruhen in Rouen ihretwegen gehört hat, trifft den
Bischof von Beauvais ihr Zorn, und es ist der Zorn gegen sich selbst. Weil
sie nicht an das Volk geglaubt hatte.'

Now Johanna reaffirms her faith in the people she had once led in battle
against the English:

JOHANNA: Aber in der Schlacht fürchtete ich das Feuer nicht, denn da war ich nicht
allein, sondern um mich waren meine Leute. Nur, jetzt zweifelte ich am Volk, als ob
ich stürbe und sie achteten es nicht und tränken ihren Wein. Sie aber wußten alles
von mir, immer, da war nichts umsonst.
BISCHOF: Was soll das, was die Faßbinder und Fischweiber wissen?
JOHANNA: Bischof, da wird ein Tag sein, da werden die Weinbauern der Touraine
mit den Schiffern der Normandie zusammensitzen und Euch wird's nicht mehr
geben.[17]

Johanna withdraws her recantation and this leads to a development in the
people from apparent apathy (because they thought Johanna had let them
down) to activity. The *Programmheft* describes the change 'das lockere
Mädchen' undergoes:

Es ist anfangs ohne jedes politische Interesse, freundlicher den englischen Eindring-
lichen gesonnen als der Johanna. 'Warum ist sie nicht daheim geblieben?' fragte sie
zuerst ganz verständnislos, um später, wenn sie im 'Fischzug Petri' den Brief der
Johanna an die Engländer hört, mit Genugtuung festzustellen: 'Die ist gut!' Der
Abstand zwischen diesen beiden Repliken kennzeichnet die Entwicklung, die das
Mädchen, dank Johanna, genommen hat. Und daß sie am Ende des Prozesses die
englischen Fremdherren zum Teufel wünscht, macht vollends klar, daß ein erst
unpolitischer Mensch sich nun einmischt.

In the penultimate scene the crowd closes its ranks to hide the young peasant
from the English soldiers — a typically visual 'Geste' to convey solidarity —
and this is evidence 'daß die kämpfend sterbende Johanna das Volk geändert
hat. Es sind nicht mehr die Leute, die gleichgültig zugeschaut hatten, wie
man sie zum Prozeß führte.' The final scene, a sort of epilogue five years
later, indicates the historical repercussions of the positive process revealed in

the trial: the English are being driven from France and there is an implied call, through hints and direct references (the last line runs: 'Das singen sie jetzt in beiden Frankreich, hüben und drüben', and Brecht's poem 'Deutschland 1952' is reprinted in the *Programmheft*), to expel the American (and Russian?) 'occupiers' from Germany now. Thus Brecht does not handle the theme of Joan of Arc in isolation but attempts to integrate the events into a continuous historical process.

This adaptation demonstrates in a simple form that a literary work can be both a historical document and a historical interpretation. As document the play does not operate as a contribution to historical truth and enjoys the privilege of not being scrutinized and answerable to demands of factual accuracy. Its meaning — and consequently its aesthetic — is not in the material itself but in the method of ordering that material. And the meaning in its turn is inseparable from the function of activating the energies of the spectator by engaging his reasoning, emotional and aesthetic faculties. Brecht's aim is to lay bare the patterns of our social reality — both past and present — and open up the possibility of understanding and coping with it better. This is a moral purpose that recalls Lessing's desire to promote 'tugendhafte Fertigkeiten' (with the etymological connotations of MHG *vertec*, 'ready to travel') which describe not an end result but a readiness to apply insights gained, a state of mind prepared to put things right. It is not surprising that Brecht, like Lessing, should have chosen as his 'pulpit' the theatre, the most public and therefore socially dynamic vehicle of literature.

Of course, no statistical or other method has yet been devised to measure the degree to which a critical theatre may influence the habitual thought processes of an audience. The task of using the theatre to the definite end of stimulating a critical attitude would appear to be gigantic, given the entrenched social prestige of a visit to the theatre and the established, unadventurous paths of response in the majority of audiences. The existing order — whatever its ideological bias — always has a protective resilience (part of its power) that enables it to blunt and even absorb uncompliant radical impulses; as Max Frisch said in his Züricher Rede in 1958, a writer begins to shout if he feels he is speaking into cotton wool. An example of the obstacles encountered can be seen in Egon Monk's failure as Intendant of the ailing Hamburg Stadttheater in 1968, his attempt to stimulate political theatre being frustrated by the inertia of the public. By the same token Frisch coined his famous *mot* that Brecht now possesses 'die durchschlagende Wirkungslosigkeit eines Klassikers' only a decade after his death; Hans Mayer describes both Marx and Brecht as having been turned into 'Requisiten der Bürgerwelt';[18] and Dürrenmatt is most biting about the predictable enshrinement of the classics 'in India paper editions' that absolves from proper interpretation:

Man interpretiert nicht immer, sondern exekutiert allzu oft die Klassiker, der fallende Vorhang deckt einen verstümmelten Leichnam. Doch ohne Gefahr, denn stets stellt sich auch die rettende Konvention ein, die alles Klassische als vollendet hinnimmt, als eine Art Goldwährung in der Kultur, und die aus der Meinung besteht, daß alles Gold sei, was da in Dünndruckausgaben glänzt. Das Publikum strömt zu den Klassikern, ob sie nun gut oder schlecht gespielt werden, der Beifall ist gewiß, ja, Pflicht des Gebildeten, und man ist auf eine legitime Weise der Nötigung enthoben, nachzudenken und ein anderes Urteil zu fällen, als das, welches die Schule einem einpaukte.[19]

Apart from audience inertia, the degree of its familiarity with the original is another hazard that faces the adaptor. Better known, more 'weighty' plays (such as *Der Biberpelz* and *Coriolanus*, perhaps) no doubt provoke more resistance to an adaptation than those like *The Recruiting Officer* and *Dom Juan* which bulk less largely in the literary consciousness. A second factor that partly counteracts the first regards the language of the original and its cultural context: Shakespeare and Molière would prove less formidable sources to a German than to an English and French adaptor respectively, since a German audience would in any case always have to experience their plays filtered through a translation and uprooted from the humus to which they belong. (But the linguistic factor is not the primary consideration: the attraction of a modern interpretation is proved by the fact that it was Brecht's *Hofmeister* (not Lenz's) that a Paris theatre produced in 1957, Brecht's *Antigone* (not Sophocles') that the Compagnie du Sud-Est performed in 1963 and Brecht's *Eduard II* (not Marlowe's) that was chosen in translation for the National Theatre.) It can be argued that there is room for adaptations precisely when they are radical, and that far from supplanting the original their function is to suggest a reading which can enrich it for that particular age. This is the spirit in which Brecht sketches in his *Kleines Organon* a politico-economic orientation to *Hamlet*: 'Diese Lesart des Stücks, das mehr als eine Lesart hat, könnte, meines Erachtens, unser Publikum interessieren.'

The horror that is so often evinced at an interpretation by Brecht is not usually produced by aesthetic considerations. The adaptor's drastic surgery is judged to be reprehensible, and yet such a view is no more defensible than that an audience should be asked to submit itself to the original and shut out from its mind and reactions the events of history, economics, literature. The loudest protest accuses Brecht of reducing the 'universal' in human actions to the mechanisms of economic forces; this criticism ignores the dialectic of continuity and individuality in Marx's view of man. A quotation from Georg Lukács identifies more accurately the essence of all Brecht's theatre: 'Nicht die Vorherrschaft der ökonomischen Motive in der Geschichtserklärung unterscheidet den Marxismus von der bürgerlichen Wissenschaft, sondern der Gesichtspunkt der Totalität.'[20] If this perspective is at all attainable, in however fragile a form, it demands that the *modus operandi* of drama be historicized, without sacrificing its unique quality of affording visual pleasure and entertainment. Brecht's method of achieving this is to structure the events in a drama in such a fashion that the audience is given an understanding of the organization of reality. Totality of understanding is striven for by employing the means of alienation to keep the picture and its depiction apart, to engage the feelings and the mind of the spectator in the widest possible range of experience. The gestic method of acting developed by Brecht is the means by which the theatre organizes its symbolic models of real events economically and significantly as analogies to these events, with the aim of inducing a greater perception of reality.

Brecht's adaptations are thus generated by the same impulse to historicizing that permeates his own plays. They are not fortuitous renderings seeking to destroy the original. Indeed, the very opposite is true, for Brecht was sensitive to the need of men for more than a present reality, for a knowledge and understanding of the activities of past generations in order to manage the complex diversity of their own life and society with awareness and calm composure. In describing a characteristic of Goethe and Schiller — whom so many consider antipodean to Brecht — Fritz Strich unwittingly confirmed the latter's intrinsic 'Laxheit in Fragen geistigen Eigentums' as a quality of all great men:

Wenn man die wahrhaft großen Menschen in ihren Beziehungen zur geistigen Welt betrachtet, so wird man immer sehen können, wie sie die Güter aller Zeiten und Völker als ihr Eigentum betrachten und in sich aufnehmen und über die kritischen Geister lachen, die ihnen vorrechnen und vorwerfen wollen, was sie von außen her sich zugeeignet haben. Sie nehmen solche Güter in sich auf, so wie sie Luft einatmen und ihrem Leibe Nahrung geben. Es ist die Luft und Nahrung ihres Geistes, und ihre Frage an die großen Schöpfungen der Zeiten und der Völker ist unbedenklich diese, ob sie es vermögen, ihre eigene Produktivität zu wecken und zu fördern. Ihre Dankbarkeit erstatten sie mit ihrem eigenen Werke, das aus der Befruchtung wächst und seinerseits wiederum die geistige Welt befruchten kann.[21]

This may sound somewhat metaphoric in relation to Brecht, but Strich goes on to describe factually the quite radical changes made without compunction in accommodating Shakespeare to the style of the Weimar theatre:

Goethe hat wohl bei seiner klassischen Reform des Weimarer Theaters eine Bearbeitung von *Romeo und Julia* vorgenommen. Aber es war eine Übersetzung aus dem barocken in den klassischen Stil . . . Er spricht von Allotria und Dissonanzen. Alle Prosa wird einer durchgehenden rhythmischen Form geopfert, von der sogar Teile in Alexandrinern gehalten sind. Die klassische Form des Weimarer Theaters verlangte solche Anpassung Shakespeares an den neuen Stil, der sich näher an den französischen Klassizismus als an die englische Dramatik hielt. Auch Schillers *Macbeth* ist ja eine totale Verwandlung von Shakespeares Stil zugunsten eines neuen Klassizismus. Auch hier zum Beispiel die Tilgung von Komik und Prosa. Goethes Übersetzungen von Voltaireschen Tragödien dagegen konnten dem Originale näher bleiben, wie auch Schillers *Phaedra* es vermochte.[22]

In terms of his own age Brecht exactly parallels Goethe's and Schiller's procedure of adapting a play to the extent necessary for it to be effective for their type of theatre. The characteristics of Brecht's adaptations are a measure of the changes in political, social and literary realities and thinking over the intervening century and a half.

NOTES

1 H. Mayer, 'Bildung, Besitz und Theater', *Die Zeit*, 20/27 September 1968.
2 T. S. Eliot, 'Tradition and the Individual Talent', in *The Sacred Wood* (London, 1920), p. 49.
3 H. Kipphardt, *Die Soldaten*, nach J. M. R. Lenz (Frankfurt, 1968), p. 91 f.
4 Op. cit., pp. 18 and 59.
5 H. Mayer, loc. cit., quotes the young playwright Peter Handke: 'Wie man etwa im Fußball Torchancen "herausspielt", so hat Brecht mit seinen Parabeln Widersprüche "herausgespielt", freilich sicher an dem falschen soziologischen Ort, mit den falschen soziologischen Mitteln: von der Wirklichkeit, die er ändern wollte, unendlich entfernt, die hierarchische Ordnung des Theaters benutzend, um andere hierarchische Ordnungen hierarchisch zu stören: keinen Ruhigen hat er beunruhigt, Unzähligen freilich ein paar schöne Stunden geschenkt.' Mayer then paraphrases this attack: 'Der Fehler Brechts bestand nicht im Unterfangen, durch schriftstellerische Arbeiten für Veränderung zu wirken, sondern in der Entscheidung für untaugliche Mittel. Brecht hatte zwischen dem — abgelehnten — bürgerlichen Theater und einem Theater der neuen Dramaturgie, Schauspiel- und Zuschaukunst unterschieden. Handke scheint auch dieses umfunktionierte Theater immer noch für ein Theater der Bildung und des Besitzes zu halten.'
6 Brecht never ceased formulating and re-formulating the fundamental concept, 'Verfremdung heißt Historisieren' (*GW*, 15/302), and illustrating it in every genre: drama, prose, lyric.
7 A detailed consideration of the implications of historicizing is undertaken by K.-D. Müller, *Die Funktion der Geschichte im Werk Bertolt Brechts. Studien zum Verhältnis von Marxismus und Ästhetik* (Tübingen, 1967), pp. 30 ff. Müller refers to the *Messingkauf* where the Philosopher suggests how a Marxist would present Schiller's *Wallenstein*, compare *GW*, 16/531 f.
8 Müller, op. cit., p. 39.
9 Quoted by Mayer, loc. cit.
10 *GW*, 16/582.
11 *The Sacred Wood*, p. 52. Eliot also describes the subtle re-ordering of the pattern of tradition that every new work effects, p. 49 f.: 'What happens when a new work of art is created is something that happens simultaneously to all the works of art which preceded it.'
12 *GW*, 19/537.
13 *GW*, 19/533 f.
14 See the lines from 'Lied des Stückschreibers', 1935:
>Um zeigen zu können, was ich sehe
>Lese ich nach die Darstellungen anderer Völker und anderer Zeitalter.
>Ein paar Stücke hab ich nachgeschrieben, genau
>Prüfend die jeweilige Technik und mir einprägend
>Das, was mir zustatten kommt.
>Ich studierte die Darstellungen der großen Feudalen
>Durch die Engländer, reicher Figuren
>Denen die Welt dazu dient, sich groß zu entfalten.
15 H. Ihering, *Von Reinhardt bis Brecht*, 3 vols (Berlin, 1959), ii, 200.
16 *GW*, 17/1256, and for the next quote.
17 *GW*, 6/2541.
18 Mayer, loc. cit.
19 *Theaterprobleme*, p. 19 f.
20 G. Lukács, *Geschichte und Klassenbewußtsein* (Berlin, 1923).
21 F. Strich, *Goethe und die Weltliteratur* (Berne, 1946), p. 113.
22 Ibid., p. 127 f.

SELECT BIBLIOGRAPHY

1. BERTOLT BRECHT AND THE DIALECTIC OF TRADITION

Brecht, B., *Flüchtlingsgespräche*, Frankfurt, 1961
Esslin, M., *Brecht: a choice of evils*, London, 1959
Hegel, G. W. Fr., *Recht, Staat, Geschichte* (selections edited by F. Bülow), Stuttgart, 1955
Hinck, W., *Die Dramaturgie des späten Brecht*, Göttingen, 1960
Kaufmann, H., *Bertolt Brecht. Geschichtsdrama und Parabelstück*, Berlin, 1962
Lukács, G., *Skizze einer Geschichte der neueren deutschen Literatur*, Berlin, 1964
Mayer, H., *Bertolt Brecht und die Tradition*, Pfullingen, 1961
Piscator, E., *Das politische Theater* (revised edition), Hamburg, 1963
Rasch, W., 'Bertolt Brechts marxistischer Lehrer', *Merkur*, 17 (1963), 988–1003
Rülicke, K., 'Bemerkungen zur Schlußszene', *Sinn und Form*, 2. Sonderheft B. Brecht, Berlin, 1957
Sternberg, F., *Der Dichter und die Ratio*, Göttingen, 1963

2. DER HOFMEISTER

Böckmann, P., *Formgeschichte der deutschen Dichtung*, I, Hamburg, 1949
Burger, H. O., 'J. M. R. Lenz: *Der Hofmeister*', in *Das deutsche Lustspiel*, I, edited by H. Steffen, Göttingen, 1968
Herder, J. G., *Sämmtliche Werke*, Berlin, 1877
Kant, I., *Gesammelte Schriften*, Berlin, 1900
Lenz, J. M. R., *Gesammelte Schriften*, edited by Franz Blei, München, 1909–13
Lessing, G. E., *Hamburgische Dramaturgie*, edited by Otto Mann, Stuttgart, 1963
Löfdahl, G., 'Moral und Dialektik — über die Pätus-Figur im *Hofmeister*', *Orbis Litterarum*, 20 (1965), 19–31
Mattenklott, G., *Melancholie in der Dramatik des Sturm und Drang*, Stuttgart, 1968
Schlegel, A. W., *Kritische Schriften und Briefe*, edited by E. Lohner, Stuttgart, 1966
Schöne, A., *Säkularisation als sprachbildende Kraft. Studien zur Dichtung deutscher Pfarrersöhne*, Göttingen, 1958

3. DER BIBERPELZ AND DER ROTE HAHN

Barnstorff, H., *Die soziale, politische und wirtschaftliche Zeitkritik im Werke Gerhart Hauptmanns*, Jena, 1938
Benjamin, W., *Versuche über Brecht*, Frankfurt, 1966
Bruck, W. F., *Social and Economic History of Germany from William II to Hitler, 1888–1938*, London, 1938

Dosenheimer, E., *Das deutsche soziale Drama von Lessing bis Sternheim*, Konstanz, 1949
Emrich, W., *Protest und Verheißung*, Frankfurt, 1960
Gebhardt, B., *Handbuch der deutschen Geschichte*, Stuttgart, 1931
Gregor, J., *Gerhart Hauptmann. Das Werk und unsere Zeit*, Wien, 1944
Guthke, K. S., *Geschichte und Poetik der deutschen Tragikomödie*, Göttingen, 1961
Hauptmann, G., *Das gesammelte Werk*, Berlin, 1942
Hauptmann, G., *Das Abenteuer meiner Jugend*, Berlin, 1937
Kerr, A., *Das neue Drama*, Berlin, 1917
Mann, Th., *Altes und Neues*, Frankfurt, 1952
Martini, F., 'Soziale Thematik und Formwandlungen des Dramas', *Der Deutschunterricht*, 5, Heft 5 (1953), 73–100
Müller-Seidel, W., *Klassische Deutsche Dichtung*, Bd. 17: *Lustspiele*, Freiburg, 1962
Naumann, F., *Ausgewählte Schriften*, Frankfurt, 1949
Reichert, H. W., 'Hauptmann's Frau Wolff and Brecht's Mutter Courage', *German Quarterly*, 34 (1961), 439–48
Rosenberg, A., *The Birth of the German Republic, 1871–1918*, New York, 1962
Schröder, R. A., *Gerhart Hauptmann. Gedenkfeier*, Bremen, 1952
Soergel, A., *Dichtung und Dichter der Zeit*, Leipzig, 1911
Tank, K. L., edition of *Der rote Hahn*, Berlin, 1959

4. DON JUAN

Adam, A., *Histoire de la Littérature Française au XVIIe Siècle*, Paris, 1948–56
Adam, A., *Les Libertins au XVIIe Siècle*, Paris, 1964
Arbelet, P., edition of *Dom Juan*, Paris, 1935
Arnavon, J., *Le Don Juan de Molière*, Copenhagen, 1947
Baumal, F., *Tartuffe et ses Avatars*, Paris, 1925
Bénichou, P., *Morales du Grand Siècle*, Paris, 1948
Bévotte, G. de, *La Légende de Don Juan*, Paris, 1929
Cairncross, J., *Molière — Bourgeois et Libertin*, Paris, 1963
Dürrenmatt, F., *Theaterschriften und Reden*, Zürich, 1966
Fernandez, R., *La Vie de Molière*, Paris, 1929
Giese, P. C., *Das 'Gesellschaftlich-Komische': zu Komik und Komödie am Beispiel der Stücke und Bearbeitungen Brechts*, Stuttgart, 1974
Grimm, R., *Bertolt Brecht und die Weltliteratur*, Nürnberg, 1961
Hoffmann, E. T. A., *Musikalische Novellen und Schriften*, Weimar, 1961
Howarth, W. D., edition of *Dom Juan*, Oxford, 1958
Jouanny, R., edition of *Molière. Théâtre complet*, Paris, n.d.
Lemaître, J., *Impressions de Théâtre*, Paris, 1890
Lewis, W. H., *The Splendid Century*, London, 1953
Mörike, E., *Werke*, Stuttgart, 1949
Mornet, D., *Molière*, Paris, 1943
Stendhal, H., *Œuvres complètes*, edited by P. Arbelet and E. Champion, Paris, 1926
Stendhal, H., *Racine et Shakespeare*, edited by H. Martineau, Paris, 1928
Sternheim, C., *Gesamtwerk*, edited by W. Emrich, Berlin, 1963–7
Weinstein, L., *The Metamorphoses of Don Juan*, Stanford, 1959

5. *PAUKEN UND TROMPETEN*

Anderson, M. S., *Europe in the Eighteenth Century*, London, 1961
Archer, W., edition of *Farquhar's Plays* (Mermaid Series), New York, 1959
Billias, G. A., *The American Revolution*, New York, 1965
Connely, W., *Young George Farquhar*, London, 1949
Farquhar, G., *The Works of the late Ingenious Mr. George Farquhar*, eighth edition, London, 1742
Farquhar, G., *The Recruiting Officer*, edited by Michael Shugrue, London, 1966
George, M. D., *England in Transition*, second edition, London, 1953
Hobsbawm, E. J., *The Age of Revolution 1789–1848*, London, 1963
Saxe, Maurice Comte de, *Mes Rêveries*, Paris, 1757
Trevelyan, G. M., *English Social History*, London, 1942

6. *CORIOLAN*

Beckley, R. J., 'Some Aspects of Brecht's Dramatic Technique in the Light of his Adaptations of English Plays' (unpublished M.A. dissertation, University of London, 1961)
Brunkhorst, M., *Shakespeares 'Coriolanus' in deutscher Bearbeitung*, Berlin, 1973
Bullough, G., *Narrative and Dramatic Sources of Shakespeare*, London, 1964
Chambers, R. W., *Shakespeare's Hand in the Play of Sir Thomas More*, Cambridge, 1923
Charney, M., *Shakespeare's Roman plays: the function of imagery in the drama*, Cambridge (Mass.), 1963
Dieckmann, F., 'Die Tragödie des Coriolan', *Sinn und Form*, 17 (1965), 463–89
Dionysius (of Halicarnassus), *The Roman Antiquities*, translated by E. Cary, Loeb Classical Library, 7 vols, London, 1937–63
Dürrenmatt, F., *Theaterprobleme*, Zürich, 1955
Enright, D. J., *The Apothecary's Shop*, London, 1957
Fontane, Th., *Sämtliche Werke*, München, 1967
Grab, V. L., 'B. Brecht's Adaptation of Shakespeare's Coriolanus' (unpublished M.A. dissertation, University of New York, 1965)
Grass, G., 'Vor- und Nachgeschichte der Tragödie des Coriolanus von Livius und Plutarch über Shakespeare bis zu Brecht und mir', *Akzente*, 11 (1964), 194–221
Hazlitt, W., *The Complete Works*, edited by P. P. Howe, London, 1930–4
Hoffmeier, D., 'Notate zu Bertolt Brechts Bearbeitung von Shakespeares *Coriolan*, zur Bühnenfassung und zur Inszenierung des Berliner Ensembles', *Jahrbuch der deutschen Shakespeare-Gesellschaft*, Weimar, 1967
Kleinstück, J., 'B. Brechts Bearbeitung von Shakespeares *Coriolanus*', *Literaturwissenschaftliches Jahrbuch*, N.F. 9 (1968)
Knight, G. Wilson, *The Imperial Theme*, London, 1931
Knight, G. Wilson, *The Sovereign Flower*, London, 1958
Kott, J., *Shakespeare our Contemporary*, London, 1964
Kuczynski, J., 'Coriolanus: Plutarch–Shakespeare–Brecht', *Theater der Zeit*, 16 (1961), 43–52

Leonhardt, R. W., 'Können wir den Shakespeare ändern?', *Die Zeit*, 2.10.64
Livy, *The History of Rome*, translated and edited by D. Spillan and C. Edmonds, London, 1849–50
MacCallum, M. W., *Shakespeare's Roman Plays and their Background*, second edition, London, 1925
Palmer, J., *Political Characters of Shakespeare*, London, 1945
Phillips, J. E., *The State in Shakespeare's Greek and Roman Plays*, New York, 1940
Plutarch, *Lives of the Famous Romans*, edited by J. Langhorne, London, 1805
Rülicke-Weiler, K., *Die Dramaturgie Brechts*, Berlin, 1966
Schiller, F., *Die Räuber: Vorrede, Unterdrückte Vorrede, Avertissement zur ersten Aufführung*, facsimile of 1781 edition, Leipzig, 1905
Spencer, T. J. B., *Shakespeare's Plutarch*, London, 1964
Stirling, B., *The Populace in Shakespeare*, New York, 1949
Symington, R. T. K., *Brecht und Shakespeare*, Bonn, 1970
Thomson, J. A. K., *Shakespeare and the Classics*, London, 1952
Traversi, D., *Shakespeare: the Roman Plays*, London, 1963
Wekwerth, M., *Notate über die Arbeit des Berliner Ensembles 1956 bis 1966*, Frankfurt, 1967
Wilson, J. Dover, edition of *Coriolanus*, Cambridge, 1960
Zéraffa, M., 'Shakespeare, Brecht et l'histoire', *Europe*, Special Brecht volume, 35 (1957), no. 133/134

7. CONCLUSION

Eliot, T. S., *The Sacred Wood*, London, 1920
Ihering, H., *Von Reinhardt bis Brecht*, ii, Berlin, 1959
Kipphardt, H., *Die Soldaten* (nach J. M. R. Lenz), Frankfurt, 1968
Lukács, G., *Geschichte und Klassenbewußtsein*, Berlin, 1923
Mayer, H., 'Bildung, Besitz und Theater', *Die Zeit*, 20/27 September 1968
Müller, K.-D., *Die Funktion der Geschichte im Werk Bertolt Brechts. Studien zum Verhältnis von Marxismus und Ästhetik*, Tübingen, 1967
Strich, F., *Goethe und die Weltliteratur*, Bern, 1946